A CLOUD OF FORGETTING

A CLOUD OF FORGETTING

PAMELA COOPER

QUARTET BOOKS

First published by Quartet Books Limited 1993
A member of the Namara Group
27/29 Goodge Street, London W1P 1FD

Copyright © by Pamela Cooper 1993

The poem by Freya Stark on page 180 is reprinted with the permission of John
Murray Ltd

A catalogue record for this title is available from the British Library
ISBN 0 7043 2731 7

Phototypeset by Intype, London
Printed and bound in Great Britain by
Bookcraft (Bath) Ltd

'It is called, not a cloud of the air, but a *cloud of unknowing*; which is betwixt thee and thy God. And if ever thou shalt come to this cloud and dwell and work therein as I bid thee, thou must, as this *cloud of unknowing* is above thee, betwixt thee and thy God, right so put a *cloud of forgetting* beneath thee, betwixt thee, and all creatures that ever be made . . . But, to speak shortly, all should be hid under the *cloud of forgetting* . . . And thou shalt step above it stalwartly, but listily, with a devout and a pleasant stirring of love . . . And smite upon that thick *cloud of unknowing* with a sharp dart of longing love; and go not thence for aught that befalleth' – *The Cloud of Unknowing*, chapters 4–6, edited by Abbot Justin McCann (Burnes & Oates, 1924)

Foreword

Most of us like to think that our lives can be made to appear tidier than they really are, that deskfuls of letters, diaries, jottings – the flotsam of memory – may be burnished and stacked into a gleam of order. It is an illusion, perhaps, but one worth holding on to: part of being human is to try to shape some order out of the chaos of actual experience.

This book tells what happened to the daughter of a prosperous, settled and seemingly secure Anglo-Irish family in the twentieth century – born ten years after it began, writing ten years before its end. It was written because of another little girl, a very small girl indeed, dark curls caught in two pigtails, wearing a red frock, whom I watched after a night of devastating bombardment in West Beirut in the summer of 1982. She was carrying a large petrol can of water to her family in a high corner building. Every few feet she had to set down the heavy load, and once, to my dismay, she drank from the rubber tube. That was *her* childhood. My life has perhaps been more fortunate than hers may ever be, but neither of us has escaped the despair and rubble of our century, whose conflicts show no sign of abating.

For months my son Malise helped me in my purpose, wrestling with letters, diaries and memories which served only to issue in new notes, jottings, revived recollections – repetitious, no doubt, inaccurate sometimes, oddly relevant to me, hardly relevant to others. Eventually he handed what he found and sifted to Peter Ford, who shaped it into this narrative. Peter's skill and humour, his uncanny gift of getting to know people he never met, finally reconciled me to the telling of this story, to the tracing of that thinnest of threads connecting the rectory child with the child of West Beirut.

Others who helped in the preparation of the book, by providing information about events I did not witness, or by helping to dispel the cloud of forgetting, include Henriette Abel-Smith, David Beaufort and Anne Rasche, Roy Foster, Paul Harper, Hugh Hodgkinson, Peter Hodgson, Tony Lothian, Peter Smithers and Sydney Watson. Ruth and the late Tony Dulverton housed us in the west flat at Batsford during the years I started my research, encouraged by Penelope and Lucy Hughes-Hallet, who read my Beirut diary, while Derek, my husband, imposed an impressive degree of order on the crumbling folders and tin trunks where this story lay dormant for many years. Michael and Pattie Hopkins provided the cottage in Italy where the real work was begun. My son Grey assisted in its completion by putting a roof on the barn we now live in. Heartfelt thanks to them all.

Pamela Cooper

July 1993

Contents

1

Piggyland

Early in the twentieth century privileged babies were reared in the nurseries of their mothers, grandmothers and even ancestors. These nurseries were usually situated at the top of the house, up long linoleum-covered stairways, often with barred windows to prevent such deathly tumbles as those which befall the more adventurous members of a bird family.

My first visual memories are of tree-tops and sky from the windows of my Grandmother Hodgson's houses in Sussex and London. The steep stairs to the nursery were an Everest for small fat legs. I remember negotiating the stairs of the Chelsea house, No. 51 Cadogan Square, astride a Great Dane, held on by Henry the footman in dark-blue livery with gilt buttons. Even when we reached the billiard room, there was still a long way to go, with the constant danger of slipping back over the animal's haunches.

It was to this narrow, dark Victorian red-brick house in Chelsea that my siblings and I were brought, to be born and subsequently for occasional visits. I arrived by mistake, the outcome, I was told, of the 'safe period', eleven months after my brother Michael's birth. In those days nannies still wore black bonnets with ribbons tied under their chins and long grey coats and skirts. They walked or pushed us in our prams to Hyde Park, where we would strain at our straps to watch the women squatting on the lower steps of monuments, selling balloons and great basketfuls of flowers.

Once there was quite a long stay at No. 51, when my brother and I were to have our tonsils removed. The billiard room had been converted to an operating theatre. I remember crying out as the

1

handsome doctor lowered a gauze mask, doused in ether, over my face, 'Darling Dr Longstaffe, darling Dr Longstaffe, don't do it!' Consolation arrived in the shape of postcards – dogs and cats dressed as soldiers, policemen and sailors, the work of Louis Wain. I treasured them with passion.

When we were not at our grandmother's we lived at the rectory at Merrow, near Guildford, where my father was rector, until he volunteered to serve as a chaplain in France. He was a passionate admirer of Napoleon, and his study, the largest room in the house, was walled with books and prints and busts of the little Corsican. I can just remember the day war broke out. I was standing by the bird bath in the rose garden my mother had made outside the wide french windows of the rectory study, when I heard the grown-ups talking about war being declared on Germany. The day is sharp in my mind: there were still rambler roses out on the trellises, the grown-ups gathered around the study steps with unsmiling faces. From then on we would look through the *Illustrated London News* for pictures of the Kaiser to spit on, and when we sat on our pots in the night nursery with a bed between us, my brother and I were urged to have 'one big try for the Kaiser'. Nanny would leave us after this exhortation, and we developed the very tricky skill of moving between the beds to visit one another, dragging the pots with us like dogs with worms.

One morning, shortly before he left for France, my father, who was not much encouraged in the nursery, for Nanny said he made us wild, seized my brother from his bed and carried him to the front gate to watch the soldiers in khaki marching by. I saw one lying in the ditch beside the road to the common. 'He's drunk,' said Nanny. 'What a headache he'll have in the morning.' I worried many hours about that soldier's headache, never having suffered one myself.

Our parents were usually indulgent, but discipline was strict. All scolding and punishment was inflicted by Nan or the nursery maid. I once broke a chamber pot, playing the doggie game. I was pushed round the door into my mother's bedroom in great apprehension, carrying a flowery piece attached to the handle. She was putting up her hair at her dressing table, a converted spinet, by the window. She appeared to be completely unperturbed by my crude and shocking crime.

Nan, however, often smacked us, and hard. She always walked

aloof down the street and she was looked on as over-severe, I believe, by the village. I don't think we minded, and we really loved her. I used to be called the Waterworks, so I must have shed an unusual amount of tears. Once I crept to the washstand in the night nursery and spat on Nanny's tooth-brush, but I think this was a response to my sister Romola's arrival, when I was five. The new baby was entirely nursed by Nan. My father once sponsored a subversion of nursery discipline and, despite our Nan's protestations, allowed us to play in the garden with no restrictions. Naturally we made straight for the coal store behind the greenhouse and returned black from head to foot.

My elder sister Diana shared lessons with Muriel Laing, who brought her excellent governess to the rectory each morning. This lady was called Miss Bowden. Her brother was a famous horsemaster in the British cavalry. Muriel was a red-haired Scottish girl with a very tall, reserved and alarming mother, whose high prominent cheek-bones were covered with tiny purple veins. Her husband, a businessman, was brother to the Archbishop of Canterbury, Dr Cosmo Laing. I was allowed to sit in on their lessons and do some pothooks. I have no memory of actually learning to read. A time just came when words suddenly took on a familiar and friendly look, probably from much-loved books being read to us aloud.

On one occasion my father lost his temper in the nursery and became very Irish, denouncing us as thoroughly mollycoddled. His upbringing had been tougher than ours. He had run wild with his three brothers – all of whom became clergymen – on the family farm in Waterford, while his father, Dr Fletcher, travelled to and from America, where he regularly went on preaching tours. A photograph of the good doctor shows a patriarchal figure with fine aquiline features and white flowing beard. His wife, having buried at least six children, suffered a stroke and took early to a bathchair.

On Sunday nights we used to sing songs and hymns round the piano. My mother played well and powerfully, in a manner that belied her seemingly gentle nature. The only time my father ever beat us was one Sunday evening after Michael and I had sabotaged her performance. Every time she started the opening bars of a hymn, Michael and I stared at each other and burst into 'All the Best Girls Love a Sailor'. Nellie the nursery maid had recently become engaged to one.

The night nursery at Highlands, my grandmother's house at Bolney in Sussex, looked down on to wide lawns and through huge oaks to the unbroken, unploughed horizon of the South Downs and the beeches of the Chanctonbury Ring. We generally visited Bolney in August and September. I cannot remember seeing the oak trees bare. I would jump out of bed first thing to watch the red squirrels running up and down the trunks and cutting capers on the lawn around circular beds of pampas grass. We washed at a double wash-stand behind a tall glass screen, decorated with a stork and a frog in a lily pond. Two of my mother's sisters had created this monument to modesty.

Those high nursery windows, looking on to tree-tops and clouds, made for an early recognition of winged creatures. The first stage I invented and acted on was with fairies, angels, flying boats, even before 'Winken and Blinken and Nod' became a favourite nursery rhyme or the story had been read to me of the princess who flew out of the castle window to hatch the rooks. Maybe it also made for an acceptance of heaven as not too distant, but, as it were, just above everyday life. At ground level, you walked through grasses which were a forest, puddles which were little lakes. In the nursery, we invented Piggyland, where we all came from. It was somewhere akin to where the Lost Boys and Peter Pan lived, our features being swineish but not unattractive. 'When I was in Piggyland,' my brother would start off.

From the Highlands day nursery, which faced the drive, you could hear the noise of gravel being raked – almost the first sound I can remember. There was a little desk with a flap lid and brass rail, while the cupboard held a few toys in good order: a whipping top, blue, red and yellow, and some clockwork animals, which, when wound up, walked drunkenly on the linoleum, tiresomely bumping into chairs or table legs. The best fun to be had upstairs was the wide landing with its door leading out on to the lead roof. Here we helped the younger maids dry their hair in the sun behind the chimney pots, while the head housemaid, a redhead with frizzy locks, sang to us, accompanying herself on the mandolin.

After breakfast I was dressed in striped knicker overalls – blue or pink – and loosed in the garden with my brother and sister. Being well-behaved children, we crept silently down the front stairs, through the back half of the drawing room, past the china cat playing timelessly with his ball beneath the piano, through a door into the conservatory to inhale the very special smell of maidenhair fern and geraniums, carnations and watering cans, then up some steps to the covered way that took us to the squash court.

Among the croquet mallets and garden chairs we then played at being cripples, suffering and hobbling in pain, subject to rough hospital regimentation until disablement lost its glamour and off we galloped past the beech maze, up wide grassy walks flanked by herbaceous borders to the walled garden. Here a shimmering row of glass-houses nurtured black and white grapes, peaches and nectarines hung along the warm brick walls and vegetables and salads and asparagus were planted among the fruit trees. Adams, the head gardener, terrified us. He was the epitome of Mr McGregor, arch-enemy and persecutor of Peter Rabbit. It was hard to like this efficient hard-working man, who could never be dissociated from the sickly smell of the burning lime from the kiln behind the squash courts.

We would wander up the grassway to the woods, snapping the snapdragons or gathering flower-heads to make dyes. As we grew older we were given jam-jars in which to drown the caterpillars of the cabbage white for pennies. I must have gazed for long summer hours across that meadow to the downs, because every fairy story I read later took place in Bolney wood and the surrounding fields. The wood held two summer houses: a dear little gazebo of faded blue, and a dark tattered hut with a thatched roof where witches and their familiars were presumed to live. It needed courage to tramp up that path by oneself. Beyond grew a wood of huge oaks. These must have been planted long before Barnard Becket Hodgson, my grandfather, brought his rich bride, formerly Miss Margaret Thornton, down from Yorkshire and cleared the Sussex woods to build his gabled Victorian mansion with its gardens, shrubberies and stables near the Brighton Road.

After war was declared, Bolney wood was turned to chaos, as teams of cart horses, their huge feathery feet stuck with clay, trampled the wild flowers, their massive haunches dragging the chains that hauled the fallen giants on to the wagons. I can still hear our nannies bewailing this desecration, nodding together in their long white uniforms and straw hats. My heart became filled with hate for the war effort, patriotism and the Kaiser. Those horses must have been the same, friendly animals which pulled the hay wagons we rode on at the Home Farm.

The Home Farm lay some way from the house, across a little stream with pools overhung with elder trees, where moorhens and frogs congregated. We would linger there a while, throwing the odd stone or stick, then take the beaten track to the farm, where there was always kindness and welcome. Beyond the Home Farm came the London to Brighton Road, where a public house stood by a clump of the estate cottages. We were immensely impressed to know that our grandmother owned a pub, and looked upon it with awe every time we crossed the road to buy sweets at the shop opposite. There was no ploughed land on the whole estate. Later I learned that my grandfather had been wont to meet his cronies in London or Brighton, where he also owned a house, and boast with them about the cost of their estates. In those days, there was then no need to destroy the countryside in order to make it pay. Landowners lived off other revenues.

The adjoining estate to Highlands was Wykhurst Park, on the farther side of the London Road, a far grander foreign-looking pile inhabited by a banker of Austrian origin called Huth. A deer fence surrounded the park full of fallow deer, dappled like my treasured chestnuts. The two Huth grandchildren, Sylvia and Roger, played with us, but the old man made the greatest impression – his white face and beard and elegant European clothes and figure. What made him doubly memorable to me was the rumour that when he travelled he took his own lavatory seat with him.

Grandmother Hodgson was a round old lady in black. She wore a lace cap in the manner of Queen Victoria. She used to sit behind a screen in her boudoir with Coley, my mother's former governess. Every now and then Grannie would gather up her skirts and fumble for a little gold chain bag to give us each a sovereign engraved with St George and the dragon. She had very light, bright-blue eyes and high apple cheeks and pale little hairs on her upper lip. I remember her rather harsh deep voice saying, 'The child looks a little peaky' – everyone thought I was peaky because of large blue eyes set in a pale face.

Another of the great joys of Bolney was the little room through the green baise door which led to the back stairs and servants' quarters. There sat Miss Johnston, my grandmother's personal maid from the North of Ireland. She stitched at a huge treadle machine or at a round table covered with a moss-green velvet cloth fringed with big tassles. I suppose it was there that we learned Granny surprisingly wore long combinations like us in winter, under those voluminous petticoats, and no knickers. The room was completely surrounded by glass bookcases containing the Hodgson children's books, beautifully bound and engraved. Fairies and children peeped through capital letters in decorative illustrations by Walter Crane or Kate Greenaway: little girls dressed in white frilled pinafores and thick black stockings, boys in sailor clothes and knickers covering their knees. There were bound volumes of children's magazines – the *Boy's Own Paper*, the *Blue* and the *Violet Fairy Books* of Andrew Lang. Miss Johnston would invite us to tea to choose a book. The children in these books were closer companions than any we met and picnicked with: one of them, the eponymous hero of *Froggie's Little Brother*, I encountered again in the streets of Beirut in 1982.

I always identified with the boys in stories, or the animals. A passion for donkeys could be attributed to a little pink paperback I was given, entitled *The Story of a Donkey*. When I lost a jointed, chocolate-coloured donkey in the laurel bushes at the rectory, I searched vainly for it day after day with a tenacity foreign to my nature. *Daddy Darwin's Dovecot*, *The Story of a Short Life*, *The Cuckoo Clock* – these were some gems from Miss Johnston's library. Certain stories had to be remembered, produced and acted next day, when the moment of release came early in the morning with dew still on the grass. The production of these was hard work, better performed before noon. Thereafter the sun made one hot and sticky and it was preferable to roll in the cut hay or make a house – something that didn't require much brainwork, nor entail the disappointments of unrealized ambition.

In late autumn and winter, back at the Surrey rectory, my young sister Romola begging to sit up in the pram, we went for long nursery walks, through the twin lodge gates, guarding the great elaborate wrought-iron gateway of Clandon Park, where sometimes we were joined by Joseph in the bright-blue uniform of a wounded soldier. He was one of the inmates of the Earl of Onslow's great house, which was a hospital throughout the war. I loved everything about Joseph: his ginger moustache and hair, his limp, his voice. The only doll I ever had was an exact replica of Joseph.

In colder weather, all nannies believed in children being taken for long walks. At least, they seemed to be long. There was little traffic, and the butcher, the grocer and the milkman drove around, respectively, in a high two-wheeled boxed-in cart and a float, delivering goods and leaving coveted horse droppings to be hastily scooped up outside the cottages. The long chestnut palings to the north side of Clandon Park made a satisfactory noise if you carried the right stick, and there were holes into which to drop treasures, which then became impossible to retrieve, although somehow they remained in one's possession. The verges were home to white violets and celandines, cow parsley and cuckoo-pint. The wheels of the farm carts sank no very deep ruts. Consequently, in good weather, a pram could take a cart track or lane. Water ran clean and free down the ditches into iron grids, this making for most interesting dawdling, and more stick work.

In the winter we and our Nan must have walked miles. My sister, growing into a striking-looking child with yellow curls, orange cheeks and bright-blue eyes, sat in her pram scowling at any human who stopped to speak with us, or went purple in the face with the effort of viewing a dog or cat, putting a dangerous strain on the much-used pram harness.

The most exciting walk of all was outside the park along the road to Clandon and up Ashentree Walk, where the gnarled beeches met overhead, flanked by long, deep pits of chalk. Shuffling through the leaves, the pram bumping over the exposed roots, was like walking into *Grimms' Fairy Tales* as illustrated by Arthur Rackham. As our legs grew stronger, we could reach Merrow Downs by way of Todd's Lane above the church. There were huge yews, close-cropped turf of thyme, and wild flowers and juniper bushes all the way up to Newlands Corner and, most romantic of all, the little church of St Martha on its hill-top. Trees had been hurriedly planted around it, because it was a path-finder for Zeppelins. Beyond the woods lay the common, where Mary, our fat under-housemaid, lived with her equally plump mother along with several goats. To reach the common we had to cross the railway. Sometimes we climbed a stile and put halfpennies on the rails, then waited with glorious suspense for the London train to come rumbling along through the trees and turn them into pennies.

My Grandmother Hodgson's fortune originated with forebears

who owned a fleet of merchant ships. Lawrence and Richard Thornton became merchants when Napoleon's blockade of England excluded English shipping from the Baltic. The King of Denmark was even more rigorously excessive than Napoleon, and Baltic trade grew to be extremely dangerous for English merchants, but was of vital importance to the maintenance of the Royal Navy. Richard Thornton was commissioned by the Admiralty to buy as much hemp as he could get out of Russia for the rigging of the Fleet. He armed one of his own merchant ships, sailed on her himself and fought off a Danish gunboat, both sides putting up a vigorous cannonade. Landing at Memel under an assumed German name, he penetrated Russia and succeeded in making vast purchases of hemp. His brother Lawrence, when in Memel later, managed to convey a message to Richard in England that Napoleon was turning back from Moscow. Richard went through the City of London, making large and advantageous deals for the forward delivery of hemp, tallow hides and other Baltic produce three days before even the Cabinet had heard the news of Napoleon's retreat.

The Thornton fortune was considerable, but little of lasting value seems to have come of it, except for the portion that went to Richard's nephew, Richard Thornton West. He not only gave the money to build St David's church in Exeter, but also built Streatham Hall as his Devon home, and laid out its magnificent grounds, which later became Reed Hall and the impressive campus of the University of Exeter.

My grandfather saw his chance to while away most of his married life driving coaches and four-in-hands between London and Brighton, fox-hunting and going to race meetings. He sired nine children and was a kindly, benevolent parent. He died just before my mother married, and must have been tall and good-looking, like his sons, the elegant, immaculately dressed cavalry uncles who in due course appeared at my wedding. The eldest, Barnard Thornton Hodgson, became a barrister and Commissioner in Lunacy. He was the least good-looking, but it was said the 'loonies' loved him.

Henry, the second son, commanded the Australian cavalry under General Allenby in Palestine. He dismounted and joined his chief on their triumphal march into Jerusalem in 1917. (Quite recently I spotted him in some old film.) My grandfather loved him and paid for his polo ponies and his debts. I last saw him in a flat in Hans

Place shortly before he died, sitting in a high-backed, leather chair with one leg on a stool. He had my grandmother's brilliant-blue eyes and her deep rasping voice. Admirals, generals and Intelligence officers were always to be found lunching at Hans Place, one of whom was Major Gilbert Clayton. In Cairo years later I met his younger brother, who greatly regretted having to travel through the Middle East by car, for, he said, intelligence was more easily garnered from the back of a horse.

My youngest uncle, Walter, who was also the youngest child, was a constant part of our lives. He joined the Royals and after the war commanded the Cavalry Brigade at Aldershot. For many summers running there was an evening when we drove to the arena between the pine trees for the Tattoo. It was an annual event which never failed to create excitement: the oncoming darkness, the bands, the gloriously decorated horses and men of the cavalry in scarlet and gold, blue and silver, riding directly towards us in the brigadier's box, while the massed bands played operatic tunes. Pat Hore-Ruthven, my future husband, would have been in an adjacent box belonging to the Household Brigade, which his father was then commanding.

The sister closest to my mother, and only a few years older, was Aunt Margaret. She was married to Uncle Willie Campbell, a most dapper, exquisitely dressed man, always with a cornflower in his buttonhole. They lived at Brantridge Park at near-by Handcross. I have only a very dim memory of Brantridge, for they left soon after, to live at Harewood Park in Herefordshire. But the house seemed in those long sunny summers to have an elegance that Highlands, with its Victorian gables, lacked. I can just remember shiny chintz and pink rhododendrons, silver trays and teas on the lawn. When I came to read Oscar Wilde's plays, Brantridge became their backdrop. We called the cousins the 'Campbell Kids' – two boys, two girls, all with hair the colour of newly hatched chicks.

Aunt Margaret was tough, chain-smoking, full of lively witticisms delivered in my grandmother's rasping, throaty bass. She had a difficult life with Uncle Willie, who seemed to spend most of his time standing in front of the fire in immaculate shooting breeches and jacket, blinking and winking his bright-blue eyes and talking politics. I don't remember his ever doing anything else. After his death the grand piano was found stuffed with uncashed cheques, long expired, for sales of cattle, corn and rents. For years the family estate had been run on my aunt's portion – no wonder she smoked so much! The Campbell Kids were down to earth compared to us rectory children. They had ponies, ferrets and rabbits. The sisters fought, as we seldom did. I enjoyed teasing them, to fan the flames.

My mother was the youngest girl of her generation. She used to describe the agonies of shyness she had suffered while descending the same stairs we dashed down each morning when we were at Bolney, to meet her four tall brothers back from Eton. Her duties were to look after their ferrets and report on their welfare when the holidays began. Very early on I connected her with the pleasant scent of her skin, of her hair that she washed in a cotton bag of herbs. She seemed always to be beautifully dressed in soft pliant materials.

When we were being bathed before bed at the rectory, we would be held up to watch the tennis party going on below. My father, a competent player, would punctuate his shots with threats and ejaculations, making a circus out of the game. My mother, in contrasting style, had a strong swooping underhand service and was swift on her feet.

She was so slight and shy, with her great bun of golden hair, her green eyes the colour of gooseberries covered by large, heavy lids. I never saw her in an ungraceful position, except once, at Bognor, when the bed collapsed beneath her. It made such an impression that for ever after she became the Giant.

The Giant had two accomplishments dear to us. One was a kind of Russian dance, performed by squatting on the floor and shooting out her legs straight, to the front and to the side. None of us could emulate her in this. Another was her ability to close one lid over one eye while the other remained open in a calm unwrinkled stare. She also had a habit of getting the giggles, uncontrollably. For a woman of great dignity, this was of peculiar fascination; whenever she saw her sister Margaret, they had only to look at each other and an attack might begin. It happened one day in London on the tube, something to do with a little man sitting opposite. We armed her out at the next station with mingled shame and pride.

At some point in her life she must have become truly religious. I still have some of her books, much read. *The Cloud of the Unknowing*, Evelyn Underhill's *The House of the Soul*, *The Mysteries of the Mass in Reasoned Prayer* are among those which have survived. I can't imagine such a private person ever arguing or confessing her beliefs with the ebullient, curious and inquiring Irishman she fell in love with. Even as a child I could tell she was much loved in the village, especially by the humbler parishioners or the bereaved from the Great War, as we called it then. I think her family, her garden and the countryside were her chief loves, but looking back I doubt if she was very tough; could it have been simply a true spirituality which made her withdraw, or rest on a sofa before tea? Maybe if she had married a weaker man than Harry Fletcher, she would have shown her strong character to the world. My father was twelve years her senior and far more robust. Except in matters of domestic living, she was content for him to take the lead.

But even when we were grown, she was never waiting or appearing anxious. Whenever we came home she would usually have disappeared down the garden or around some obscure corner of the house where we had to go to seek her out. 'Where is she?' we shouted on arriving back from school or travels, and when we kissed her she screwed her mouth away and offered a cheek. After the war had changed domestic life, when she had to let the chauffeur and lady's maid go, when Nanny had no nursery maid and my father was still away except for leave, Giant became a wonderful cook. She also emerged as a companion to everyday life. There were walks with her across the fields under the great elms opposite the rectory front gates, holidays by the sea in 'rooms' taken and administered by the owners, who generally moved into a hut at the end of the garden.

We went often for rides in a parishioner's dog cart, but for ourselves, in the early days, usually rode in a car driven by Mulley, the chauffeur. We started with a large, open Renault with green leather and a great big hood like a pram. Later, with Mulley long gone to the wars, my mother learned to drive and was given a smart two-seater by Uncle Arthur Hodgson, who suffered from asthma, which blocked a military career in his case. Instead he worked with Tommy Sopwith, building aeroplanes. He had a model farm near Horsham, in an exquisite sixteenth-century black and white building. His cart horses, labradors, pigeons and Bentleys were all golden coloured. I was rather a favourite of Uncle Arthur's, until I was about sixteen, when I cut off my long fair hair. After that he transferred all his interest to my cousins, the Campbell Kids, and we were never, as they were, invited up to his house in Scotland to shoot and fish.

It was my future husband Pat Hore-Ruthven who christened my

father 'the Reverend'. When we became engaged someone asked him, 'Why are you going to marry her?' 'Because what my family needs is a little reverend blood,' was Pat's reply. So the Reverend he became thereafter, and retrospectively.

His nanny, when he was a child in Waterford, had a small beard and smoked a clay pipe. When he was fifteen, he briefly ran away from Ireland to see the London Dickens wrote of; he returned to the capital in his thirties as curate at the fashionable High Anglican church of Holy Trinity, Sloane Street. I have a photograph of a handsome almost aesthetic young man. The dark hair is brushed in a quiff, the very blue eyes look steadily and there is a deep cleft in his chin. He wears an elegant frock-coat and, in gleaming black, the all-embracing clerical waistcoat only seen on bishops today.

On coming to England he became part of the theological élite, revelling in Higher Criticism as well as High Churchmanship. He utterly deplored the hostility which underlay relations between the Church of Ireland and the Roman Church. He had many tales to tell of young people, secretly coming to him for instruction, who had made the fatal mistake of falling in love with 'one of them'; of Catholic brides being abducted before they could cross the threshold of the hated older and more solid building. It was at Holy Trinity that he met my mother, who stayed with her parents in Cadogan Square when the family were not in Sussex. She rejoiced in his broad churchmanship: he was absent-minded and often made mistakes in performing the unaccustomed rituals at Holy Trinity. Her soldier brothers must have thought him a strange choice for their pretty, graceful sister. But the old lady, in her 'alpaca' skirts, was always pleased to see him, and I believe we were the favoured grandchildren. Before she married, my mother had never put on her own stockings, and whenever she went out 'a little maid' accompanied her. This led to a joke between them. He must have asked to see her home on one occasion and she had answered, 'There is a little maid.' He liked all mankind so long as they weren't boring or pompous: if they were, he would mock them relentlessly or ignore them. He could easily be hoodwinked by rogues. I recall a tramp who stayed a night and went off with money.

The ups and downs of mundane existence seemed to have little impact on the Reverend. He found it hard to be solemn for long, he continuously told jokes against his cloth and the bloodthirsty chronicles of the Old Testament; he possessed a zest and absorption in living which I wish he had passed on. He had a fund of stories of the eccentric Protestant clergy of the Ireland he grew up in, of how they addressed their congregations and their maker, of the often beautiful churches and cathedrals reserved for the worship of the ascendancy alone under the patronage of some landlord, a fact he came to criticize sharply when we went to Ireland for summer holidays.

When he did grow angry or excited, his beginnings came through with a strong Irish brogue. Though utterly unpractical in everyday matters he never forgot how to handle a scythe or pruning hook. I often wondered why he never rose further in the Church, as someone who had been scholar of Trinity College, Dublin, in the days of the legendary Professor Mahaffey. Maybe his superiors and bishops were never quite sure of him: he broke rules, I know, for later at San Remo, when the Bishop of Gibraltar came to visit, we were using a revised prayer book strictly forbidden. Typically that bishop, however, became a close friend of our parents. I do not doubt that my mother smoothed over many an irate superior.

In a corner of the garden at Bolney, next to the beech maze, stood three or four great oak trees where my father, on leave from France, would sometimes read from *The Jungle Book*, the lilt of his voice rising and falling with excitement as he related the adventures of Mowgli and Sheer Khan. At other times, in the more formal setting of the library, he would try to teach us about the journeys of St Paul. I suspect I was too young to understand: all I can remember is the golden glow of the room from the leather-bound volumes lining its walls, the great desk with the lion pawing the ball of the world. St Paul was no match for Kipling.

On Sundays we went to church. Sometimes we drove in the carriage. It had a peculiar fusty smell and was lined with navy-blue felt held in by black buttons. We sat on the little seats, our backs to the horses, opposite the grown-ups. It meant wearing a white dress, hated frilly knickers and a floppy hat. I preferred it when we walked across the fields along the hedgerows of dog-roses and honeysuckle, to arrive at church by way of a stile and a little path through the graveyard. I liked church – the stained-glass windows could be made into stories, the choirboys were fun to stare at, individually recognizable despite the uniform surplices. Now and again I would actually listen to the liturgy: its incomprehensible words and sentences could be made into images or personal stories and chants. Each Sunday service culminated in the drama of the collection, when my brother or I would have to scrabble among the hassocks for the pennies that insisted on escaping to the bottom of the pew.

The Brighton house had been sold when my grandfather died, but I remember a day trip there in a large Daimler which, like the carriage, was lined with navy-blue felt. It was breathlessly exciting, as the road started cutting into the downs, to smell the sea; then came the descent to the beach, the encampment on the wide flat stones, the hurry and worry of undressing; the screwing up of eyes against the sun and whipping strands of hair, the sea water nibbling at toes and ankles, the collecting of seaweed and storing of treasures for the long twelve miles' drive back. Has one ever been so busy since? Have mere objects ever again been so important?

Fishing was another source of excitement, reserved for special days. We would take our picnics across the meadows to the mill ponds where we watched the red and yellow floats bob in little clearings between the alders, worms and mealy bugs threaded on our hooks. Our catches were usually perch, tench or eels. They were cooked and sent up to the nursery. They tasted wonderful, of bones and mud.

We also went fishing at Barnfield, home of Uncle Ted Hodgson. Here Nanny Clara reigned over the fishpond. She was a favourite with us, tiny and always shouting with a funny squeak voice. Her special care was Cousin Barbara, whose mother had died at her birth. Barbara lacked a thyroid gland, remaining mentally a child for life. Tall, with very dark hair, Barbara used to come galloping towards us like an unschooled filly. I loved her big dark eyes and wide mouth, dribbling with kindness. Uncle Ted had remarried and had a daughter, Elizabeth, who was younger than me. Later she became a most beloved cousin, but at that time I rather despised her for her curls, smart clothes and reputed literary achievements. Her mother, Aunt Nancy, was a pretty woman who had been courted by both Uncle Ted and Uncle Arthur. She once told my mother not to smile too much because 'it was so ageing'. When she died she left me a brooch – pearls and diamonds set in the shape of a question mark. It had been given her by the unsuccessful suitor.

At a later stage we spent some holidays at Lea Place, not far from

Bolney. Uncle Bob Helme had married my mother's eldest and most alluring sister Ettie, and taken her to live in a large house he had built next to old farm buildings and stables. To reach Lea Place from Wisborough Green you had to negotiate a long, winding track between fields and hedgerows and coppices. The road was gated and crossed the river Arun. In winter it often flooded and Lea Place was cut off, but in the summer the Arun was a brownish-green, sleepy old river with steep banks of clay and gnarled roots of oak trees to sit on while watching for the bobbing of the green and red float.

I remember Aunt Ettie as a slim, elegant figure in a blue riding habit and black veiled tall hat, walking swiftly through the communi-cating oak-panelled rooms whose windows all looked out on the blue expanse of the Sussex Weald. She had the family voice and manner of speaking – she always addressed children as equals. Uncle Bob was round and bald, but he possessed the fairest skin imaginable and eyes the colour of aquamarine. There were three grown-up sons, and a daughter, Molly. The household was ruled by 'the Oracle', a nanny-turned-housekeeper named Venn.

Lea Place was altogether more haphazard and less spruce than Bolney. The large hall was surrounded by window seats for old chintz cushions and dogs. Molly, I suppose, was almost grown up. She made us sets of furniture out of acorns and matches, peering through thick lenses with her pale-blue Helme eyes. I found her husky voice and laugh – her wavy fair hair and transparent skin – most attractive. She had literary leanings, organizing a play in the village – *The Princess and the Swineherd*. Somehow she made me learn my lines, and one hot summer's afternoon we performed on the lawn at a house in the village. I was not particularly proud to be chosen for the princess, but I liked my swineherd.

Uncle Bob owned several farms, which stretched away to the Toat Tower and the downs beyond. There were oak woods and hazel coppices where wild strawberries crept everywhere among ferns and little orchids. It was high, open country, with wider horizons than Bolney. Every year the Helmes held a farm supper in the stable yard. All the nannies, who met frequently for picnics and fishing, would the following morning discuss this noisy celebration, placing much emphasis on thick heads. There were regular picnics under the trees, when we would run for help or just to chat, from one nanny to another. My favourite, other than our own Nan, was Venn, the

Oracle of Lea Place. She looked so stern with her frizzy hair and the little hairs sprouting from the mole on her chin. It was all the more satisfactory when one received only help and kindness from her after that first very quizzical look.

While I was still very young, tragedy struck Lea Place. Guy and Barnard, the two eldest sons, had only lately left Eton. Guy, dark with grey eyes, and handsome like my brother, joined the Coldstream Guards. Barnard, with the Helmes' fair curls and skin and aquamarine eyes, enlisted in the Royals. Both were killed within weeks of joining up. The mud, the roaring cannon, those shiny pictures in the *Illustrated London News* which set my teeth on edge as if sticky fingers had walked over them, suddenly stopped being just pictures. My mother was summoned. Aunt Ettie was distraught. Neither Uncle Bob, Molly or Nigel, her surviving son, nor the Oracle, could console her. She died not long after her sons, having joined the Roman Church.

Lea Place began to become quite different, colder yet more sophisticated. There were purple and green patchwork cushions in the schoolroom, pierrots and harlequins, a flavour of art deco, and later the gossip of Molly and Nigels' friends among the Bright Young Things, and cocktails before meals.

Uncle Bob loved my mother. He evidently preferred her to his other sisters-in-law, so we often went to stay with him. When Nigel was down from Oxford, I fell in love with everything about him – his lazy sleepy voice, the way his breath hissed through his teeth. He used to play the ukulele, singing:

Twice one is two, twice two is four,
Twice three is six and the twins on the floor.
There's Lil and there's Bill, and there's Algernon,
There's Mable and there's Abel, and of course there's John,
So having kissed little Mabel through the twelve times table
He would start all over again.

In the morning I would peep into his bedroom to see the Oracle shaking him awake – 'Come along my sweetie, wake up my sweetie. It's ten o'clock.' Throughout mealtimes he ate tiny Huntley & Palmer rusks, continuously, out of a silver-lidded trophy. His voice was deep, his tone self-deprecating. He would screw up his aquamarine eyes and make endless disparaging jokes about people and life. Nigel hunted and shot, of course, but I don't think he was devotee of racing like his father, who had a box at Goodwood, with his name on a bench in the members' enclosure.

The most indelible image of Lea Place that stays with me is of the large oil painting of a woman on the passage wall outside Uncle Bob's bedroom. She lay on a couch, plump and blonde and naked. To me she was somehow related to the lonely and inarticulate widower in his bedroom behind her.

Our English uncles used to leave us to ourselves, unscathed; but the Irish uncles, all of them clergymen, expected conversation, answers to questions and jokes. My father was himself the jokiest of men: neither very subtle nor witty, but always finding reasons for laughter in solemn people and occasions. At times it could be disconcerting, but it was often pleasant to have a receptive audience for one's own idiocities. The Reverend never giggled or chortled; he just threw back his head and laughed from his belly. I remember him reading *The Young Visiters* aloud with tears of mirth pouring down his face.

The grown-ups seemed to regard one another with mutual esteem and affection, which left us children free for adventuring in a secret land without being hauled into their dramas of anger, jealousy or passion. I never once heard my parents quarrel when I was small. On the other hand, I don't remember other children in those early days with any great affection; all my ardour was concentrated on my handsome and most courteous brother, under a year older. We used to attend children's parties together. The best moments came when, poised at the top of the line, it was one's turn to dance between the two avenues of children, watched by everybody, to meet one's diagonal, grasp crossed hands and whirl for several bars of Sir Roger de Coverley. Such terribly brief ecstacy was ruined if one's counterpart was slow of foot and fell during the tugging and circling. I wore a dress of net over sateen, coloured with tiny moss roses of pink and green, my hair arranged in bobbles, tied up the night before with linen strips. Michael, better looking, in his white serge suit, than any of the other boys, always kindly obliged when I insisted on dancing with him. But he already had one eye roving beyond his younger sister.

Life was to change dramatically when Michael was sent to board at a preparatory school. At about the same time, my elder sister

Diana developed a 'murmur' in her heart. A great, long basketwork pram was brought in, on which she lay flat. She even went to the dancing class in it. When my brother's big black trunk and tuck box arrived in the nursery, one life came to an end. The nursery broke up. There was to be no more hunting for the Kaiser in the bushes, or digging for Australia. Privately I had for some while addressed myself as Teddy, in homage to a handsome village boy who walked past the rectory gate on Sundays in navy-blue serge and who lived in a cottage down on the common. I discovered I was now a girl, not a pony or a boy or a fairy. After my brother went to school, I sometimes slept in his little room, watching the moon ride across the sky, not knowing why I felt sad and lonely; yet, in the agonies of each return to school, when he would creep up to the night nursery and hug our baby sister, the tears coursing down his cheeks, I have no recollection of sharing his misery.

It was round about now that I decided I would adopt the Greek gods and would pray to Hermes or Mercury instead of Jesus. My heroes and saints were Jason, Perseus and Theseus. My sister Diana and I spent very many happy summer hours being nymphs, hung with daisy chains and buttercups in the nutgroves at the bottom of the garden. She grew stronger again quite quickly. With my father constantly abroad, Diana and I were prepared for confirmation by his locum, Father Denny, a High Anglican, devout, humorous and scholarly priest, who bore a close resemblance to Mr Punch. I can still see Father Denny's elderly face, smiling and serene as he walked about the village in his black cassock and beretta, as the battles and slaughter raged across the Channel. Under his influence, my sister became genuinely devout, reading Father Andrew, and other advanced mystical books. I abandoned my allegiance to the pagan Greek deities; I was confirmed at eleven – a more sensible age than the teens, given the disruptive effects of hormones on the psyche. To this day I can recapture, if only faintly, the elation experienced when kneeling before the Bishop of Guildford and feeling his hands rest on my head. However foolish, sinful and neglectful my subsequent behaviour, nothing can take away from me that moment of dedication to the hidden world. The Armistice came. We celebrated outside, jostling children and grown-ups with bands and singing. Each child was given a mug with the soldiers of the Allies marching round it, carrying their countries' flags. My father stayed on for a time with the Army of Occupation in Cologne.

When he finally did return, our life was changing even faster. I was now in the lower school at Guildford High, where Diana and I were both enrolled. Nan was mostly occupied with Romola. We ate downstairs in the dining room. I had been moved into a large attic bedroom above the nursery floor, close to the hissing, gurgling water cisterns. Mary the housemaid slept near by and there was a faint, peculiar smell of goats, but she never came to bed until I was asleep. The evening climb up the flight of linoleum-covered stairs, emphasizing the severed contact with the nursery, created a glorious sense of freedom and selfhood. I had my first full-length mirror. Naked, my yellow hair flowing around me, I could dance and caper, and shout and sing all the poems I learned and read: 'Hyperion', which I pronounced 'Hiphooray', 'The Forsaken Merman', 'The Jumblies', Wordsworth and Kipling, nursery rhymes. I made tunes for the psalms, and thus, through Father Denny, the wandering lamb returned to the fold.

In the morning, I washed in cold water, dressed in a navy-blue gym-tunic and long black stockings and ate breakfast. Then Diana and I either bicycled to Guildford or caught the private bus. This vehicle stood waiting for us, various other scholars and Miss Tweed each week-day morning outside the Horse and Groom. Miss Tweed, who taught at a primary school in Guildford, was tall and gaunt and possessed a remarkable bouncing walk. She kept the bus waiting, she clowned and talked incessantly, never smiling, in a loud voice for all to hear. But the bus ride could never rival the excitement of the bicycle on those early mornings of spring, summer and autumn. Then we rode through empty roads, spinning downhill past the familiar village shops and houses as we left the downs and entered the suburban streets lined with the sedate homes of our school-fellows. Sometimes we took the muddy lane where Ethel M. Dell, epitome of a child's idea of a governess, wrote her novels of Passion in the Empire, and who sometimes held children's parties with superlative food, music and dancing. Thence we would join the London road at a corner where, opposite a small railway halt, the brick and slate high school, with its limes, its shrubberies and concrete playgrounds, received its pupils. We entered by the side-gate, pushed our bikes into a shed and proceeded into the cloakrooms to change shoes, hang up our hats – felt in winter, straw in summer – and retire into evil-smelling lavatories. I hated those lavatories with a violent detestation. Their odour permeated the entire cloakroom. The very high intellectual standard of the school under its head, Miss Stocks – I am told now the best of its kind in the country, with its imaginative and varied curriculum – did not extend to toilet hygiene.

Every subject was well taught at Guildford. Up to twelve years, boys and girls were mixed, and I almost excelled in class, sitting most happily next to a curly-headed boy called Stewart, the son of a local builder. I repeatedly won the reading and poetry prize – once with a rendering of 'The Burial of Sir John Moore at Corunna' which almost reduced the judges and my fellow pupils to tears. Gym was always enjoyable, with horse, ropes and shipwrecks; so was netball in the playground and hockey and lacrosse in playing fields along the London Road. After I reached the senior school, about half a dozen scholarship girls were to arrive as non-fee-paying scholars. There was much whispering, and doubtless snobbery. There were critical comments from other parents, though never from mine. The scholarship girls were worth the experiment. Thelma, an engine driver's daughter, was a good musician and generally came top in maths and French; Connie was a brilliant athlete and soon put me in my place as a fancied sprinter, becoming Captain of Games; Lisa, with her lugubrious, basset-hound features, became a private friend.

Willey (Miss Wilson) was the oldest teacher. She wore her white hair in a net above her pince-nez, trailing navy-blue skirts. I never cheeked her or read a book under the desk during her classes, or passed books around. She instilled in me a lasting love of Milton and Shakespeare and the early English poets. I doubt if she ever knew what a great teacher she was.

In Miss Nye's lessons, by contrast, I giggled and dawdled, gossiped and fidgeted. She taught mathematics, chemistry and botany in the long upstairs lab. In one botany exam I distinctly remember being handed a Brussels sprout and a sheet of foolscap. I drew the vegetable with some care, but could think of absolutely nothing to say in analysis. Miss Nye took me for extra maths, and treated me with kindness. But by that time the dangerous teens had taken over, or I had a block. Meanwhile Diana had prospered academically, to reach the sixth form. Only my extra subjects – elocution, the piano and later the violin – held me, but even those I never practised to the degree my talents merited. Small vanities and rebellions took on increasing importance. I had to wear a bow tie, with my gym tunic high on my thighs and the plaited waist-band tied around my hips; I wore my hat at a saucy angle, or bent, like an Australian digger's; I had to cheek the prefects – one of whom was a very clever girl with huge sea-blue eyes, appropriately named Thalassa Crusoe. She sang with gusto and was a brilliant, co-operative creature. Despite her fascination for me, I did all I could to be irritating and defiant. Climbing over the high chestnut-paling fence out of the playground was no mean feat on summer afternoons, and it was fun to lead a little troop up and over into the forbidden long grass, away from the tennis and netball courts.

The school was divided into houses, each with its debating society and orchestra. Though I was appointed conductor of mine, by now I was incapable of carrying anything through. I think it was for this reason that I was often given responsibility. We collected money for 'the starving children of Europe', pulling in our cheeks and tummies in imitation of their plight. By the end of one term I had left my scattered funds on the sixth-form table without bothering to add the total up or seal it in the prescribed envelope. Somehow I wonder if the journeys back and forth from home to school, traversing, as we did, the busy world of streets and shops and people, was too much of a daily distraction. There was a handsome man whom we passed on his way to the office, who always solemnly raised his hat and winked at me, doubtless recognizing the rakish angle at which I wore mine atop the yellow plaits; there was also a forward and cheeky porter at the London Road station who needed to be put in his place. But I do not remember gossiping much about boys, or talking to my schoolmates about home life.

Wartime friends of my father came to stay. He must have brought home with him the horrors of France, of the hospitals he had served in among the streams of dying and wounded. I heard them discussing the Armistice; he banged on the table hard, shouting, 'It's wrong, it's wrong!' as he told of the terrible plight of defeated Germany. He would still sing a favourite psalm or hymn while shaving, as if forcing the Almighty to listen to him; he was still as jokey as before, acting the fool at mealtimes, reciting Edward Lear's nonsense verses in mime, with knives and forks and wine glasses, or expounding some book he was reading, such as Ball on the Universe, or the new passion that

22

had taken over from Napoleon, Joan of Arc. He made a pilgrimage to Domrémy, walking the last few miles, as Allenby did into Jerusalem. He plotted with the Dean of Winchester to erect a statue to her in the cathedral; he even suggested I change my name to Joan or Jeanne.

But in the parish, I sensed, things had changed also. One day the choir walked out on him, probably over the introduction of the *English Hymnal*. There was a stout, round-faced grocer of a man who sang in the bass. He and Mr Pleece, a touchy schoolmaster, must have found it difficult to stomach the robust eccentric Irishman. I think the Reverend's influence on the choristers was much the same as on ourselves in the nursery – he wasn't the least interested in discipline. Rather he wanted alert minds and questions and laughter. He did not mind being cheeked – by us or by them. I got into the habit of doing silly 'unsuitable' acts for him – the village idiot – or singing quite ribald songs, like 'No Wonder She's a Blushing Bride'.

The Reverend took us to stay with some friends of his called Acland, a large and well-known family of liberal intellectuals who had rented a school in Scotland. We went swimming in the loch in the nude. I had never seen a naked grown-up before, and was pleasantly surprised, but the men, I think, kept to another bay. It was my very first house party: we loved the charming, talkative young men and women, with us the only children there. My father was a fine swimmer as well as a tennis player, and had run for Ireland while at Trinity College. Now, however, his health suffered a set-back. It was on a later visit to the Aclands that he became ill with pneumonia, which in those pre-penicillin days carried a far higher risk of mortality than it does now. My mother rushed to his bedside, and soon afterwards, when the term time came around, Diana and I were sent to stay with 'Anne Dan', a former parlourmaid from the rectory who had married the local postman. We shared the big bed in their front bedroom and ate in the kitchen. There seemed to be no room anywhere: the low ceilings made us huge. Anne Dan was pretty and gay, caring and spoiling and utterly changed divested of her black dress, crisp white apron and cap. Later we moved to Mrs Bowles, who lived farther into the village beyond the church. We experienced cereals for breakfast for the first time, and condensed milk.

Near to Mrs Bowles's house was the village hall, where all kinds of junketings took place: dances, sales, mothers' meetings and Sunday school. My mother taught at the latter, and as we grew older we helped by giving out cards and settling the children at their paintings of texts and bible stories. I felt happy and useful, my tiresome urge to be different submerged in observing my mother so sure of herself. We had been more accustomed to seeing her at a distance, entertaining in pretty, expensive clothes – evening dresses and furs, the wide-leafed hats she bought at Woolands and elegant hand-made shoes from Peter Yapp; or watching from the bathroom window as she played tennis with her guests or drove off veiled in the open car behind Mulley. Now I saw how loved she was in the village, where my father had many critics.

At Merrow I had one friend close to my own age. Audrey Neil lived with her mother and nurse in a cottage in our lane, opposite the schoolhouse. The cottage was white with black beams and a tile-hung roof, and had a pretty garden with apple trees. Her mother, Eleanor Neil, was a tall, rangy woman whose husband had been killed early in the war. Audrey, an only child, was unusual and, to me, somewhat eccentric. She lived with an enormous family of stuffed animals who sat in a circle while she talked to and taught them endlessly. She had an unbounded imagination, but her games had to be interpreted practically: sometimes I felt embarrassment at the continuation of her imagination with the sticks and stones of everyday life. Eleanor was a Theosophist. She also played the piano. Audrey learned the cello. The three of us would go for long walks on the downs – Eleanor always striding ahead. She left a lasting impression on me, that of an interesting and distinguished mind. She must have been poor. I knew no one else who lived alone in a cottage with the nanny doing the cooking. Sometimes a handsome sister was around, married to General Sir Hugh Ellis, whose father, Sir Edmund Ellis, lived in the village. The general's advent always created a stir – he had invented the tank.

After my parents had gone abroad, I sometimes stayed with Eleanor Neil so I could continue at the Guildford High School. Audrey was by then away at boarding school. In the small drawing room leading out of her dining room, Eleanor played with discernment on the grand piano, which nearly filled the room, and accompanied me on my fiddle. She smoked Turkish cigarettes beside the fire and drank China tea. There were big blue cushions on the chairs and sofa. On the window ledges, blue hyacinths grew in blue and white china bowls.

One day she told me she was to have an operation. She had another and another, and finally, after an interval of a year or two, I went to a London nursing home to sit with her and write her letters. I found her utterly changed – querulous, gaunt and yellow, imagining persecution from within the home, impossible to please. The Ellises decided it was better for Audrey not to see her so ill and altered under morphine, so I continued my visits until she died. At her funeral I walked with Audrey behind the coffin.

A few years later I learned that Audrey was studying music in London and frequented the London College of Psychic Science. She told me how she frequently spoke with her mother and discussed her life with her. Would I like to attend a séance? I went to an upper room in Queen's Gate, where I found Audrey and a little woman with fair, fluffy hair, who sat quietly in her chair facing Audrey. I sat in a corner by the window. Some contact spirit came through, whom the medium seemed to know well. I imagined a kind of Ariel to her Prospero. He 'fetched' Eleanor and she started talking to Audrey – telling her she, Eleanor, was intensely busy since a number of people had just 'come over' completely unprepared. This was a reference to a recent earthquake in the Far East. Then she stopped and said to Audrey, 'Someone else is with you today.'

'It's Pam,' said Audrey.

'Oh, Pam – it's so long.'

Although it was the voice of the medium speaking, as I walked down Queen's Gate pondering, I was, and still am, convinced it was Eleanor Neil who spoke to me.

We vacated Merrow rectory when I was about eleven. My father's illness so soon after the years in France had culminated in a swap. The chaplain of one of the two English churches at San Remo on the Italian Riviera was to take on Merrow while my father was to convalesce in the Italian sun. Never again would we sing and pray in the familiar old Norman church, whose every pew and footstool I knew. There would be no more family prayers in the dining room after breakfast, the maids rustling to kneel or rise in their morning print dresses as we peeped at them through our fingers, to see whose bottom was biggest.

Nor would we be with our Nan. Shortly before we left Merrow

rectory for ever, Nan asked my mother, with a burning face, if she could go to Guildford to meet a friend. It was something that had never happened in fifteen years. 'Why don't you bring her here?' said my mother.

'It's a he,' said Nan.

Nan was late for her own wedding. She had hidden in the nursery bathroom, where she was found washing Romola's white socks.

It was autumn when we took the Train Bleu to the French Riviera. The carriages smelled of coal and soot and were very warm and stuffy. There were attendants and porters, for all luggage, great trunks and round hat-boxes, travelled in a special van. There was an elderly lady also travelling on the train, on her way to join a daughter who lived in San Remo. Tall and stately, with sable furs and a veil, she made friends with my mother. During the night she must have mistaken the carriage door for the lavatory and fallen on to the line. My mother, who had not slept, evidently visited her compartment and found her missing. She pulled the alarm cord, causing a wave of consternation to spread the length of the train as it ground and shuddered to a halt. Men in uniforms came and went. My parents found themselves at the centre of a fearsome argument. At first the officials had refused to believe them and threatened to fine them for pulling the communication cord. When my parents finally convinced them that the old lady was indeed missing, they were told rather callously that she must have fallen into the path of the oncoming Paris express.

This tragedy of the night hours only temporarily dampened the excitement of venturing with my family towards an unknown destination. The first sight of red-tiled roofs and olive trees in the morning rapidly caused my spirits to soar. We exercised all our well-proven wiles to comfort our parents and make them smile again. We had to spend one night at Mentone as there was no connection to Ventimiglia on the Italian frontier. My father disappeared for hours to try and telephone the old lady's daughter. The smell of the hotel garden – mimosa and heliotrope, warm sea air – was unlike any I had breathed before. I stepped down from the next day's train as into a theatre, a light-hearted comedy where nothing was real or urgent or important, a sensation enhanced by the utter foreignness of the people and place.

2

Les Visages et les Derrières

The Italian and French Rivieras of that era were an enchanted land. There were no large towering buildings; villas stood in luxurious gardens beside the sea or higher up, back towards the mountains. San Remo, like all the Riviera resorts, had retained its old town, set on a hill behind the Casino, above the railway and the main street where the trams trundled, ringing their bells under the tangled branches of plane trees. In the old town the streets were so narrow that some of the houses were connected by overhanging archways. Women screeched at each other as they hung out the washing. Everywhere there were tiny dark shops and stalls, barrows and babies, handsome dark-eyed men and women; there were flowers and vegetables unknown to Surrey or Sussex, and an all-pervading smell of drains. Steep, cobbled streets led from the Grand Promenade and the large hotels to the villas and pensions above. It was with amazement that I came across men or women urinating or squatting along the front or in one of those leafy laneways outside my father's church of All Saints. Beggars sat under the date palms, parting their ragged garments to show sores and wounds, or even leprosy.

The railway ran half-hidden by the promenade, and below it were the small limited beaches of sand and artificial fishing piers. At midday and early evening the promenade came alive with well-dressed people just walking up and down and less well-dressed people trying to sell them flowers – carnations, violets, roses and marigolds. The newspaper and magazine seller each had his own individual chant. I had never seen so many handsome people, descendants, no doubt, of the Ligurian tribe and Saracens.

27

A Cloud of Forgetting

The young men strolled in bands apart from their sisters. The boys and older men offered comments on the girls as they went by. I soon came to expect compliments – 'Una vera piccola Botticelli.' Before long many of the elegant, well-dressed youths would become tennis and dancing partners at the sport club. In no time I acquired a taste for continental ways and the high living-standards of the pre-war Riviera. I sometimes wonder at the months and years of my life spent with such profligacy on playing tennis and dancing. Diana and I became quite proficient at tennis: we played in the San Remo team all along the French and Italian Rivieras, even consorting with the Wimbledon great when they arrived for international competitions. We loved Fred Perry, who wasn't too grand to play with us.

Our education meanwhile continued on a basis of seasonal migration. In the summer weeks of term, when the Germans descended on the Riviera, I went back to England to continue at Guildford High. During the winter, we attended lessons at the Jeanne D'Arc Convent, an association that greatly pleased the Reverend. There we sat with the Italian pupils in their black uniforms and wrote French dictation, reading and spelling each word afterwards – 'Maître Corbeau sur un arbre perché!' Later we took Romola, aged about seven, with us. But she would not co-operate. I tried hard to remonstrate with her, but her only answer was a cryptic, terrified scream, 'The pottitoe nun, the pottitoe nun!' Long afterwards she explained that the kindly old nun in charge of the infants had a huge nose with enlarged pores like a potato.

My father's duties were to succour and call on the English-speaking visitors at the hotels or the residents in their villas. Not all were respectable, or necessarily attended either of the two English churches. Wintering in the luxuriant villas above the sea-front were assorted drunks of both sexes, 'gay' peers who had been blackballed by London clubs, divorcees or incipient divorcees, affluent English families who came to enjoy the mild climate. In more modest establishments were retired domestics living on legacies.

We were to have three or four seasons of lodging each winter in various pensions or flats which my mother contrived to make habitable enough to entertain any motley individuals the Reverend might bring round. Then the invitation came for my father to stay at San Remo on a permanent basis. Miss Coat, the church's chief supporter in the town, had died, leaving her villa and garden on the hillside on the western outskirts for the use of the chaplain of All Saints. Below the Villa Graziella, Miss Coat had built a cottage for her two old maidservants, Sarah and Hetty, to retire to. With their cats and dogs and parrots, they in turn provided a refuge for my youngest sister, lonely for the English countryside and already a budding naturalist. Romola never learned much Italian; but she soon knew individually all the horses harnessed to the fiacres, obediently trotting along the sea-front or struggling up the steep lanes to the hotels and villas. Most of them answered to names like Bobbie, Clumpy or Black Captain, having been left behind by the British cavalry at the end of the war.

There were those among the English who took an excessive interest in animal welfare. Up the road above the Villa Graziella I once came across an English lady literally beating an unfortunate man with her umbrella while he loaded up his big black mule. An interesting exception, who gave priority to human needs, was Mrs Kenneth Grahame, wife of the author of *The Wind in the Willows*. She spent much of her time collecting for the Italian poor. The creator of Rat, Mole and Mr Toad stood by, white-haired and gentle; when he and his wife were together he seldom got a word in.

Shortly after we arrived in San Remo, the old Italian verger at the church had left, to be replaced by Mr Prestige, a retired butler who had lived for many years with a rich expatriate and spoke fluent Italian. By day he might be seen gossiping with his Italian cronies as he swept the porch; we found his round red face under a cranium of sparse red hair always ready for a joke or a grumble. It must have been Mr Prestige who reported that the priest at the near-by Polish church, who used to converse in Latin with my father in a thoroughly friendly way during the week, regularly abused him from the pulpit each Sunday, denouncing him as a heretic and a mortal danger to Catholic souls. Mr Prestige, who kept the church so beautifully, also kept my parents on tenterhooks: he used to disappear for days on benders, and once was found in the crypt, drunk in charge of a corpse.

All Saints had been built by those English residents who had tired of the humble little evangelical church that stood in the shadow of the flamboyant, gilded dome of the Russian basilica, next to the English tea-room at the farther end of the promenade, just before the elaborate precincts of the Casino. The Reverend was blissfully happy at All Saints, free to indulge the Anglo-Catholic tendencies denied to him in Ireland and Merrow. He collected finely carved saints and a large crib from Bolsano in the south Tyrol; he gathered together a choir, which Diana and I joined, and robed us in saxe-blue gowns and veils. We attended week-day choir practices, laying our tennis rackets among the footstools. I sang mostly seconds, but Diana had a lovely pure soprano voice like a boy's. It was sadly neglected by the Reverend, for in one of the hotels he had discovered Mrs Dyson, a general's widow, within whose ample bosom lived an instrument which could rise without a tremolo to top A during a hymn solo or chant and contained a pathos and spiritually I can never forget. After every such performance, she would turn a pair of large moist Pekinese eyes on us, as if asking for our approval. She never questioned the Reverend's untutored direction. How rewarding it must have been for him to have such a soloist after the rasping tenor of the stout grocer in the Merrow choir who led the insurrection there.

The organist, Miss Hood, lived in a shady villa with her mother and was cast in a very different mould. Musically competent, if uninspired, she clearly detested the Reverend. Once, towards Christmas, when she was asked to play the hymn, 'Jesus, good above all other', she flatly refused, proclaiming it an irreverent dance tune because it was composed in waltz time. I expect she loathed the introduction of the *English Hymnal*.

In the early 1920s, our congregation was large, often augmented by Italians who would stand at the back, thinking my father's services were conducted according to the full Latin rite. I remember one Italian deploring that so many attractive young women in the choir should have taken the veil. Three quarters of the way up the right-hand side of the aisle, a few arm-chairs were kept roped off. These were reserved for Princess Beatrice and her Lady-in-Waiting, Miss Minnie Cochrane. The elderly princess, a widow and the youngest daughter of Queen Victoria, stayed at a villa at the eastern, German end of town, belonging to the Graysons. Lady Grayson had formerly been Louise Dale, a singer and actress of some fame. My father used to visit the old princess regularly and read to her as she had failing eyesight.

One memorable Sunday, when the congregation sang in an especially lacklustre way, abetted no doubt by the witch at the organ, the Reverend banged his fist on the lectern so hard that even Miss Hood felt obliged to stop. 'This is no way to praise your Maker,' roared my father. 'This service is at an end. For the remaining time we will practise the hymns and canticles for next Sunday.'

There followed a deathly hush. I felt the familiar, acute embarrassment the Reverend so often engendered without warning. In the reserved area a dignified figure in dark red rose immediately to her feet and opened her prayer-book, followed by Miss Minnie in stately black. Slowly and rather sheepishly the rest of the congregation followed to take their punishment.

The Reverend was well supported by his churchwardens, by contrast with Miss Hood. One was a retired senior officer, General Sir Foster Reuss Newland, who had served in the Middle East with Allenby and Uncle Harry. He was separated from his beautiful young Italian wife, but a small girl of enchanting looks would sometimes come to stay with him. The general had the gait of a man more used to riding a horse, and there was something poignant in the two of them stepping hand in hand along the promenade before the child with the dark curls and large black eyes disappeared again and left the old soldier to his lonely Italian winter.

Long, long after, when I knew her as Tony Lothian, she said that on one of those visits she asked her father if he thought God was an Englishman. He gave it careful consideration before replying, 'My dear child, I wouldn't be surprised.' The lonely little girl grew up to become a renowned journalist, a friend of the first Russian woman cosmonaut. She had married Peter, Marquis of Lothian, and had numerous issue, so bringing the Latin Rite into many of our aristocratic and landed families. I hope the general hasn't been upset.

Many of the winter visitors to the hotels, villas and pensions of San Remo came to improve their health. Always a good listener, my mother was regularly regaled with stories of ailments and treatments while taking tea in flats and pension bedrooms with lonely ladies to whom injections and suppositories were a new and exciting element in their lives. Her one great dread was to see the washing flannel being used as a kettle holder.

Betty Weingartner, the estranged wife of the conductor Felix Weingartner, was a devotee of Dr Fava and the treatment he offered. The doctor was a plump, swarthy Italian physician who enjoyed an enormous reputation along the Riviera. According to Betty, instead

of using a stethoscope, he would lay his balding head on the patient's
bosom to listen to heart and lungs, concluding his investigation with,
'Tomorrow I will come and massage your little pink abdomen.'

Betty, who used to appear at San Remo from her wintering
ground at Monte Carlo, had known my father when he was a young
locum curate in Switzerland and she a fascinating, quicksilver minded
Jewish teenager and budding actress. She still had a wonderful swagger
and self-assurance from having lived and travelled at the side of the
maestro, her former husband, but the general opinion seemed to be
that she brought trouble wherever she went. 'Poor little Betty,' my
father would say as she arrived. She had converted to the Roman
Church, and tried unsuccessfully to become a nun. I suspect she came
to San Remo to consult and perhaps be shriven by the Reverend.

Sometimes she would drive me back with her to Monte Carlo,
where she lived in a suite at the Hôtel de Paris. I sensed that she was
unhappy, did not like my mother and still held a romantic image of
the Reverend. Monte Carlo was far more beautiful than San Remo,
I thought – an architectural fantasy of terraced sugar cakes, decorated
with angelica for the palm trees, facing a dark-blue looking-glass sea.
The great grey rocks of the mountains hung above the town. Poor
little Betty was eventually to die lonely and rather alcoholically,
reduced to an inexpensive room at the Hôtel de Paris. That was
where I last saw her alive, summoned, as I had often been over the
years. She insisted I be an executor to her will, to distribute her
furs and clothes, her prayer-books and collection of Weingartner's
gramophone records, all of which she thought to be of immense
value. When it came to it, her lawyer told me there was no estate to
administer, she had died in debt to the hotel. It was a sad ending for
the brilliant girl who had once charmed Weingartner with her voice
and acting. There is a photograph of her and her husband on the
wall in Sacher's Hotel in Vienna, among the famous.

There was a lot of gossip when the Sitwell brothers came to stay
at the big hotel below our villa. The flutter they caused had something to do with their wearing baggy flannel trousers at parties; they
seemed to us quite old and unexciting and certainly did not dance
or frequent the tennis club.

Our parents found it hard to lure us away from the young Italians
in order to help entertain some of the British visitors. Thursday was
'At Home Day' at the Villa Graziella. The Giant would assist in the

baking of cakes and scones, and the cutting of savoury sandwiches for a truly British spread, never knowing who or how many would come. These feasts were in no way confined to the congregants of All Saints. Many of the Russian émigrés, recently scattered in their hundreds along the Riviera coast, came and ate hungrily; along with Englishwomen unhappily married to Italians, governesses, nannies and ladies' maids and lonely misfits. One of the latter we particularly appreciated was an ex-jockey with a wooden leg. He came and played cards with us and taught us how to cheat by sleight of hand; I suspect my father lent him money. I used to wait on the guests, circulating the plates and tea-cups between the drawing room and the dining room, the big double doors drawn back. My sister Romola would sidle up beside me and whisper loudly, 'You've got that silly look on your face again.'

About two years after we began our life on the Riviera, my parents decided that I should attend an expensive boarding school in Camberley. The headmistress, Miss Remington, was a friend of the Reverend's, her school being especially for girls from Scotland and overseas, and had agreed to take me at half-fees. The arts were stressed, with much of the autumn term being given over to performing one of Shakespeare's plays. During my term it was *The Tempest*, and as one of the company of 'elves of hills, brooks, standing lakes and groves' whose pastime was to 'make midnight mushrooms', I slid up and down steep planks at the back of the stage.

The English mistress was not of Willy's standard, but she gave great encouragement to our essays. I gathered a commendation for one which owed something to my father's declamation of 'Maud', a poem he knew by heart. I played in the school hockey team and made friends with a tall Canadian with whom I walked in crocodile across the sandy Berkshire pathways on frosty afternoons. After supper we would be invited into Miss Remington's large chintz drawing room to learn how to conduct ourselves with proper decorum. It was clear that most of the Beaufront pupils were destined to take their place in the highest ranks of a privileged society.

It was the second mistress, Miss Tillyard, who really ran the school. She was an enormous woman who appeared to suffer from some form of elephantiasis, or more probably dropsy. She was passionately attached to the gentle, elegant headmistress. I took a violent dislike to her, for when the local doctor gave me the routine examination and found me skinny, I heard Miss Tillyard say: 'We'll soon fatten her up.' From that moment on I planned to end my career at Beaufront.

I expect I transferred all the homesickness and isolation I felt at leaving my family the other side of Europe on to that unfortunate woman with her unwieldy body and booming voice. When the Christmas holidays came to an end, I refused to leave Italy. My parents had to write what must, in the light of the half-fees concession, have been a most difficult letter, explaining that it was impossible to reason with a child who would have to travel to England without a grown-up to see she actually arrived.

It was soon after my father had decided to stay on at San Remo that Granny Hodgson died and Uncle Barnard inherited Highlands. The Giant found a pretty little Regency farmhouse at Moushill among the oaks and millponds of Milford Common on the Surrey-Sussex borders. Each April she would begin to miss the English spring, and we would bundle ourselves into the familiar second-class, four-bunked compartment of the PLM (Paris-Lyon-Marseille) express. The guard's van invariably contained a trunk full of large fir-cones she had collected during drives in the mountains. At the customs, which were very strict after the war, she would declare her innocent cargo, which invariably amazed the officers. Meanwhile my father, respectably clad in clerical grey and dog collar, would walk ahead of us, two bottles of his favourite Strega liqueur hidden in his coat-tails. He was never caught, and always refused my mother's pleas to declare his contraband. He never lost his Irish distrust of authority, and would invariably defy notices saying 'trespassers will be prosecuted'.

There also came about the first of our summer holidays in Ireland. One of my father's best friends was Henry Patton, the Anglican bishop of Killaloe. (My father, when he later became canon at Killaloe, felt shamed by the small congregation in the beautiful old church, whereas the Roman Catholic faithful had to crowd into a small tin-roofed building.)

We stayed on that first and other occasions at the Bishop's Palace, and a donkey cart lined with hay came to collect our luggage at the station. The narrow streets of the town were still cobbled. The Shannon was in flood, and we bathed in the fields surrounding the palace. The bishop had a very pretty daughter, and my brother spent most of the time with her in a hayloft. It was at Killaloe that I had my first period. Bewildered, I told my sister, but she was most unhelpful, saying only that it was something to with Adam and Eve. She did not advise consulting Mrs Patton. My mother had stayed behind in England with Romola.

We went on to have a riotous visit with Uncle Lionel Fletcher, a renowned fox-hunting parson who lived in Kildare, where we played tennis on emerald-green turf. Uncle Li was in effect private chaplain to the Barton family at Straffan House, and lived in a charming glebe house full of Sheraton furniture. He had a good thoroughbred mare and hunters and always exhibited at the Dublin Horseshow. He was very Irish and ribald. He drove the rectory car appallingly danger-ously, urging it up the steep hills and lanes with rocking movements as if he were in the saddle. We didn't much care for Aunt Bessie. She was pretty and well dressed, with very round blue eyes, but also a crashing snob. She never left Uncle Li alone for a moment. She came from the North and had no children.

The tennis parties at Straffan were famous: all the ascendancy played pretty well. I fell in love with Ronald Barton, who danced with me and held his umbrella over me after church. Ronald was up at Oxford. He had a handsome Frenchwoman in tow, whom I thought very old. The Bartons lived in considerable state at Straffan House, the grandest house I had ever then seen. It was a kind of Gallic palace. To run it Ronald's father, Bertram Barton, employed sixteen servants, including three footmen. The family owned the famous Barton claret vineyards in France, but by the time Bertram died in a hunting accident in 1927, only five years later, the estate was deep in debt. The eldest son, Derek, cut the house down to a reasonable size and became an official Irishman – no longer a member of the ascendancy. Ronald inherited the vineyards, though he thought he had lost them when I met him in Lebanon in 1941, serving with the Free French. He returned after the war to revive and promote them and become the first English Mayor of Bordeaux.

During our time in San Remo, unknown to me, my future war-time boss Freya Stark was tramming into San Remo to learn Arabic, from L'Arma, the cottage at La Mortola where she had settled with her mother after her sister Vera's marriage to Count Mario di Roas-cio. It was an unhappy time for Freya and her mother, who was engaged in an expensive lawsuit against the count; he had swallowed most of her private money in a disastrous business venture. Freya told me that she had to make her own clothes at this time – which probably accounted for her later obsession with *haute couture*. Do we ever forget childhood disappointments, especially over the clothes we are made to wear? It is interesting to speculate what might have happened had we met at San Remo. Would she have tried to lure this foolish flapper towards higher education?

The culture gap was partially to be filled by a friend of my brother's. Michael, firmly integrated into the British private school system, only came to San Remo in the holidays. When he first appeared at the tennis club he was already long-legged in immaculate white flannels, a great asset to his sisters. With Granny Hodgson and her bounty deceased, and my mother's inherited portion in trust, money became tighter. To his eternal disappointment, Michael had to abandon a prospect of Eton, where he had long been enrolled, for Lancing. A natural athlete with a good eye for a ball, my brother might otherwise, like the Etonian Hodgson cousins, have been diverted from classics to the playing fields.

At Lancing, Michael made one special friend, Desmond Flower, the son of Dr (later Sir) Newman Flower who owned the publishers Cassell's. Desmond was an athlete but had the mind of a true scholar. A year or two older than my brother, he appeared at San Remo one holidays, staying at the Royal Hotel. Michael would disappear to join him in a sophisticated glamorous world and float amid company we only heard of through the gossip of other well-heeled parishioners. There was, for instance, a Spanish grandee confined to a wheel-chair who invited Michael to Spain as a companion for his much younger and handsome *duquesa*. For me, Desmond became an important addition to my spasmodic education. For years he chose and sent me books accompanied by exquisitely engraved and illustrated letters; through him I read *Moby-Dick*, David Garnett's *Lady into Fox, Go She Must!, The Grasshoppers Come*. I still have the white velum and gilt volume of William Morris's *Earthly Paradise* he sent me. He dug deep into my childhood when words meant rhyme and rhythm and cadences and he led me in due course to the poets of the years between the wars. Eventually he invited me to Eights Week at Cambridge, chaperoned by Lady Flower. There were long days on the river, long nights at the balls; but I was too immature to contribute to or benefit from Desmond's circle of erudite friends at King's.

Back in Italy, the ritual of courtship, as in all peasant societies, was conducted through dance, so dancing became an essential part of our education. A plump sleek man smelling of violets held a class for the foreign young ladies while, throughout the hour, his unremarkable wife sat against the wall as duenna. He taught the foxtrot, the two-step, the tango, the blues, and a dance I particularly enjoyed, 'L'Apache', the tune of which had become immensely popular. It began 'La notte invita l'apache'; one covered most of the floor and at the climax bent over backwards beneath the arms of the marauding *apache*. Although the dance-master never smiled and seemed made of flock rather than flesh and blood, he taught us well. I always looked forward to my turn for dancing with him, even though the heady rhythms of the blues and the contortions of 'L'Apache' had to be performed with unsmiling decorum. The Giant sometimes accompanied us to lessons in the early days. A Frenchman sitting next to her whispered: 'Regardez, Madame, les visages si graves et les derrières si gais.'

Thus were we made, first, fit for the fancy-dress parties, where children could join grown-ups, and finally to qualify for *thé dansant*, sometimes held at a private villa or hotels or in the gilded palm-fringed ballroom at the Casino. Those lessons were a good invest-ment, for the boys too had learned the art. As we sat around the walls on small gilt chairs, an unknown young man would detach himself from a small company on the other side of the dance-floor and approach one's parent or chaperone and bow to her. Nearly all the young Italians danced well, the weight laid back on to the heels of their stylish, polished shoes while we danced round those shoes on our toes, twisting and listing to the subtle orders of their right arms, their shoulders hunched a little, their bottoms slightly promi-nent. It was exciting and, in my case, utterly addictive, for this was before Fred Astaire popularized dancing cheek to cheek. The bands were excellent and intimate, the leader holding a special position in the hierarchy.

The best band in town was at the Royal Hotel, where dinner dances were held twice a week. One Christmas holidays we were invited to the 'Five o'clock'. I was wearing my first dress from Mme Marthe, designed and chosen by myself, a very dark-green silk slip heavily fringed. During one number, the god-like bandleader set down his baton, walked across to my chair and bowed. It was like being given the fox's brush after a hunt. In later years, when I was promoted to the dinner dances at the Royal, he became a little amorous and waylaid me on my way from the ladies' cloakroom. That particular hunt thereafter had to be renounced, for it wasn't done to dance with the leader of the band at the Royal. You were captive at your hosts' table for the evening: the stray young men would not even ask you to dance unless they knew them well.

Noel, the young man I shared a tutor with, was often asked as my partner. His parents had a villa at the German end of town, an imitation French *château* with gardens and vineyards running down to the shore, where there was a Moorish bathing pavilion. His father was an industrialist from the Midlands, with a yacht and a string of racehorses. An extremely pretty daughter used to come out from England, elegant in short skirts, a cloche hat pulled down over an Eton crop. Noel was younger, having just left Harrow. The Reverend befriended Noel, knowing his father to be a heavy drinker whose wife was unable to control him. Noel was tall and well dressed and always smelled good. One day I was taken to lunch with his parents at the villa with my father. It was there that I drank my first cocktail. We took our cocktails up at the villa and then had to walk through the tunnel under the highway and down a long path between the vines to where we were lunching at the pavilion by the sea. It was like walking the plank for five hundred yards. No one had prepared me for grown-up drinks and habits.

Eventually the spirits killed Noel's father. I overheard the Reverend telling the Giant about the terrible state of the body. His mother burned herself to death while dyeing her hair. All of that came later; Noel meanwhile cleared a path for my adolescent party life through the maze of polyglot grown-ups of varying backgrounds. He gave me endless boxes of chocolates and a pair of green and black crêpe de Chine pyjamas such as his sister must have worn. When I was sixteen, he proposed to me. It was good for my self-esteem, but not perhaps the best preparation for the tougher battles of life.

But even as happy, rather spoilt teenagers, we gradually became aware of larger events unfolding. The effects of Mussolini's attempts to condition the everyday lives of the Italian people began to show. The railway station was refurbished to impress foreign visitors; the evening *passeggiata* was regimented. The citizens of San Remo were instructed to walk up one side of the street and promenade down the other. Girls who joined the Party wore elegant black cloaks to match the boys' black shirts.

Mysteriously the beggars vanished from their station outside our church, the little cobbled *salitas* became less smelly. On my way to a friend's villa, where twice a week I gleaned a few rules of Latin grammar or read Ovid's *Metamorphosis*, I no longer had to pass by ladies or gentlemen performing their morning defecation. 'Nel Fascismo e la salvezza della nostra libertà,' I yelled to the Reverend, capping it with, 'Yes, we have no bananas, we have no bananas today.'

3

Dog Days and Travels with K.

Diana had seriously trained as a secretary and found a job. I was supposed to be training for the stage and was being tutored by Kate Rorke. To settle us in London the Giant had rented a large flat at the corner of Cheyne Walk and Flood Street, where we were joined by 'Mo' Lecky. Mo's family lived at Bally Kealey in County Carlow and she earned her keep by fine stitching, making and selling the most beautiful underwear of crêpe de Chine and satin. Mo had long thin legs and dimples in her cheeks and chin. She wasn't exactly pretty, but she had a mad kind of *joie de vivre*, a deep chuckle and a reputation for being rather 'fast'. In fact there were remonstrations from some of our Irish relations about letting her share the flat; however, she loved the Giant and the Giant reciprocated. Mo's sister was very handsome; she had married Ronnie Barton's eldest brother Derek, the heir to Straffan House.

Mo's clever fingers found work fashioning the costumes of Douglas Byng, London's most popular cabaret star of the 1930s. He was renowned for his comically grotesque female impersonation sketches, such as 'Minnie, the messy old mermaid'. In another of his songs, 'I'm a mummy', he used to be wheeled on stage in a sarcophagus, wrapped in Egyptian graveclothes of Mo's invention. We followed him round the clubs. Douglas Byng never smiled when we met him with Mo, and his famous sideways head-jerk from left to right was constant. One day Mo made a mistake: she laughed at one of his boy-friends, whom she thought comic. From that day on he never spoke to her or employed her again.

Another cabaret artist, and a true friend, was Ronald Frankau. He had a daughter our age and a new young wife. Like Douglas Byng, he wrote his own lyrics. I only remember one:

> Down by the river
> Where the reeds go a-shiver
> And the white folks' hearts are black,
> Makes my liver
> Go a-shiver shiver shiver,
> And I'm never never never going back.

Entertainers I disliked were the Two Barkers. A husband and wife act, they were much in demand for private balls, at which they sang lewd verses with innuendoes that I found embarrassing, especially since one was probably squatting on the floor, expected to laugh, beside a young man one hardly knew:

> How could
> Red Riding Hood
> Have been so very good
> And still kept the wolf from the door?
> Don't let me ask it,
> Who filled her basket,
> The story books never tell.
> But you know, I know . . .

The great stars were still in circulation and at the height of their powers: Gertrude Lawrence, Bea Lillie and Tallulah Bankhead, who was finishing her eight years in London, and Florence Desmond, who mimicked them all. The London we knew and played in was criss-crossed with their footprints.

Mo came to stay with us for Galway race week when we had hired a lodge on the shores of Lough Corrib for a whole summer. She swam round Galway Bay, clad in a dishcloth, shouting that she was 'Minnie, the messy old mermaid', then rode on the wall of death at the fair. Romola and I were there on our own for most of that holiday, and lived off the trout and pike we caught, Romola becoming a cunning and proficient angler. We were ostensibly under the wing of the Reverend's friend, Canon Dunlop, though our companions were the local farmers rather than the quality, and the miller, the young bachelor who owned the lodge. From time to time the latter turned up with a member of the Garda and a bottle of first-class poteen confiscated from a local still. There was a fancy-dress dance, given by a local family, to which I went as a scarecrow, a tattyboggart with a face mask of newspaper. The only word I spoke all night was 'rooks'. I enjoyed myself vastly, and as the moon was setting we all ran across the bog, jumping the turf drains. I cannot think I made a good duenna for a younger sister.

I had also been to stay with Mo in her family's big old Georgian house in County Carlow. Her mother seemed unwell and was hardly visible. Her father, the tall elderly General Lecky, was always courteous and attentive. Mo showed me her home, the woods and fields, displaying an almost poignant love for them. Her brother Rupert, who was in a cavalry regiment, used to drop in at the Cadogan Gardens flat with his friends, but it was when General Lecky came to London that Mo grew really excited, like a child. During the summer, when the general was staying at his club, he would take us to watch the polo at Hurlingham. Mo eventually married the son of an Irish baronet. She joined the WAAFS and learned to fly, but died in a plane crash at the beginning of the war. Almost the last time I saw her I found her utterly stricken. She had learned that the handsome general, the strength and stay of her youth, was not her real father at all. 'As if it mattered,' I said. But to Mo it did.

With my parents still abroad for half the year, I was led to spend more time with my godmother Kathleen Rees-Mogg, known as 'K.', at Clifford Chambers, her house in Warwickshire, and on the journeys she took me abroad. When I remember my godmother, I see her in grey: hunting in a pale-grey riding habit and bowler the colour of old man's beard; or dining in smokey-grey chiffon, with black and fire opals on her corsage and a bandau round her already grey head, wearing a long chinchilla cape, her grey-green eyes twinkling and sparkling above a long thin nose and lighting her face in humour or anger. Her health was always poor. Already when I first met her, she had undergone some serious operations.

Born Kathleen Mary Wills, K. was the youngest daughter of Sir Frederick Wills of the Wills tobacco dynasty. In 1909 she bought the manor house of Clifford Chambers near Stratford-upon-Avon, and that same year, in September, she married Edward Douty, a fashionable physician who counted Joseph Chamberlain among his patients. She had met him while visiting Cannes with her parents. Together K. and Douty improved and expanded the estate and the house, buying the Manor Farm and most of the village that stood outside the iron gates and red-brick walls of the manor. Their only son Gilbert – known as Tim – was born, like me, in the autumn of 1910. Two years after his birth his father died of tuberculosis.

As befitted the chatelaine of Clifford Chambers – a monastic establishment before the Reformation – the lonely widow and her small son were much under the influence of the Church, in the person of the Reverend Hodson of Clopton Hall. He and his wife, and his daughter Avis, became for K. close friends and counsellors. Clopton was converted into a hospital when the First World War broke out; a ward was named in memory of Dr Douty and the Hodson family moved to the Mill House, near Clifford Chambers.

I have a book whose plates show the manor as it then was inside and out, but that was before the disastrous fire of 1918, which broke out, I believe, while the family was away. The flames devoured the Renaissance staircase, the Elizabethan oak panelling and the Jacobean oak panelling of the dining room. In that pre-inflationary period, the damage was estimated at £30,000. The house, as restored by Sir Edwin Lutyens, retained the lovely Queen Anne façade, but he made his mark across the courtyard with his total rebuilding of the medieval south wing, known as the Grange, which had once been the abbot's lodgings. Here the formerly narrow passages were widened, the bedrooms made wonderfully luxurious, each with its own bathroom and dressing room, and new beams and plaster supplanted the charred ruins of the old. For the dining room, Kathleen found dark linenfold panelling on which to hang silver sconces.

The house which gave affection and dignity to my erratic teens was therefore not the same as the one K. bought in 1909 with her marriage to the delicate, older and fascinating doctor in mind. Avis Hodson told me years later how she remembered her family's move from Clopton to Clifford, swimming in the river Stour by the Mill, and roaming round the island across the moat from the garden side of the house, just as I was to wander in turn when the snowdrops were thick under the tall limes, whence the rooks had ominously departed. She recollected Dr Douty as friendly and kindly, writing children's rhymes to amuse. There is a photograph of him standing in knickerbockers and Norfolk jacket, his back to the camera as he admires the gazebo he designed.

K. had actually acquired me as a godchild by marriage. Her second husband, Graham Rees-Mogg, the chief veterinary officer to the Life Guards, had shared digs with the Reverend in his days as a London curate and hence became one of my godparents. Moggie, as he was generally known by the family, was a remarkably handsome man, over six foot tall with black hair and large dark-blue eyes inherited from an Irish mother. He had an elderly widowed reverend father, a member of the West Country family of Rees-Moggs, and a younger brother Robert, who was very different from the stern and almost puritanical Moggie, being constantly indebted to the bookies. Moggie had been an assiduous godparent, sending me toys throughout my childhood, though I scarcely knew him then.

In 1922, Kathleen had brought Moggie to share Clifford with herself and Tim, by then a schoolboy. For a while Moggie stayed on in the army. There was a house in Prince's Gate, conveniently close to Knightsbridge Barracks and to Tattersalls, at the corner of Brompton Road. Moggie sometimes took me to watch the auctions there after attending matins at St Michael's in Chester Square, where Canon Elliot's sermons packed the church each Sunday.

Tattersalls auction ring would be filled with men in top hats, frock-coats and shammy-leather gloves throwing knowledgeable glances at the circulating horses. Presiding over the scene was old Somey Tattersall, sporting a well-fed white waistcoat with morning coat and black top hat. The horses' hooves made a rhythmic clatter as the lads, smartly accoutred in breeches and bowlers, followed one another decorously round the ring. Someone should have thought to preserve that triangle of old London, with its circle of cobbles and loose boxes beneath the plane trees.

During my first visits to Clifford, I was much alone with Kathleen, for Moggie spent the week in London while Tim had just left Eton and was 'cramming' to get into Cambridge. Each morning K. would be closeted with Miss Thame from Stratford-upon-Avon to sift and answer the daily pile of mostly begging letters, addressed to her as a well-known heiress. There were no tax-free covenants or charitable trusts in those days to lighten the burden of wealth. Sometimes she would tell me about the odd requests and demands she had for her money; one family of royal descent wrote that unless given a new

Daimler they would be unable to carry on with their own charitable work. She never grumbled, having received a stern Nonconformist upbringing. 'Who would you like to ask for your birthday?' her parents used to ask her. 'Your little friends or those poor children from the workhouse who never have a party?'

At Clifford I slotted effortlessly into the smooth-running household. K. called me 'Pom' and I became a surrogate daughter. I would accompany her on visits to Batsford Park, the Gloucestershire home of her brother, Lord Dulverton (whom we knew as Uncle Gil), to consult him as head of the family regarding Tim's shortcomings. Tim was looked upon warily by his Wills relations, as rather flash and spoiled. All his bills were paid, but his actual allowance was little more than my brother's. There was no preparation or instruction for the great inheritance awaiting him. We used to stop to pick bluebells on our way, ostensibly to arrive at Batsford Park with a gift, but really to delay the somewhat painful interviews.

Many years later Uncle Gil told me, sadly, that he never knew his nephews and nieces at all well, seeing them only when they were in trouble. He had worked immensely hard for the family firm, as well as being an MP and master of hounds. He had a pale ascetic face with the same long nose as K. He sculpted well and composed music and limericks. I loved him and his pretty wife Victoria, but then I was never a subject for his concern or duty.

My flirtation with the stage continued. 'Don't put your daughter on the stage, Mrs Worthington,' sang Tim. There was much encouragement from Kate Rorke, and I must have some talent. I was even given leads in an offshoot Ben Greet touring troupe, playing Portia, Viola and Oberon: Shakespeare as a missionary endeavour, sponsored by the LCC and other educationally minded authorities. We travelled far and wide in a huge bus, the costumes and props strapped into laundry baskets. Subsequently I joined the newly established Guildford Repertory Theatre, now the Yvonne Arnaud Theatre. But other great distractions beckoned, especially the custom of 'staying away', as it was known. For whole weekends, or even for several weeks in the hunting season, one could be housed, fed and thoroughly entertained as a guest in the country. My plans for the stage slowly evaporated as I came to spend more and more time in K.'s company.

A year or so after I first stayed at Clifford, K. invited me to travel down to Exmoor for a month's stag-hunting during the summer holidays. The Giant, having been a hunting lady in her youth, managed to unearth a bowler hat and bought me breeches and boots. Thus I joined the exodus from Clifford, along with the cook, a footman, a lady's maid and a housemaid and most of the hunters with the head groom, Few, and his second groom. Tim drove down in his own car, a Chrysler coupé. K. and I drove in the big old Daimler behind Hasty, the chauffeur, who was so small you could hardly see his little hunched back behind the wheel.

We lodged in Dunster High Street at the Pink House, an old house belonging to the Misses Luttrell, aunts of the owner of Dunster Castle, Walter Luttrell. Here, free from Moggie's dominating shadow, since he remained on duty at Knightsbridge Barracks, Kathleen became 'Miss Wills that was'. Whenever she rode to the meet at Webber's Post in her grey habit, through some farmstead or Exmoor village, such as Horner or Luccombe, Brendon, Dulverton or Exford, someone who knew her was sure to approach, mounted or on foot. There would be recognition, an invitation for tea or drinks, or rest. Her delight at being back on the scene of her youth was unmistakable: I never saw her looking so happy in Warwickshire or with the North Cotswold Hunt. Exmoor was her country, were she had been reared to the song of the river Ex below Northmoor at Dulverton and the burr of the West Country voices she imitated so faithfully.

Riding on Exmoor was an excellent and demanding school for a novice like myself. We spent long hours in the saddle, cantering across the Dunkery heather or clattering down the steep combs to the water below; if a stag decided to make for a sanctuary near South Molton, we would have to hack all the way back to Exford. The hound trot, the gait hunters adopt in order to keep just behind the hounds, gets one firmly down in the saddle.

During my second season hunting with K., I was invited to ride out early with the 'tufters', a special honour, granted me no doubt as Miss Wills's protégée. The tufters represent a kind of reconnaisance party who seek out the stag before the main party gives chase. We met with the 'harbourer', or stalker, who told us where we would find a mature 'warrantable' stag suitable for hunting. (Old and wise stags retire to cover at the first glimpse of dawn.) An animal marked down for hunting can move up to a dozen miles overnight, into another country and another woodland. The harbourer therefore goes out at dawn to 'slot his stag' by following his tracks.

After we had found a warrantable beast, we rode back in triumph to the meet. It was then that the hunt began in earnest, with a full panoply of horns and hounds in tongue. Many people today condemn stag-hunting as even crueller than fox-hunting; it was certainly a bloody sport in the days when the hounds tore the animals to pieces limb by limb. By the 1930s, however, it was customary for the huntsman to carry a small gun with which to dispatch the stag once the hounds had him at bay.

Red deer have bred on Exmoor since prehistoric times, long before the farmer reclaimed the moor and forest. Having no natural predators, they need to be controlled, as we see today in Scotland, where their numbers are causing environmental havoc. From the farmer's point of view, they are wasteful and mischievous animals. They will root up a crop of turnips, taking only a bite from each, and nip the succulent tips of corn from a field, raiding by night and bedding there by day. They break through fences and destroy young trees.

During the nineteenth century, when the royal hunting preserve on Exmoor fell into disuse, the deer almost died out. With no regular hunting to protect the breeding cycle, they were shot and slaughtered in and out of season, their meat salted down like a pig's by the country folk. E. W. Hendy, a journalist and field naturalist who was not himself a hunting man, claimed that only the hunt ensured the survival of the red deer through the two world wars.

There is little in life to beat coming down to a breakfast of cold grouse, cold ham, kedgeree or bacon and eggs, already dressed in one's breeches over laddered silk stockings, maybe a waistcoat. We wore ratcatchers, tweed or whipcord coats, collars and ties or coloured stocks, brown boots or gaiters. Sometimes there would be a thick blanket of mist over the valleys, and it would be freezing on Dunkery or at Brendon Two Gates; on other mornings the sun would shine from a cloudless sky, and by noon the horses would be sweating, breeches would feel tight and boots irksome, while the quarry remained in the valleys whose friendly waters carry no scent. When the saddle finally began to betray its wooden tree beneath the leather, Few or his number two, the young brother of the pretty Mrs Few, would be there to say, 'You've done enough, Miss Pam, give him to me. Hasty is here with Madam.'

The Pink House, only two storeys high, gave on to the street, a room straddling each side of the front door. The drawing room at the back opened directly on to a walled garden with a gate through to the churchyard. The church sat square-towered, its blue and gilt clock facing our windows so that there was never any excuse for being late for a service, a meet or a meal. The garden was planted with magnolias, with tender shrubs along the walls, with tulips and begonias. Right above us in the park, on a hill surrounded by great old trees, sat the castle the Luttrells had owned since Domesday, the family being the oldest recorded commoners in England. Walter Luttrell was a large, impressive man with blue-grey eyes. He had a charming Australian wife and a well-mannered small boy, also called Walter, who came out hunting on his pony.

Below the castle, within the park, there was a polo ground; it was fun to stroll there on a non-hunting day, honour satisfied since one had been on a horse the day before and would be again tomorrow. Most of the polo players were housed in the Luttrell Arms at the far end of Dunster High Street. They appeared to be old, with wicked pasts, dubious presents and, unlike us, no futures. Like a race of centaurs, they were a breed apart with straddling, thin legs in shining brown boots and white breeches fanning out like elephant ears from tightly buttoned knees. They had names like Keith Menzies, Philip Magor, Maurice Kingscote; they talked in loud confident voices. One of them, Archie David, who was short, round and Jewish, often visited us at the Pink House. Later he would invite me to dine at posh restaurants in London. I remember longing to be shorter and trying to shrink for his comfort.

Minehead was then still a modest seaside town, where there were polo and hunt balls to reap in money from the rich summer visitors. We mingled with the local county folk, the centaurs and other house party guests around the neighbourhood. The Munningses sometimes stayed on Exmoor. One would come across 'A.J.' behind his easel, while Violet Munnings, a visual treat riding sidesaddle in a dark-blue habit, would delight us with her stories of 'Ai Jai', as she used to call her husband in her inimitable cockney voice.

My father used to tell his choristers, 'The Church of England is built upon rhythm.' The same applies to horsemanship. I reckon it an art every bit as demanding as music or painting. The ruddy outdoor faces of horsey people belie their sensitivity and intuition. A connoisseur of art or music need not paint or play; but I doubt if any man or woman can be a good judge of a horse who has not at some time or other known the movement and rhythm of those bones and muscles between their thighs.

My life among what my mother used to call 'those young bloods who exhaust you', gave a new and absorbing satisfaction to someone who had hitherto loved mainly music and dancing. The 'bloods' did not dance like Ugo, Fabiano and Enrico; nor were they as flirtatious. But it was exciting and, for the time being, entirely satisfying to belong to a gang.

One day during the 1933 season K. came into my bedroom as I was changing for dinner and sat on my bed. This was unusual in those days of personal modesty, when we dressed and bathed alone. I had never even shared a room with my mother or sisters. K. said, 'Pom, I need your help. A friend of Tim's from Magdalene has come to stay at Holnicote with Lady Stucley. His name is Pat Hore-Ruthven. He has a reputation for being extremely wild. There's been trouble with the police, I believe. I don't want Tim to see too much of him.'

Pat's parents were away in Australia, where his father, Brigadier-General Sir Alexander Hore-Ruthven, was Governor of South Australia. I had, in fact, glimpsed Pat the previous winter, when Dick Cadbury, another Magdalene friend of Tim's who often stayed at the Pink House, asked me up to Cambridge for the Harriers Ball, he and Tim being joint hunt masters. I was sitting in his rooms with his party when the heavy oak door opened a crack, revealing a long, a very long nose peering in before the door closed again. 'That was Pat,' said Dick, 'looking for anyone of interest.'

Later, at the ball, I asked Dick who the strange young man was who spent most of the evening dancing with a cushion. 'That's Pat Hore-Ruthven,' he said.

The Holnicote party was to consist mainly of Lady Stucley's relations: her niece Angela Manners, who had married Pat's uncle, Colonel Malise Hore-Ruthven; Ange's twin sister Betty, who was married to Arthur Asquith, son of the former prime minister; and Lady Stucley's sister Mrs Hamlyn – known as Aunt Chris – who lived at Clovelly Court, above the picturesque coastal haven. When we arrived one afternoon for tea and tennis, Ange's two small daughters were turning cartwheels on the lawn. It was a lovely English afternoon, with Holnicote, enchanting as its name, standing amid garden, lawns and trees under Dunkery Beacon, above Porlock and Selworthy. Arthur and Diana Fortescue, about our age, were there, and so was Maurice Baring, the author. In the illustrations to Baring's charming book, *Forget-Me-Not and Lily of the Valley*, Ange and Betty Manners were personified as the sweet peas who 'danced all night' at the lizard's ball, while the geraniums who frequented the bar were their brothers and boy-friends.

We played tennis and had tea on the lawn. Pat chased cabbage-white butterflies instead of tennis balls, then went off to fish. He didn't look very ordinary, but I doubted he would seriously endanger Tim. The younger set all met up again two or three nights later at a polo ball at the Town Hall in Minehead. This time Pat fancied me as a partner rather than a cushion, whereas I rather fancied the middle-aged loud-voiced polo players. When the band played 'God Save the King', Pat suggested we all return to Holnicote, where delicacies awaited us. When we got there we raided the larder and, I suppose, made a disturbance. At the next meet of the Devon and Somerset it was intimated that the Pink House party would no longer be welcome at Holnicote.

Afterwards I learned that Malise Hore-Ruthven, who acted as one of Pat's guardians in his parents' absence, had pronounced Tim to be an unsuitable friend for *his* charge. This, of course, only incited the Holnicote undesirables to frequent the Pink House undesirables, with Tim offering to mount Pat (illicitly, since Pat was supposed to be studying and had been forbidden to hunt). Few and a selection of hunters from Clifford lodged at the White Horse at Exford, while we, Cambridge friends and girl-friends, stayed at the old Pink House.

I had a green Connemara tweed jacket, similar to that worn by the foxy-haired gentleman when he seduced Jemima Puddle-Duck for love of her eggs, made for me by the boys' favourite tailor, Mr Forster of Savile Row. They all had their suits made there at fourteen guineas a time. Unfortunately, unless one was a hunt servant or a farmer, the hideous bowler was *de rigueur*.

Tim was not strong. At Eton they had cut away half his neck while looking for a tubercular gland. It must have been a terrible grief to him, for he was a handsome boy with dark chestnut-brown hair and large sloping spaniel eyes. Although Mr Forster built his suits and jackets along the prevailing horsey fashion, Tim's very slight figure made the waist seem narrower and the skirts of his coats more flared; his breeches were yellower, his boots shinier than a newly opened chestnut.

We hunted three, sometimes four days a week; the other days we fished or picnicked, joined by friends from houses in the neighbourhood, or watched polo. Some evenings the boys shot rabbits on the cliffs above Minehead or drove to Lynton and Lynmouth to inspect the bank manager's daughter. It was all very different from the Casino and the tennis club at San Remo, but much more diverting. Once mounted we felt like young gods. Few pronounced stag-hunting the best way to get the hunters fit for the galloping Warwickshire country and the unploughed North Cotswold hills. At the end of a hunting day we rode back to Exford (the horsebox never came west), and there would find half the gang already in the bar, drinking the strong still local cider.

Not long ago I met a man who had been a companion of those summers. 'Were we awful?' I asked.

'You came out hunting with cutting whips,' was his reply. I doubt if I ever did, but it does sound rather like Tim.

On the most memorable of those days, our quarry, an enormous seven-pointer stag, took us all the way across the moors to South Molton. The hunt lasted four and a half hours, by the end of which time we were absolutely beat. There were only about a dozen of us in at the finish, including several local farmers who had joined the hunt as it progressed. After the kill I found myself riding back to Exford with Pat. He looked very dark in his tweed breeches, brown laced-up gaiters, a blue bird's-eye silk stock and dark-brown whipcord jacket. Black curls escaped indecently from under the hairiest of Lock bowlers. Yet he seemed a very different person from the erratic dancer at the polo ball. During the long hack home on our two tired horses, we came upon a mutual recognition, a companionship of the spirit as we talked of the books and poetry we liked. I wrote to my mother: 'I have met a boy who looks just like a black fox.'

The following day, as I was sitting in the garden with Godmother having tea, Pat was announced. He introduced himself to K. and said he had called to thank her and Tim for mounting him. He was candid about his Uncle Malise banning us from Holnicote and said 'my aunt's Aunt Marion' (Lady Stucley) had nothing to do with the ban. He would shortly be leaving to stay at Clovelly with Mrs

Hamlyn and the Asquiths. 'He has great charm,' K. commented afterwards. 'One wouldn't mind if he found one washing one's hair.'

At the end of that holiday, Pat managed to borrow Arthur Fortescue's car, to drive me back to Moushill to rejoin my family. Outside Minehead we drove into a bus. I realized he was not a reliable chauffeur – in fact he had barely learned to drive. By tea-time we were still on the Somerset-Dorset borders, trying out hunters and likely 'chasers with Harry Duffosee, the steward at Stalbridge Park, well known in chasing circles in the Blackmore Vale.

When the woods and spinneys of the North Cotswolds hung with curtains of hazel catkins, when the buds of oaks, beeches and elms traced a changed pattern against the sky, when the first primroses struggled up through the carpet of dry leaves and the clever foxes of those hills and woods barked their eerie mating call at night, K. would take her doctor's advice and travel for a month beyond the reach of the bitter Midlands spring winds. Punch, who cleared his fences like a rubber ball, sturdy Martel and the Band, who made any fence seem two foot high, and lovely Slieve-na-Man; all were given time off to recuperate from the cuts, sprains and rigours of the winter's chase.

Tim had by now left Cambridge. When he was twenty-one, the Chrysler coupé had been changed for a Rolls Bentley. At the same time, his home had become more and more the domain of his stepfather, after he left the army. Moggie ran the farms and the stables at Clifford, chose the hunters and insisted on having his name inscribed on the farm carts. Tim nevertheless always treated Moggie with forbearance and courtesy, calling him 'Father'. It had been arranged that he should join the staff of the British Embassy in Baghdad as honorary ADC to the ambassador, Sir Francis Humphrys. Sir Francis and Lady Humphrys, and their children, who were our age, had been tennis-playing companions at Clifford. Lady Humphrys, in white piquet shirt and shorts showing her strong brown legs, played a good fast game. Tim joined them in Iraq in the autumn of 1934, and the following spring K. and I set out on what would be the most memorable of our journies: a pilgrimage to the Holy Land, to see the wild flowers there and to meet up with Tim in Jerusalem. H. V. Morton had recently published his best-seller *In the*

Steps of the Master; it was arranged that we should have his dragoman in Palestine, Michael Khoury.

To travel with K. was a gloriously luxurious adventure. Trains were still the great steaming dragons of childhood, hissing and puffing their way into the platforms with ear-splitting shrieks, their vast cylindrical discs protruding like gaudy bosoms, gleaming with black, red, green and polished brass, as they came to rest on the patiently awaiting buffers. Engine drivers and their stokers leaned from the cabs with smiling, smutty faces. The noise was deafening, but the platforms for the continental trains leaving Victoria Station were pleasantly uncrowded. There were plenty of porters to lift your trunks from the taxis and watch over them until the time came to find the white ticket with your name on it pinned to a dark-blue window seat. When setting off on a journey with K., there would be a little group to look out for at Victoria: K. and her travelling maid, the resourceful Last, a cousin or friend who acted as a kind of lady-in-waiting, a couple of porters and, of course, Thomas Cook's representative.

Everything was arranged by 'Mr Cook'. He brought the tickets, kept the numbers of the seats, cabins on the cross-channel steamer. At Paris, his French counterpart lifted us from the Train Bleu, heading for the Riviera, on to the Orient Express, which was to be our caravan for the two nights and three days it took to reach Istanbul. Each of us was allotted a comfortable *salon lit*, each with a large armchair upholstered in the same navy-blue buttoning as Granny Hodgson's carriage. In the corner near the corridor a mahogany door opened to reveal a good-sized wash-basin with brass taps, a large mirror, shelves and fittings; while below, most convenient and modest, the 'article' was easily extracted by a handle and tipped at a perfect angle for emptying when reinserted. There was plenty of space to sort out books and night-clothes, none of the hazards of climbing into a sleeping-bunk aloft. As the countryside rushed past the windows, one's own life came to a stop. It was like being inside a picture: the dancing feet resting, the thrills and fears of the hunt stilled, decisions delayed and those all-important love letters from home not to be found until Jerusalem.

At mealtimes we met in the restaurant car, where good traditional French menus were served. We drank the same Beaune, Pommard and St Julien wines I always associate with journeys to and from San

Remo in the PLM. As we dined in the evening, the 'brown nanny', with his gold-braided uniform, would make his way along to transform the armchairs into full-sized beds ready with clean linen sheets and blankets. Being under particular instructions from 'Mr Cook' to take good care of Mrs Rees-Mogg, the 'brown nanny' became one of our party. K. would flirt with him and flatter him outrageously, so that in the end he almost deprecated the 'sweetener' pressed into his hands as we said goodbye.

K. always carried watches, pens and other small presents as rewards for care and kindness. She would ask apropos of a possible recipient, 'Do you think he is penworthy, Pom?' Once, as we left a hotel in Luxor, a small boy waving a cloth jumped on to the running-board of our car, shouting in agony, 'Lady, lady, you have not seen me.' K.'s largesse was scattered with sense and sensibility, in contrast to that of the transatlantic voyagers of the period, but I often think I should have helped her more as she fumbled and sorted those coveted handouts. In Venice, after Mussolini had taught the Italians to think of themselves as Roman citizens instead of beggars and organ grinders, even the lift boy refused a tip.

On that 1935 journey to the Middle East with K., I sat like a princess in my *salon lit*, viewing Europe from west to east as we headed for Asia by way of the Taurus mountains towards Aleppo, benefiting from those brief years of peace when only the privileged travelled for pleasure: the poor journeyed from stoic necessity on wooden slatted seats. Gladys Alington, a Hamilton cousin of K.'s, was in attendance, and made the perfect travelling companion. She had born six sons, two of whom she had reluctantly given away to childless friends and never saw. She wore her hair *en souffle* above the full grey-flannel skirts in which she clad her pinkish white skin. Nothing daunted her or seemed to impair her enjoyment. She never voiced an opinion on any subject beyond commenting on the people we met, yet she had earned her pilot's wings and had in her time performed a number of daring exploits. Our threesome of obviously well-dowered females attracted acquaintances and would-be hangers-on all along the route. But whenever we stopped or changed carriages, Thomas Cook's courier would be there, the name written clearly around his cap; and any unseemly fellow traveller swiftly faded away.

When we crossed the frontier from Bulgaria to Turkey in the

middle of the night, there had been deep snow, and strange-looking soldiers boarded the train. Then there was more and more snow, and the wildest and most desolate country, stiff with magpies and grey crows. We arrived at Istanbul at 8 a.m.

Our short stay in the city made a distinct, rather odd impression, perhaps because it was half Eastern and half European. At the time the secular revolution launched by Kemal Atatürk, the 'father' of modern Turkey, continued in full swing; and memories of the old imperial regime of the Ottoman Sultans, abolished by Atatürk in 1926, were still quite fresh. I recorded my impressions in a letter to the Giant.

We stayed at the Pera Palace Hotel which the President [Atatürk] had only left the day before. The President must be a man of tremendous force to revolutionize in under ten years such a stronghold of Muslim imperialism. He has no religion and doesn't encourage it. The women go unveiled and wear European dress; so do most of the men. No one wears the fez any more and only a few wear the old Turkish baggy trousers. The bazaars were amazing: people kept seizing you by the arm and forcing you into their shops. Nothing intimidates them. The city is swarming with Russian refugees, you feel its population belongs to the whole world.

After lunch we went to the ex-Sultan's palace [Topkapi]. It stands overlooking the Bosporus and opposite St Sophia. I had the creeps from the moment I walked in under the gateway . . . Outside the gate we entered, trembling ambassadors used to wait four and five hours to be received; there too was the queer stone beheading machine where some would die should they bring unfavourable dispatches from their countries. The palace is charming with a garden of lawns, pavement and cypress trees, and one or two fountains. The huge vaulted kitchens are turned into museums where I suppose are kept some of the world's finest treasures . . . We saw the world's largest ruby and emerald, the royal cradle of solid gold and the children's satchels, studded with diamonds and pearls. Everything was set with precious stones; it seems unbelievable that any human beings could prepare such magnificence for themselves.

Then we were taken to the harem which was luckily open that

day. It was awful. I could hardly talk at all the whole time. It is a series of rooms, the private apartments of the Sultan; . . . Most of the rooms are tiled with brightly coloured tiles, some painted by Italian workmen; others are hung with silks and heavy brocades. Everywhere [there are] enormous couches and of course, carpets and carpets and carpets, so I imagine you would never hear anyone coming. The Sultan's bathroom was lovely: high white vaulted plastered ceilings, white walls and bath – with just the corners of the mouldings tipped with gold. It was so hot that everyone had to wear cork slippers lest the floor burn their feet. In the 'cooling off' room stood a beautiful white and gold satin couch.

Beneath all these rooms, underground, lived the wives with only Nubian eunuchs to attend them, going up only when called for by the Sultan. Once a year they assembled together in the throne room at the annual installation of a new wife aged thirteen or fourteen. From one window we saw a row of underground half-grilles: these were the dungeons where any misbehaving wives were kept. The black eunuchs were responsible for their pleasing the Sultan and thrashed them at will. When the Sultan fled the wives were freed and had to run from the palace; some of the younger ones were lucky and married officers in the town and live there still in their twenties.

The custodians of the rooms and the treasures are the saddest-faced men I have seen. Their eyes were quite hopeless. Under the new regime their pay is halved, they stand saying never a word in the corners of the rooms and I suppose brood upon the past. There were two wrinkled old eunuchs talking to each other in high, squeaky voices and an uncanny little eunuch dwarf-hunchback who skipped about the courtyard. He never leaves the palace but orders everyone about. He was formerly the Sultan's court jester and does no work. During our lifetime the Sultan ordered 1,000 men to be beheaded and his orders were obeyed. It seems impossible: it is a mercy it is all over now. I think it will take centuries to get that awful, sinister smell of intrigue and bloodshed out of the precincts of the palace.

To proceed to Syria and thence to Palestine, we had to cross from Europe to Asia, taking a launch up the Bosporus from the Golden Horn Bridge to Üsküdar. At the station we found a detachment of

Turkish soldiers standing to attention, along with many military figures in red hats, their women and civilian relatives. They were seeing off one of Turkey's most prominent generals, who turned out to be travelling on our train, the Taurus Express, to a larger frontier garrison at the opposite end of the country. His compartment being next to mine, we came to know him pretty well, and he was, as I wrote to my mother from Aleppo, 'most charming but spoke only poor French'.

> However he had a most attractive ADC who spent the morning taking my photograph in the corridor when he thought I wasn't looking. The scenery was so spectacular that we spent most of the time in the corridor. The general wore his pyjamas throughout. He has been in England and knows Ramsay MacDonald and the Prince of Wales. He fought against General Townshend [in Mesopotamia] during the war. He said he was a charming man and they got on well when they met.
>
> We were the only women travelling and I fear his attention went to our heads somewhat. He asked us to stop off and go hawking with him, an offer we had to decline. K. enjoys every minute but the money has been dreadfully confusing. She wants to tip everyone. I cannot imagine what she must be spending on this trip. In every place we go to the best hotel. Now we have a dragoman all day who stays with us along with a private car and chauffeur. Today we had two cars. Of course people always make a beeline for us. Last, the maid, is perfect. She is unobtrusive but efficient and very intelligent to talk with. She is much travelled and has been all over the world as a temporary travelling ladies' maid. She was in Spain with the Carisbrookes, staying at the Spanish court just before the revolution. She knew Minnie Cochrane's maid and Princess Beatrice's staff. She is just that type.

Aleppo provided my first true view of the East. We arrived at night and had four horse-drawn fiacres to carry us and our luggage to Baron's Hotel, where we went straight to bed. In the morning I stepped out on to my veranda and watched a procession of camels and crowds of men in fezes. Doves and pigeons flew around in flocks overhead against the blue sky. Later, a charming Armenian boy from the hotel took us up to the Citadel, from where we saw the whole town laid out before us. The souks were full of silks, lovely copper pans and all kinds of things to eat. The Arabs sat curled up in their stalls, never coming out to pester to buy as they had in Constantinople. Some, from the country, looked just like the Shepherd Kings in bible illustrations, and seemed such gentlemen compared to the city Syrians, Armenians and Jews.

At Beirut – said in those days to be a second Paris and certainly very French in some parts – we stayed a night at the enormous St George Hotel, which made me feel as if I was aboard the *Olympic*. It stood overlooking the town, its foundations practically in the sea, the view from the windows, up the coast to the snow-clad Mount Lebanon, being quite wonderful. We had driven there from Tripoli, along a road, more precipitous than the Grande Corniche, that twisted among grey rocks which had spiky asphodel and wild cyclamen growing among them. 'I long to send you the bunch I picked yesterday in the hills above Beirut,' I wrote to my mother. I did not know the names of all of them, but there were tiny blue irises, anemones of all colours, cyclamen and little yellow plants which turned the mountain-sides into rock gardens. The olive groves had been a sheet of pinks, with blue and white beneath.

Leaving Beirut at 10 a.m., we motored over the mountains to Baalbeq, a journey that took three hours. For the first hour we climbed 5,000 feet above sea-level, almost to the snowy slopes where the cedars grew. We travelled for nearly another hour among the heights where snow lay about between the red and mauve rocks. There was no grass, no trees, the only sign of life being large square buildings used for storing snow in summer. Rounding a corner rather suddenly, we saw Mount Hermon for the first time, his snow shining like glass as he rose majestically from the lovely fertile plain between the Lebanon and Anti-Lebanon ranges. 'Some people say he is the mountain of the Transfiguration,' I wrote to my mother; 'he might well be – I have never been so impressed or awestruck as that moment we came round the corner and saw him rising above the whole countryside.'

Dropping down to the plain, we found it all green and blue: wide tilled fields, streams lined with poplars and willows, children playing in waterfalls. As we passed out of the plain, there were strings of camels, generally led by an Arab on a donkey, their heads in the air as if to avoid bad smells. The road shone white as it led across a stretch of desert to Baalbeq, and here came by far the most amazing part of the drive: no tree in sight; the soil deep red; the mountains the colours of precious stones, amethyst at the top near the snow, below topaz and ruby red. Oxen tilled what seemed a desert waste, herds of black goats grazed what appeared to be stones.

We arrived at Baalbeq in time for lunch at our hotel, which stood in a grove of pine trees at the end of a long drive. It was very homely, with clean, primitive bedrooms and large stoves to heat the rooms, since the town stands 3,000 feet above sea-level. As soon as we had eaten, we drove straight to the Roman temple, built in A.D. 170 'of such size and splendour, and in such a situation, looking down on green gardens and fields, surrounded by red desert and snowy mountains, as would turn anyone to worship the Roman gods', I wrote in my letter to the Giant.

> There are only seven pillars remaining out of the 54 belonging to the famous temple of Jupiter. It is said that 100,000 slaves worked on it for a hundred years; the carvings and ceilings of some sections look as if they were just made. An Arab workman on the excavations lent me his scraper and I spent a blissful five minutes removing the dust of centuries from a section of frieze with the egg and arrow motif representing life and death which decorated the priest's bath. We returned to tea and heavenly home-made quince jam, the fruit cut in large chunks and tasting rather like one of your special preserves. We shall go to bed early. Tomorrow afternoon we motor to Damascus, where our luggage has already gone in a private car.

The dragoman we were to have in Palestine, Michael Koury, I added, had escorted the author H. V. Morton back in the bible lands a week or two earlier, taking him to the towns visited by St Paul, whose life he was now writing. 'Tell Father I am reading his book and loving it,' I said, referring to *In the Steps of the Master*.

From the Orient Palace Hotel in Damascus, on 10 March 1935, I wrote to the Reverend:

> It is not every day one can write to one's father from Damascus. Yesterday we motored from Baalbeq, the Roman Heliopolis which they built high among the mountains across the wide plain

which lies between the Lebanon and Anti-Lebanon ranges. In the middle of this plain, now a fairyland of blossom and thin poplar trees coming into leaf by rushing streams, there are villages of Christian Arabs who work on the land, ploughing the dark-red soil. They are the most charming and contented-looking people; the women work in the fields with the men, even the Muslims; all go unveiled, wearing light-coloured frocks and white muslin twisted round their heads like wimples.

In the valley we turned off the main road through the wildest rocky gorge where the robbers used to hide. Not a blade of grass anywhere, no trees and the rocks set in the most extraordinary formations and positions. There are shepherds tending flocks of black goats. The kids are enchanting, they have long black ears which hang down like ribbons. The government of Syria has built the most wonderful road, sometimes the caravans of camels and asses use it, sometimes you can see them below, taking a short cut through the rocks. The names are impossible to remember but the car climbed round a mountain where there is a ruined Muslim shrine on the spot where Cain killed Abel. From there we dropped down into the valley that leads to Damascus . . . The apricot trees were in full bloom. Some have dark-red flowers, others white and pink, we smelled them through the open windows of the car. Tables and chairs sat under the trees along the river bank where the Damascus people come pleasure-making in the summer. We saw some kneeling towards the east, saying their prayers.

The road into Damascus is a grove of eucalyptus trees, very straight, you can see the white buildings and the mosques from afar. The river runs straight through the town, which is very French. The plump provincial *madames* of the French Mandate forces drive around looking smug and supercilious in open carriages. Round our hotel are large new houses, shops and gardens.

K. had asked our dragoman to take us to mass at the Greek church at 8.45 a. m. We went down the street called Straight, the oldest street in the world, very narrow and lined with shops nearly meeting overhead. The Muslims were selling at stalls and the street was crowded with laden donkeys and children. There is a narrow doorway on the right hand belonging to Judas' house, where Saul lodged, now a tiny mosque.

Half-way up the street we went under a small archway and

followed the dragoman through one cool courtyard after another. These were the presbyteries where the patriarchs, the bishop and priests live. Every little courtyard had orange and lemon trees growing in the middle. It was warm and sunny and everywhere comic little black-eyed children were playing. In the church the service had already begun; we sidled into an empty pew, but a young novitiate in a black cassock with his hair done in a bun, told us the children would be coming later. He led us up to the stalls in front of the altar, where boys and young men were grouped round two young priests who led the chanting. The bishop was reading the service robed in white and gold with a huge gold mitre on his head set with precious stones.

Our stalls were set sideways by the altar steps; but that wouldn't do, so we were marched to another just behind the bishop and below the cantors. I knew Godma was suffering agonies of shyness and shame, I wasn't feeling very pleased with myself either. The service was immensely long. On either side of us the young men and the two priests answered one another with the most extraordinary, uncanny wailing and chanting with no accompaniment; the ritual was more elaborate than any Roman service. The gospel was read in Greek, then a man up in the roof proceeded to read it again in Arabic. The children had arrived by now, while the women were behind the screen on the side isles and in the gallery behind another screen. K. and I were entirely out of place among those chanting men and long-haired priests and novitiates.

The church was tawdry, I was longing to do a bolt, I rather hated it all. It seemed far from the early Christians who received Paul after his conversion, more like a kind of devil worship. The entire congregation are Arabs, as are the priest, bishops and the patriarch, but it seemed a barbaric worship compared to the quiet squatting men we have seen in the mosques reading their Korans.

After a much delayed breakfast we drove into the old town where the Muslims and Jews were working and trading as usual; we went out of the Eastern Gate round the old city wall, which is shining white, and to the Roman archway. Above it is the window from which Paul escaped. It was a biggish drop: instead of the orchards and fields of crops which now surround the city walls, there was desert. We have come through the country he travelled on his way to Jerusalem.

A Cloud of Forgetting

As we crossed into Palestine, we showed our passports at a frontier created by the European powers when they carved up the land won from the Turks in the war. Lebanon and Syria came under the French Mandate; Palestine and Transjordan, with all their miscellanies of confessions and ethnic groups, were administered by the British. Palestine was divided into provinces run by district commissioners to whom the village chiefs or *mukhtars* were answerable. The League of Nations Mandate, following the disastrous Balfour Declaration of 1917, specifically allowed for Jewish immigration: by 1933, 92,000 Polish and Russian Jews, and about 63,000 from Central and Eastern Europe had settled, mostly in the new city of Tel Aviv. In Transjordan, the British had established the Amir Abdullah, son of the exiled Sherif of Mecca, in Amman, plying him with money and advice. When we arrived in 1935, the tension that would culminate in the Arab rebellion of the following year was doubtless evident; but as we were mainly visiting religious sites, and were protected by our guide from unwelcoming encounters, little of the rumbling dissatisfaction reached our ears.

Palestine still seemed a biblical land, with terraces of ancient olive trees and peasants tilling the soil using primitive wooden ploughs pulled by camels and donkeys, much as in Jesus' day. Thanks to the relatively benign neglect of Turkish rule, the country was considerably less built over than during the time of Our Lord. Many of the cities described in the gospels had long been reduced to hamlets, perched above mounds or *tels* which testified to grander, imperial pasts. In other respects, the houses, the farms, the animals, the implements and the peasants themselves could scarcely have changed. Even if a majority of the Palestinian Arabs now professed Islam, they all bore the genes of their forebears – whether Canaanite, Hebrew, Assyrian, Persian, Greek, Roman or Crusader. The early spring flowers were the same, the mountains and plains filled with anemones, hollyhocks, irises, tulips, oleanders, asphodels and lupins, while small creeping plants found out every crevice in the rocks.

Galilee gave me my happiest time. We visited the Church of the Miracle of the Loaves and Fishes, and saw the newly discovered mosaics depicting the plants and animals of Roman times, while all around the country seemed much as it must have been in Christ's day – lovely and untamed, like the west of Ireland. Leaving Galilee, we drove to Acre to pick up our guide, Michael Khoury. He lived with his wife and child in a roomy old house built into the pale limestone walls constructed by the Crusaders to protect the Kingdom of Acre against coastal attack. The frontier with Lebanon lay a few miles to the north.

The roadside was lined by flimsy cafés with unsteady trellises, where men in baggy Turkish trousers chatted and smoked hookahs while their women worked the fields. Michael told us that those on the south side of the frontier cursed the British for letting the Jews into Palestine; while those to the north cursed the French for their high-handed arrogance. All along the way their children and grand-children held up flowers and herbs for us to buy. At Nablus (the Shechem mentioned in the Book of Genesis) we stopped to visit the Samaritans. The town was largely Muslim, but the Samaritan community, a pathetic remnant of the kingdom established by Jereboam in 926 B.C., still claimed to be the only true descendants of the Children of Israel. On their holy mountain at Gerizim above Nablus, they celebrated the Passover exactly as Moses had done, erecting tents to camp in and waiting for the moon to rise, before slaughtering their sacrificial lambs by slitting their throats. The high priest intoned the prayers, the tents were smeared with blood and the lambs were roasted and eaten in extra-large mouthfuls, the Children of Israel having been in a hurry to get out of Egypt.

Their high priest, who received us in a sparsely furnished upper room, was extremely tall, with a finely curved nose above a jet-black beard. His brother, a paler, more languid version of himself, served us deadly-sweet coffee in tiny cups. The community was reduced to some 150 souls; they were not only impoverished but were also, to judge from the appearance of the younger men, extremely inbred, and their babies were all boys.

In Jerusalem Tim joined us, and we dined with the High Commissioner, Sir Arthur Wauchope, a small, dry Scottish bachelor. Sir Arthur was rumoured to be biased towards the Zionist settlers, but he showed a great appreciation of the Palestinian arts of embroidery and pottery. Palestinian notables invited to dine at Government House – a fine modern villa set amid pine trees on one of the hills above the city – must have felt reasonably comfortable there, despite the presence of their Jewish counterparts.

At dinner I sat next to a boy from Northumberland who knew Pat. He shocked us with some alarming news. Taffy Nicholls, a friend of Pat's, had died after the car in which they were both travelling collided with a tree. That evening I wrote to Pat:

> All of me, except my miserable body, is with you. I shan't stop thinking of you and Taffy for one moment. I don't know how you are going to get through but you will. It's all right with Taffy, you must realize that; I know it for certain, I don't have to worry for him at all. But I know the agony I am feeling now is one millionth part of what you are suffering and I would give my soul to be away from here with you or somewhere near you.
>
> I hate the futility of this paper and pencil – remember there is a God who bothers about all this and it is not an awful thing at all that has happened to Taffy. The Hell is all yours.

During our time in Palestine, the chief of police, Colonel Roy Spicer, sometimes provided us with an escort. We thought him charming. He took us to watch his constables training the Alsatians used to track down Arab dissidents. I do not remember feeling any outrage when told how the Palestine police blew up the homes of rebels – a policy later perpetuated by the Israelis. But among the many fascinating details I did learn as I read Morton in bed in the King David Hotel, was how the Roman troops involved in the destruction of Jerusalem by the Emperor Titus in A.D. 78 (fulfilling Christ's prophecy that 'Jerusalem shall be trodden down by the gentiles') had been trained in Britain, where Titus' father, Vespasian, distinguished himself. It was a terrible story of a stiff-necked people, beseiged by the mightiest army in the world, continuing to fight each other to the death inside the city while refusing to surrender so as to save it and their lives. As we made our pilgrims' way through the labyrinth of cobbled lanes and alleys, kneeling to pray in the churches built down the ages, each with its different, unfamiliar rite, nuns and priests from different sects whispered complaints against each other (inspired, I suspected, by jealousies fuelled by K.'s largesse).

As a child I had been given a bible, illustrated with coloured prints from German galleries. The Good Shepherd was a dark young man, surrounded by pure-white fleecy sheep of the kind one still sees in Wales. The Palestinian Arabs suggested more plausible versions of Jesus than the religious canvases of Europe. It was easier to imagine him among the farmers and small-holders with their camel and ox ploughs, or among the urban folk of the Old City – the water carriers, the gold and silver smiths, the vegetable and fruit sellers, or in the dark, fly-infested butchers' shops among the bloody, hanging carcases.

Paradoxically it was more difficult to visualize him in the city's Jewish quarter, among the wide fur-trimmed hats of the ultra-Orthodox or the Agudath Jews, who dressed in Victorian black. With pallid faces, framed by corkscrew curls, they rocked back and forth as they prayed at the Western Wall, muttering sacred words. To me they seemed uncompromisingly European, and still looked like foreigners in the city they had been trickling back to since medieval times. They gave me an uneasy feeling: they never stared at or greeted one, as did the Arabs, not even their children. We wondered how they would assimilate with the new Zionist settlers, mostly Ashkenazim from Central and Eastern Europe, the plump girls with their light-blue bloomers, the men in Western clothes. Did the Orthodox Jews hate the British as much as the Arabs did? How had they felt when General Allenby walked into the Old City with Uncle Harry Hodgson and his Australians?

Christianity was reassuring; Judaism, and to a lesser extent Islam, I found disturbing. It seemed more comforting to believe that the Messiah had come, and that he would if you followed him lead you towards God and Eternity, than to be constantly waiting, alert, unsatisfied. Yahweh I revered because of the messages he sent through the prophets in lovely poetry and prose. Allah it was impossible to reject, since he was the object of such trust and devotion in those cool uncluttered mosques; but the rules set by both Yahweh and Allah seemed finicky and increasingly untenable. As for the complexities of theology, I did not really mind if the Master I was following round that wicked Holy City was God, or represented the nearest one man had lived to God. In the calm of the basilica built by Constantine the Great at Bethlehem, I was happy. In St Pierre en Gallicante, I was enraged by his suffering. In St Anne's, the great church built by the Crusaders, where cool white light filtered through alabaster windows, I met his challenge. In the garden of St Anne's, which adjoins the Pool of Bethesda, K. and I talked long with the white father in charge. His hairy cassock was as white as his hair and beard. Before we left he placed his hand on my head. He said he thought I 'could' be good. I often remember him, and wish I had been.

That spring in Palestine, the recipient of my childhood prayers and teenage confessions took on human flesh and bones. I saw him as a young man striding around the shores of Galilee, picking a gang of friends, fishing, eating and drinking with them, mingling with the polyglot folk who lived around the lake, and in the Greek towns of the Decapolis, newly linked by the highways built by the Roman occupation. Speaking Aramaic, he was a despised Galilean with a funny accent laughed at in Jerusalem, a Palestinian of the Jewish rite, rejected in the Jewish town of Nazareth, but welcomed as a healer among the people, the poor and the sick of the northern regions, teaching in the local synagogues, in the market places and by the lakeside, a new sympathetic version of the Creator – but one that proved to be anathema to the authorities in Jerusalem. He dined openly with drunks and unbelievers, had non-Jews among his followers and, most heretically of all, spoke with women, whereas no Orthodox Jew would acknowledge even his wife, daughter or mother outside the home.

One afternoon we drove out of Jerusalem, 'three score furlongs', to the village of Emmaus, represented in modern times by a small Arab village called Imwas, built high on a salient with two others not far away called Jebo and Jelo. We arrived before sunset, to be there when 'the day was far spent' – the time when Cleopas and his friend were interrupted in their sad ruminations on the happenings of the previous three days in the city by the arrival of a third man, and asked him to tarry with them. As the sun settled gently down among attendant pink and gold clouds low over the plain and the Mediterranean beyond, I became lost in the story of the resurrection, the doubting men and the believing women; the peace after tracing the harsh stones of Calvary, the Via Dolorosa, the terrible black hush and worship in the Church of the Holy Sepulchre with its conflicting custodians, the controversial British site of Gordon's Calvary.

Here in Imwas, houses had been built and people had lived, farmed and gardened since before Anno Domini. It could be no other than where the three arrived at sundown. K. was wonderful. She left one to private cogitations and prayers, never intruded with her own disillusionment, sensations or visions, but remained ever-ready to relapse into our funny-ridiculous peregrinations with Michael, once we were settled sipping our evening wine. I never remember her once correcting or berating me, yet I must during our journeys often have been tiresome and have trodden on toes.

In Transjordan, where we went on to from Jerusalem, we notched up a social success when the Amir Abdullah was persuaded we were worthy of an audience. This contrasted with the occasion on a later journey when we were travelling via Albania and stayed in Tirana in the only hotel considered suitable for clients of Mr Cook. King Zog, we were told, regularly surveyed the hotel terraces through a telescope to discover if any guests looked likely for a game of poker at the palace. The summons never materialized. Evidently we failed that particular test.

The Amir we found in a large bedouin tent among the pine trees in the royal grounds of the small but imaginative palace the British had built for him above his new capital, Amman, then scarcely more than a village of white-washed houses among flaming pomegranate bushes. The son of the ill-starred Sherif of Mecca, he had been handed a small patch of desert by T. E. Lawrence and Winston Churchill in order to thwart French ambitions in Syria and Zionist claims east of the Jordan. The bedouin guard surrounding him looked stunningly exotic in khaki cassocks and scarlet cross-belts, with long black curls escaping out of their headcloths. It was said that, used to desert ways, the Amir Abdullah preferred his tent to his palace and insisted on sleeping there. A neat, elderly man, with sharp eyes and a trim beard, he wore Arab dress surmounted by the triple gold *aghal* or headropes befitting a *sherif* or descendant of the Prophet. The Assistant British Resident, Alec Kirkbride, introduced us, along with some other visitors. After we had drunk little cups of bitter black coffee, each of us had a few courtesy exchanges with the Amir.

Early one morning we set off for Petra, travelling in two ancient but well-sprung limousines. The hot tortuous drive along bumpy dust-ridden tracks seemed to go on for ever. We broke our journey at a police post where we were welcomed by an immaculately uniformed member of the desert police patrol; we were given glasses of sweet tea and allowed to engage in what Michael insisted on calling our 'toileting' – an activity necessarily conducted in the open, with Michael mounting guard with his back turned to us. At Ma'an – a small huddle of mud-brick houses among palm trees – we met another equally courteous policeman, a few children and dogs and a man on a camel. Soon we came upon the weirdest range of mountains

I had ever seen: bizarre, jagged shapes in blue and purple, and completely dead, as if left out at the creation of world. At Wadi Musa – the place, according to Michael, where Moses struck water from the rock – we left the cars and changed to horseback; our bags were loaded on to donkeys. There was considerable argument over the mounts. I was given a stallion, who proved unexpectedly uppish, considering he was in poor condition. Refusing to allow the bedouin guides to lead our horses, Tim and I galloped on ahead; but as the way became narrower and stonier, and the great sandstone cliffs of the Sik – the narrow gorge forming the only entrance to Petra – closed in on us, we were forced to slow to a walk, allowing the rest of the party to catch up. The Sik is more like a crack in the rock than a gorge. At some places it is so narrow that you really think you will get squashed: at others there is room for two to ride abreast. The cool, rather sinister silence was disturbed by an argument that erupted among our bedouin escort when my stallion tried to bite Tim's mare in the rump. The row was still going on, creating fantastic echoes, when we suddenly came on the first of the great temple façades that stands at the end of the Sik and which the Arabs call Pharaoh's Treasury.

As the sun was going down, we had to ride about two miles farther on, to the camp at the far end of the city. Our horses made a beeline for an area of crumbling masonry, grass and oleander bushes, where stood a collection of white tents: here, just as at Victoria Station or the Gard du Nord, the ubiquitous 'Mr Cook' was waiting, the mess tent already laid for dinner. Asked to state a preference for a tent or a cave, K. and Cousin Gladys opted for tents, but after dinner Tim and I climbed up the mountain behind the camp and took temporary possession of two tombs large enough to accommodate several generations of Nabateans for their eternal sleep. 'Mr Cook' had provided basins, ewers and comfortable camp beds. As the moon came up over Petra, there were eerie sounds and strange calls; but I slept as one should in a tomb. I wasn't, however, alone. An Edomite flea visited me that night, and despite every ablution and blandishment, insisted on staying with me throughout the Egyptian part of our tour, only departing when we finally made it back to Europe.

At Petra I got up at dawn, and climbed a steep rocky stairway leading to the place of sacrifice, perhaps the 'high places of Baal' mentioned in the Bible. There was a pool for ablutions, flanked by two stone obelisks and what looked like two altars – one for sacrifice and one for burning. Standing alone in the High Place, and feeling rather hungry, I remembered John Lewis Burckhardt, the Swiss traveller who discovered Petra in 1812. His disguise as a bedouin having been uncovered, he had to sacrifice his boon companion, a goat. Nor was he able to scramble down again, like me, to 'Mr Cook's' ample breakfast.

That evening the bedu held a feast to entertain the mighty Peake Pasha, founder and commander of the Amir Abdullah's army, later, under John Glubb, to become known as the Arab Legion. We watched the Pasha arrive in camp, looking thoroughly at ease on his Arab stallion – a scarlet cloak draped over his blue patrol jacket, his famous black lambskin cap on his head – and escorted by some of the men he had formed into the region's most effective fighting force.

Peake was already a legend. He had commanded the Egyptian camel corps which co-operated with the Amir Feisal and T. E. Lawrence in the desert campaign against the Turks. When the Amir Abdullah was granted the 'wild, unwanted territory' east of the Jordan that had never known effective civil government (except for a brief period after the construction of the Hejaz railway), he engaged Peake's services. Within a few years the gentle-mannered, blue-eyed Englishman succeeded in subduing, by a combination of diplomacy, cunning and sound military tactics, the toughest and most rebellious Jordanian tribes, beating off the fanatical Ikhwan warriors from Nejd whom Ibn Saud used in his ruthless campaign to eliminate the Sherif Hussein, father of Abdullah and Feisal, from the Hejaz. He established the highly efficient system of police and army posts that survive in Jordan to this day. His successor, Glubb Pasha, relates how despite his natural good humour, Peake sometimes thought it sound policy to appear angry. 'The word Thundercloud was passed from post to post when the Pasha was on tour, and feverish polishings and sweepings would ensue.' To his men, he appeared the 'Centre of the Universe'. Yet for all his obvious authority, he appeared to us to be informal and friendly and quite without affectation.

There was feverish activity in the tents as the feast was prepared. The result was unlike anything we had tasted in Palestine. A great cauldron of boiled sheep was carried in and set on a vast bed of rice

– the two sheeps-heads grinning with open jaws at the top, their fat tails draped between them. Over this culinary tableau was poured the juice, a kind of melted butter fat. Once the great had been served – we all ate bedouin style with our fingers – the bedou fell on the rest, mingling with our escorts and grooms. The children hovered about, waiting their turn to gather up the remnants. As the sun went down, a huge bonfire was lit, and dancers and singers appeared. The songs, so Michael told us afterwards, made frequent mention of 'The Mighty Thundercloud' and his heroic deeds. There were also complimentary references to 'Mr Cook's' guests, including 'Sitt Bamela', who had a special song to herself. The singing and dancing continued for a while after we had climbed back into our tombs, exhausted by a day spent inspecting the remains of the crumbling city of Edom. The feast had quite banished the unquiet, sinister mood of our necropolis. Even the distant howling of the jackals seemed less disturbing as the performers crept silently away, their poor bellies full.

At the end of our visit to Petra, my stomach began to rumble ominously with gastric portents. Feeling an acute sense of disappointment, I abandoned plans to drive across the Sinai with Tim in his car, and instead joined K. and Gladys on the train to Cairo. We rattled down the narrow-gauge track from Jerusalem by way of El Kantara, following the route taken by the Holy Family on the flight into Egypt.

I have a book about Egypt, by the Rev. Samuel Manning, lavishly bound in heavy brown leather with gold tooling and published in 1877. It contains, among many other illustrations, a picture of the Prince of Wales and his party at the pyramids. The Egypt depicted by the good reverend in his pen and pencil sketches is not far different from the Egypt we found in 1935: a seeming earthly paradise, filled with smiling, dark-skinned people happily working in the fields of that great, winding swathe of cultivation that was already flourishing when Abraham set out from Ur of the Chaldees.

We inhabited Mr Cook's Egypt, far removed from the desperation of a peasant population seeking a livelihood in the city, continuing to breed the children they hope will safeguard their old age, and of a clerical class of effendis bitterly resentful of Europeans and their privileges. We rode camels to the pyramids, sailed up the Nile in elegant, feather-sailed feluccas and were treated to a private viewing of the Tutankhamun treasures by a professor from the French school of archaeology. The same professor conducted us round Luxor, Thebes, Karnak and Sakkara. I ceased to look on the ancient Egyptians as gloomily obsessed with death, but came to recognize them as a people who lived close to the wild life that abounded in their meandering oasis, planting and tilling the little square fields, eating well from fish and game and constructing tombs of monstrous even hideous dimensions, creating and gathering up the treasures their dead would take with them to the wonderful unseen world from whence they came. I developed a special affection for Anubis, the jackal god who leads humans across the chasm from this world to the next, who can cross the desert without benefit of stars, leaving tracks for others to follow.

In the palm groves of Luxor we listened to the sad tunes of the snake-charmers and watched the tricks of the gully-gully men, who caused chirping new-born chicks to suddenly appear, then vanish. In Cairo we went shopping in the Muski, buying rugs and scarabs, icons or brass trays, like countless tourists before us. I bought a black wooden Anubis with a gold collar and sharp little ears. In a dark shop near Shepheard's Hotel, hung with carpets from roof to floor and heavy with the smell of scents and spices, my fortune was told by a highly regarded seer. He said he saw horses, that I would bear two children and live in the shadow of waving flags.

Both Tim and I were relieved when the time came to board the ship from Alexandria to Naples. His months with the Humphrys in Baghdad had failed to entice him into a diplomatic career. I was missing my friends and the rather more bohemian life I enjoyed with Diana in our Chelsea flat, and worried about the unmarriagable Pat and the recent tragedy of Taffy.

We usually returned by way of Italy from our journeys with K. At the close of our last trip in 1936 we looked out of the window as the train drew into the station at Rome to find a high-ranking delegation, brimming with pomp and *fascismo* flourishes, waiting to see off Sir Oswald Mosley. Mosley took possession of the *salon lit* next to mine, but he was not friendly and forthcoming as the Turkish general had been. Instead he sat alone, silent and brooding, throughout the journey. As he tells in his autobiography, he was in the habit of paying an annual visit to Mussolini, his great original inspiration in founding the British Union of Fascists. In 1936 he provoked a rift with his hero when he married Diana Mitford secretly in Germany at a time when the Italian leader was on bad terms with the German Nazi party. 'Il Duce' took offence and refused to receive him, and they never met again.

It was also in 1936 that the Reverend decided to quit San Remo. The sun-loving Germans had become more popular than the British or American visitors on the Italian Riviera and All Saints had virtually lost its congregation. The large villas along the Berigo were closed and eventually sequestered. La Graziella was shut up, along with the church.

4

The First Dilemma

The Fletchers returned from Italy to Moushill, the small farmhouse the Giant had bought on the Surrey-Sussex borders on the edge of a long strip of heathland preserved through having been one of the earliest gifts to the National Trust. It was a happy period in England for anyone with at least a little money. As a result of the depression and gloomy forebodings about Germany, everything was cheap. It was a most propitious time to buy antiques and pictures. My mother's trust income went further than for a long time. Even after paying my brother Michael's Oxford debts and seeing him into the army, and educating my younger sister Romola at Downe House, there was still plenty to spare.

We spent weekends at Moushill, playing tennis with local families, including the Corbetts, who were half-Greek. They lived on top of a hill near by, and the father was a towering, handsome man, black-haired and dark-skinned – something big in the tea business. Dick, the eldest son, was the first person I knew to have a library of records and a good gramophone. After he left university to go to Ceylon to learn about tea, he wrote me long homesick letters and poems. Sometimes I took up gardening. It became a family joke that whenever I was in the thick of romance, I would dig a water garden under the old pollarded poplar adjoining our meadow.

The Giant leased a large flat at 87 Cadogan Gardens. As was her way, she found faithful 'daily' maidservants who never wanted to leave. First there was old Harriet, an accomplished parlourmaid who wore a black pinafore with frilled apron and cap with little streamers. Then came Isobel, who took a very personal interest in all our friends. 'Mr X and I are jolly pals,' she would say. Finally there was Alice, a devoted Cockney who always told stories against absent members of the family and remained with my mother until she died. The flat had two large communicating rooms, with a balcony facing south as well as a large den where my father wrote his sermons. Most Sundays he stood in for overworked priests, not only in London churches but all over the Home Counties.

The flat was a real benefit for me. At last I had somewhere to invite and entertain all the friends so important to one's early twenties. There was a day and a night porter, both ex-servicemen, one fat, the other thin, in blue uniforms and peaked caps. They were useful in helping to keep suitors from unfortunately colliding on the doorstep as they came or went through the wide swinging doors. The night porter knew it was dawn when a bedraggled sleepy figure crept through those same doors and up the stairs, shortly before the milkman shouted from the area behind, 'Number one, the fun's begun.' 'Wasn't it all fun?' I said to my sister Diana not long before she died.

'But they were always *your* friends,' she protested sadly.

In the West End or on the hunting field, Pat Hore-Ruthven continued with his crash–dash–splinter life. When offered a present he asked for a train and boat ticket to get him to Castle Martin, the Irish estate where his Aunt Sheela and her husband Freddie Blacker bred horses. After he came down from Cambridge in 1934 he would have liked to join a racing stable and become a professional jockey, having begun riding on the flat. But a racing career was considered somehow unworthy, and despite the favourable report he had received at Eton on his literary talents, an army career was the only approved option he was given. Here, too, his own preference – for the Scots Grays, in which he would have had a horse – was thwarted. Instead he was given a commission in the Rifle Brigade, the old regiment of his grandfather 'Rivvie' Ruthven ('Ruthven' being pronounced 'Rivven'). For the next three years he was stationed mostly with his batallion in Malta, and returned to be with us in the Cambridge gang only when he was home on leave.

There were nightclubs dotted around Mayfair to suit all purses and inclinations. If I was with Pat we generally went to the Florida. It sported a gyrating floor, with fifteen black jazz musicians in white tuxedos playing tunes like 'Bye, Bye Blackbird'. We sat at heavily shaded tables, each with a telephone under a silk lampshade so one could talk or wisecrack to any friend sitting on the other side of the dance-floor.

Pat liked to stay until breakfast of bacon and eggs or kedgeree was served with the first editions of the morning papers. Eventually a weary waiter would bring the bill; in his spiky 'kitchenmaid' hand, Pat would fill in a cheque for thirty shillings. However short of cash he was, I never remember it entering my head to help out. All the current débutantes frequented the Florida, by far the most attractive being Alicia Browne, whose brother Henry was with Pat in the Rifle Brigade.

Sometimes we went to the Café de Paris, haunt of Douglas Byng. Up top, at the balcony tables, dinner jackets were allowed and it was not obligatory to dine, this putting the balcony within reach of poorer boy-friends. Downstairs was really posh. There you had to be accompanied by a gentleman in white ties and tails. But I disliked dancing with a crackling, bulging stiff shirt. Pat invested in a double-breasted dinner jacket that he wore unconventionally with a dark-cream silk shirt and satin bow tie, so we didn't often make the downstairs.

After dinner, during a pause in the dancing, a kind of worldly Nanna Venn would take the floor – Douglas Byng in another of his cabaret Dame roles:

> Old Nanna,
> The keeper of the manor,
> In and out the lodge all day.
> A-popping and a-bobbing
> When the gentry come to call,
> Stopping little boys from writing
> Rude things on the wall.
> All the village knows me,
> Everybody owes me
> Money which they don't intend to pay.
> At Easter when the vicar
> Calls to ask the squire for alms,
> He calls in for a cuppa
> – I still have my hidden charms –

And he always leaves his prayerbook
With ten shillings in the Psalms.

Nightlife with the older generation consisted of private dances and charity balls. K. and Moggie would have tickets for any number of these to dispose of. The charity occasions were for the most part gastronomically disturbing dinner dances. Just as one delicious course arrived – and the food was invariably of the highest class – some gentleman at the table would suggest dancing. Down went the knife and fork; a gulp of wine and you were back on the dance-floor. These opportunists were often young men who frequented débutante and charity balls and were called 'La-di-di-poops' by the Cambridge boys. There were many wasted occasions that literally went over one's head. One evening Robert Byron, the dazzling travel writer of the day, destined to die in 1941 when the ship on which he was travelling to Egypt was torpedoed, talked across me to my other neighbour all through dinner.

On a less elevated level, there were our pub crawls and cat hunts round Mayfair: a sort of projection of those daring childhood games of 'Bears' and 'Hide and Seek', ending at the coffee stall at Hyde Park Corner or in an underground nightclub, the police keeping an eye open for reefers or illicit drinking. The *de rigeur* custom that a girl should be 'escorted' by a man was ridiculous and strange, seeing that our seniors had all worked during and survived the Great War. Perhaps our rebellion was a reaction to those heartbreaking goodbyes to the troopships.

Violet 'Bunnie' Branfill, née Persse, was an Irish cousin of Pat's, whom he called the 'Kinswoman'. She had joined our party in Devon for two or three hunting seasons, and had made life fun for K. and hilarious for us all by taking a lot of the nonsense of our 'horseyness' out of us, turning the whole business into an Irish farce. I never in those days met any other woman who rode with such effortless ease and co-ordination with her mount. The day she pronounced casually that I 'had a good seat' I felt born again.

I sometimes went up, with or without Tim, to stay with the Kinswoman in Northumberland after her husband, 'Branny' Branfill, had taken the mastership of the Haydon hounds. They lived at Threepwood, a tall house beside the kennels among taller scotch firs. This was a different style of fox-hunting: I was no longer a follower or subscriber but an honorary member of the master's hunt servants. On non-hunting days we exercised hounds, learning their names and their characters, while riding the hunt horses, who knew their job and what was expected of them, or other young ones, fairly green and newly acquired, who didn't. Branny was a good huntsman, very tough with a fine flow of language, a good-looking but, I thought, insensitive man. Bunnie ran his establishment with two or three very young local handmaidens, entertained as mistress of foxhounds, rode all the young horses and whipped in. There was nothing tough about her. Her Irish classlessness and humour among all the farmers and foot-followers made her as much loved as Branny was respected and feared. She would equally have made an outstanding parson's wife or a vicereine.

The Northumbrian walls were black, and sometimes carried a lethal coating of snow on top, to put the fear of God into any horse. One day when the hounds got away across open country, the master's horse twice refused at the intervening wall. He shouted at me, 'Go on, yours'll take it!' Sure enough he did, with a great leap and me still uncertainly a-top the farther side. That day I was given the fox's mask; it hung on a hook in my bedroom in Cadogan Gardens all through the war. When I returned it was riddled with moth.

At his departure for Malta Pat had to leave behind the best horse he ever owned, a chestnut thoroughbred named Imported which his great-aunt Rose McCalmont thought would be a good ride at Sandown in the Grand Military. Pat wrote of the horse,

I have never been so delighted with anything. He is the most awfully good ride, with perfect mouth and, except for a tiny bit fidgety, perfect manners . . . He feels like a really flippant little horse and . . . was admired by all the Fitzwilliam friends, and he looks like a lot of money when he is titupping along – I feel like the King of the World!

He gave Imported to me to hunt until he could come back and race him. It was on this little chestnut that I really learned to ride astride. He had run at Punchestown; he stood back at his fences and jumped the smallest Cotswold wall as if it was a great Irish bank. At Clifford, Few, the groom, was excited when Imported arrived. He had always wanted 'that there Mr Hum-Ruffian' to race Tim's lovely bay from Tipperary, Slieve-na-Man. But Moggie refused to stable Imported. He was becoming increasingly jealous of his stepson and his friends, forever criticizing Tim and continuing to insist that his, Moggie's, name be written on all the farm machinery and vehicles.

Pat always felt uncomfortable at Clifford, in any case. It was altogether too English for him. Once the gong to change for dinner had gone, there was no time to visit the stables. Tim, when he was at home, became equally correct, and sometimes selfish. There was a scene one night when Pat wore bedroom slippers at dinner; another when Tim didn't feel like hunting, so all the horses were cancelled.

K. was sympathetic to the problem of Imported, but her health was declining and she was powerless to intervene. It was the Kinswoman who came to the rescue and found stabling for him next to Hartwell, her old Cotswold farmhouse near Bibury. There he summered for the time being in Bunnie's flowery meadows, in front of the house and the duck pond. By 1938, Pat was with his regiment in India. I spent the season with the Bathurst hounds and exercising around the Gloucestershire lanes in what was to be my last year of freedom to dawdle in the still waters under the bank while the main stream hurtled towards war. Sometimes I hunted four or five times a week, riding back in the darkening afternoons through Hatherop, Coln St Aldwyns and Quenington, to George Dibble and his warm efficient stables; then on to where I lodged. The Cadogans, the Lakins, the Bazeleys – none could have been kinder to a not very proficient or well-endowed member of the hunt.

Pat, home on a short leave from India, also hunted Imported that season. He had a talent for 'setting his mount alight' – very useful if riding a slug, but it reminded Imported of his Punchestown days, and after Pat departed again I found him hard to handle. It was from Gloucestershire that Pat sent a cable to Australia saying 'WANT TO GET MARRIED', without mentioning to whom. Addressed to his father, who was on tour, it was opened by Dan Ranfurly, his ADC, and was the cause of what my sisters later called the 'Gowrie Conversations'.

Pat's father had been created the 1st Baron Gowrie of Canberra and Dirleton in 1935, and in the following year was appointed Governor-General of Australia. I first met the Gowries at the old Guards' Club in Brook Street. On leave from Australia, they were giving a small party for a young Australian heiress. Pat had telephoned me a few days earlier, ordering me to attend, and should I do so, 'not to sit like a poached egg'. (Nothing sinks more immovably on to its toast than a poached egg.)

There, among the rosy chintzes of the Ladies' Annexe, stood two tall, elegant people of unique charm and humour. Pat, unusually tidy, hovered near Sandie, his father, perching on the arm of a sofa. His mother, Zara, stood in front of the fire, wearing a tight black velvet dress edged with silver braid, her curls swept across the nape of her neck and pinned in an imitation shingle. Her gaiety suffused the room. No portrait or photograph can convey her charm and magnetism: the soft voice, the deep-set shining black 'boot-buttons', as she called her eyes, and the irrepressible curls.

Zara's mother, born Florence Bingham, was the youngest daughter of Lord Clanmorris, an impoverished Irish peer who succeeded in marrying his daughters to wealthy men. Florence, at barely seventeen, was married off to a young Scot, John Pollok, whose father had bought him a large stretch of land in East Galway; she bore him nine children, boasting that she never missed a season's hunting. But by the time she was thirty she had tired of her Scot and taken a lover, Jim Barry, son of a Chief Justice of Ireland. Her youngest child – Pat's Aunt Sheela – was generally thought to be Jim's.

Zara met Sandie Ruthven in Dublin, where he had been appointed ADC to the Viceroy, Lord Aberdeen. Her mother was implacably opposed to the match, and unimpressed by Sandie's horsemanship or military credentials: the younger son of an extravagant and impoverished Scottish peer, he had no 'place' and was therefore unsuitable. Zara and Sandie struggled for years to overcome her opposition; it was only when Sandie's career really began to take off, with his appointment as military secretary to the Governor-General of Australia in 1908, that she finally relented and they married. I often felt that the years of opposition they had to endure as lovers laid the foundation for their remarkably happy and successful partnership. Zara's spirit and mind moved outwards. She shared, with profligacy, her happiness, her talents and her passionate concern for the unlucky ones or drop-outs, along with criticism of anyone ignoring their plight. She never lost her Irish youth, for she remained a rebel in many things, especially over the discrepancies between Irish and British versions of history.

Though he was not conventionally good-looking, there was an

indefinable elegance about Sandie. He looked taller than his six feet: his bones were fine, his clothes immaculate in an old-fashioned way. A small ladybird tattooed on to his right hand drew attention to small, claw-like hands. In London, or while performing his public duties in Australia, he was consistently respectful and courteous, whether he was dealing with royalty or the toughest of union leaders. But the horse was his real element. Seated on a horse, he appeared heroic, almost monumental. Compton Mackenzie in his *Gallipoli Memoirs* (1929) recalled him in his prime at Gallipoli, just before he was badly wounded.

> One afternoon I saw Sandie Hore-Ruthven riding back into the lines. He was wearing jodhpur breeches, and the picture of him on that horse against the skyline of a sand-dune remains in my memory like a figure of supreme sculpture. At the moment it was seeming to me, that nobody could look so well as that on a horse and not be destined to ride on to some historical event, that so much ease and grace of bearing could not be wasted merely on finding a few hundred yards fit for a gallop among the dessicated scrub and herbage of the promontory during the first days of that pregnant but so inscrutable August.

Sandie must have cut a glamorous figure in Ireland, with a VC won in the Sudan, a reputation as an amateur jockey, and as a lady killer. 'Huntin' all day and dancin' with the girls all night,' was his description of life at Viceregal Lodge in the Phoenix Park. He rode at Punchestown, the Curragh and all the amateur steeplechases and point-to-points; many ladies fell in love with him and retained their early affection. I know, because I used to meet some of them in later times. As an old man, he would browse through his notebooks, recalling his racing days. 'Call yourself the honourable Ruthven,' a disappointed Glasgow punter had once shouted from the crowd, as his mount, the favourite, came second. 'I call you a dishonourable bugger.'

The second time I met Zara, she was alone, and I faced her as a prospective daughter-in-law. 'Himself,' as Sandie was known in the family, following the Irish usage, had needed to forgo his leave because of labour troubles in Australia. We sat together on the chintzy sofa in the same ladies' drawing room in Brook Street. I was wearing a navy-blue serge coat and skirt made by Busvine, of which I was particularly fond, and a tricone hat. She took from her handbag a piece of paper written in a clear pretty handwriting with curly musical capitals. I saw a list headed by the word 'Dilemmas', heavily underlined. The first of these was 'Poverty'. Poor Zara. Amid those brief costly journeys home to the family she missed and the son she saw so little of, the growing storm-clouds over Europe and the loneliness of Himself in Australia, I represented a new dilemma which must have bitten deep. 'Who *is* this Miss Fletcher?' exclaimed Aunt Maud Brassey, OBE, during dinner at 29 Berkeley Square, where Zara always stayed, dropping her monocle into the soup.

The dilemma anxiety had first been raised in a letter Zara wrote to me in response to Pat's telegram.

Pam Dear,

You and Pat have scarcely been out of my mind since I got Pat's cable. It is such a Dilemma for us all – as you would be so welcome as a Daughter – but we can't let you both starve. We just think and think all of us – I cheer myself by saying so many other mothers must have faced a much worse situation than this as there is only one very serious problem and that is the absolute lack of money. You know poor darling Pat can never nearly make both ends meet, not because he is really extravagant but all the things he loves cost something. Of course his allowance is very, very small but it is just about half what I have got, and that is the only 'real' money we have; the rest our Breadwinner, Pat's father, makes for us and everything dies with him – so really Pat and I would be almost penniless. It seems so ridiculous when you see us here living like minor Kings! But every penny is spent on the show. It is quite impossible for this to be otherwise.

When Himself was offered the job he rubbed it into the King that he wasn't the right selection because he was a poor man and could only spend the pay and nothing else – this was made quite clear. We try to do it on the pay but have to use a little of our own sometimes to keep heads above water. Every other Governor-General has spent about £10,000 a year apart from his pay, except for Sir Isaac Isaacs. It is often the most awful problem trying to do what is expected of us on the money. I am telling you all these family secrets so that you should know the real situation . . . Himself always said from the time Pat was born that he would struggle to give him a good education but that was all, he could leave him nothing . . . It's so terribly sad but it is the truth.

When Pat gets on in the army he will be making a little more all the time and his pension, but he probably may not be a captain for some time still. When I see Dan [Ranfurly], Percy [Blacker] and so many other boys with no jobs at all, I feel so thankful that small as it is you can't starve in the army, but the awful problem is marrying . . . Of course Staff College would have to be faced and got into . . . There isn't a soul in my family who can ever leave me anything. I have £150 a year from an uncle but that dies with me so our only chance is to make it.

I know how much Pat loves you and would say 'I will give up everything and never look at a horse again' and he would mean it and would want to do it, but that might distress you and the regiment if he couldn't play any part in the sport side. I write like this rather assuming from what Pat said that you are in the same boat as regards money. I can see Pat being in despair if you two couldn't do all the things you both love doing with your friends. One simply has to think of all these sordid details, I am sure you have thought of them all but I know that Pat, in his great wish to marry you – will be unable to think calmly unless you can help him to do so.

I can't believe that between us all, weighing and exploring every avenue, we will not be able to think of something, as long as you can wait till we have thought it all out and talked it all over. We are so longing that it would be possible, I believe we are as bad as Pat! Yet we can't have you both in debtors' prison, and the end of the poor Ruthvens and Gowries for ever more.

I wonder what made Pat cable? I dare say your family may be very worried and wanted to chase Pat off, and this cable was sent in despair and he couldn't wait to write. A great deal must depend on the regiment because if they stuck their toes in, it would be very difficult. Pat would really be on the dole then, so at all costs they must sanction it or we are done . . . You can perhaps think what my feelings would have been if you had been an Undesirable! I really would have broken my heart then.

As it is I am only sad that things don't look at all easy, but we are not absolutely beaten yet. I rather fear you may both be terribly worried and I should love to think of you free of care. What a Dilemma life is from cradle to grave. Much Love from Pat's Mother.

PS. It is quite possible Pat might make his way in the world as his father did, but he is young to put aside everything and work like a Black at the exams as Himself did. If he could it might be the making of him.

Dilemmas of another kind continued at Clifford. As Moggie had steadily advanced his hold over the estate, so it seemed K.'s asthma had likewise increased its grip. Each year she seemed to become more delicate; was increasingly disabled by nervous oedemas. She would come down some mornings, her poor face all puffed and purple, the eyes like slits so she looked like someone else. The point was reached when her lady's maid, dear old Flattie, who waddled around the house after her mistress, her frizzy hair trapped in a hair net, could no longer cope and a series of nurses arrived to stay. One I remember disliking: it was easy to see she was dishonest, making up to Moggie, who was worried sick about his wife, and upsetting the other staff as only nurses and nannies are able.

K. had for a long while been a governor of St Bartholomew's Hospital. They lent her a tall, late middle-aged women from Cork, whom we called Paddy. Paddy brought a benison with her to Clifford. There was never a word of criticism of her from the staff or Moggie after she took charge, and she was to stay throughout the rest of K.'s and Moggie's lives before finally retiring to her native land.

A shadow meanwhile fell across my wedding plans. After Tim had abandoned the prospect of a diplomatic career, he flirted with the idea of joining Hamish Hamilton to be a publisher, but nothing came of that either. At Clifford he had his tiny study upstairs, where a large portrait of his father, handsome, forceful and quizzical, took up one of the walls. Apart from his large bed and bathroom, his hunter and a young footman to mind him, there was little else at Clifford Tim could call his own. Eventually, when there was talk of finding him a farm in the Cotswolds, Tim went up to the Feversham Estate in Yorkshire to learn about husbandry. He was there in 1938 when the country first woke up to the need for civil defence.

One evening he drove with some friends to a Civil Defence Anti-

Gas dance at a local village hall. They arrived in Tim's Rolls Bentley, wearing dinner jackets. The room was full of villagers in their day clothes, some of them already lit up with beer and spirits. An argument developed between Tim and a young off-duty policeman. Tim's two companions persuaded him to leave, but just as they were passing through the doorway the policeman threw an empty bottle, hitting him just above his poor scarred neck. The others bundled him into the back of the car; it seems they drove around for a long while, frightened and undecided, before finally getting him to a hospital. He died there without regaining consciousness. At the inquest, it was said that his skull had been unusually thin. The young policeman was married with children. He was never charged. The newspapers had a field day with this story of class conflict and the violent death of a scion of the famous tobacco family.

That September I travelled with Zara and her sister and brother-in-law, Ruby and Louis Fleischmann, to Aix-les-Bains, where Louis loved to take the waters. A merchant banker of German origin, Uncle Louis was a wise old bird, very cultured, something of a gourmet. He kept a magnificent table and collected fine paintings, which he hung in Chetwode Manor, the large, rather gloomy Jacobean country house he leased in Buckinghamshire. Aunt Ruby resembled Zara with her exuberant grey curls and 'boot-button' eyes, though her manner contrived to be stiffer while less urbane. Somehow she looked like the great gardener she was. My task was to occupy Uncle Louis so the two devoted sisters could have the time of day together. He and I would discuss the menu seriously, and at great length, as the Irish sisters chatted about their tribe. It wasn't done to treat food frivolously in front of Uncle Louis. Once, when dining at Chetwode, I made the gaffe of asking for the salt. Uncle Louis gave me a look of withering contempt as he said, 'Ach, Pamela, I zee you cook at ze table.'

From Aix I took a mountain train to Schuls Tarasp, a Swiss spa K.'s doctor had recommended as she was pronounced well enough to travel. It was a season in the Alps I had never known before. The train climbed so slowly you could have reached out of the window to pick the autumn gentians. At Schuls Tarasp Moggie was there to meet me, and escorted me to a large, luxurious, gloomy hotel built above the mountain with healing waters.

Each morning, after breakfast, I walked up the mountain paths between the glowing beeches, the rigid firs and the autumn gentians. Then we all took the baths in rather nasty smelly bubbling water. Afterwards K. would retire, looking wan and white in her sickness and sorrow, to spend the rest of the day in her room with Paddy; and I went to play tennis with a group of Italians, sometimes with Moggie. Paddy came down to join Moggie and me for lunch, but I had to dine with him later on my own. Tim's death seemed to have deranged him. Throughout the delicious Swiss soup and fish or fowl, he blackguarded his stepson, accusing him of killing his mother by causing her nothing but worry and trouble. All the pent-up jealousy of those years since Tim, aged twelve, had welcomed him to his mother's bed and board came pouring out.

There was an Englishman staying alone, to whom I expect I confessed my dislike of these outbursts. He had a black patch over one eye and a quadruple-barrelled surname, Plunkett-Ernle-Erle-Drax. We used to sit together outside the hotel below the tennis court. He was a great comforter. When I married, he sent me a charming pink porcelain coffee set.

After talking with Paddy I realized that Moggie was in some ways less well than his wife. Remembering how each night, if we were late home, Tim would tuck a little note under her bedroom door to reassure her we were safely back, or to say good night if she was not sleeping, or how he had asked me to marry him in order to make her happy, I wonder I never hit Moggie. I never felt the same towards him again, knowing that from then on he would gradually close in on K., suffocating her with his devotion.

K. and I agreed that when one could no longer pray or reach God it was best just to repeat the Lord's Prayer or something familiar and beautiful from the liturgy, until the icicle of sadness melted. She died in 1949; while her coffin was being lowered beside Dr Douty and Tim, Moggie fell weeping to the ground, calling her name.

When I returned to London from Switzerland I found a cable from Pat, saying he would prefer an uxurious Christmas. He had to wait until 4 January 1939. I insisted that if I must be married in London, it had to be Westminster Abbey. This was because I disliked organs and knew the choir would sing unaccompanied. The rules were bent and we were allowed the Henry IV Chapel, partly, no doubt, because an old friend of my father's was chaplin at Sandringham. The Reverend was permitted to perform the actual marriage.

My younger sister Romola drove Pat around London to make the necessary arrangements. I took up the job of choosing the music seriously: here was a wonderful opportunity to hear my favourite hymns and carols, and pieces by Bach and Buxtehude. My parents had the tricky task of allotting the limited stalls in the chapel among relations and people whose names flew back and forth in a stream of cables between England and Australia. The Gowries were expected to be home for good shortly, after being relieved of their viceregal duties by the Duke of Duchess of Kent. This and the usual poverty prevented even Zara from being with us for the wedding. We were to travel to Australia for the honeymoon.

I insisted on spending the night before the ceremony on my own at Prince's Gate, while Pat had his bachelor party. I supped with Dick Corbett, who was back from his tea-planting in Ceylon, and stayed the night alone at 42 Prince's Gate. The service was just as I wanted it, though many of the relations, especially Pat's Brassey cousins, pronounced it unusual. In his stall near the altar, Aunt Sheela's husband, Freddie Blacker, broke into a strange fit of wailing. So it came about that, after seven years of wild and turbulent romance, I finally married the dark young man who looked like a black fox I had met hunting on Exmoor. When I first met Pat, he had been temporarily rusticated from Cambridge for biting a policeman on the nose.

5

Moon Voyagers

K. had suggested that we join her and her Wills nephews and nieces
at St Moritz, then pick up our ship at Marseille, but Pat was against
it. Pat had hated the snows as a child. In any case, he was unwell,
having contracted anaemic dysentery in India; so after spending two
or three nights at Vern Leaze, Malise and Ange's home at Calne in
Wiltshire, we boarded the P. & O. ship *Strathmore* at Southampton.
'You can be sure,' said Pat, 'that whatever port we call at, we shall
find either one of Daddy's or Mumps's lovers to meet and look after
us.'

We found ourselves in a large double cabin on the deck, a present
from Zara's sister-in-law, Aunt Gladys Pollok, who had been a Mc-
Kinnon, of the shipping family. The ship's hold contained our carefully packed wedding presents: saddles and horse-rugs from Pat's rich
Brassey relations, 'something out of the cupboard' from the poorer
and discerning. This latter dictum of the groom's paid off; among
the cheques, the saddles, bridles and horse-rugs we raked in some
very pretty pieces of china and old silver.

Our ship took a leisurely route towards Australia, its ports of call
being Tunis, Malta, Suez, Bombay and Colombo. Pat declined to sit
at the captain's table, preferring that we should have a private one to
ourselves in the corner. The P. & O. food was English and ordinary,
with a very British curry and rice served at least twice a week. At
first I was chagrined when he insisted on returning dish after dish.
Far from being upset, the head waiter was only too happy to come
across someone who complained. A junior chef was put in charge
of our table and a choice menu offered at each meal. Pat was

delighted. He instructed me not to gobble, but to enjoy the fare and produce good conversation.

Evening dress was *de rigeur*; but by day we reverted to the uniform of our Cambridge group – narrow whipcord trousers, open silk shirts with knotted handkerchiefs, trying to look as much as possible like Irish stable lads. Pat played deck quoits with great agility, having had much practice on previous voyages; I was pretty fair at deck tennis, but was unprepared for his bitter disappointment when I failed to win the tournament.

At Marseille we had a whole day ashore, found a fiacre with a wise-cracking coachman and a black mare called Minèrve. He drove us into the Provençale countryside where sun brought out the smell of thyme and rosemary as we scrambled over red and grey rocks. At Tunis we almost lost each other in the flower market. Pat spent a fortune buying flowers for our cabin, but the young Arab tried to short-change him; I was left standing with a posy of tiny pink roses as my groom chased the boy between the stalls, then belaboured him with and ruined the large bouquet. At Bombay a detachment of sepoy peons from Government House, resplendent in braided uniforms, climbed the gangway to collect our luggage. We were to stay a few nights with Sir Roger and Lady Lumley in a guest bungalow.

We were met by Nathoo, an elderly Indian servant who practically belonged to the family. As a young man he had accompanied Sandie Hore-Ruthven on foot on an intelligence-gathering mission in Afghanistan and Persia; later he acted as bearer for Malise, and finally for Pat. Nathoo had travelled all the way from Meerut to meet us. He slept at night, as was his wont, outside our door. When we left Bombay, Nathoo waved goodbye at the quayside with tears falling on to his thin white beard.

Colombo was less grand and ceremonial. In 1939, Ceylon was a magical country, filled with graceful, musical people, silver sand and waving palms. There was no time to travel inland, but I remember wonderful nights in our high-ceilinged room, the moon floating between the palm leaves with huge black bats weaving to and fro between them. From Colombo we sailed eastwards on the gentle bosom of the Indian Ocean. At sunrise and at nightfall it was an absorbing pastime to watch from the deck as the flying fishes made sudden little arches of silver, curving in and out of deep-blue phosphorescent waves.

We made friends with three young Italians, travelling to Melbourne. There were two brothers from Milan, Claudio and Orlando Alcorso, and a nephew of the minister who had signed the Treaty of Versailles for Italy in 1919. Having served with Mussolini's son Bruno in the Italian air forces supporting Franco in the Spanish Civil War, they had all become disillusioned with Fascism and were emigrating to start a silk business in Australia. Once, as I was sitting with Claudio, reading Dante or d'Annunzio, Pat came upon us. Looking more Italian than any of them, he said: 'Beware, my ancestors used to knife people like you!' His forebear and namesake, the ailing Patrick Lord Ruthven, had been the first to plunge a dagger into the hapless David Rizzio at Holyrood House in 1566. Claudio and Orlando spent long hours arguing about the men controlling all our destinies.

None of us could know that our Italian friends were heading for internment in Australia, or that Pat would die from Italian bullets in the same North African desert we had steamed past a week or two before. The news from Europe hardly reached us. Lovely long lazy days were interrupted by swimming and deck games, and always a return to poetry. At night, Pat would identify the constellations to me. He knew his stars. Two years earlier he had written from another P. & O. boat: 'Orion sleeps in these far latitudes; idle and sheathed his sword hangs by his side.'

In Sydney 'Their Exes' (as we often referred to Himself and Herself) lived at Admiralty House. It was a far smaller establishment than the state governor's residence, though it had a large garden leading down to the bay. Government House, the Governor-General's principal official residence, which stood in the district of Yarralumla in the federal capital of Canberra, was being reconstructed and redecorated in preparation for the Kents.

Lord Dudley, who was Governor-General from 1908 to 1911, once wrote a long letter of advice to his successor Lord Denman, which went into every detail of life at Government House, including travelling, carriages, horses, golf, interior decorations, staffing and even the problems of laundry. His concluding remarks about Australian social life provide an important clue to the Gowries' success: 'It is very difficult for the wife of a Governor-General to make friends among the ladies here, and so if I may be permitted to say so, I think that Lady Denman would be wise to bring out some relation or friend with her who would be a companion to her out here. We were lucky that way because my military secretary, Sandie Ruthven, had a charming wife who was a godsend to us all . . .'

Sandie, appointed to Lord Dudley's staff as a bachelor, then had to confess to having just married. Zara told me how, because she had studied in Florence, she was often encouraged to sing to the company after dinner, but had to give up the practice because Lady Dudley always wanted to follow, blissfully unaware of creating an embarrassing anti-climax. Zara must have been captivating, standing beside the piano with her unruly black curls and shining black eyes – her 'boot buttons' – shy yet completely unselfconscious and perhaps with a hint of self-mockery. She had a true high range, in contrast to her low soft speaking voice, though I only ever heard her sing in church. She and Pat used to behave outrageously, sending up the hymns and psalms, even in the viceregal pew, in the manner of those who have grown up in the affection and familiarity of the Anglican communion.

At Admiralty House we were given the best suite of rooms over-looking the harbour and the bridge. Throughout the household I was known as 'The Broide'. Among the ADCs, Jim Windsor Lewis was the most mature. He came from the Welsh Guards, which Sandie had joined as colonel during the Gallipoli campaign. Jim was immensely popular. He knew the Australian cricket team and would regale the dinner table with stories of Bert Oldfield and Don Brad-man. Being a true Welshman, his stories lost nothing in the telling; nor did his accounts of tours in the Outback, as he described how Binghams and Persses and other descendants of Zara's less reputable Irish kin would suddenly emerge from the bush, holding new babies aloft to be kissed and shouting, 'Good old Cousin Zara' and 'Cousin Sandie'.

Qualifications for ADC-ship at Government House were unusually flexible: in most cases it was enough to be one of Pat's friends or Zara's relations. Dan Ranfurly (Thomas Daniel Knox, Lord Ranfurley, our best man, married just before we were), was elder brother of Pat's Cambridge friend Corky Knox, and had been recruited mainly as a result of a need to put as much distance as possible between himself and the bookies in England. Percy Blacker, Aunt Sheela's elder son, owed his short appointment to nepotism in the strictest sense. He spent most of his time smoking on the sofa, and drove everyone mad, except Himself. Sandie's private secretary was Brigadier-General Austin Anderson; his literary-minded wife, Ethel, became a close friend of Pat's, and after his death edited his letters into the book called *Joy of Youth*. The military secretary, Captain Leighton Bracegirdle, was a stern and efficient naval officer who had done long service with His Ex.

On the domestic side, there was an English butler, and an Irish footman from Kilcullen, the village next to the Blacker's Castle Martin estate in County Kildare. Mrs Donald, Zara's lean, nervous but formidable Scottish cook, presided over the kitchens, having begun her career with the Hore-Ruthvens as Maggie the kitchenmaid. She and Miss Stacey, Zara's lady's maid, seconded from the Brasseys and McKinnons, stayed with them for nearly half a century. Mrs Donald and Miss Stacey, who were never known to address each other by their first names, were still looking after Zara when she died in 1965.

Her Ex's private secretary was Miss Park – known simply as 'Park'. Technically she was not of the household and had to be termed a 'clerk'. She had her own suite of rooms, and since these occupied a limbo-land between the dining room and the staff hall, her meals were brought up to her on trays. The ADCs gave the impression of thinking her rather vulgar; she had come from commercial circles. But there never was a soul so generous, devoted and unself-seeking. She served Zara with great devotion, and then adopted Pat and me. She lent me a skirt and boots to go skating in; she typed Pat's poems and retyped them through successive drafts with numerous corrections, including poems he sent from the Middle East after the war broke out. Their Ex's loved and always supported her; I was once detailed to choose tactfully a dress for her to wear at a ball. We also protected her from the wiles of the ADCs, who had to work closely with her and sometimes made disparaging remarks about her in the office at the end of a long corridor, where we all forgathered. Sandie, having been an ADC himself, was ever the soul of tact. When approaching that office he would whistle 'Yankee Doodle', or whatever, so that whiskies and sodas or anything else unseemly could be rapidly stowed away.

There was a charity concert to which the Alcorso brothers were invited. They arrived immensely well groomed with red buttonholes, and sat directly behind the viceregal chairs. To the delight of Pat and

Zara they hissed, '*Cane, cane,*' down the backs of our necks at the efforts of the performers, and were ever after known as the 'Canes'. (The Gowries did what they could to minimize the hardship of their incarceration during the war, and eventually they prospered with their silk factory. Claudio, the elder brother, became director of the Sydney Opera House.)

The Gowries arranged for Pat and me to take part in the annual muster of cattle being brought down from the Bogong high plains in Victoria before the snows fell. These were not cattle from a single large station, but the property of several small farmers, mostly of Scottish origin, who banded together to bring them down each year. Our hosts were Mr Blair, his son Frank and daughter Marjorie, the latter having been persuaded to come as my companion. Pat and I spent the night at a small, very rudimentary hotel at Bright. The following morning we met Mr Blair and some of the other cattle owners, climbed into our stock saddles, and rode away to the high plains.

For hours on end we rode uphill, through steep miles of eucalyptus trees and wattle bushes, lit by the glaring Australian light which blinds English eyes even in winter, a silvery light that floods the grass and the trees, washing out colour, painting every contour the same yellow-grey monotone. When night fell, we rode by moonlight, travelling faster as the land flattened out while the yellow, flowery fronds brushed our faces. We slept in a hut on wooden bunks stacked above each other, as in a train. No one undressed. Pat and I came bitterly to regret our well-cut Newmarket jodhpurs: until the last steer had been mustered from the high plains above, we were never to take them off. We soon got through the meagre rations brought by our single pack-horse. Fortunately Pat managed to catch some trout in the stream where we washed by tickling their bellies with blades of grass. Mostly we were sustained by billy tea brewed in the open. I vowed I would get a silver billy kettle to take to Meerut in India, where we expected to go when Pat rejoined his regiment.

Pat had ridden horses since before he could walk. He had raced over hurdles and on the flat, had played polo and gone pigsticking. During the previous year, I had hunted up to four times a week. But neither of us was prepared for the gruelling craft of cattle mustering: in the saddle for nearly nine hours a day, riding up to the high plains where only snow gums grew. Having found the beasts, we had to bring them down to the stockyards near our hut. Some of the steers were extremely unruly after being left in the highlands for a season or two. One particular brute had evidently eluded muster for years and exercised a satanic influence over the more docile members of the herd. He was probably behind a disastrous break-out one night, when most of the steers escaped back to the highlands and the operation had to begin all over again.

After the mustering came the cutting out, as other owners arrived to claim their beasts. Marjorie Blair and I were only tolerated on the periphery of this fast and furious operation, from standstill to gallop, inside and outside the yard. Pat acquitted himself better than some and learnt to use the stockwhip, but he admitted he could not compete with the more seasoned hands. We rode back to Bright, tired but triumphant. At the hotel we inspected ourselves in a mirror for the first time in a week. Pat had a silky, pointed Elizabethan beard; 'the Broide' resembled nothing so much as Strewwelpeter, the boy with wild, matted, straw-like hair in the fierce German nursery verses.

A later visit was to the Bedford Osbornes at Bowylie, their station in New South Wales. The Osborne family were among the closest friends the Gowries made in Australia; and during the three antipodean visits Pat made to his parents, Bedford became his 'real cobber' in turn. His wife, the tall and beautiful Mollie Osborne, had just had a new baby, and I remember thinking it strange that she should be bathing it herself – I cannot have made a very sympathetic guest. I joined the men at dawn and rode round the station before returning for a huge breakfast of mutton chops with giant mushrooms picked from the sandy soil. Bedford's first love was the sea, which he had to abandon to run the family station. When he and Pat once went sailing together on Sydney harbour, and were late returning, Sandie got in a real fuss and insisted on sending a motor-boat out to find them. Bedford was a most charming personality. Of all the men close to Pat whom I knew, I would – had fate permitted – have taken Bedford closest to my heart.

A week or two before we were due to leave Australia, the dysentery Pat caught in India returned. Fortunately it meant an extension of his leave: now he would not need to rejoin his regiment till July. He spent each day in our rooms at Admiralty House, reading books and writing poetry, which made him an easy and contented patient. I wrote home to the Reverend on 5 May 1939: 'We have such a lovely comfy suite of rooms and the long veranda to wander about on; the fleet are in and lying all around us. It is quite usual to see Himself crossing the harbour in the Admiral's barge in full regalia, to inspect the ships.' A dance given in our honour had been a 'proper party', I said,

only spoiled by Pat having to sit upstairs in his dressing gown entertaining only a few favoured friends. Our Italian boy friends from the ship arrived three strong and were a great success. They all fell for Herself and next day sent an enormous basket of flowers redolent of 'Sole Mios' and the passionate south. I have bought myself a guitar, have had it strung with gut and hope eventually to be able to play Bach and our XVII and XVIII century friends. It is an instrument with a lovely rich tone. It will be a perfect accompaniment to Harry Fletcher's voice. The co-adjudicator at the cathedral is . . . an excellent preacher, but most of the churches are very Prot.

Pat's illness meant he missed the journey I made with Their Exes to Queensland and the Great Barrier Reef. I resumed my letter to the Reverend on the 7th:

This was to have been such an interesting letter but alas it was interrupted by my leaving for Brisbane for the last few days of Themselves' farewell tour in Queensland. The concert given in their honour the Saturday night was unique. Such a variety they had collected, with even a troop of Aboriginals giving a most peculiar performance of their own. As we were in the front row we got the full blast of the BO.

Himself gave a charming farewell speech. He has an excellent delivery and hardly mentions himself but speaks mostly of his successor designate the Duke of Kent: he works unceasingly to pave the way for him and Princess Marina.

At 6.45 Monday morning Herself and I and Jim Windsor Lewis climbed into a little machine and flew nearly 900 miles up the coast. It was a wonderful flight, we landed twice and could see all the eastern seaboard and, for the most part, virgin bush the whole way. We arrived at Dunk Island in the afternoon: almost the first people to use the new landing-strip Hugo Brassey, Zara's cousin and godson, has made there. He lives on the island, has built little bungalows for people to stay in and does one most awfully well. Mum would go dotty. Dunk Island is ten miles off the Great Barrier Reef, emerald green with the strangest tropical plants, luscious fruits and butterflies the size of sparrows: blue ones which are made into brooches and emerald admirals, among hundreds of others; one finds them far out to sea. The beach is fringed with coconut palms. Looking towards the mainland one might be in West Killarney, it's extraordinary what a resemblance there is.

A customs patrol boat was laid on to take us out to the Barrier Reef:

There is a tiny heap of shells and sand where one can land. We spend the day in our bathing suits swimming about looking at the wonderful coral and the coloured fish and queer beasts. I remember learning about it with Miss Gough. It is quite, quite unreal. Hugo is the oddest card I ever came across. Tremendous charm, looks like a blond Apollo, wears patterned shorts or a sarong. He is at his best with his godmother, Herself. Some of the family crack that goes on would make you bust your sides. He married a German baroness and sent her back to England after six months and proceeded to get a divorce. She has left a sad little ghost in the island. Our rooms are charmingly done with locally made bamboo furniture and materials which she designed after the Bavarian things she was used to.

Hugo has set up a big fish-trap; his fleet of little fox terriers catch them at low tide. Tomorrow we take a boat and go four miles around the island taking the dogs on a wild-pig hunt. I am looking forward to this enormously; the pigs make excellent eating, very gamey . . . Love to all and lots to your dotty old self.

By now we knew Pat's battalion was leaving India, most probably for Egypt or Palestine. It seemed likely I would go with him since Themselves were to be away on tour for all of July and part of August, before departing for good on 29 September. We went to stay at Government House, Brisbane, for what was arranged as Their Exes' farewell visit. The governor, Sir Leslie Wilson, had, like Sandie, a son in the Rifle Brigade. Lady Wilson was extremely large, with an addiction to eating. After serving everyone, the butler would place the dishes on a trolley beside her at the head of the table, for a second helping no one else was offered. The most compelling image I retain of Government House, Brisbane, is of the last of the luscious strawberries being popped one by one into Her Excellency's capacious maw.

The afternoon we had spent in a small motor launch on the great expanse of the Brisbane River. There was a festival and a boat race. Sir Leslie was popular, and in action was hilarious, not very regal but noisy and 'hail fellow'. He was embarrassing yet touching in his presentation of the Governor-General. Themselves sat erect in the stern, watching and missing nothing. I noticed how, almost out of sight, they held hands.

Back at Admiralty House we received the news that the 2nd Battalion of the Rifle Brigade was indeed moving to Palestine. By early June we had re-embarked on the P. & O. liner *Strathmore*. I was by now more than four months pregnant: this, combined with the deteriorating world situation, made our plans less certain than ever. We were to part in Egypt, Pat leaving for Palestine and I remaining for a brief holiday in Alexandria. Here, before returning to England, I had the experience of sailing up to Mersa Matruh in an Egyptian battleship with Admiral Sir Gerald Wells of the Ports and Lighthouses Administration.

Shortly before Pat and I parted, Pat had written to the Giant, addressing her as 'PM' (for 'Pam's Mother'):

July 9th (Black Sunday) 1939
    P. & O. *Strathmore*.
Dear PM
    Pam says it's high time I wrote you my bi-annual letter and that it is to be a funny one, but really I don't feel very funny, as we have come to the parting of the ways; hence Black Sunday at the top of the page. Actually I have one day's respite as my train doesn't leave Port Said till Monday evening and Pam will go down to Alexandria also on Monday night; so we will be able to smell our way round the gateway of the East together.
    If only you were installed in the charming little house on the Suez Canal, that Pam tells me you have in mind, how useful you would now be to your family (and 'in-laws') streaming as they are

through the canal in shoals! Your son Michael is just astern of us in the *Circassia*. We met him at Port Sudan which was a great bit of luck, unfortunately our ship only stayed in about an hour, but he and two shipmates came on board and we plyed them with gin and sandwiches, till long after the shore bell had finished ringing; then we went down to the gangway which had already been drawn up, so we had it put down again, and pushed them off in a Police Boat! I trust they were not whisked straight off to a Sudanese Dungeon for delaying the departure of the ship! Michael looked very fit, possibly a bit thin after the hot weather, but seemed in very good heart. Anyhow you will see him and be able to judge for yourself almost as soon as you get this letter.

Your daughter (my wife) is, I regret to say, in a non-planning mood, so I don't quite know when you will see her. She is by way of going to stay with somebody called Admiral Sir something Wells who is a friend of Herself, until my plans are a bit more settled. I think she will probably get home early in August, but I cannot guarantee her movements. I seem to be the most unsatisfactory and 'undomesticable' husband, never being able to provide a home; in fact like the cuckoo, incapable of building a nest, but always having to use other peoples, for the accommodation of my belongings. My 'nest-eggs' in the shape of packing cases of wedding presents are still at large and likely to remain so until Himself's things reach India on the way home, when I hope mine will join them. Have just heard that my Battalion is at Nablus. I shall probably turn into a Samaritan (non-good variety). Pam tells me they are very queer.

My racial origins are already deeply suspect on the *Strathmore*. The other day when I was sitting by the swimming bath, faultlessly attired in a Sarong, and a Mexican Hat (with nothing in between) two ladies were heard discussing my probable descent. Eventually they gave up the anthropological problem and decided that I must be a 'native' which to the English means, I suppose, anybody who lives in a south-easterly direction from Dover!

This parting is terribly sad; however, such things happen in the Army, and we have had a very good six months. Best Love to Rom. I am terribly sorry that Rory died, as I always thought him such a grand little dog – I am glad she likes her new puppy. Love also to His Reverence and Diana.

Elegant preparations were in hand at 87 Cadogan Gardens for the arrival of my first-born, including a christening robe made out of family lace with a bastinet of matching net. Daily the news grew more ominous. Pat's letters caught up with me at irregular intervals, after long sea-borne delays. One, from Nablus, was dated 14 July:

Went out on a raid with Tom Pearson (our Intelligence officer) and the police, just for 'divarshun.' Had a long walk in the dark to surround a tent where a Bad Man was supposed to be lying up. He wasn't there but we took three of his pals for investigation. Just before we left a crescent moon set through the battle-red after-glow and looked like a bloody dagger. I couldn't decide whether it augured well or ill for Islam; but as our rebel eluded us I suppose that his God was guarding him . . .
I love you very, very much and miss you dreadfully.

16 July
Today is Sunday and there is no battle on, consequently I am missing you dreadfully and am going nearly mad with reaction; do write to me hundreds of times a day. I want to go on leading my 'inner' life with you; although Ruthven the Outer Man is sitting in an Arab house in Nablus, R. the Spirit would sail away with you to wherever you choose. This is very difficult if I can't visualize your temporal activities. The day before yesterday we went in search of a secret arms dump belonging to Mr Abu Omar, the local Michael Collins. The total bag was one automatic pistol, broken, one army pattern circingle and one dinner knife, property of the NAAFI. For this four aeroplanes, four officers and about one hundred troops, to say nothing of Interpreters, Informers and Arab Irregulars, spent about ten hours in operations. When I got home I was told that one of my merry men had dropped a bandolier contained 45 rounds of ammunition, in or near the suspected village, so I can't help feeling that that round of the contest went to Abu Omar. In one house we were searching, we found the photograph of one of the rebel leaders, now deceased, also an empty Turkish ammunition box.
There were some large granaries at one end of the room and I suddenly had a hunch that there might be rifles concealed in the grain. So we pulled out the bungs at the bottom of the granaries

and let the grain run on the floor; suddenly to our intense excitement, the end of a belt appeared through one of the bung holes; accompanied by throaty British cheers it was pulled out. It turned out to be the army circingle already mentioned. Most disappointing and my imagined MC (Medal for Cuteology) vanished into thin air. Meanwhile in another part of the village some troops had found suspicious looking boxes on top of a house. "'Ere, Bill, empty one of them things there might be ammo in 'em.' But far more deadly, bees poured out, with results that need no description. The boxes were beehives.

During this time of operations at Nablus Pat composed his poem 'Biddya':

> At noon they fell upon Biddya,
> Fariz Assoni, Hamid Zwatta,
> And forty of their fighting men.
>
> The heat of the day gave way to heat of battle;
> Blood added scarlet to the grey of dust;
> Bullets woke the village
> With sudden song,
> With strange, untoward exhilaration.
>
> The negro from Kap Dih fought splendidly,
> Knifed two of Hamid's followers, then,
> Himself shot, died immediately,
> Ear-ringed in jet magnificence.
>
> After this (leaving ten dead
> And a girl's body underneath the ilex),
> Fariz Assoni, Hamid Zwatta,
> And thirty-five men
> Vanished through the olive groves.
>
> This the Mukhtar reported, clamorously excited
> When I arrived, too late, to his assistance.

Despite her excited preparations for a grandchild, I succeeded in luring the Giant off to the McGillicuddy Reeks in Kerry towards the end of summer. The fuschia hedges spilled their blooms like drops of blood against a backdrop of mountains that turned first gold, then blue. Along the seashore the wrack gave out the smell of fishy decay, familiar since childhood. The diet in our lodgings was extremely limited: mostly porridge and blackberries.

On 25 August Pat was writing from Palestine:

I don't know what to say. War looks absolutely inevitable. Is Civilization to be crucified as surely as Christ was? On this great tidal wave of chaos, what happens to 'spindrifts' like ourselves is of little importance in the scheme of things. If we both happen to be cast up on the same shore we will certainly find each other. Only remember, my darling, that our love will survive anything in this world.

If anything happens to me you must help this 'Pig' and love it just as you always loved me. Teach it that courage and honesty are the only two things that matter in the world. I love you beyond this life or any other.

PS. If war breaks out we stay in this country for the time being.

On 1 September he wrote: 'Am expecting to learn that war has been declared at any moment'. The next day he added:

Just got in from patrol. Went out at 10 p.m. and my alarm clock for a new day has just sounded. I thought about you a lot while I was out but am too sleepy to write it all down . . . Hear rumours that war was declared at midnight but can't get a confirmation. Whatever happens I love you more nor life, but please, please look after yourself.

The rumours, of course, were true. The outbreak of war meant that Themselves would stay on at Government House in Canberra for the duration, while the Duke of Kent took up the work in RAF Home Command that would lead to his death in a flying accident in 1942. Urged by the Gowries, I had decided it would be wiser to have the baby in Ireland. At the same time the Reverend, after more than half a century's exile, returned to his native land and church of his beginnings: his old friend Henry Patton, Bishop of Killaloe, appointed him Canon of the Shannon at the parish of Castleconnel, a once popular salmon fishing resort on the banks of the river. The Giant packed up the flat and Moushill Cottage, neither of which she would see again for several years. 'Well,' Pat had written on 5 September, 'the worst has happened and God knows how it will all end.'

> I don't think I have ever been quite so miserable. Wish to God I knew where you were – suppose all the mails have gone astray. Meanwhile there is a press censorship in force so can say nothing. Lack of news is the worst feature . . . Wish I was in the know. Suppose the thing will drag on interminably like the last one, and what will be left of our world then? . . . The mood will pass I suppose, but cheer me up by telling me that you are in Ireland and out of all this. Tell me how it smells and what the wild things are saying, that I may know that life is still worthwhile. I love you terribly and when the black mood is on it is to you I look for courage.

In fact I waited for the child at Ongar, near Dublin, home of Zara's mother, known as 'The Honourable', and her Jim Barry. They allotted me a study hung with portraits of Binghams and Persses in hunting pink. It was, for me, another brief, happy interval out of the mainstream, under the bank.

Jim would come and sit with me after cub-hunting, or riding his roan cob Hippo to mass – he being a Catholic. He flirted with Giant, telling her Pat had 'chosen the wrong girl'. On coming down to breakfast and seeing her already sitting at the table, her golden hair parted at the centre, he would say: 'This morning, PM, I feel loose and careless – but then, you see, I too part my hair *à la vierge*.' He told me stories of his rakish youth in the 1880s, and sang me the old music hall ditties:

> There's a little pink pettie from Peter,
> And a dear little blue one from John,
> There's a green and a yellow from some other fellow
> And one which I've never put on.

He sported waistcoats made of 'Manchester' corduroy, of the kind embroidered by admiring ladies for their favourite sportsmen. He told me that for all his passion for the sail and the saddle, there was no pleasure greater in this world than making love to a woman.

The Honourable had by now become muddled after her long life of romance and adventure; but she was still a fund of witticisms, and backchatted relentlessly with her aged butler during meals. Sitting in the front pew at church, she once pronounced audibly at the beginning of the sermon: 'Take no notice of him, he's only an old visiting fumbleyboo!' We were sitting in the drawing room one day when she saw her son Ian, killed in the South African war, pass the window. Together, we looked at photographs of the *Sunbeam*, the famous Brassey yacht, in which it was easy to spot her staring out to sea from the old sepia prints. 'You look rather wicked, Gran,' I said.

'I was,' she replied with satisfaction.

In Palestine, Pat's prospects of promotion had suffered a blow through a feud with his colonel. As a result, he was putting in for a transfer to the Welsh Guards. The first mention of his fury and disappointment came in a letter of 8 October:

My commanding officer has seen fit to pass me over for promotion to temporary captain having previously said he would recommend me. This means I will lose a lot of seniority . . . We are in camp at the moment for battalion training and my dispositions in a defence scheme were considered incorrect, which was given as the reason . . . This was purely an excuse as I know what he feels about me and so do you . . . I don't often feel I have been badly used, but this time I do, more especially as my company commander has just gone round the position which was criticized and said that it was quite all right.

After the scheme I was sent for by the colonel and told that though I should probably be a good leader in war I should never be given command of a company while he was commanding the battalion, so in applying to transfer I think I did the only thing possible . . . Do hope pig-making isn't too horrid, we seem to have troubles between us but I am sure we'll get the better of them all yet.

PS. Here is some pig-money, I am very rich.

On 18 October, he had left the 'horrible sandy camp' in the Jewish sector and was trying to write 'by the light of two stable lanterns and a candle and the remains of my servant's ink pot in a hut in one of the most beautiful places I have ever been to . . . fine wild country about 300 feet up'.

But there is no you to share it with and I am so miserable these last few days as I know how you would adore it here, but without you is like wine without company and has the same depressing effect. Also I haven't heard from you for about a fortnight, suppose there are letters held up somewhere, but O God I get so lonely sometimes now, especially when I feel that all men's hands are against me . . .

At the moment I long to get to the war and if I could stand beside you on the way, I could look without fear into the unknown and everlasting. I think that loneliness could make me a coward very easily, especially loneliness of the heart. Do be near me always, always in spirit anyhow, which is all we can count on now. I sometimes feel you are very far away and I suppose it is something to do with the pig . . . I haven't felt you near me now for many nights and haven't been able to dream my way into your consciousness. You know how I could generally tell what you were thinking about whenever you came into a room, and distance seems to have quickened, rather than deadened that instinct, so please be near me again; that is the only wish of my heart.

On the 20th his heart had lifted again:

Got a heavenly letter from you this afternoon . . . and a new me is singing all over Palestine and the big mountain beyond is skipping like a young sheep and I don't feel downy any more for all they won't make a captain of me. A letter from Pamela in haversack is worth more than the baton of a Field Marshal. So to hell with rank and fame say I, while love of the world is mine . . .

Last night as I was driving home from road patrol (combined with dinner at battalion HQ) an old hyena slid over the road in front of me, and went on about his business into the night. Tonight there is no wind, but the moon half-risen shines in a mackerel sky and all creation, which even warring man cannot destroy, cries out with me for my own, own heart.

The mood of pessimism was back again by 16 November:

Somehow everything seems so unreal, your being in Ireland and not beside me especially at this time, but the world has gone so utterly mad that I suppose we must adapt ourselves to its moods and vagaries. I feel that this war is only a beginning of a New and Dark age, and is more likely to be a War to end Peace than a War to end War. (All of which is very unoriginal and pessimistic I know.)

Our bodies, yours and mine, may not survive this upheaval, but pray God some spark of our courage will, if only we have that courage. I believe that Heaven or Hell are only created by what trail of good or evil we leave behind us. For the bulk of humanity there is only annihilation, so don't let's be nonentities. This is only a theory but there is no one here with whom I can discuss these things, so don't be shocked or astonished by any of my dissertations. I wrote to PM all I could think of about pig-making, godparents, etc., she really is a ducky the way she writes to me. Let this love of ours survive. Perhaps through that alone we shall be accounted 'candidates for Immortality'. I fear this last phrase is borrowed. It is much too good to be mine.

'The sun never shines so bright as when he bursts through a rift in the clouds,' wrote Pat on the 25th, 'and today after a black week he came to lighten my life with two letters from you at Ongar, and such grand gay letters they were, that they made me feel a coward and a cur'. His personality clash with his colonel was still having consequences.

I simply haven't been able to write as things have been going so damnably badly, and all my patience, never very great, and courage seem to have melted at the futility of dealing with a man like X . . . The crowning blow came when volunteers for the BEF or transfer to a training unit at home (preparatory to going to France) were called for and I was the only volunteer and still was not accepted, but someone else was persuaded to go. It's enough to break a lion's heart and I only put it down to the fact that he never had any use for me and never will. I only hoped that he'd take the chance of getting rid of me, as it would probably mean being sent to whatever regiment wanted a reinforcement. However, patience may win in the end but it's very foreign to my nature. O God I am unhappy as nothing seems to go right – it's no good my trying to reason or argue as I know I should only loose my temper, so I just have to sit tight and hope that the luck will change, but at the moment it's a nightmare. Everyone is much too terrified of X . . . and there is no one to help in the matter . . . However, if I go on volunteering I must get taken in the end. I cannot seem to develop a 'riflemanlike' attitude to life and never will. They are all much too busy trying to be gentlemen, which ought to be unnecessary.

Haven't had a letter from Australia for ages. Horrid of me to write like this when you've probably got a brand-new pig by your side as you read it. Do hope my being out of luck at the moment won't have any bad effect on P–. It's so utterly unruthveny and unmeltonian to be down on one's luck and I don't think I show it but I have to tell you. I wouldn't insult you by writing you 'bedsidey little letters' now as I suppose a good Husband would. I have to tell you what my thoughts are as always and I hope you won't take it out on the poor pig in revenge! Most of the time I am with you but in a queer impersonal, almost unwanted kind of way and I suppose I hover in just the same sheepish way that a Father (not small f) does hover on these occasions. I think it's just as well that I am not there with P– stealing all the thunder. I am glad anyhow he is going to be the last of the exquisites. I shan't mind a bit if he's a she or even a frog providing you're all right . . .

The moon is full tonight but now the thunder has come and engulfed him. I started a kind of nursery rhyme all about someone called 'His Fullness the Moon'.

I will try and finish it for the pig when he is old enough to understand. I love you more than any pig in the world. Don't give too much of yourself in making him.

My doctor was Ninian Faulkner in Dublin, so with the baby due I took an attic room in a nursing home in Lower Hatch Street, just off St Stephen's Green. To be on hand, the stalwart Giant booked herself in at Slattery's Hotel opposite. One afternoon I went to see Leslie Howard and Humphrey Bogart in the film, *The Petrified Forest*, and walked back across the green in the rain. Later that night, on 26 November, the baby was born, with a thatch of black hair, looking for all the world like a small Arab raider. From Palestine a jubilant Pat responded to the news:

28 November

Simply don't know what to say! Wireless messages keep arriving about Raiders.* Black and Big and Lusty and the camp is in an uproar of apprehension with all guards doubled not knowing what danger threatens. Intelligence officers are tearing at their non-existent hair in perplexed anxiety as information is pouring in from a variety of sources and in a strange language for which there is no interpreter available. All that one of the chief co-instigators of this foul and dastardly plot could do during its nefarious culmination, was to borrow a gun from the nearest policeman and shoot a snipe. With this gun of French ancestry and anarchic tendencies the Father of Iniquity downed the highest snipe that has ever fallen victim to the inexplicable. The 'fusil' all but exploded to leave a widow and new-born orphan at large in the world.

Later (30 November). At this stage the original letter (posted in the egg book) got over-excited and was quite illegible two days later . . . I simply don't know what to say or how to thank you for my nice baby. You are a clever old stick, and me not there to share the triumph. But it is all yours this triumph as my contribution was only the great joy of loving you. Now I am stepping from Mountain to Mountain over the world, not so much because I have a son, but because you loved me enough to make one for me. I feel now that however I may fail the Ruthvens they will be always in my debt, 'cos I will have brought your blood into theirs . . . All the love in the world to both.

PS. Has he got a long nose?

* The 'raid of Ruthven' (1582) is a well-known episode from Scottish history, when the second Earl of Gowrie, known as Greysteil, held the sixteen-year-old James VI captive in his castle near Perth.

After a leisurely stay in Lower Hatch Street, I returned to Ongar, where I nursed my new and charming companion in an old rocking chair beside the turf fire in my bedroom, or lay in bed, pulling him up from beneath the bedclothes, where he burrowed like a mole. Cables flew round the world. I thoroughly enjoyed the excitement. One, from Australia, asked: 'Has he good bone?' – a term which, in horses, denotes sound confirmation, this being tested by the knowledgeable through running a hand down the animal's fetlock to check that a man's finger and thumb can only just meet around the straight cannon bone. Ninian Faulkner, a sailing man not a horseman, took minute and complicated measurements which were cabled back to Sydney.

The christening was held in St Patrick's Cathedral, the Reverend officiating. The boy was named Alexander – after Sandie; Patrick – after his father; Greysteil – after the Ruthven ancestor who fell foul of James VI and I. A week or two later, Ian Blacker, Percy's younger brother, who was staying at Castle Martin preparing for the Foreign Office exam, drove me to Killaloe, and a house by Lough Derg I had rented, complete with staff and gardener, its owners, the Butler Stoneys, having departed to do war work in England.

My sisters came to stay. Rom had joined the Fannys, Diana the Wrens. A young local nanny was found; milk was to be had from the Dean's wife's cow. Maria, the cook, called the baby 'Proudie Browneyes'. Rom named him the 'Yellow Pigeen'. They were happy, contented weeks, but by January 1940 I was already plotting how I would get back to the Middle East.

6

Grey Pillars

> I kiss you and kiss you,
> My pigeon, my own;
> Ah, how I shall miss you
> When you have grown.
>   – W. B. Yeats, 'A Cradle Song' (1912)

In the churches and art galleries of Europe are countless canvases and sculptures showing babies being wrested from their mothers' breasts by soldiers intent on murder and ravishment, or trampled under foot by mounted cavalry. The scene depicted in most of these works of art, 'The Massacre of the Innocents', is merely incidental: what is portrayed and affecting is not so much a remote incident from the biblical past, but the eternal contest between love and war. Nowadays the media assault us with comparable images of children torn from their mothers, starved, massacred or otherwise abused by armed men. In this contest, women pay a terrible price: torn, not just between love and war, but between the love of men and their children.

Pat's regiment having moved to Cairo, I determined to rejoin him there. Because I had stopped off in Egypt on my way home from Australia, I was termed a borderline case, unlike many other wives who had to resort to devious ploys in attempts to join their husbands. In London, Uncle Malise pressed my case with friends in high places. I drove back to Ongar from the shores of Lough Derg with my son, the nanny and the émigrée Giant: the little party which, I hoped, would remain comfortably in the Georgian house by the lake till better plans could be made. In Ireland we knew little of the progress of the war; but it seemed that if I hoped to reach Cairo, I would have to hurry, before the military passed a prohibition order on wives.

There came a day in March 1940 when I stood at the upstairs bedroom window at Ongar with Greysteil in my arms, looking at the trees waving naked branches at the encircling rooks as if daring them to alight. He was wearing a fine lawn gown with a green ribbon threaded through the embroidery, part of a christening trousseau given to Pat by his godparents, the Hardinges, the then Viceroy and Vicereine of India, where Pat was born. We watched cheek to cheek as the birds flew round the ancient elms, already grown purple and pregnant beneath the scudding clouds. Then I laid him in his cot. By the time I had dressed for travelling and gone back upstairs, he was asleep. I kissed the small arm that lay outside the blanket and went downstairs again. All were gathered in the hall: the Honourable and Jim, dear Bolger, the lady's maid, the old butler with his red, kindly face, who stood such abuse from his mistress, the brave Giant about to take up my small burden.

In a confusion of resolve and discomfort – it is unpleasant to have to wean a child at short notice – I somehow reached Poole Harbour, where I was to board a sea-plane. We were delayed, and spent three days in Bournemouth, listening on the wireless to the agonies of Finland invaded by the Soviet Union. On 15 March I wrote to Giant from the Haven Hotel, Sandbanks:

> I have been kicking my heels here, having had a dreadful scramble to get here with my papers in order . . . However, a lovely sunset last night was filled with promise . . . The view from this place is lovely. There is snow on the hills opposite. It reminds me of the Côte d'Azure around Toulon, small squat pines and heath surround luxurious houses with steps leading down to the beach. It was horrible sitting in extreme comfort, consuming what could have been an enormous meal, listening to Finland's initiation. Of course we and the other democracies are to blame . . . My fellow passengers seem pleasanter now that we are going. How is your wild husband?

The next day a small boat took us alongside the great grey machine floating like a huge gannet on the water. One of my more pleasant fellow-travellers was Philip Jordan, war correspondent of the *News Chronicle*. We had a rocky landing on the waves outside Lisbon: It was then quite tricky descending the ladder into a little boat below. I tried not to think of the 'kindly peace' I had left behind in Ireland. This was no time for dwelling on three tranquil months of nursery life: the rocking chair, the smell of turf from the glowing red heart of a fire, a brass fender with small clothes drying upon it, the rooks floating above the bare trees like fragments of charred paper, the mewing gulls of Dublin Bay, or the loving concern of those who had ministered to us, each manifesting a special, personal kind of interest in me and 'the Raider', 'the Little Dote' or 'Yellow Pigeen', each preferring to use a different, special name. All such thoughts now had to be buried in the 'deep heart's core'.

Cairo in 1940 was still a handsome city. The teeming millions who today crowd its streets, having invaded the roofs and gardens of elegant villas or spacious apartment blocks, their chickens, goats and children in tow, were still tilling land made rich by the Nile and its annual flood. The king was in his palace, the pashas in their residences, or feasting and gambling at the Mohammed Ali Club. In the British Embassy, whose gardens rolled uninterrupted to the Nile, there reigned, more powerfully than the young King Farouk in the view of certain nationalistic Egyptians, Sir Miles Lampson, brother-in-law of Uncle Gerry Ruthven, Sandie's elder brother, with Jacqueline, his much younger, pretty, half-Italian wife.

Miles was a huge man, standing six-foot-six in his official grey frock-coat and spotted bow tie. Expansive and hospitable, he took a liking to Pat, even confiding to him his difficulties with the court and the military. His was an extremely awkward position. Representing a country deeply resented by the majority of Egyptians, he had to try to ensure that the ever-swelling Army of Occupation could fight its war against a European enemy, protecting its vital route to oil and India, without disturbing the official neutrality of its host. Much of the time the army kept him in the dark, adding to his difficulties with the Egyptians.

Jacquie was flirtatious, and loved to be amused by young men; when I first arrived in Cairo she still had no children. She was a target for malicious gossip, especially from the palace. Her father, Sir Aldo Castellani, one of the world's leading experts on tropical diseases, had been surgeon-general to the Italian forces during the

Ethiopian war and would later become medical advisor to the Italian High Command. When Sir Miles tried to put pressure on King Farouk to get rid of his pro-Axis cronies, the monarch was famously said to have remarked: 'I'll get rid of my Italians when he gets rid of his.'

The Rifle Brigade was stationed in the Citadel, which dominates the city under the great squatting dome of the Mohammed Ali mosque. I found a flat in the Sharia Amir Fuad, on the shady isle of Zamalek, a short walk from the Gezira Club with its racecourse, swimming pool and tennis courts. Beyond came the botanical gardens, where the two generals lived: 'Archie' Wavell, Commander-in-Chief, and 'Jumbo' Wilson, commander of the British Forces in Egypt. I sent a bulletin to Giant:

My flat is beginning to take shape. It is a little like La Graziella. I found some old French prints gathering dust in the drawer of a shop belonging to a Romanian, and at last a big picture frame for a large mirror . . . I have bought some old Turkish silver from the Mousky and some blue Persian tiles out of a mosque for table mats . . . We have bought a ten-year-old open Buick for £28; it is yellow, has a good engine, and is just like the cars of the 1900s. We sit side by side, very high at the rear, and have a temporary chauffeur who wears a fez. He is known throughout Cairo as 'The Prince'. Our cook is good but idle, the house-parlourmaid hardworking and rather sweet, but not really able for valeting Pat. I feel The Prince might turn into an excellent chauffeur-batman, but each of them wants £4 a month – we spent £94 this month on our ordinary living. One dines out a lot, but this is counteracted here by entertaining at home . . .

Pat has bought The Pig a set of old French pictures for a nursery frieze, 'The Return from the Fair'. The nicest part of the flat is the rather high, Italianate entrance hall. I have furnished it with two bay trees, a trestle table and rush seat chairs I had made. Down below there is a fascinating gathering of *bauwabs*, the Cairene equivalent of Porter Brown at Cadogan Gardens. They sit all day on a seat outside our main entrance, their shoes in the middle of the footpath. Ours is very charming and efficient, he carries one's parcels, something which Mr B. would never do.

Cairo was one vast, exciting railway station. Practically everyone we had known or heard of was already there, or about to arrive. Although Pat's haversack and tin helmet lay under our bed, life was hardly warlike: more like the Cambridge days, without the hunting. Mohammed Jahn, the tailor at the Citadel, was kept busy, with each regiment ordering subtly different shades of khaki for its service dress. He made me a dark-green coat with skirt and trousers to match so I would not look very different from the ladies of the Interpreter Corps who had recently arrived in the leafy suburb of Maadi, a few miles south of the city. I had grown very thin: Pat said I looked like a stick of celery. Our Buick and the Prince saved us a lot in taxi fares, as Pat had to drive to the Citadel every day. Known by some as the 'mad Ruthvens', we lived a wild and careless life among a huge company of friends. After dark the restaurants and bars would be crowded with riflemen in green and silver uniforms, members of the 60th Rifles with an added touch of scarlet, cavalrymen in navy-blue or cherry-coloured overalls, Irish regiments in bottle green and a new influx of British yeomanry furbished as for a crusade, in full dress uniforms of great dash and elegance, all sporting chain-mail epaulettes. We borrowed polo ponies and rode round the racecourse, or in the fields of the Cultivation beyond the city.

Exhausted by the constant round of parties, nightclubs, the glorious company of young men at arms and the attention of ambitious Cairene hostesses, I sometimes found refuge in the garden of the Watsons in Gezira. Sir Frank Watson was financial adviser to the Egyptian government. There was a family connection: his brother had married the widow of Philip Ruthven, Sandie's younger brother, who had died of tuberculosis before the First World War. Sir Frank once told me, with infinite satisfaction, that he had never entertained an Egyptian in his house. Going to tea with the Watsons was, I wrote to my mother, 'like walking into paradise. You never, never saw such a garden, with all the old San Remo friends, and many Australians too – teturas, fresias and irises, lawns and pools surrounded by mimosa and jacaranda. I am brushing up my French with Philippe Stoloff, Victor's brother.'

Victor Stoloff, a film director who was shooting in the Siwa Oasis, had married Pat's first cousin, Rosemary Fleischmann, earlier that year. His parents, who were Jewish émigrés from Russia, invited us to share their Passover meal. As Professor Stoloff drank to the 'deliver-

ance out of Egypt', he remarked drily that he was determined 'to
stay in the Land of Bondage for the rest of his life'.

My letters to the Giant came to be filled with concerns about
money and safety.

I sent two cheques for £10. Does that cover Grey's expenses? Will
it take you to the seaside? Can you manage through the summer?
The Nazis are so obviously out to bomb Britain that I feel you
mustn't move from Killaloe. Added to the difficulties of getting
home I think I must stay near Pat while I can. I promise you some
relief in the autumn. Himself's time is officially up next January,
but it looks less and less likely that he will be able to leave. I had
a real 'Sandie sunbath' the other day when I was told by 'someone'
that Sandie and Jellicoe were the two great men he had known.

Other opinions of Sandie, however, were less flattering: there was
an elderly colonel resident in Cairo who had known him during the
Sudan campaign. I tried to get him to describe to me the battles of
Omdurman, and Gedaref, where Pat's father, a humble militiaman,
won the VC that first brought him to Kitchener's and Queen Victoria's attention, laying the foundations of a brilliant career. All I ever
got out of Colonel Elgood was that Hore-Ruthven and his crony
Freddie Guest had given him a lot of trouble and he had had to
suspend their leave. When I pointed out that Hore-Ruthven had
done rather well since, he didn't exactly enthuse. 'Give a dog a bad
name,' Sandie once wrote in Zara Pollok's commonplace book.
Senior officers have their favourites, and their victims: if you come
up against one, as Sandie himself knew well, it is wiser to move
elsewhere. He had been a Highlander and a cavalryman and had
commanded a regiment of footguards as well as served as a militiaman
in the Egyptian army: yet as he grew older he became more cautious,
urging his son to 'stick it out' under a colonel whom Pat believed
would always block his promotion.

Letters from neutral Ireland contained vivid and comic descriptions
of life beside Lough Derg. Those purporting to come from Alexander
Patrick Greysteil himself delighted Pat especially. He had been invited
to watch one of the few new-born British babies being bathed at
Abbassia, to prepare him for fatherhood. For my part I dreaded the

idea of returning to a plump, blond baby. 'Dined with Pat's charming brigadier and his wife,' I wrote to the Giant.

> There were dreadful photographs of babies lying about the room . . . They are planning to bring them out in the autumn. Light brown hair? How dull! I want to know what his voice is like. What do you mean by 'greeny-black eyes and brown hair?' Pat kept muttering 'Too peculiar'. I can't bear it if he's going to look like me. But Pat loves all the nauseating details, and the letters are to be kept for the archives.

I suppose this bantering rejection of nursery news was the armour behind which we hid from ourselves, and others, that unnatural cutting of the 'silver cord', knowing that, as each month passed, a special small part of ourselves would never look the same again. One of my friends, Elisabeth Oldfield, who worked at the censorship office, kept a picture of her dog on her desk. Only a few intimates knew she had also left a baby at home, or even that I had a child of my own.

At dawn on 2 May the order came for Pat's regiment to move to the Western Desert. The haversack and tin helmet from under our bed went off with him and his battalion towards Mersa Matruh, where only a year before I had alighted with the Admiral of Ports and Lights and his family for a few days of swimming in the blue lagoons. The posts were highly variable. On the 15th I wrote to my mother:

> Your letter of the 6th arrived with Alexander (Greysteil's) daisies sewn into it. It brought an awful lump to my throat to think you have had none of my letters. I fear some may be lost. Yours arrive quite well and the Australian ones are quick and regular . . . I reign alone in Gezira as most wives double up and are mostly up at . . . Abbassia. I may let the flat for a month, to save a bit: I can't live here for under £40 a month, which seems absurd for one person in wartime. I am signing on for work here. I hope it will be using French and Italian . . . H.Q.s are very short of clerical staff: it's a shame that Diana and Rom aren't here. Today is unbelievably hot. I wonder what the summer will be like . . . Now Pat's away I shall play some tennis; everyone gets up early and keeps the siesta

habit . . . I keep thanking my lucky stars I got here, although if I shut my eyes I can nearly see the loveliness of Lough Derg. The sadness is I can't smell it with you. Aunt Ruby [Fleischmann] writes that she will go over . . . soon . . . and call on 'the Tiny Raider'. I do think of him sometimes, but not often as a relation of mine. It is extraordinary how your letters bring him and all of you very vividly to mind. I'd rather like to have seen you picking those daisies together. I'm afraid I'm rather like AHF [the Reverend], not really a family woman. Isn't he lucky to have you and Nanny to love him? Pat put at the bottom of his last letter 'Any Pig news?' I think he loves even the rudest details. I am glad Nanny is going to look smart when you go calling.

Over the next three weeks the news from Europe could not have looked blacker, with the evacuation of the BEF from Dunkirk over the turn of the month, the entrance of Italy into the war on 10 June and the fall of Paris on the 14th. The next day I wrote pessimistically to the Giant, 'I have no conviction that this letter will ever reach you, it has rather a hazardous journey ahead of it.'

When Italy entered the war, Pat's patrol had been one of the first to cross the 'Wire' – a triple line of coiled barbed wire and mines, stretching hundreds of miles between the Mediterranean and the Libyan sands, which Marshal Graziani had constructed against an attack from Egypt. The British were vastly outnumbered and poorly equipped: ammunition was in such short supply that Pat and his soldiers were told only to fire when absolutely necessary. Their real task was to discover what the Italians were up to. Did they intend to invade Egypt? If so, how and when? Months of patrolling across the rocky desert, of faces seared by the scorching *khamseen* wind, of sand driven into the skin like a thousand needles, of desert sores and bully-beef boils, had begun.

I told the Giant:

There was a great letter from you which I sent on to Pat. I fear it may have to last him a long time: you can probably make a shrewd guess as to what he is up to. I am starting work any day now. I gather the hours will be fairly long . . . I can only tell you Pat is very well, and I expect enjoying himself. Last time he wrote he was commanding his company. I keep on thinking of Themselves.

She [Zara] wrote that the one thing that kept her going was the thought of you and the Raider together 'all snug'. Now they, too, will get very delayed news.

As leave became disappointingly scarce, I sacked our cook, and kept on Abdul Aziz and a houseboy of his choosing. When the boy was found drinking Pat's whisky, Abdul Aziz decided to run my flat alone, calling on a cook when help was needed. The arrangement worked well: he became my most trusted friend and stayed until I had to leave. Sometimes I visited his family in the single, scrupulously clean room they inhabited near the Bulaq Bridge, where there was always a new baby which only seemed to survive a few weeks. I also kept the Buick and the Prince.

I had volunteered to work at 'Grey Pillars', otherwise known as GHQ, a vast building near the British Embassy where General Wavell established his headquarters. I was assigned to an Intelligence branch which handed out situation reports to the press. Many of the young reporters I met, like Alan Moorehead, were to make their reputations. The office was miserable: long stifling hours of intense heat in airless rooms smelling of sweaty khaki. I learned that men were every bit as prone to jealousy, if not more so, than women. It was irritating to see how young officers insisted on taking the credit for work I had done, or could easily have carried out alone. Women's jealousy seemed less corrupting, focused harmlessly on eyelashes and ankles.

There was a rumour that Jim Windsor Lewis had been killed at Dunkirk, but no way of checking since we saw no official lists. It turned out that he had been wounded and captured, but escaped via Paris, disguised as a nun, and made it back to England. I had earlier been urging on my mother that she and the 'Pigeen' should seriously think about taking wing on the 'Yankee Clipper' for the safety of Australia. 'There can be no doubt now that it will be . . . a long war, and Ireland might have to be put to some use: he could soon travel alone with Nanny and I could join them the other end, if you didn't want to leave your old man. All the love possible to the three of you. We'll smash 'em yet.' By 27 June the picture was already looking very different, but, 'Great luck!' I wrote to the Giant. Philip Jordan, the *News Chronicle* correspondent, had whispered to me that he hoped to leave the next day, and could take a letter.

Tantalizing to think I shan't be able to get one back from you. I am working in GHQ Intelligence. As we do journalistic work I hope they will think this is an article I am writing. I dined last night on a houseboat with the Dawnays, a charming Anglo-Irish family. They had just received a cable saying their three children were off to Canada. I imagine your Friend is becoming an increasing burden and anxiety. I nearly cabled 'SEND HIM TO THEMSELVES', but when France fell I felt uncertain. If we lose the war, which of course we won't, Australia will be pretty vulnerable. You know local conditions, so I will just have to leave it all to your judgement. I imagine you can avoid bombs in the West of Ireland, and there will always be a drop of milk. Poor darlings! It is lousy for you and AHF to have another war to survive.

Pat writes that it is like the best pheasant shoot, only the birds spit back. He is so obviously enjoying himself and is lucky to be fighting the Italians rather than the Huns. Cairo has been unbelievably hot. It is terribly interesting working here. I have some 'jolly pals' which is a great help. I long to write you about it all but daren't. There is a political crisis going on here. Things are tricky, including HM [King Farouk]. We have a good many air-raid warnings, but I think they only drop leaflets. Wives may be evacuated to Palestine, but I hope my work may get me out of that.

I love to think of you among those gorse bushes. I suppose he is growing fast and getting more and more bouncy. Hope there is some hair at the sides. What a bad old letter. I can't think for long about anything except how, with so many blunderers about, we are going to beat these Nasties. A big hug for Daddy, an even bigger one for you and a kiss for that dreadful Greytail.

PS. Mark Chapman Walker is back. He has been with Pat, so I know all about his doings. Pat was caught in an air-raid without his trousers or tin hat. He wrote and told me he was doing his great big business when it started.

The letter Mark brought from Pat contained a sprig of thyme:

Herewith Mark who got bombed till his back teeth rattled up at Salum. He was taken away from me and sent on liaison work at the forefront of the battle where he was duly plastered. He will tell you all about it, as a reward for his remarkable achievements he has got ten days' leave and will probably get an MC out of it. Great work altogether. I told you about our raid in my last letter but you will probably get this first by Mark's hand. One of the bombs fell on a bedouin encampment killing three young women and two children, another fell about seven miles from where we are and got three men, one camel and three donkeys. The Italians are very quiet this morning. We had an air-raid warning about 6 a.m. I was still in bed (magenta pyjamas) so I reached out for my tin hat, put it on and turned over again: this was not cowardice but the safest thing to do. Nothing happened, then I dressed with caution under my tin hat. Now I am sitting in a glorious hot sun drinking cold beer (we have a cellar consisting of a petrol tin full of water sunk in the sand) with Frank and Mark, who is recounting his experiences.

Yesterday there was talk of a dawn attack to be carried out by the Rifles but they decided that the position was too strong, thank God. So I am smelling of thyme, enclosed, instead of fertilizing it. What a world of chance it is, but what fun getting up in the morning with no idea what the day will bring, a dawn attack and an air-raid or the smell of thyme and the underlying presence of the sea.

I don't feel that I have ever lived so fully or consciously before. When every breath one draws may be the last, how brave and sweet it is. I know it doesn't worry you, my living or dying, not the real you. I don't mind writing like this. My only dread is Hugo [Viscount Garmoyle, Pat's company commander earlier] coming back and having to hand over my command, especially if he arrives in a fault-finding mood. I would so much rather give orders than see they are carried out, I don't mind obeying them but I loathe being responsible for their exact execution . . . I feel like a 1st whip who has been carrying the horn while his huntsman is getting over a fall – if only I could show them a real good hunt, as it is I have got through some patchy scenting conditions fairly well. No use your waiting near the telephone, Dick Poole has just brought up your 10 June letter after I had tried to telephone you the last time. I fear it's only through your heart I can reach you now . . .

I have heard talk of wife evacuations to Palestine. Have you heard rumours your end and is there any means of dodging it through your job? Would Christopher or whoever your boss is let you have four days off or would it prejudice your chances of avoiding evacuation? I have lost my watch in action, also Hugo's flask. Could you look around for a nice fairly large one for him and a good luminous wrist watch for me, cheap ones won't go in the sand. I have stirring tales to tell you if and when I get away. Don't set too much store by it as the hazards of war and that uncertainty which I so enjoy may well intervene . . . One loses all sight of the real war out here. Haven't seen a paper for weeks, nor have I heard from you or anyone else. Am thrown very much back on to myself as you haven't been around for a day or two . . . maybe it's only constipation in the postal service.

This afternoon as I lay by the sea there was a light surf running and kicking up the sand, which made the water shine like shot silk, pink and green. The lap of the waves harmonized perfectly with the base of distant gunfire a curious orchestration of destination with the indestructible. I have found that I am quite brave, but curiously enough much more frightened than I ever thought I should be. The great thing is that the best antidote to fear, which is always worse in retrospect, is a further encounter with danger. I am sure you have felt the same thing jumping a series of big places out hunting, but I had never looked at it in the light before. So it goes on and each day brings its new problems and divarshuns and worries and laughs . . .

Bless you my only heart, all the love in this strange and rotten world.

Pat's next letter to reach me from the Western Desert was dated 25 June and described 'a day like burnished copper – too hot even for me'.

There was a hot South Wind when we got up at four, but it veered northerly at noon and fell away. I spent a lazy afternoon alone on the beach and the sand hissed when I touched it with wet flesh. I started thinking, which is always a horrid thing to do nowadays and it left me rather downy. Where will it end and what of our world will we save from it all? What will Pig inherit but a dusty and outlived tradition? Will you or I ever be able to show him the things that we love? Will the same things thrill him that thrill us and shall we ever know what he grows up into and what his world will be? An aeroplane has just gone overhead, but too light to be worth firing at. Haven't had a shot at one for several days now – it's about the only divarshun we get. I miss Mark dreadfully and am bored being back at my old job as I miss all the sport and am only a rather inefficient housekeeper. Almost perpetual thirst is our worst discomfort. I get a bath nearly every day and have now acquired a cake of Marice Soap. Before that I massaged all cosy corners with hard white sand which was just as good. My hair is in great if somewhat disordered beauty and apart from a slight discoloration of the teeth I am extremely handsome and very lean. I don't look nearly as prosperous as my son, to whom I must write some timely advice on care of the figure. All I require from you is your presence, every hour of every day and night and as many little blue razor blades as you can afford, £10 in cash and some Bromo. Sorry for such a disjointed letter. I am awfully conscious of onions a-frying for my dinner. Have lost all my former prejudices and sometimes even ride a motor Bi-coicle. Such are the horrors of war.

The Free French volunteers arriving from France and North Africa had been formed into a separate unit attached to the Rifle Brigade Support Group and Pat was appointed their liaison officer. It became one of his happiest times. He called them *mes braves et mes gloires*, relished the ingenious meals they created out of Eighth Army rations, and sent them to call on me whenever they visited Cairo to pick up medical supplies. I would buy cases of rosé wine for them to cool by burying in the sand. They wandered round Cairo with no news, or even knowledge, of wives, children or parents. All of them wanted to join the desert operations.

Miles and Jacquie Lampson had meanwhile, with infinite kindness, drawn me into their diplomatic circle. In those days there were no high-rise buildings overlooking Lord Cromer's spacious Edwardian villa. The Embassy grounds, uninterrupted by Nasser's Corniche, reached down to the Nile. At lunch or dinner I found myself seated beside visiting dignitaries, foreign secretaries or ministers. These included General de Gaulle, who, despite my best efforts, remained aloof and silent. I tried to interest him in Pat's *braves et gloires*, but though perfectly polite, he never really turned towards me. The general even declined an invitation to visit them at the front – because they were attached to the British Army. I found this hard to forgive.

A letter of 25 July to my mother described my routine at this time:

> I rather look forward to being on my own. Half my work is making contact with people and trying to get material for a magazine we are producing primarily for the troops and indirectly as propaganda . . .
>
> I feel you may not be invaded after all and are right to stay put. What would old Pigeen do without the Giant? I have made jolly pals with Freya Stark and am getting to know a lot of the Arab world . . . The enormous numbers of comings and goings keeps one's interest up, but we only get one afternoon, night and the following morning off each week. The long morning – 8 a.m. till 1 p.m. – can be trying.

Among the first people I met when I arrived in Cairo had been one of my oldest childhood friends, Sylvia, granddaughter of Banker Huth of the portable lavatory seat. She was now married to Peter Hobbs. In fact there were very few wives in Cairo, most having been prevented from travelling to the Middle East in the first place. Of those who were there, many left when the army finally took the decision to evacuate wives in August, though Sylvia gave birth to a son in the American Hospital in Cairo after Peter was killed in the Western Desert. Those few of us who got permission to remain lived well above our station. I rode round the racecourse before breakfast with generals, embassy officials and officers on leave. General Wavell, our much-loved 'Chief', always took the trouble to tell me when he had seen Pat and how he was faring. 'Looks like a terrier who's been down after every badger in the county,' Pat said of the C-in-C after spotting him in his desert outfit.

An exiled wife who crept back illicitly was Hermione Ranfurly, née Llewellyn. Well trained, she had been working as a private secretary to Lady Wakehurst at Government House, in Sydney, where she met Dan during his term as Sandie's ADC. Hermione was enormous fun, but something of a tease, though not an unkind one.

She had a plummy, rather muffled voice, and a unique jaunty walk. She often said outrageous things, always prefacing her remarks with 'Darling' or 'Little ones'. While many evacuated wives went to India to weep on the Viceroy Lord Linlithgow's bosom and enlist his aid, Hermione flew to Cape Town, borrowed money from a bank and took the next plane back to Cairo, telling the service people aboard that she was so secret she couldn't even hint at her mission. Anyone who tries to tell Hermione's story in the Middle East will get it wrong.

The first we knew of her arrival was a ring at the door of the flat, which Pat opened, being back in Cairo at the time. I heard his high-pitched astonished laugh, and in came Hermione. She was unable to pay the taxi waiting below. Freddie Hoffman, manager of the Continental Hotel and mutual friend to most of the Eighth Army, had given her our address. While she started to look for a job, she remained with us incognito, sleeping in Pat's dressing room and sneaking up and down the iron outdoor staircase used by the *bawwabs*. She even had to give up driving around behind the Prince in the old Buick. Hunted by the Provost Marshal, she was top of his list for deportation. But unlike most of us, she was a highly trained secretary – a species in desperately short supply at GHQ. She managed to get herself a job in a branch where she soon knew too much to be sent home – though the Provost Marshal, Brigadier McCandlish, never gave up his campaign to banish her. 'Looking for me?' she once asked him defiantly at the bar of the Continental, as he stood there, surveying us all with a baleful eye.

Pat and I went through some tricky moments on Hermione's account. After a lunch party at our flat, the guest of honour, Air Vice-Marshal Sir Arthur Longmore, who was C-in-C Middle East Air Forces, followed Pat down the passage to his room, where he was changing to go riding – to discover Hermione eating her lunch from a tray provided by Abdul Aziz. Not long afterwards, Wavell intimated to me at a dinner party that he was aware Hermione was in town. After that she could go public: she took a room at the Continental. There, when I was visiting her after she went down with chicken-pox, I ran into the strange little figure of Orde Wingate. He had been trying to persuade her to join him in Abyssinia, but she had declined. She told me she felt that if things went wrong on a mission, he would never take responsibility for the fate of any of his staff. Dan had by then been made a prisoner of war. Hermione left for Palestine, to become private secretary to Sir Harold MacMichael, the High Commissioner in Jerusalem.

'Such excitement yesterday,' I wrote to my mother on 10 September, 'letters arrived with pictures.'

I could hardly contain myself, having had only one p.c. dated June 24th. Well, it was heaven to hear from you and your Friend. I just sat up in bed – had a gorgeous tiny illness and three whole days in bed with nothing to do and now at least two days' sick leave from the office to sit about at the Club under the trees, so that I look twice the person I did. – Well, I sat up in bed and stared at APG in his pram and burrowing around in his bed, and it wasn't any use pretending that I didn't know who it was . . . I shall try to get the pram one copied. I must send it to Pat as he gets so hungry for the Killaloe news. I think he'll be rather pleased you and APG have his photograph. Tell Nanny I thought he looked a really well turned out properly nourished baby in his pram . . . All that long hair! . . . I hope by now you will have my letter Dermot [McCalmont] took back and it will help pay for the cattle crate and the high chair and all the endless things. How long will his frocks last? I should never be surprised if I found myself on my way home before Christmas (not voluntarily). A wonderful cool summer going on here. Lots more 'people' arrive. I think it was the nightlife that laid me low. I plan to go down to Suez with the Lampsons.

Life is almost too full. I am trying hard to get to know something of Egypt – tell the Reverend. People tell such conflicting tales of what is being done and what is not being done . . . It is quite incredible how separated the British are from the people of the country. It seems such a bad policy, that we never do anything to try to make people like us. Of course it is easy enough to meet the usual Upper Ten [per cent], but for the most part the British and the Egyptians might be living on different continents.

One feels thankful that winter is coming upon us and will make things more difficult for the Hun planes, and keep them from coming your way . . . I get nostalgia sometimes for my Giant and those poor ones, my sisters, in London and Portsmouth; so thankful

I got you and AHF to Ireland and stuck you there. Will Gwan and Jim ever see the Pigeen? . . . Very long time since I saw Pat.

By 10 October, Pat was back in Cairo for a month, on light duties:

It will give him time to build himself up again. He came in fit except for one nasty desert sore, but no bigger than a snipe in the bog, which makes Pigeen look all the more over-fed. I have never known him in such heart, he is enjoying every minute, especially dining out and seeing people. I had four days of leave on his arrival and we went down to Suez for the weekend with the Lampsons. It was great fun. We had to borrow a friend's car as ours would never have kept up with the Ambassadorial convoy . . . Last night Arthur Longmore had a birthday party so we all forgathered again . . . Geoffrey Goschen, Sheela Blacker's nephew, has won an MC, and a real good one. Tell Daddy the old bishop is a ducky.

At this point I must slip in a comment to say I have yet to read a book on this period in the Middle East which pays a tribute to this great Anglican churchman. The Rt Rev. Llewelyn Gwynne, appointed Bishop of Egypt and the Sudan in 1920, filled the now vanished Cathedral of All Saints in Cairo with men from the desert, administering courage and hope along with the sacrament. He had begun his career as a missionary to Khartoum in 1899, and had stayed with the Gowries in Sydney. My letter continued:

I am afraid I am making absolutely no attempt to come back to you. It is just everything to be here in the flat when Pat comes in on leave. I am in close touch with Australia and I know they want me to stay on. I long to get a letter from the sisters, but I don't suppose they ever get a moment . . . Pat says Grey is a charming name, but I say you'd have to be something of an Adonis to wear it successfully. Anyway, I think they all want to call him Greysteel – that's the way to pronounce it, so you had better start soon . . . Pat sends very best love. I wish you could see him as he is here. I never saw anyone enjoy life so fully.

While staying at the Embassy resthouse at Ismailiya we attended the Ambassador's private duck shoot at Ekiad in the Delta. As Wavell was there with a party of VIPs, we were allotted an outlying hide where few of the duck would venture. Crouched beside Pat by a wall of reeds, I watched the duck come over us, wave upon wave like clouds of the heavenly host, just as the first light was dawning. I was thankful my gun wasn't 'on form' that morning.

Before lunch each gun was required to lay out his tally of birds and return unused cartridges, since cartridges were extremely expensive and had to be paid for. Pat's haul of birds looked ludicrously meagre alongside the mounds of limp feathers, each set out in separate clumps. Fortunately, his ratio of birds to spent cartridges was not unimpressive: he'd not shot badly, but very few birds had come his way. At lunch he stole the limelight by recounting how he had survived the rigours of the desert with all its discomforts, only to discover the marriage couch infested with bedbugs. Once, when asked how he found me, Pat told a brother officer, 'As a companion, charming, as a housekeeper, a disappointment.'

7

Freya and the Brotherhood

It had been at an Embassy lunch some time in that summer of 1940 that I first met a very round small person with a pair of the sharpest, most knowing little brown eyes beneath a fantastic hat. Freya Stark was on a brief visit from Aden, where she was employed by the Ministry of Information to make propaganda for the war effort and interview Italian prisoners of war. Sir Miles had suggested Freya should come to Cairo. After the capture of an Italian submarine, which surrendered to a small trawler-turned-minesweeper with one gun, Aden seemed relatively out of danger from the Fascists; but in Cairo Italian was to be heard in shops, cafés and restaurants, not to mention the Palace, where one of King Farouk's favourites, the electrician Antonio Pulli Bey, was rumoured to be a Fascist spy. In the desert, Wavell, with his handful of regiments, and Longmore, with his scanty air arm, faced an army of 300,000 Italians under Graziani.

After lunch Freya asked me if I would help her unpack. Together we climbed upstairs to her bedroom overlooking the Nile, and there she told me she had agreed to come to Cairo to try to counter the Italian and German propaganda and would need an assistant. The prospect intrigued me. I was growing tired of Grey Pillars – the long hours spent rewriting dreary situation reports from East Africa amid the sweaty khaki shirts. I had looked enviously at our rivals at MEIC (Middle East Intelligence Centre) across the way, who seemed to operate in a far more imaginative mode. Kenneth Grant, a naval officer who worked there, had put forward plans to recruit the local whores to undermine the French Fleet bottled up in Alexandria harbour: warships rendered harmless when Admiral Godefroy agreed to discharge their oil tanks and remove gun firing-parts after the destruction of much of the rest of the French Fleet at Mers el-Kebir. Their docked crews had then watched impotently as Admiral Cunningham, in command of their old rival, the British Fleet, took control of the eastern Mediterranean, despite the numerical superiority of the Italian naval forces. They remained anti-British, anti-Free French and loyal to Vichy, meanwhile being well-fed and paid by the British. Kenneth's idea was to encourage the Alexandria prostitutes to convert their clients to the Allied cause.

Our boss at GHQ, Brigadier Shearer, a former executive at Fortnum & Mason, took himself immensely seriously. Even in uniform he moved around rather silently, like a shop walker, speaking in a low soothing voice. He would work late into the night, rewriting reports from the battle zone – quite unnecessarily, but just so he could put his signature to them. When Pat or any of his friends called, they were searched and questioned assiduously: I suspected that the presence of these young men, so lean and sunburned, was not welcome at Grey Pillars. Brigadier Shearer had been offered uniformed female staff from home to work at GHQ and had firmly declined, saying there were plenty of well-trained and intelligent young women among the regimental wives already in Cairo. As proof he cited another of the wives, Susan Hambro, and myself, though both of us had adamantly refused to don uniforms. I told Freya that I was doubtful whether I would be released from my IC branch of Intelligence by the brigadier.

Little did I reckon in this with the iron will that lurked in that round diminutive body, so much abused by her earlier travels in the Near East. Within weeks, Freya was back in Cairo, installed in a charming flat on a small arm of the Nile. Working contrary to suggestions that she should hold a salon where good pashas would meet Britons of note, she instead started Al-Ikhwan al-hurriya, the Brotherhood of Freedom, a movement devoted to spreading democratic ideas among the young effendis and merchants of the souk, the camel drivers round the pyramids and country families of the Fayoum oasis and the Cultivation. In Sir Miles and her immediate boss, Reginald Davies, she found – as she would write – 'imaginative men with minds refreshingly unorthodox . . . [who] even permitted Pamela to be plucked out of the severe grey marble arms of GHQ'.

This last *coup*, I suspect, was clinched at one of her breakfast parties, when Freya, resplendent in silken Hadhramaut robes, entertained People of Importance to listen to her ideas about How to Keep the Egyptians on Our Side.

My co-assistant was Lulie Abu'l Huda, a princess of the old Otto-man aristocracy who had been at Oxford. Lulie's mother was the widow of a Syrian Arab, a former prime minister of Transjordan. A wise and charming woman, swathed always in black, she herself was a Turk and owned an old palace in the centre of Cairo. She had a host of influential relations and friends throughout the Arab world. When Lulie, her elder daughter, insisted on studying at Oxford, she went to live there with her and Lima, her younger daughter. Now they were back in Cairo and Lulie had volunteered to work for Freya under Reginald Davies. It was wonderful for me. When Freya was away (as she increasingly tended to be), Lulie and I wrote the bulletins for the Brothers together, often with Pat's help if he happened to be on leave. Lulie had pretty dark eyes and beautiful skin, burnished wavy hair and a great sense of humour. While Freya put her heart and considerable intellect, as well as her rather fragile health, into what she chose to call the Art of Persuasion (she disliked the term propaganda), our hearts were usually elsewhere. I remembered one happy morning wrestling with the bulletin for Mr Samaha, our Coptic clerk, to print out, when Pat asked Lulie whom she was going to marry. 'Only a Turk,' she declared. Years later she kept her word, becoming the wife of Prince Feuzi, her cousin.

Some have complained that the story of our activities as recounted by Freya in *East is West*, and later in *Dust in the Lion's Paw*, presents an exaggerated picture, with too many names being dropped, but this was how she worked. Those were the days before young women could act as newspaper correspondents in dangerous places, or analyse the financial markets as well as, or rather better than, their male contemporaries. Freya had an exceptional mind and grasp of the complexities of the Middle East, where we stood alone at that time. Much of what she wrote is still relevant to our policies today. If, under her influence, I became somewhat isolated from my friends and contemporaries, I would never again be justified in complaining that I knew no Egyptians. For hours on end I listened to Freya's earnest 'young effendis', the junior bureaucrats who worked for the government, as they explained their ideals and aspirations; or rode in the Cultivation to meet the villages with hordes of noisy children at my horse's heels; or went with the Minister of Agriculture to one of his experimental farms, or sat with him over dinner at the Mohammed Ali Club as he complained how the war effort was forcing up prices until the peasants could barely afford to eat. In every case I faithfully reproduced – suitably edited for the audience concerned – the essence of Freya's message to the Egyptians: Britain would win the war in the end; better the British devil they knew than the Axis. There would be evenings with a tutorial from Freya, or from Mr Samaha, who wrote the bulletin we distributed to the Brothers at their various, disparate gatherings, so they could discuss the same news and ideas.

Once allowed to join Freya and her *Ikhwan*, I began to learn a great deal more about the British role in the Middle East than I had ever glimpsed when travelling with K. Listening to Freya and her friends among the Egyptian intelligentsia, I gained a clearer picture of how our work was haunted and hampered by the Balfour Declaration, by the blundering parsimony and downright dishonesty of our politicians. This Second World War was being conducted by the very man who had, as colonial secretary – in his own words – taken on the burden of the Mesopotamian entanglement. When the Jews were promised a homeland by the British government, Churchill had striven to convince the Arabs it would be to their gain. We gave away a freehold when we ourselves had only the leasehold, then kept down the inevitable native revolt with air power and superior arms, as we had been doing throughout the region, as we set up our nominees to rule over newly invented states. It was a policy that was bound to leave a legacy of trouble.

Beside my boss, who issued patient instruction to 'this daughter of the Church and Cavalry', I could call on the friendship and wisdom of John Hamilton, Oriental adviser to the Embassy under Sir Walter Smart. There was also our immediate chief, Reginald Davies, a big, kind man of vision. I motored into the Western Desert with him to visit Bourg el-Arab, where Colonel Jennings Bramley had restored an old fort on the Libyan frontier. The colonel planned to make it a centre where the bedouin tribes could meet and sell their wares. There had been an opening ceremony at which the nomadic sheikhs met King Farouk. Towards dusk we realized we were lost. Reginald stopped, and seeing a horseman riding towards us asked the way. 'Yonder, under the Pleiades,' said the Arab, pointing to the stars. We followed these instructions, and sure enough came to the fascinating habitation. My quarters had a sunken bath like a large Belfast sink – sufficient for ablutions from top to toe, using a minimum of precious water. Our host was one of those Western characters the Arabs have made their own. The colonel, for certain, now worked for British Intelligence. He could be seen on occasion trotting into Grey Pillars wearing khaki with red tabs.

Our message began to prosper. As General Graziani's vast army – which, at a quarter of a million men, outnumbered Wavell's by five to one – was lured towards Egypt, the months of patrolling and probing began to pay off. Early in December, General Richard ('Dick') O'Connor retook Sidi Barrani, on the Egyptian side of the frontier, where the Italians had penetrated and established a fortified post. Within three days he had rounded up over 38,000 prisoners and captured vast hauls of munitions, vehicles and petrol. With Freya I visited a hospital full of Italian wounded. They were mostly from the Mezzogiorno and, after talking with them, I angrily blamed our government and diplomats for having let Italy join the Axis.

At Christmas, buoyed up by the splendid news from the desert, Freya and I took the train to Luxor to join the Ambassador's party at the Winter Palace Hotel. Officers of the Royals and Yeomanry from Palestine were present – as was almost anyone on leave who could get there: but no Pat. We rode around on donkeys, and picnicked near the tombs. Sir Arthur Longmore, with Collinshaw, his Number Two, came up between victories. I attended midnight mass. The church, filled with shiny dark worshippers from the upper Nile, resounded with their Arabic responses.

Back in Cairo, we heard on 5 January that O'Connor had pressed home his advantage to enter and take Bardia, having invaded Italy's Libyan province of Cyrenaica on Boxing Day. In conducting this daring campaign, O'Connor had the full support of his chief, General Sir Archibald Wavell, who gave him permission to forge ahead in hot pursuit of the ranks of the demoralized Italians. Tobruk was taken by the 22nd, and by the end of the first week in February the British had captured Benghazi and secured Cyrenaica, of which General 'Jumbo' Wilson was briefly appointed military governor. It seemed a wonderful New Year. Our Brethren were able to tell the doubting Ahmeds, 'I told you so'; while Mr Samaha's bulletins, like the army magazine *Parade*, made for rosy reading. I would dragoon anyone on leave to address any gathering of the Brethren I could get together. Tom Pearson, a neighbour of the Campbell Kids in Herefordshire, was one who obliged. Looking every inch the future general in khaki and black buttons, he described with humour and élan conditions in the desert. I doubt whether the Brethren understood much, but they certainly took to him.

Early in 1941, Pat was given leave. He arrived to join in the rejoicing round the bars and dinner tables with which we celebrated our victories: not only were we beating the Italians in the Western Desert, but good news arrived from East Africa, where General Alan Cunningham, launching his offensive from Kenya in February, soon reached Kismayu in Italian Somaliland. It looked as though the Italians were being knocked out of Africa. Momo Marriott, daughter of the financier Otto Kahn, whose husband Sir John was one of the commanders in East Africa, threw the best parties in the luxurious house she rented from a wealthy pasha. 'To be seen at her parties,' writes Artemis Cooper in *Cairo in the War, 1939–45*, 'in the company of generals commandos and celebrities, was to be at the heart of Cairo's wartime society.' While her mother worked indefatigably for the welfare of the troops, Momo's principal war work consisted of entertaining anyone she considered important, interesting or engaging. When I brought Pat along, fresh from the desert, looking like a bedouin in khaki, I overheard Momo telling him: 'Darling, I hope I shall see you incessantly.' Thereafter Pat would do a chant, accompanied by a little jig: 'Momo is going to see me incessantly! Momo is going to see me incessantly!' We borrowed polo ponies and rode round the Gezira racecourse, Pat wearing the same brown whipcord jacket, blue-spotted stock and check dog-robber breeches he had worn on the long hack home from Exmoor that now seemed aeons back in time.

With things appearing to go so well, kings, prime ministers, chiefs of staff and diplomats dropped in from all around the world. From Australia, Bob Menzies brought me a present from the Gowries. He produced it from his waistcoat pocket during lunch: a large aquamarine stone, designed, he said, to 'keep me cool' while Pat was in the desert. A local silversmith made it into a ring for me – I have it still. Hermione and I took him to the Kit Kat Club, where Australia's wartime prime minister seemed to enjoy himself, watching the cabaret and wise-cracking with the girls. But the greatest sensation at this time was caused by a new face in Cairo: that of an attractive Englishwoman, Joyce Britten-Jones.

Mrs Britten-Jones, mistress of King George of Greece, supposedly had her passage to Athens 'facilitated' by the Embassy, which regarded her influence over the monarch as wholly beneficial. Her stop-over in Cairo, the subject of urgent messages from Anthony Eden, was meant to be very hush-hush. In the event she arrived in a blaze of publicity, landing at Heliopolis aerodrome on the same flight as General de Gaulle, who gallantly let her precede him from the plane. Peter Coats, representing Wavell, was waiting on the runway, along with the leading Free French dignitaries. As Artemis Cooper describes the scene: 'the door of the plane opened, the band struck up the "Marseillaise" – and out stepped Mrs Britten-Jones'.

I met her at lunch with Michael and Esther Wright. Michael was counsellor at the Embassy, a great francophile, one of whose duties was to take care of the prickly de Gaulle. Not having been briefed as to who she was, I kept asking her what she was doing in Cairo and how long she would be staying. The perilous situation of Greece meanwhile kept everyone busy. There were endless Red Cross fund-raising galas and Red Crescent galas, while the Greeks themselves made feverish collections for their ill-prepared and ill-equipped soldiers. At one such event, the British wives were enlisted to sell drinks at a stall. This gave grave offence in a Muslim country, and caused a lot of stiff tails. I should have known better than take part.

It was Greece, of course, that was responsible for the disasters that overtook us as 1941 went on, just as things had appeared to be going so well. One day, at very short notice, I was invited to dinner at the Embassy. Anthony Eden was there, accompanied by General Sir John Dill, the recently appointed Chief of Imperial General Staff, along with General Wavell, Admiral Sir Andrew Cunningham and Air Marshall Sir Arthur Longmore. Jacquie Lampson and I were the only women present. At the round table on the veranda I sat between Dill and Longmore. Eden, sitting next to Jacquie, looked relaxed and confident; but it was Dill who made the greatest impression on me – so wise and courteous, yet seemingly sad and worried. During the meal Eden was called out to speak to Hermione on the telephone: the Lampsons were rather miffed, and I felt apprehensive, knowing Hermione.

Military matters were not discussed in front of us. But soon afterwards I learned that Dill and Eden, representing the Foreign Affairs
Committee, had brought with them Churchill's decision to halt Dick
O'Connor's advance. With only 500 miles to go, the Eighth Army
was already half-way to Tripoli, having driven the Italians an equal
distance and by now captured 130,000 prisoners, some 850 guns,
400 tanks and thousands of lorries with thousands of gallons of petrol,
not to mention drinking mugs and billy-cans that did not leak their
precious fluid as ours often did. With Tripoli gained by the British,
the Axis would have retained no foothold in Africa. I suspect that
Dill's air of sadness arose from the fact that he disagreed with his
orders, as any good soldier must, seeing he was being asked to
withdraw a victorious army to untenable positions, while his seasoned
troops were replaced with inexperienced recruits. Rommel himself
later confirmed that 'no resistance worthy of the name' could have
been mounted by the Axis if the momentum of the advance had
continued.

There was much bitterness in the desert army as to why so decisive
a series of victories was never followed through. It seemed to us that
all the advantages we had gained, at the cost of many courageous
friends and comrades, were being heedlessly thrown away. For
example, the superb Australian division that had captured Bardia,
Tobruk and Benghazi was withdrawn, to embark for Greece. Years
later, the historian Arthur Bryant summed up our point of view in
Jackets of Green, his study of the Rifle Brigade. 'Instead of continuing
to hold the ring of salt-water and desert round the all-powerful
enemy who had overrun Europe, and so keep him imprisoned as in
a cage until Britain's rising strength, and that of her potential allies,
could enable her to enter the cage and destroy him, she thrust a
finger through the bars and had it bitten off.' Some of us never
forgave Churchill, who among other things deliberately ignored the
warning delivered by the Greek Prime Minister, Metaxas, shortly
before his death on 29 January, that if we went into Greece, we must
do so in strength, otherwise we would only be making a bad situation
worse. I suppose the decision was a political one: Eden and Churchill
thinking that if Britain were seen going to the aid of a small nation
in distress, the United States might finally be persuaded to join us
against the Axis.

On 28 February, I began a letter to my mother after spending all morning in the Mousky, where the Brothers of Freedom held a meeting of sheikhs and members of Al Azhar – the ancient Muslim university and religious centre.

We were told it would be impossible to get in there. Freya can accomplish anything and it' is fascinating to see her sitting among them all in her quaint clothes, they in their delicious robes listening and eventually melting and smiling. We have just returned from Fayoum, a lovely district like a great oasis in the desert. There is a big salty lake, surrounded by bog. The birds would delight Rom's heart . . . We stayed with the squire of the village, who is also an MP. We ate roast turkey with delicious vegetables at every meal.

I would have loved one of my relatives to have seen me. We were taken to inspect the first power station built to drain the marshes. One of the young engineers had been in Limerick with the Shannon Scheme in 1939. My little dog, which I rescued one night and brought home, was bitten by a bigger dog and had to be put down. Poor Sir Frank Watson died suddenly: it is tragic – they were our first resident friends here . . . I long for news of Gwan, and whether you have been up there . . .

Pat has a charming distant cousin, Charles Gairdner [later Sir Charles Gairdner, Governor of Western Australia], who has done great things in the desert. He says he was at our wedding. Peter Fleming was here too. You can imagine the fun of having him and Freya here together. It looks like an interesting time ahead . . . Freya is off to Iraq and I shall be left in sole command. I dread to think of the results.

2 March
I'll finish this off now as it is a horrid cold windy morning, by the fire . . . Next week Freya and I visit the tribes toward the Canal, accompanied by two young men who come from that district. We set off in my old car, and then take to camels. These are the high spots of our work. It is the first time I have done a real desert tour with her. When she gets into the desert it is like the Fletchers arriving in Connemara . . . Please, please take Greysteil's piano education in hand from the earliest possible stage and *teach* him. I couldn't bear another strummer in the family. He would learn a lot from you by the time he is seven.

When, later in March, Freya went off to Baghdad, the idea – backed by the incoming Ambassador to Iraq, Sir Kinahan Cornwallis – was to establish the Brotherhood there, as pro-Axis feelings, encouraged by the German advances in Greece, were running extremely high. While she was away, Lulie and I were left in charge of the Brotherhood in Egypt – under the benign authority of Christopher Scaife, a professor of English at Cairo University.

In April I wrote to my mother:

Darling Giant,

Such a long time since I wrote and no letters from you since the bunch from you, Nanny and Grey and one forwarded from Australia which Aunt Ruby had written saying he was just like a fat Pat. Poor old Pat never got back for his leave as the Huns started coming on. But I have news of him, he had a pretty exciting trip back across the desert [leading to safety a group of men who had been cut off]. The Greek campaign is hell, and I think they have bought it here. I feel we have a pretty beastly three or four months ahead, and then the RAF will start knocking them hard. Our pilots and machines seem better than theirs – anyway it will draw the stuff away from all of you.

Otherwise we are still untouched here . . . I . . . am off tonight to visit the Brothers in Luxor. They wrote to say 'all but a few insects believe in a British victory', so we are to convert the insects . . . The countryside is too lovely, the barley is ripening to platinum blonde; the corn is darker and the bersim the emerald of Irish grass. I still ride a lot but seldom if ever play tennis. I ride Lady Watson's pony . . . I miss the Watsons terribly . . . I do wonder if you saw Bob Menzies when he was over. I meant to cable Daddy to go up to Dublin and try to persuade him to spend a couple of nights at the Lakeside Hotel, but thought I had missed the bus. I wonder how those sisters are standing all this awful blitz. I get out of all the bother, don't I? Can't help laughing at the way you have been completely landed with your Friend. The Egyptians think it is most unnatural that one should leave a son to come to a foreign land and see one's husband once in a blue moon. The boys here are very much mother's darlings.

Grand letters and cables from Themselves arrive. Himself longs to see Grey and is always talking about him. It brings rather a

lump to one's throat. I think this war is hell for them and you.
Here one feels so in the thick of things and it is all so intensely
interesting that despite anxiety the weeks flash by. But that's easy
enough when one's daily life is comfortable.

I bought some charming prints at the Watson's sale, also an old
rug and a few odd bits such as flower vases. They make all the
difference to the flat. The flowers are at their best now and
the desert blossoming with funny little wild creeping things. I love
all your letters and the Pigeen's. Aunt Ruby says he has bright
brown hair. How dull. I want to know what his voice is like –
and more photographs, please, for Pat . . .

Arriving in Baghdad on 2 April, Freya had been caught up in the
coup d'état mounted by four Iraqi generals, popularly known as
the 'Golden Square'. The pro-British regent, Abd ul-Illah, who ruled
on behalf of the six-year-old King Feisal II, was deposed, and replaced
by one more amenable to the Axis. Parliament was summoned and
the government entrusted to the veteran nationalist Rashid Ali al-
Gailani. Freya had entered the town in a horse-drawn carriage under
a parasol just before the gates were closed, and taken refuge, with
other British residents, in the Embassy, under the wing of the
Ambassador, Sir Kinahan Cornwallis. The Iraqi police who watched
over their seige allowed in supplies of chocolate, whisky, beer and
cosmetics, but marvelled that people so soon to have their throats
cut should be concerned with such luxuries. 'I mean to be killed, if
it comes to that, with my face in proper order,' wrote Freya in her
diary.

Meanwhile, my forebodings about Greece were more than justified. By the second half of the month, the evacuation of Greece had
begun. By May, King George of Greece was back in Cairo as an
exile, having been driven out by the German invasion. He settled in
with Mrs Britten-Jones at Mena House, the royal villa next to the
pyramids. 'I must say,' Miles Lampson confided to his diary, 'I thought
this slightly *infra dig* on his part. In the days of Charles II there was
no doubt a recognized protocol for royal mistresses, but nowadays I
have a strong feeling that kings should keep that side more submerged.'

The rebellion in Iraq received a boost to its cause with the arrival in
Baghdad of Dr Grobba, the German minister charged with resuming

diplomatic relations. Rebel Iraqi forces moved to threaten the RAF base at Habbaniya, whose commander, Air Vice-Marshal Smart, launched a bold pre-emptive strike. The formation of a collection of units, known as 'Habforce', was scratched together, and joining with troops sent from India, caused the collapse of the Iraqi rebellion. The Embassy seige was lifted within a month, and in the end the incident provided a rare chink of light amid the darkening gloom.

By the end of April, Rommel's tanks had cancelled out all the gains of Wavell and O'Connor in the Western Desert. On 1 June we withdrew from Crete. On the 22nd, Hitler invaded Russia, which further threatened our oil supplies. Egypt, including the Canal, and the refineries at Abadan were endangered from east and west; communications between Palestine and Iraq, with whom we had a treaty to safeguard our oil, were in danger of being cut. Glubb Pasha opined that most of the Arab world, even those who remained loyal to Britain, thought in the summer of 1941 that we were finished, and that Germany would take over in a matter of weeks. We had lost our victory in Libya and our standing in Egypt and Iraq, while the Greek expedition had been a disaster.

As these epoch-making events unfolded, Pat and I were able to spend some time together in Jerusalem, where everyone was agog as the operation of 'Habforce' leaked. Dr Grobba was said to be trying to stir up the Iraqi tribes, and Major Gooch of the 1st Household Cavalry was sent off with his column to try and capture him. But Dr Grobba evaded his hunters, his escape thus marring the success of the Iraqi campaign. On his way back from the campaign, Gooch exchanged courtesies with the commander of the Vichy French garrison in Syria, Capitaine de Buisson, who demanded to know why the British had violated French territory. The captain, amused by Gooch's explanation, said that the German official had been in Syria, but had now left for the coast. What neither of them knew was that, even as they talked, the British were advancing into Syria with the compliance of General de Gaulle and his Free French forces. By July, General 'Jumbo' Wilson, charged with occupying Syria and Lebanon in the face of active resistance from the Vichy French, had forced the Vichy forces to agree to an armistice; while in Iraq a new pro-British government was established under General Nuri el-Said.

Pat had obtained a staff post with Wilson. 'I really have been lucky getting this job galloping for Jumbo,' he wrote to his mother. 'It is

really an absolute plum . . . plenty of variety and travelling and yet
with a comfortable base to come back to from time to time. I have
already been to Iraq twice in the last ten days, and never know where
I am off to next.' The morning I arrived from Cairo, he was already
out at work, but I soon found his room in the King David Hotel. It
looked as if there had been a party the night before. The King David
had virtually become a branch of GHQ, which had taken over the
whole of one floor. About midday I heard Pat's voice in the huge
foyer asking, 'Where is my wife?' Asked to describe me, he shouted:
'She wears her hair like a lion!'

We stayed at the hotel while my search commenced for a flat that
we could walk to through the wild flowers and olive trees, and
treated ourselves to one of the more expensive rooms. There, within
a few days, we both succumbed to jaundice, which caused Pat to
miss the fighting in Syria. When we were at our most yellow, Prince
Aly Khan, son of the Aga Khan, leader of the Ismaili Muslim sect,
popped his head round the bedroom door, wanting to borrow Pat's
jodhpurs. Pat replied impolitely in the negative, and when Aly's head
had disappeared from the door, turned to me and said, 'If Aly thinks
he can get his fat bottom into my jodhpurs, he had better think
again.'

While working at Grey Pillars, I had often met Aly and his English
wife Joan; after I joined Freya I continued to see him, since he
helped us with the Persian brothers in the Cairo souk. Sometimes I
accompanied him on these visits, which usually meant dancing afterwards at Groppi's, the famous café rendezvous. He was charming,
and I later understood how the tribes in the mountains of
Lebanon, and throughout the East, came to love and adhere to him
as a leader. However, he suffered from the problem that afflicts so
many rich men: an inability to concentrate. There always seemed to
be something more interesting or alluring round the corner.

Aly had been ordered to ride into the Druze strongholds in
Lebanon to raise the tribes for the Allies, having been seconded to
a British Yeomanry regiment. It seemed to me he was neither welcomed nor made full use of. I knew Aly thought so too. It was not
until the Syria–Lebanon situation became really serious that he was
called upon to exploit his position as an Ismaili leader on behalf of
the Allies. Had he been allowed to operate in the desert or with one

of the forces which invaded Iraq and Syria, his life might have taken a different route.

Many British officers, including friends of Joan's and mine, were frankly beastly to and about Aly. He had one important ally, however, in Colonel Wintle of the Royals, who headed a section of British Intelligence in Jerusalem. Years later Colonel Wintle told Aly's biographer, Leonard Slater, 'Old Aly was a bit of a Zulu, but he would have made an excellent cavalryman.' Wintle had moved his office to Jerusalem, bringing Aly with him, with a view to organizing some kind of cloak and dagger outfit to use the Syrian Ismailis against the Vichy French. I don't know how the plan fared, but I well remember that whenever I tried to defend Aly to my colleagues in Intelligence, they always produced the same old excuse – that he couldn't be relied on, since he would take out Jewish girls as well as women like the beautiful Druze Amira, who inhabited the floor above us in the Kind David Hotel. I merely thought of him as being very Italian, like his mother – except that he did not dance like an Italian. On the floor he held one in a sort of bear hug that made rhythmic movement difficult, so revealing his Persian ancestry: the only other man I would meet who danced that way was the Shah.

The Druze princess, Amira Hassan al-Atrash, was just then the talk of Jerusalem. Green-eyed and beautiful, she was estranged from the Amir, her husband, the new Syrian war minister appointed by General Catroux when the Free French, accompanied by British and Australian troops, crossed into Syria and in effect abolished the French Mandate. I doubt whether the Amir's salary was sufficient to support his princess in the suite she took in the King David Hotel – any more than Pat and I could afford the luxurious room we inhabited on the floor below. We never attended the famous orgies to which General Spears refers in *Fulfilment of a Mission*, but the Amira could down the whisky in unrivalled style, and we often had drinks together. To Military Intelligence she seemed important because it was supposed that her people would respond to her call to support the Allies. Both the Ismailis and the Druzes were Shi'ite sectarians; hence Aly's mission and his interest in the Amira coincided.

At the time the Amira, or Esmahan as she was known by her stage name, was still recovering from her affair with a handsome British cavalry officer, Lieutenant-General Sir John Evetts. He was a charming man, but thoroughly infatuated, while Esmahan was not discreet.

A Cloud of Forgetting

When Evetts was packed off on leave to his family by General Jumbo, he left the lovelorn princess in his house with instructions to his ADC to cherish her. But the general never returned. Soon she was regularly to be seen dining in the King David, or ordering whiskies from the barman, reputedly an Axis spy.

In *A Story Half Told*, Anita Leslie describes driving on a winter's night into the mountains of Lebanon, where the Amira was staying at a hotel and there was to be a party with 'one of those mysterious Beirut millionaires . . . on the edge of a gorge with a sheer drop into the valley below'. The Amira, and Anita in her khaki ambulance-driver's uniform, were the only women guests. There was a lavish champagne supper, and after a few cigarettes (laced, no doubt, with hashish), Esmahan huskily sang Arab songs, a talent inherited from her mother, at which she excelled, and debated with the assembled company on her lonely future without the general. 'Should she become a film star in Egypt [she asked them], or remain in command of her forces for the Allies!'

Like the Isamilis, who were said to hedge their bets and pray to God and the Devil, the Amira, notwithstanding her penchant for Englishmen, had her doubts about Britain winning the war. After failing to borrow money from either Catroux or Spears, she was picked up heading for the Turkish frontier by British Intelligence. Evidently, despite my recent training at Grey Pillars and with Freya, I failed to recognize a double agent when I drank with one. The King David was abuzz with rumours: the Druze had offered to send an assassin to remove her from the scene; Sir Harold MacMichael, the High Commissioner, had replied that, since British law applied in Jerusalem, her assassin would be convicted and hanged.

Esmahan opted for the fleshpots of Cairo, where her husky voice and songs of war and passion could be expected to sustain her without recourse to espionage, blackmail or protection. We heard she had been driven south, accompanied by a 'curious little woman' who described herself as a Hungarian countess, and in Cairo she did indeed start a new career as a film star. It all came to an end within a couple of years. A car in which she and the 'countess' were travelling overturned and went into a canal in the Nile delta. Her chauffeur, presumably a Druze, survived by leaping from the car before it left the road. Everyone suspected foul play. Both the French and the British secret services were implicated by rumour, but she had caused her own people much outrage.

One night Pat and some others arrived for dinner at the King David in their shirt-sleeves, having just returned from Syria. The *maître d'hôtel* said they could not dine without jackets and ties. I never saw Pat so angry. He sat on a chair in the prohibited dining room and, with his hands either side of the seat, levitated into the air, the four legs of the chair hitting the floor like a lamb in the springtime. He won, and we dined together with the other warriors among the staff officers and PAs and ADCs – not to mention the spies!

Jumbo took me in his staff car with Pat to the top of the Anti-Lebanon. We all climbed out and surveyed Syria beyond and below. Jumbo hardly needed his binoculars, so long was the sight from those narrow eyes. I knew he loved Pat, among other officers from his own Rifle Brigade: he was sometimes accused of surrounding himself with 'Black Buttons'. In due course, Hermione Ranfurly was also working for him in Jerusalem. 'Tell Pat's father,' the general once said to her, 'that his son is still the worst dressed man in the desert.' Hermione and Mark Chapman Walker jealously guarded Jumbo against rival commanders. She once, it was rumoured, put sticky paper into Monty's beret while he was conferring with the C-in-C.

I finally found us a little flat overlooking King David's Tower, outside the Old City. It soon became a gathering point for strays from every battle zone. Charles Wood, the son of Lord Halifax, was one: we drove with him and Hermione down to the Dead Sea one day. Geoffrey Keyes, a brigadier at twenty-six, whose death was to inspire one of Pat's most moving poems, was a regular visitor. Henry Weymouth arrived with his broken nose, and two close friends of Pat's came: John (Shan) Hackett and Mark Chapman Walker. Later Shan married his wife Margaret in Jerusalem after much difficulty; Pat, who should have been at the wedding, arrived late.

The interminable drives in a staff car to Syria and Iraq were increasingly exhausting for Pat, but Jumbo was pleased with him. Whenever 'John the Baptist' returned – as Pat referred to himself in the role of 'galloper for Jumbo' – we breakfasted on our corner balcony looking towards the Old City walls, or supped with Steven Runciman in his Byzantine corner off the chickens who lived in his kitchen with the cook. For diversion there were open-air cinemas under a trellis of vines, with bars and small restaurants. We heard Vivaldi played to perfection by a new Jewish chamber orchestra.

At Government House the MacMichaels presided. Sir Harold, a great-nephew of Lord Curzon, had a strong Curzonish look, with thick white hair and black eyebrows. No one knew more than he about Palestine and the Zionist problem. In contrast to the style set by Sir Arthur Wauchope, who had, despite his Zionist sympathies, given Government House an Oriental look, Lady MacMichael transformed it into a chintzy English country house. Sir Harold was one of the great ones of those years. I enjoyed sitting next to him at dinner: he could talk about everything. He loved stones and gems, and presented me with a handsome pair of topaz cuff-links.

Always, too, there were the chance meetings with hunting or racing friends from home. One of these, Anthony Palmer, had been around in the Clifford days. A very good-looking regular soldier, he married Henriette Cadogan from the Old Rectory at Quennington, whose family befriended me after I rode Imported over the Cotswolds to the care of Georgie Dibble's farm and livery stable. That was the winter when, regardless of regimental, parental or financial dilemma, I found within myself a resolve to marry Pat, as he always foretold I would. Anthony had been caught up in the evacuation from Dunkirk. When he came to the Middle East, he left a baby daughter at home with Henriette, and another child was born in that year of 1941: his son Mark, whom he would never see.

When Pat took some leave that summer, we spent part of it in Lebanon. As we drove along the coast road to Beirut, lingering at the rickety little wayside cafés, Anthony could well have been below us on the coastal waters, heading toward the dangerous mission from which he would not return. He had been placed in charge of a commando raid, code-named 'Sea Lion', whose object was to blow up the oil refineries at Tripoli. For covert operations like this, the British command often used Arabs and Jews, the latter trained by such officers as Orde Wingate. None of the personnel on Anthony's mission survived, and his widow subsequently had to endure a never to be relieved silence from the War Office on how and where he died.

Lebanon was good riding country, and here I took my last ride with Pat. We rode past the Beirut racecourse under the trees where there were huddled mile upon mile of sordid shelters of corrugated iron and sacking and petrol cans in which the poor of the Middle East were condemned (as they still are) to live. These were the homes of Shi'a Muslim families (grandparents of today's militiamen) who had migrated from the south to find work. As in Egypt, the army tried to pretend such homeless people weren't there. I felt some empathy with the migrants. As the military authorities were against married men on principle, officers and their wives had no help from the army in searching out somewhere to live. We lodged for a time with an old judge and his housekeeper mistress. It was all very dainty and restrictive for someone on leave. Later, we stayed with John Hamilton in his house near the Lighthouse. John had become a very good friend through helping us a lot with the Brothers of Freedom.

As the Australian and Indian troops fought their way up the Levantine coast, we felt part of this war, not estranged from the battlefield, as we did in Cairo. General Catroux – the only five-star French general to join de Gaulle – was happy with a war of his own at last; the blonde, vivacious Madame Catroux – known as 'la Reine Margot' – set up her *foyer* for the troops and asked me to join her. The American-born Vassar-educated Lady Spears arrived with her husband, Major-General Sir Edward Spears, who headed the military mission. As Mary Borden she had written novels I had greatly enjoyed in my teens, concerning wicked and dashing fox-hunting men and their ladies. The Spears had a charming house and garden near the sea. Following the surrender of the Vichys in July, they landed in the thick of the arguments with de Gaulle about the future of the Levant. The Free French trusted General Jumbo, who spoke schoolboy French with a very English accent; but Edward Spears, who spoke French like a native, they looked upon with the deepest suspicion. Such suspicion was not unfounded, since Spears sympathized with the Arab nationalist cause and was anxious to prevent the French from reimposing the Maronite supremacy through which France had sought to safeguard her interests in the Levant. Though Jumbo and Spears were not always the greatest admirers of one another, the thought of all those poor Shi'as in their hovels left me in no doubt that they both stood on the side of the angels.

But for us younger ones, the feuds and animosities of our elders took second place to the enjoyment of gardens and parties – and to making love. Lebanon was still a most lovely country, its capital full of the old shuttered, Ottoman houses with red roofs and fretwork verandas where we were lavishly entertained. Freya had forbidden me to visit one family, the Sursocks, because they had sold much of their land in Palestine to the Zionist settlers and had made a killing out of wheat during the famine in Syria in the 1920s when thousands died of starvation. During a few days Pat and I spent together in the mountains at Ain Sofar in Papa Georges's Grand Hotel, Pat began work on a play, *A Post-War Principality.* The cast included our particular friends in Palestine and the Lebanon at that moment; the scene laid 'in the independent Principality of Crede in the Hither Levant'.

The Characters:
ALEXANDER, PRINCE OF CREDE
PAMELA, HIS PRINCESS
THE EARL OF ALEY, GRAND VIZIER (Shan Hackett)
THE MASTER OF SKIRMISH, Scottish adventurer and Captain General of the Prince's Bodyguard (Fictitious, based on Master of Belhaven late Aden Levies)
DUC D'AIN SOFAR, VICE MONOPOLIST (Mark Chapman Walker)
BARON BHAMDOUN, MINISTER FOR PERFIDY (Peter Smith Dorrien)
THE EARL OF BRUMANA MASTER OF THE HORSE (Dan Ranfurly)
THE COUNTESS OF BRUMANA, COURT FAVOURITE (Hermione Ranfurly)
LORD CHROME OF CARLISLE, GRAND EXTORTIONER (assisted by Armenian Secretariat, George Carlisle)
COLONEL BONAFIDES, PRESIDENT OF AIR VITALITY INCORPORATED (Colonel Bonner Fellers, American Attaché, Cairo)
KENNETH BASILDON ESQ., PRESIDENT PROCUREUR TO THE DOG'S BROTHEL (Basil Kennedy)
M. MENACE, A LEVANTINE ROUÉ (The Druze Amira's Attaché)
THE PRINCESS FARUCHE, VISITOR FROM AN ADJACENT PRINCIPALITY

I remember Pat starting to write this scandalous piece, but little more than the cast-list has survived. He conceived another nostalgic play called *Ease.* Its first scene showed the Ladies of 'Ease' in their stillroom. His return to the Western Desert took toll of that as well.

The last of the Cavalry Division horses were in the Lebanon, and with them an assortment of some of the top jockeys and horsemen of the British Isles. At the Beirut rack-track, in the shade of the umbrella pines that extended their branches over the red earth, they organized a race in aid of the Red Cross. The gentlemen and professionals were all mounted on mules. The course was run over very small hurdles, and the finish was most spectacular. Not one jockey was able to control his mount, and they all ended up in a great heaving heap of men and beasts against the rails, like an unmanageable mass of football fans.

So many good friends had arrived in the Lebanon, I would have liked to settle for a while. Bill Astor, son of Waldorf and Nancy, had taken a house; Joan Aly Khan was working in a hospital; I could always stay with John Hamilton; Hermione was working with Jumbo. I thought of trying to get work there, too: perhaps I could have picked up a job like Anita Leslie on the *Eastern Times*, since I had written pieces for *Parade* in Cairo; and thus, in between his 'galloping', I could have got to see Pat. I would dearly have loved to continue helping Mme Catroux with her *foyer* for the 'boys'. Like Jumbo's French, her English was a delight.

But as it was I was committed to Freya, who was badgering me to join her in Baghdad, a move strongly resisted by Pat. An inundation of cables from Australia forbad me to go there before October, Pat having reported my jaundice and anaemia. Sandie, who had once made a spectacular walk from India to Persia with his bearer Nathoo, knew the climate and wasn't impressed by Freya's needs. As Freya struggled on alone, what only Pat and I knew was that I had started another baby.

By the time we drove back to Jerusalem, Freya had arrived. But she had contracted sand-fly fever and gone straight to bed in Government House. Pat and I gave a party in our flat, which she dragged herself out of bed to attend. She wrote to her mother from Government House:

> I went to Pat and Pam's farewell party, a very good one. Quintin Hogg, who is delightful MP to talk to, and Lord Feversham, whom I knew before, and a lot of good-looking modest young soldiers who made you feel our poor old country may do some good yet in the world. Then Jumbo came in with his nice, kind, comfortable face . . . it was sad to hurry away to be punctual here, as the C-in-C [Auchinleck, by then] is staying. He looks much

younger than General Wavell . . . with a Scotch face like a rough rather untidy bit of rock, and a great directness – you feel that is to say that he is thinking of what is said and not of the person who says it . . . you feel here is a soldier who would remain a soldier in any circumstance or difficulty, a man who thinks out a situation with his own brain and not with formulas.

Later she would write: 'I found Pam in Jerusalem and her husband who has rather a bad conscience as he had been trying to keep her there just for himself. I saw at least half a dozen people, they are all very gloomy at the prospects of my getting to Baghdad.' This was a reference to her plan to drive herself back to Iraq in a tiny Standard Eight, having hardly driven uphill before. Mark Chapman Walker, Pat and I and others literally pushed her off from outside the King David Hotel, the boys having arranged some kind of water supply for the journey. The car broke down several times, but by dint of charm and persuasion she always managed to get help and eventually to arrive.

A few weeks later I joined her in Baghdad. Late summer by the Tigris was desperately hot. Initially we found shelter with Judge Pritchard, in a shady garden among his roses. A perfect host, he let us go about our business without interference or criticism. But it was essential that Freya should find a comfortable house where she could entertain. We hoped for one on the river, 'to look out at people splashing or eating water melons in the shade with the red furnace of the sunset across the wide water . . . and lighted candles floating downstream on Thursday evenings in honour of the Prophet Elias'; but had to make do with an official bungalow in the suburbs of Aliya.

Our garden of date palms and pepper trees was large. In the cool of the early morning an old man came with his scythe to cut down the exuberant growth around the lawn of buffalo grass. Alone I wandered through the souk, choosing furnishings: yards of striped black and white ticking for curtains, a glass tea set for the ladies' tea parties, bedspreads and bed linen, kelims and objects I would have loved to have bought for my own home wherever it was going to be. Despite my absurdly blonde English appearance, never once did I meet with discourtesy or intimidating behaviour from townsfolk who had so lately lived under the shadow of two conflicting *coups*.

There were many colleagues in the propaganda or public relations field operating alongside us, all of them erudite and fascinating. Among them were the political officers of the British Embassy and the British Council members, E. C. 'Teddy' Hodgkin, Aidan Philip, Seton Lloyd and William Jones, as well as dear Adrian Bishop and his group. Bishop, formerly with the Anglo-Iranian Oil Company before he became an Anglican monk, was literary and amusing company; destined to be killed in 1942, alas, by a fall over the stair railing in his hotel in Tehran. He 'helped everyone except myself to understand things like the Beveridge Report', wrote Freya in *East is West*. The Ambassador, Sir Kinahan Cornwallis, had accompanied the Amir Feisal to Iraq in 1921 and then stayed as adviser to the Ministry of the Interior till 1935. He was a man of insight and resolve, having lately presided over the embassy seige – as a later generation of diplomats would face a similar ordeal from the forces of Saddam Hussein. Like Freya, to whom he gave his support, Sir Kinahan believed we should seek to win friends among all ranks of society.

Freya wrote to Oliver Lyttleton, Minister of State for the Middle East:

We have one, and only one, really useful platform at the moment – the encouragement, given to the ideas of Arab unification, recently in England. We think of using this for all its worth; it is the only cry which will waken any positive enthusiasm here. If there were to be a set-back to Arab hopes in Syria and the promised independence not forthcoming or so gallicized as to be unwelcome to the Arabs, British stocks would sink very low; emphasizing Arab hopes now would make the later disappointment even more damaging. If therefore, there is a prospect of disappointment, we should avoid making use of a line of propaganda which otherwise at this time can be most valuable to us. The same question is open in regard to Palestine. Iraq is still like a volcano with rather a thin crust.

Overwork, too much travelling and a constant anxiety about her mother – by now in the United States following a gruelling experience of internment by the Italian Fascists – were increasingly undermining Freya's stamina. She suffered headaches and could be difficult.

One evening our host, Harold Pennyfeather of the British Embassy, placed me, as a married woman, on his right hand. It thoroughly upset Freya and spoiled the evening. (I later had a strong suspicion that the incident prompted her decision after the war – unwise as it turned out – to marry Stewart Perowne, her former boss in Aden.) We came to know the young King Feisal, his mother and her brother the regent, who had re-emerged into public life. On the surface, life in the capital was peaceful and even gay. The heroine of the revolt was Miss Borland, the king's English governess. She tasted every mouthful and drop of liquid before it passed the royal lips. General Nuri, now prime minister, became a real friend. I enjoyed dining in his old house with its fretwork windows and balconies overhanging the fast-flowing boils and eddies of the Tigris.

Later in October Freya took sick-leave on Mount Carmel, where I joined her at the Spa Hotel. It did us both good. 'Pam is such a darling,' she wrote; but she scolded me when I made a scene in that very Jewish hotel about the dispossession of the Palestinians and the violation of the lovely country I had visited with K. in 1935. I left her there and went off to join Pat and General Jumbo. Everyone had suffered sand-fly fever; while a Scots doctor I consulted in Jerusalem told me I had secondary anaemia.

I arrived back in Baghdad in time for the end of Ramadan. The British Embassy ladies called on the queen and the regent's two pretty sisters. The boy King Feisal was very fine looking, and the wonderful Miss Borland was on hand. We had our first 'Ladies' Day' at the British Embassy. The ladies of the court and city were just beginning to thaw and enjoy themselves; in certain cases their husbands, having been on opposite sides during the revolt, had killed each other. We were shown a film of Roosevelt and Churchill meeting in mid-Atlantic, along with a simplified version of *Lassie Come Home*. The Ministry of Information in London arranged for these films to be projected, not just at court, but for the people at large, on the white walls in the old city. Who, I wondered incredulously, were those ignoramuses who had chosen a film about a sheepdog with which to woo a Muslim audience? Mickey Mouse would have been infinitely preferable.

One day in November there was a lunch at the embassy to meet Fakhri Bey Nashashibi, a Palestinian leader whose broadly pro-British stance and moderate views had made him a mortal enemy of Haj

Amin al-Husseini, the pro-Axis mufti of Jerusalem, lately fled from Baghdad to Berlin by way of Iran and Turkey. After a long wait for the guest of honour, the Ambassador's Oriental secretary, Vyvyan Holt (later Sir Vyvyan Holt), came in and whispered to Lady Cornwallis not to wait further – the missing guest had been shot dead by a man on a bicycle on his way to the Embassy. The lunch commenced – without comment. Holt was a strange, silent and attractive man, like an Ethel M. Dell hero, an Oriental adviser of the old school. I suspected Freya of having a particularly soft spot for him.

This incident unsettled me. I asked myself what I was doing among all these older, more important people, so far from Pat and the war. One evening there was a conversation in which Freya criticized women who did not do war work or play a useful role. I responded angrily that it was soldiers who won wars and it was our job to love them and make them happy when they weren't fighting. I loved that beautiful country, and found the Iraqis quick and vivid after the sleepy Egyptians, but saw I must leave soon.

Later I would learn that my successors had a far tougher time with Freya than I. Barbara Graham, the daughter of Colonel Jennings Bramley, who not only spoke Arabic but also had considerable mechanical training, had the misfortune to be attacked while resting in the garden of the bungalow. Freya's only comment is said to have been, 'Well, Pam never got hit on the head.' It may have been a fable, like other 'Freyaisms' that were tossed about in Cairo, Jerusalem, Beirut and Baghdad during those years, but Caroline Moorehead, in *Freya Stark, a Biographical Portrait*, writes of my successors that 'sometimes they felt like slaves . . . Freya set them a punishing routine'. I could never understand, then or now, how Freya put up with my goosiness, my inefficiency and lack of Arabic.

My last journey with Freya for the Brotherhood was to the holy Shi'ite cities of Najat and Kerbela. We were given a police escort. It was the time of the date harvest: along the canals men slashed great shiny branches laden with dates, which fell into receptive sacks that their womenfolk, shapeless black bundles, loaded on to waiting donkeys.Throughout the date groves there was much traffic in camels and donkeys coming and going. We called on a sheikh, a relative of Aly Khan's. His medieval house had walled courtyards filled with orange trees and old-fashioned roses. Though old, with a long white beard, he made us very welcome and introduced us to his young wife, who appeared dressed from head to foot in exquisite black lace, with two rope-like pigtails falling down her back. Her son was in his teens; the daughter younger and very pretty. It would have been pleasant to linger, but our escort took us away, beyond the cultivation and across the desert towards the holy city of Najat.

I was feeling rather sick, but suddenly to see the golden dome and minarets on the horizon ahead, where before there had been nothing, made me forget my discomfort – the sight was so overwhelming. We were met outside the city by a small deputation, and led through narrow streets beneath high walls till we reached a large colonnaded building built around a courtyard. Freya and I were allotted the strangers' quarters, which led off a balcony on an upper floor. Each visit to wash, or, in Michael Khoury's vernacular, to go toileting, had to be made in full view of our police guard and our hosts not far below. There was little privacy even in our sleeping quarters, while all night long the smell of coffee and cigarettes and the sound of male voices rose up to us.

The old houses in Najat still displayed the delicate brickwork first used by the Sumerians, later adopted by the Abassids. They were built ingeniously, with rooms many feet below ground level, around the deep wells of water. Our days were spent visiting the mullahs, sitting next to each other, cross-legged, on beautiful carpets, myself humiliatingly garbed in one of Freya's voluminous blouses, my own, far cooler and perfectly decorous dresses having been deemed too loose and revealing. The rooms were cool, with playing fountains and orange trees in pots, their only furnishings mats or carpets or cushions and the niches filled with beautiful bound books. During the long arguments that flowed back and forth and were quite beyond my kitchen Arabic, Freya would raise her right hand whenever she pronounced the word *democratia* and lower it as she said 'Mussolini'. I observed the old men and waited for the little boys to bring sustaining bitter coffee on brass trays. Never once did our hosts look at us. The holiest man we met wore a white robe under a brilliant emerald turban. Surprisingly he touched our hands on departing, but with obvious repugnance. In the evenings Freya would recount to me the gist of her arguments; the highly spiced meals we were served made sleep very hard to come by.

Sometimes we visited the harems, where I felt ashamed of the hideous blouse and skirt Freya made me wear. The older women were far gayer than their menfolk, but it all seemed rather eerie and there was no sense of angels' wings. Freya wrote to her mother, 'Nearly all the holy men are of Persian origin. They live in an atmosphere of intrigue, theology and greed. When they get very, very old they are run by their sons and their disciples, unsavoury looking people, sallow and fat for want of exercise.'

On our way back to Baghdad, we passed by the ruined 'Tower of Babel' ziggurat at Borsippa; the whole mound appeared to be strewn with molten red rather than fire-blackened bricks. Then we came to Babylon. The Ishtar Gate still stood, its buttresses decorated with dragons and bulls in low relief. We wandered around the ancient ruins: even the river Euphrates, which once lapped the city's walls, had abandoned it to desert and scrub.

I wrote to the Giant: 'Freya has given me an enchanting pair of delicate red–gold Sumerian earrings. She has bought several kelims and carpets for Asolo. I wished I could have done the same, but Pat and I have many expenses ahead.' Freya was ever adept at cadging and cajoling transport around the war zones of the world.

Soon afterwards I said goodbye to the most remarkable and indomitable little person, and flew back to Jerusalem. News from the Western Desert was bad, as was news from home and, by now, from the Far East. The Japanese assault on Pearl Harbor on 7 December marked the entrance of both Japan and the United States into the war. Three days later, the *Prince of Wales* and the *Repulse* were sunk off Malaya by Japanese aerial torpedoes. 'We had lost command of every ocean except the Atlantic,' as Churchill wrote in his account of the war. Pat began to think he should leave his staff job and rejoin his regiment. In September he had sent Grey an Arab sheepskin coat and a letter from Jerusalem:

Dear Grey. All the *really* smart men in this part of the world (myself included) wear these sort of coats in the winter-time, and it seems only right and proper that you (as the smartest man in Killaloe) should wear one too. It should arrive in time for your second birthday with any luck, which is, after all, a very important occasion and one which I hope will be suitably celebrated with a cake which your PM will make you (if she can steal anything better than turnips to make it from). Your mother and I have just returned from Syria, where all the very nicest goats look rather like you will in your coat. We had a lovely time and hope to go back there soon.

Now for the hats. The really smart one with a blue tassel means that you come from the Western Desert and was given to you by one of the tribesmen called Ali Sultan Bey, who now lives at Ismailia, so I suggest you write and thank him for it. The other is called a Kitzie Cap and is what the men and boys wear in Upper Egypt and was bought for you by your mother in the Luxor market.

The waistcoat is a present for PM, and your mother says she hopes it will arrive in time to stop her getting that 'tucked up' look.

I greatly admired your photographs which arrived the other day – they caused a great stir, and comments were varied – most people say that your hair is too long, but to show you that I do not subscribe to this view I am sending you one of myself in return, from which you will see that I also favour a generous coiffure.

I find it keeps me warm in winter and neutralizes the more penetrating rays of the sun in summer – it is only those with a less abundant harvest that profess to scorn crops such as ours.

Well, I hope you have a pleasant winter and that the Dean's cow won't dry up on you or do anything else unladylike. Ever your loving father.

One morning, just before dawn, he drove away from the door of our flat.

8

The Lost Ones

Alone in Jerusalem, I packed up the flat with my few treasures, restored it to its German owners, then took the now familiar noisy train to Cairo, where I stayed at the Continental Hotel. There were more possessions to collect from the Egyptian flat, and Aziz to be said goodbye to – almost the saddest of my farewells. I have an indelible heartbreaking memory of his round cheeks, his spiked moustache and his great dark eyes under a spotless turban.

Geoffrey Keyes was on leave from the desert. On my last hateful night in Cairo he and a fellow officer took me to see a film. I sat dumb and stupid between them in the cinema, and the next day went to the railway station where, months before, another me had watched a troop train moving west as Pat, in his green forage cap, leaned and waved from a window. Now my train was bound, stubbornly, and with grumbles and rattles, for Suez, where I would embark for Durban.

Geoffrey would very soon be dead, killed at Bada Littoria leading a commando raid intended to capture Rommel, who wasn't there. This loss of a boyhood friend was to inspire Pat's hawking poem, 'To a Young Man Who Died', which was included eventually in the collection called *Desert Warrior*.

> On his wrist,
> On his wrist,
> With a hawk upon his wrist
> As the dawn was breaking clearly,
> A gentleman rode early,

A Cloud of Forgetting

With a hawk, a hooded hawk
Upon his wrist.

At a hern,
At a hern,
He flew her at a hern
And her strike was like the frightening
White wickedness of lightning;
With a cry of deadly anguish
Fell the hern.

From the sea,
From the sea,
He struck out from the sea
And as heron falls to peregrine
They fell before his unforeseen
And sudden blinding slaughter
From the sea.

Oh, he died,
Yes, he died,
As other brave men died,
But for valiant quenched vitality
Deeds spring to immortality:
A young man lingers lightly
Where he dies.

On his wrist,
On his wrist,
With a hawk upon his wrist
In a dawn that breaks more clearly
A young man still rides early
With a hawk, a hooded hawk
Upon his wrist.

At Durban I was met by Cora Lyons, an Irish cousin of Zara's,
married to a sweet old doctor. The British Fleet was just in, and as
we drove out from the port a multitude of sailors were copulating
with local ladies under the trees. 'Oh dear,' said Cora apologetically.

I spent several days with the Lyonses at Ispingo Beach, sleeping in the sub-tropical garden, bathing in the warm sea and being looked after by their friendly Zulu servants. Daily I waited, as Pat had bidden I should, for news of leave or a wound. I toyed with the idea of staying on and having the baby there.

Then, one day, I was contacted by Naval Headquarters and told to prepare to leave. Accommodation had been found for me on a ship, part of a convoy heading for Britain. Cora wrote to Zara:

> . . . we had about six happy days together and I lost my heart to her! She was to lunch with Admiral Colville one day and I lent her the car to do all her jobs. When she came back she said, 'The news is very bad for I must go tomorrow, it is all very secret, I can't tell you anything.' I wasn't even to take her to Durban, she was being met. We had planned so much together. I got a cable from Pat to say stop her going as he was coming on sick leave.

Cora made a dash into Durban to try and find me, but it was too late; I had disappeared into a smokescreen of security. In fact I found myself allocated a huge cabin with bathroom all to myself, but hardly was my unpacking done before we were ordered to disembark. Singapore had fallen with dismaying speed by 15 February. It was decided the ship was needed in the Pacific; every sound vessel in South African ports was being rushed to the Far East. Memories of that time were revived in 1992 with the accusation by Paul Keating, the Australian prime minister, that the British war government calculatedly left Australia defenceless against the Japanese. Sandie must have known as well as anyone how badly the war was going, how vulnerable they were. I realized only later that invisible guardian angels were doing their best to secure me as safe a passage back to Britain as was possible in the circumstances.

My ship home in the end was an aged tub of iron and wood, whose elderly Scots skipper had been promised she would never have to put to sea again. We stopped off, I think, at every South African port. There was quite a long stay in Cape Town with family friends alerted by the Gowries. I saw Parliament and did some shopping among enormous ladies who walked down the streets like huge wardrobes. The smallest-size garment bought from a cheap store was enough to disguise my condition.

At Freetown we joined our convoy, where frequent radio messages from the leading ship showed that the Gowries were monitoring my progress as we started on an Atlantic voyage lasting several weeks. From that point on, the old skipper never left the bridge: and one bright blue day, when none of us had a clue as to our whereabouts, our comforting silvery companions slipped beneath the horizon astern of us and we found ourselves alone. It transpired that an obscure mechanical eccentricity meant that our ship's engines were unable to go slowly enough for the rest of the convoy.

I was lucky in my travelling companions, who included Charlie Wainman, the brother of an 11th Hussars hero, and a mother with a small child, who encourage me to start what is known as a layette. There were also Jon Dalrymple and Tom Bevan, who played poker continuously whenever Tom and I were not chewing the cud of the Western Desert, and a nice young man called Winn, later to become Lord St Oswald. None of us were the slightest importance to the war effort at the time. Sometimes the old skipper invited me up to the bridge for a noggin of Drambuie. We were shadowed by U-boats, but evidently none of them considered us worthy of a torpedo. Then one morning, just as breakfast was being served, the signal for action stations rang out: I ran to the upper deck as if the devil was on my tail. I had time to glimpse, and recognize, the distinctive hog-back shapes of Muckish mountain and the hills of Donegal as a plane appeared from the east and chased off the submarine before escorting us into Liverpool.

To forestall anxiety, I had not warned my parents, nor anyone else at home, of my journey. When I arrived in Dublin, the first person I telephoned was Dr Ninian Faulkner. I told him I was going straight to Ongar and would come and see him soon. 'But I think Mrs Barry has died,' he said. 'Come and stay with us.' It turned out to be true. The old house where I had waited for Grey while the Honourable joshed with her butler; the haven I had been counting on during the long and hazardous voyage, was gone. Pat and I knew Jim had died, but we had not heard about Gwan. The house, garden and stud farm were to be bought by Aly Khan and his agent installed there.

I took the train to Limerick, then drove by taxi north to Lough Derg and Killaloe, where I hoped to find the comfortable Georgian house I had rented for my parents and Grey. But like the sheltering walls of Ongar, this too had dissolved as a haven. Finding they were not needed by an England at war, the Butler Stoneys had returned. The Giant had instead taken a suite of rooms in the Lakeside Hotel, a rather busted-down establishment on the opposite shore of the lake above the old bridge where the Shannon rushes out of Lough Derg towards Limerick and the ocean. The hotel was modern, bare and fairly hideous, but the Giant had settled herself, along with the Canon of the Shannon and Grey, in the west wing looking out across the lake to the woods and the mountains of Clare beyond. The nanny I hired had left to marry the baker. To replace her the resourceful Giant had found Nan Fitzpatrick, a middle-aged woman with red hair and brilliant blue eyes, reported to be good with gun-dogs.

The hotel was owned, and the land around it farmed, by Mr Jim; his sister, Miss Maureen, did the cooking. The fare was monotonous – meat and two veg for lunch, sausages, bacon and eggs for supper – but a lot better than one got in England at the time. Mr Jim was charming and hospitable; Miss Maureen most kind, but not often in view. She had a weakness for the bottle.

I had last seen Grey sleeping in his cot at Ongar, three months old, wearing the fine embroidered baby clothes gifted to Pat by Lord and Lady Hardinge. In Cairo I had received a small snapshot of him standing by a chair, walking for the first time. I could not bring myself to look at it then; I still cannot do so today. I had taken the precaution of bringing with me from Dublin a red pedal car with which to soften our encounter. I met him upstairs, in the bare hotel corridor outside the sitting room: a dark two-year-old with huge eyes and curling hair. For a full minute he looked me in the face. And then he screamed, as he had promised my mother he would. 'Get that girl out of the sittyroom!' he shouted for several days, each time I appeared. When Giant drove the Reverend to Castleconnel on Sunday mornings, he would lie outside her bedroom door like a grieving spaniel. I had disrupted his life, his days and his nights.

It took many hours of walks and stories for us to become friends. Giant was the soul of tact; every Sunday the car had to be surreptitiously driven to church so he shouldn't see them go. Day after day, dressed in a pair of his grandmother's bloomers, or wearing one of her wide-brimmed Woolands hats, he pedalled the little red car along the corridor to the housemaid's cupboard. There, among the brooms and dustpans, he intoned prayers and chants, just as he had heard the

Reverend do in church. In the lush meadows, among the dandelions and daisies, we eventually consolidated our relationship during the few weeks left before I must return to Dublin to hatch the obstreperous child I had carried back from the Middle East.

Mail from the desert took a long time to filtre into neutral Eire. A letter dated 19 January arrived written from 'Jumbo's House' in Jerusalem, where Pat was recovering from a bout of malaria caught duck shooting in Galilee.

Here I am, out of hospital, but as weak and miserable as a half-drowned rat, and missing you so terribly that it absolutely hurts.

Jumbo asked very kindly if I would like to spend part of sick leave here, so I jumped at it as there are no ghosts of you up here and everywhere else will be filled with them . . .

Baghdad won't be so bad, as, tho' it will be full of you, we were never there together. I never knew it was going to be as awful as this or I would never have let you go; it's the awful endlessness of it all this time which is so frightening; you just can't look ahead and count the days and the hours. Sometimes I feel that we were fools, when the hazards of war had thrown us together, ever to let them separate us, yet in the end I feel we were right, and it would have been selfish of us to keep together with all the considerations and I am sure that you will be happy in Ireland once this horrid baby business is over and done with. Please, please for my sake try and love your children as I fear that I shall always owe them a grudge for this, although I will try and fight any such selfish feelings. Loving somebody so much seems to bring an awful lot of pain as well as pleasure into life, but please go on loving me as it seems the only thing that gives any purpose now. After all, this New World for which we are fighting holds out so little prospect to us that knew and loved the Old (however wicked it may have been!) and I sometimes wonder if for us this war will be worth surviving. I envy so much the Herm[ione]'s of this world with their gallant and assured conviction that things will be better after the war than before, but from a purely selfish point of view I am afraid they won't. I don't think it is disloyal to have a purely selfish point of view, as of course one knows that if the little people who suffered in London and elsewhere are going to be better off, then the war will have been worthwhile. They are the people who have suffered most so their reward must, in justice, be greater; but in the post-war rearrangement I foresee a continued striving between conscience on the one hand, which will demand that one does one's best for the greatest number and memory on the other, which will keep grudging at the glimpse of a red coat in a winter woodland and bring insistently the cry of hounds over Exmoor, and the clink of a bit at evening in a puddle-shining land.

In the last war our kind were fighting to defend the things that they loved – in this we are fighting for the things which we know to be right but of which we are still afraid. Oh why must I wait until you are a thousand miles away before I can talk like this . . . and yet it is easier to talk to you, albeit on paper, for all the distance in between, than to anybody else nearer at hand and yet not so near. Please, please stay near whatever the intervening miles may say, and help me with your heart to flout their temporary ascendancy.

News had reached him of Gwan's death, 'peacefully from a heart attack just before Xmas'.

In a way I am glad, as her 'fade out' was extremely graceful and befitting to one who had lived as passionately and intensely as she did, and who, for all her superficial faults, did much more good to those around her than most of us do. I hope that some of her unconquerable tenacity will survive into the fourth generation, and I hope she is with her Jim and that he won't always leave her behind him on his expeditions! . . . I think it is much better if your mind goes before your body – especially in such a 'bodily' family as ours!

He had also heard about Geoffrey Keyes being killed leading the commando raid on Rommel's desert HQ.

He was Lt. Col. at the age of 24. Makes me feel old and useless, as he came to my house at Eton the half after I had left. That led to the 'egg' which I enclose . . . I have no other news for you except that I love and miss you desperately. Please love me as much as I love you but don't miss me in the same way. Feel I am always near and a fig for the miles between. More nor life.

The 'egg' was his hawking poem. Shortly before Easter 1942, Pat's Uncle Freddie Blacker died at Castle Martin.

Aunt Sheela came at Easter and left today [I wrote to Aunt Ruby on 9 April]. I felt she could have settled down to the sad letters here but she had to go to Dublin and see the solicitors. I go up to Dublin in a fortnight to three weeks' time. She was terribly brave and good company. Killaloe is such a dopey place one goes quite silly in the head and one's bothers seem to float away up Lough Derg. Grey was enchanted with Jim's little chair she brought him; he sits in it and sings hymns from what he calls the score and recites 'Mary, Mary, quite contrary' to pictures of the Virgin.

A letter from Pat arrived before the new baby and confirmed he knew by now of my safe return.

AW.HQ. 9th Army
MEF. 6th April 1942

Look now I don't know what you'll think of me and no letters for ages, but I didn't dare write Air Mail until I heard that you had got in, in case my letter arrived before you did and caused a panic. Then when I did hear you'd arrived I could do nothing only cable as my right arm was in plaster having been broken at the elbow joint and quite unless as a result. Now it is out of plaster again but still very wobbly and weak.

    Oh thank God you have got there all right – I was beginning to worry a bit in spite of everything – can't help it somehow. Result was that I was working like Hell all day and never going to bed at night what with nag, nag, nag of worry and pain from broken elbow; ran up rather light in consequence . . . Actually in every other way I was very fit, flying over the mountains all day. Hills were an absolute dream of beauty with the wild flowers and everything green where it wasn't blue with iris and lupins and hyacinths, or gold with gorse and broom. Now that is all over and I am back at my old job again, having completed my mission at the other end, to the satisfaction of all concerned. Since coming back I have been away almost the whole time, first with a nice man in Dick's HQ to whom I sent many messages and also to the effect that you had got home safely. I couldn't write owing to the arm. After that I went round with the Great One of all again [Auchinleck] who came up on a great trip. I took him down to where we dined with 'Ab' [the Emir Abdullah]. Just your cup of tea it was – wish you'd been there, though it was boys only. The two of them had about 2 hours crack after dinner and apparently hit it off very well indeed. Wonderful dinner, course after course, and I overate grossly . . . Next day rushed round Palestine with the Great One and finally left him at Lydda. He would keep stopping the car and picking wild flowers which he knows a lot about. He was in grand heart and I think enjoyed his trip greatly . . .

I have not yet answered your letter about godparents and names. Here are my suggestions within the framework of what you said. Unfortunately I have lost your letter but think I remember most of them.

Boy. Malise Walter Maitland
   Godfathers. Jumbo, John Hamilton, Dan, Burgler (Curtis)
   Godmothers. Diana (Fletcher), Herm, Bets (Somerset), Nancy Connell, May Payne.

Girl. Alexandra Beatrice Margaret.
   Godfathers. John H, Dan.
   Godmothers. As for a boy.

'Maitland' of course would depend on Jumbo agreeing to be GF but it is a name which seems to go well with Ruthven. If I have left anybody out you mentioned pop them in. Do you think the boy is too godmother-ridden!?

When the time came for me to return to Dublin, the forbearing Giant once again installed herself behind the lace curtains of Slattery's Hotel, opposite the nursing home in Lower Hatch Street. The baby hurried into this world on 14 May 1942, fed up with the darkness and boredom of the womb, no cot or room prepared. I cried aloud for Pat, and bit Dr Faulkner's arm. Once again, cables flew around the world. The Gowries cabled, as did the godparents from abroad: General Jumbo, John Hamilton and Freya Stark, the latter being my choice, not Pat's. Pat was in fact the last to hear about this child of the war-torn Middle East – of Egypt, Palestine, Syria, Lebanon and Iraq. On 19 May he wrote to Zara:

> Darling Mumps, Well, I have just heard the news that Pam had had another raider! I am wildly excited but entirely lacking in any information. John Hamilton rang me up here last night saying that he had received a cable, signed Fletcher, that his Ruthven godson had arrived and that Pam sent love but that is all I've heard, my own cable not having come yet. It is agony being here and not able to find out any more details; what he is like and how the beloved Broide is . . . It is horrid, horrid being so far away and with no immediate prospects of seeing her for ages.

In Dublin meanwhile Dr Ninian Faulkner, by now Master of the famous Rotunda Hospital, was inveighing against wars. He had been torn between crossing to England and offering himself, or staying and being rather more useful to people like me. He had delivered many of my children's friends and contemporaries in the same attic room, with the help of 'the Duchess,' his formidable midwife. I prowled around under the low eaves of the attic in Lower Hatch Street, listening to the mewing of the Dublin seagulls. From there I wrote to Aunt Ruby on 21 May:

> Such a surprise when your fat cheque fell out of the envelope and in the middle of war like this. It's going to pay for my wireless which is such a boon, and curiously enough Dean Inge's essays, as I only read a very little at a time and they are good rich nourishment. Well, it was awful, much worse than before. I bit the doctor rather badly in the arm, but he says everyone thinks he did it sailing. Now I am miserable at not having stayed in Palestine or Syria and sent the baby to Australia in a KLM plane or on a Red Cross boat. I was so certain it wouldn't be very strong after my queer desert adventures with Freya and all the Arab food, but he's even tougher than Grey was. Nancy Connell is Malise's Irish godmother, she came the other day and climbed all the stairs

with her bad feet . . . she has a marketing lorry and a pony and trap. 'Fraid Ireland is going to be very lonely for people.

I miss Gwan dreadfully . . .

I turned my face to the wall and slept, ignoring baby, doctor and nurse. What seemed like days later, the Duchess stood over me, holding a bundle and angrily declaiming, 'Are you going to feed this child, or am I to prepare a bottle?' And so began a partnership which lasted almost unbroken for a year. I lingered weeks in that pleasant, now demolished street in Dublin. Dr Ninian, the bite forgiven, would sit on my bed, sipping sherry and talking with all his charm of everything except the baby. He told me that as soon as I walked into his room he knew it was to be another boy. In his view I would only bear male children. He only had daughters, three of them, so maybe he knew about these things. The Duchess admired him, but said he was hard to pin down on the practicalities of maternity: 'He catches butterflies,' she said, as if that explained much.

I wrapped the baby in the same worn Indian chuddah his father had worn at his christening at Quetta and returned to the Lakeside Hotel. There I slept in a narrow room looking south over the little town to the old cathedral across the bridge. Grey had grown attached to his new keeper, Nan Fitzpatrick. She laughed at his sallies, calling him 'the little dote'. Her ne'er-do-well brother became his hero, and for a time he adopted their patronymic. Even in letters written much later from school he still sometimes referred to one 'Grey Fitzpatrick' who had bad ways and habits.

Most of that summer Malise slept outdoors in what had been Tim Douty's massive white high-wheeled pram under its tasselled awning. When his brother was wheeled out in it from the Butler Stoney house, the school children had used to shout, 'There goes the Lord Mayor of Australia in his V8!' One of those children, now aged sixteen, was the daughter of the village tailor and a convent-reared orphan of gentle birth, once a nanny herself. Enlisted to look after Malise, May stayed with me until her charge went to school.

Everywhere I went, he came too. To Limerick city, to church, to the cliffs of Moher and the Burren, to Pat's 'wicked' Uncle Artie's house at Cappagh among the ruined towers, the grey stone walls and the scrub of the west country of the Limerick Hunt, and, of course, to Castle Martin. He travelled in a wicker cradle, decked out with pale pink and green moss roses in net: an exquisite creation given by Sandie's beautiful sister Trix to Zara for Pat's little brother Alastair; but who lived only a few days, having heard the big guns from across the Channel when Sandie embarked at Folkestone for France in 1916. Aunt Ruby Fleischmann had kept the cradle hidden from Zara ever since, but now she had produced it and brought it over.

When Malise was about to be christened by his grandfather at Castleconnel, his brother climbed into the pulpit and attempted to start the service. Although it was June, we sang 'Once in Royal David's City' in recognition of his probable place of conception; afterwards there followed a very Irish celebration in the local pub. Throughout those months I marvelled at the long-suffering patience of my parents, especially that of my gently-reared English mother. She had come over in the autumn of 1939 with nothing but a cardboard box, abandoning her large flat in Cadogan Gardens and 'the Mouse', as she called her little farmhouse on the Surrey-Sussex borders, to take their chances in the bombing.

Pat penned his response to the birth of Malise from the desert 9th Army HQ on 1 June, though it did not arrive till mid-July:

You will wonder why I have not written before since this other strange raider appeared to harass our lives and consciences, but I have been in the blackest of black moods that I have ever in my life before suffered, and in no frame of mind to write to a wife who I fear is loathing me at the moment for discomfort, indignity and such a terrible reminder of mortality. I feel this letter should be more in the nature of a humble apology than the conventional display of mutual congratulation and satisfaction which is usually apparent on these occasions.

I know, believe me, how much you hate the whole performance, but I do know also how brave you are to undergo all this to give happiness to other people. I feel that whatever happens Themselves' dynasty is now secure as is humanly possible . . . and for that I will always be grateful. Always you have had to face these things without me . . . Please, please go on loving me as never before in spite of these pigs. What is he like, black and snipey or fair and rare? Long to know all possible details of the droleen and do you hate him just as much as you used to hate Grey? Tho' now from your turfside letter, which has just arrived, you seem to

think that he is quite a nice little boy, tho' apparently this famous
mother-love phenomenon has not made itself manifest. Possibly it
will grow with greater proximity, tho' God knows proximity must
be the last thing you fancy at the moment with any of God's
creatures. If only things could sometimes stand still.

If we could have stood together at the Cross by the Col des
Cèdres for a year instead of five minutes while a strangely pre-
destined sun took suicide in a great swallowing grey cloud: I
believe we could have stood that year together and consciously
enjoyed it all. Perhaps after this life, time will stand still and we
with it, together and unafraid. Please come back near to me now,
you have been so far away lately, but this distance may have been
of my own making as I did not want to intrude and make you
cross with me. I have been in hospital off and on for a month
with wisdom tooth trouble. Very painful indeed. Off to Jerusalem
today on sick leave, then shortly back to the regiment, 1st Btll I
think as a Major, which will help.

The wisdom tooth had grown sideways in Pat's mouth and he had
it taken out during May. The army dentist cut it in half before
extracting it in pieces, and the site continued to give trouble, with
the bone becoming inflamed. By 10 June he was writing from 'Lady
M's Convalescent Home':

Look at me writing from the bottom of a very comfortable bed
in Lady M's [Lady MacMichael's] home. Came down here with
leave. Went up to see Wee Bittie [the Scottish military doctor]
yesterday and was running a slight temp. So he plunged me into
bed and then came and took it again yesterday evening and it was
still up so he insists on my keeping here today, though it was normal
this morning, in case it goes up tonight. Simply maddening, he
thinks I may be getting some poison still out of my face and is
taking no chances. Meanwhile I am waiting to be posted back to
the Regiment . . . as a Company Commander and am frantic at
this setback, as I thought I was more or less all right tho' still a bit
light – can't chew anything hard yet – now I am frightened of
missing the boat as I had already turned down a Major's job with
J[umbo], preferring the other after a year's idleness. Nothing seems
to have gone right (for me) since you left, but anyhow you have

more than made up for that, but I am downy and miserable and thoroughly cross in losing all confidence in myself ever to achieve anything. H[ermione] has been angelic and my prop and stay. Yesterday she got 21 letters from Dan so is on the top of the world. He sounds well and as happy as can be expected . . .

Later. H. has just been down having tea with me and read me extracts from Dan's letters. He sounds awfully good and patient but there is an underlying current of deep misery. Am sure I could never stand it as well as him. His address is:

> Lieut. Lord Ranfurly
> Campo Concentramento (sounds awful!)
> P.G. No. 12
> P.M. 3200
> Italy

Everybody wildly thrilled about you. 'Felicitations' from the widest variety of your friends including Abdul Nebid Haidar who I've seen quite a lot of racing, M. Georges whose eyes filled with anglophile tears at the news, Wee Bittie who feels personally responsible and says you owe him a letter . . . Jum. also very sweet and enquiring and delighted to be GF . . .

Mrs Perry who is a real duckie and runs this place has just been in to take my temp. before WB's arrival and it is up again which makes me so furious and unhappy. I went for the hell of a ride on Sunday, and being as weak as a rat fear I rather overdid it and got awfully tired, very unlike me – also had a fall jumping a wall, entirely my own fault as I half let the pony stop and we all three (pony, wall, self) landed in a heap on the far side. I wasn't in the least hurt but the pony cut his knee for which I was very ashamed.

Fear this fighting is pretty grim in the desert just now. I think it is going all right but fear there will be some bad news about people. Actually I have heard very little yet and daren't pass any on until quite sure as miracles do happen and people turn up. What are we going to call (amongst ourselves) this new Conspirator? Think Grey ought to be consulted. Malise is rather pompous for a very small boy, he can come to that later. Children sometimes have a knack of the right name, i.e. Dan named Corky (Squawk) and it stuck for life, so tell him from me as the only other male Ruthven present that I leave the matter all in his hands.

Grey duly honoured his father's wish, naming Malise 'Skimper, because he's young' – a name which, like Dan's young brother Corky's, stuck for life.

Pat said he would not write again until he felt 'less downy'. His next letter, from 'Company Rifle Brigade MEF', was dated 17 July. In defiance of his guardian angel, who had been 'putting in a lot of overtime lately by keeping me out of the battle', he had spent two days nagging his superiors until they reluctantly agreed to let him proceed on his own initiative. He hitched to the battle zone, and now had command of his own company. There was news of deaths and wounds; some posted missing later turned up alive and well.

Got my first letters since Malise's arrival yesterday – actually 3 from you; one before Hatch Street, an airgraph from there after and then an air-letter card from Killaloe undated as usual, but after you'd got back. Poor one you seem to have had a horrid time. I had hoped it wouldn't be so bad this time but thank God I can think of you now back at Killaloe getting weller and weller all the time. You said that M. was very little trouble as he sleeps a lot. I consider this very sensible of him. I wish he could store up some and send it out to me as I shall shortly need all I can get . . .

I can't tell you what a spiritual relief it is to be nearly in the hunt again. Practically all my friends are there now and I just couldn't stand being away any longer tho' Jumbo did very kindly offer me a GII job. As it is I am Major now and should save more here than my staff pay, so fat prosperity is now my lot. My face is much better tho' enormous bits of bone keep coming up into my mouth at embarrassing moments. However they don't hurt any more, nothing hurts any more except not seeing you and with no immediate prospects. We had better see what the summer brings forth before making any plans, but things should be much better by the time you get this I feel sure.

Passing through Cairo had been a 'terribly lumpy' experience, but he had lunched and dined with the Lampsons.

Jacquie was looking awfully well – really pretty again and much thinner than she used to be. Talking of which I am surpassingly beautiful once more with desert figure and complexion and all the Beyroutal look disappeared. Alas my barren beauty with no one to appreciate it . . . I am sure it will mellow like old wine against our meeting, be it by banks of Shannon or Nile. I fear my lot lies here for the duration.

Even with seven years, if we are still at it out here, it would seem rather churlish to leave 'the lads', so back you come and run Freya's show in Cairo for the winter and let those horrid little pigs fend and rootle for themselves for a bit, and when you come I shall instantly acquire some tiny little illness and come bustling back all covered in sand and it will be as tho' we were never parted. The tell-tale years will roll away from us and time will stand still. Don't let's ever be parted again. Please, please, it is too much to endure.

Love (but grudgingly) to Grey and Malise, former does look rather charming in photograph you sent. I am so pleased that Malise is fair, Black Ruthvens are always doubtful qualities I fear, but fair ones (male) are always to be relied on. Love (most sincerely and ungrudgingly this time) for poor old Grannie PM who deserves every bit of it. Last but not least my love and respectful congratulations to the Canon of the Shannon. More nor life, always
   Pat

As the months passed, driving round counties Clare, Limerick and Tipperary in my parents' small car, inventing games and stories for Grey, who thought the bog was made of chocolate, I wondered whether I could be the same person who recently lived in Cairo, Jerusalem and Baghdad, danced on the roof of the Continental, feasted with all the visiting dignitaries and travelled with the indefatigable Freya.

It was sometime in August that I wrote to Pat from the Lakeside Hotel, enclosing a photograph of Grey.

Here's a picture for you, I expect you'll be horrified, he's put on weight this summer and runs properly now, not a toddle. Is very, very funny and mad on fishing. Ian and Aunt Sheela came for two nights of his leave, I am going to try and go to Castle Martin in September, but without nanny I could never manage Grey . . . Can't think what it will be like when she leaves to get married. T'other is a perfect gent. The most thoughtful man I have ever slept with. We talk of you always. Letters are continually written by Grey. Haven't got much to tell you as I never see anyone, but there are nice things like a morning visit to the forge with Grey and finding wild white orchids along the edge of the lake. My respects to J[umbo]. Poor, poor Auk! Michael (Fletcher) went to Burma with Archie (Wavell). Wonder if this will ever reach you and what is going to happen.

Photograph and letter were to be returned long afterwards.

Auchinleck had been relieved of his command by Churchill on the 8th, and General Alexander appointed as C-in-C Near East in a rearrangement of the command structure for the area.

On the 13th, General Jumbo wrote to me from his 9th Army HQ:

I deemed it a great honour to be asked by Pat as godfather to your son in company with Freya Stark and John Hamilton, I am sending thirty-five units in War Savings certificates for the boy which should accrue into a sum to buy him a pony when he is old enough. I have not seen Pat for some time but have heard of him in the desert . . . I missed Freya in Baghdad, she is now in Cyprus recuperating as she hadn't been too fit. John Hamilton had been having a thin time with his Minister [Spears]. There have been awful rows between him and the F[ree] F[rench] resulting in a good head bashing in Cairo last week. Barring that, life in Syria has not been very eventful. Things in the Western Desert are better now but we are all so distressed about Strafer Gott. He was flying back to Cairo in a bomber on three days' leave, the first in six months. It was shot down. He will be a great loss.

Only two days before Gott was killed, Churchill had decided to place him in command of the 8th Army. His death was therefore the event that led directly to Montgomery's appointment in his place.

From then onward the arrival of news from Pat grew ever more sporadic. There were pleas for my return to the Middle East, as in this letter of 29 August, received late in the autumn:

Not much has happened since I last wrote except that we haven't been quite so hectic and busy. We are now trained to the hour, one hopes, and ready for what is to come. At the moment things are very quiet except for a certain amount of night activity in which we are not immediately concerned. It is pretty hot and the flies are beyond all. I have had the old sores again but they are more or less all right again now. Lots of friends in the neighbourhood . . .

Henry Browne [his second-in-command] and I are due for leave on about Sept. 15th Rommel etc., permitting. I have written to ask Herm to come down and help me out, as there will be too many ghosts. If she can't come I don't know if I shall take it. It will be horrid going back and not finding you to minister, but arriving almost like a stranger and living alone in a hotel, and I fear the past will come up and swallow me. Oh if only you could get out this winter. Do you think there is any chance? I feel that my own destiny is bound to the Desert for the duration now, and only a discreditable 'balls up' or a very severe wound will get me home.

Do do try always providing you are fit enough and are done with that Malise. I feel the boys have had their turn now nearly. Consult Grey about it and ask him if he could spare you for a few months. I cannot press my claim too hard as I know that it would be selfish to do so, but I long most desperately for the sight and the sound and the sense of your nearness, and I can't get used to your not being at hand, nor ever will as long as I live. Freya told Hermione that she is lost without you and deploring poor Barbara [Graham] as a substitute. You only can decide and must know the other side of the picture better than I can. I am amassing great wealth at the moment and not spending anything like my pay, so there ought to be enough by the winter!

This is a dull downy letter, but on a whole I have been in good heart. We had the new C-in-C round yesterday. Looks a good hardy one, but I do hope they don't forget the Auk and all his good work out here. When all is said and done he did save the situation.

The letter I wrote back to Pat, explaining I could not possibly hope to return yet, was another he never received.

I cabled impossibility of return to Freya. Some home must be established first and not over here; rationing is in force but badly done and black market rife so that one has no idea of what one can get. Anyway Mother is past taking them on and no nurse can work in England. I must sit tight till next spring. It's awful to say no to seeing you again soon, and such a chance, but I am still 'blackinking' [feeding] Skimper and I suppose won't be finished till after Christmas. Grey is so jumpy about partings I think I couldn't leave until he is bigger and settled in a home of his own. Herself hinted that Himself wouldn't stay [in Australia] after '44.

Here I am trying to save on your bank account, so that we can do the home-making together. At present you are quite rich and very economical with your field allowances. I watch over your finances like an old she-dragon.

Grey came into my room while I was dressing for church and did all his strange mystic hymns and chanting while 'reading' his Sunday book. I biked down to the cathedral where we had an excellent sermon about the next world from the bishop and I gossiped with the faithful Prot. minority afterwards. (The Reverend thinks the cathedral should be shared with the Papists.) Crossing the bridge I met the local Defence Force turned out in their new battledress with a flag to place over the tablets on the bridge to the memory of the three martyrs shot by the Black and Tans. Doubtless the Almighty's omnipotence is not puzzled by the conflicting prayers offered Him for the departed. The Black and Tans were at their blackest around here.

Despite foggy and frosty November mornings, Grey and I still go down to the lake fishing. He ties purple rails and orange grouse to his line, bulkyshan (ragwort) serves for flies and a dried reed for rod and line. Other times he goes hacking wood with Father's enormous axe or cuts turf. Love and take good care, I think we have great days ahead of us, Loving, impatient but decidedly dutiful. P.

PS ... Letter from John Hamilton who has gone to Jumbo in Baghdad: he says Freya is trying to snaffle Hermione. Will you go back to Jum[bo] again? If I could take the men to Australia I'd come straight on. But Himself says seas not clear enough yet.

The continuing dangers of ocean travel were brought home by news of another tragedy early that autumn. Everyone loved Grizel Wolfe Murray. Apart from her great blue eyes, dark hair and pale skin, she had a kind of radiance. She had joined her husband Malcolm in Palestine after the outbreak of war in 1939, leaving two small sons, Jamie and Angus, in Scotland. For three years at Alexandria, she then worked tirelessly in canteen and hospital for the troops and sailors. When I met her in Palestine, there was a kind of recognition of ourselves in our fated living.

Grizel was expecting another baby by 1942, and longing to see her sons again. She sailed south from Suez and, like me some months earlier, changed ships at Durban. When they were torpedoed in the Atlantic, she only had time to put a coat on over her nightie before taking to a leaky lifeboat. After two days, by which time she was clinging to a plank of wood, she was among those picked up by the crew of the U-boat that had sunk their ship. Sister Doris Hawkins, a nurse who survived to tell the tale, recorded that Grizel was 'wonderfully cheerful' and the group were treated with kindness and attention, though it was only a two-day reprieve. The U-boat captain received a warning to submerge, but first had to put his guests back in the sea. His distress was genuine, and he dropped them as close as he could to two lifeboats still afloat.

Then [wrote Sister Hawkins] Grizel and I found ourselves once more swimming for our lives with about fifty other people. As far as I know only six of us reached the lifeboats . . . We were two women among sixty-six men all British except two Polish cadet-officers. There was little water, a few ship's biscuits and a small amount of chocolate and Horlicks tablets which was all Grizel could swallow. She died on Saturday, 26 September. There were only fifteen survivors from one lifeboat, they went ashore after twenty-eight days at sea.

On 15 November I wrote to Pat from the Lakeside Hotel:

Malise and I sleep in a snug little room which looks south-east downstream to where the big square cathedral tower overlooks the houses and shops and the bridge and beyond to Africa. We see the sun rising every morning behind 'Keeper' mountain in Tipperary, and just before he comes up all the silly jackdaws go mad round the cathedral. Sometimes the swans come up to Derg from their nesting reed-beds, this morning the old heron was the first, followed by a lovely green and white barge called *St James*. We have a turf and a wood fire which never goes out. I've just had my breakfast and have time to write because May, the nursemaid, has taken him off for his bath. He slept late and has woken up all jumps and chat; unlike his brother, who sometimes warns one, 'I am a bit touchy this morning', he is always gay. There is a rush on to finish his going-away trousseau, we are expected at Cappagh at the end of the month.

There is crab and wild hip jelly to be made from the precious ration of sugar but after lunch I am going for a ride up the mountain on the dean's lovely three-quarter bred Arab mare.

You will understand what it means morning and night to know we are on the road to the end of the war and that you are well, even tho' no letters have come since one written in August and I still don't know what Special Air Service means.

It was Pat's next letter, written on 25 October from 'c/o British Field Censorship Unit No. 32 MEF' but not received by me till 22 December, which explained how he had been selected to join the Special Air Service regiment, the élite group of volunteers, led by David Stirling, who worked behind Rommel's lines, blowing up communications links and petrol dumps. Initially the aim had been to parachute them behind the lines, but after a series of disastrous accidents it was decided to deliver them to their target areas by ground transport, using the services of the Long Range Desert Group. By this stage Pat's friend, Henry Browne, had been killed. Henry's death, I felt, had much to do with Pat's decision to join a commando unit.

You will see by the address that I have moved again and am now doing what I always wanted to do when it was first mooted . . . I am now fully qualified [as a parachutist] having taken very kindly to it all, no doubt the background of Bucksbrook [a steeplechaser who gave Pat some bad falls] and his like stood me in good stead. Possibly when I went up to Cambridge the gods ordained that I should learn one thing at least which was to prove useful in later years!

Now we are doing some very tough marching and training but I am getting very fit and seem to make it as well as anybody else . . . We are all volunteers and most of us have had to come down in rank . . . but the whole thing cried out of P of O [point of honour] when the opportunity occurred. At the moment I am commanding this squadron but think this is only temporary, I have no doubt that great adventures lie ahead.

Last weekend I went up to Cairo and stayed with my long-lost cousin Melosine Cary Barnard who is married to a man called Guy Trundell in GHQ RAF. They have a flat very close to Air House (all rather lumpy). Melosine is very wild and Mo Leckyish, but great sport. I went for a ride at Gezira – all horribly lumpy and ghosts at every corner. Lunched on Monday with Esther and Michael [Wright] where who should I find but Freya, who promptly dispatched a cable to you.

O, my heart, I just don't know what to advise – I seem to be no cop at all without you, being unable to settle to anything, but F[reya] threatened Baghdad and even if you did have two months' summer leave don't feel it would ever do. Against that God knows if I'll ever see you again unless you do accept. Believe that if you bargained for not more than three months consecutively in Baghdad or something, she would probably play as I know she is mad to have you and would have you flown out. What would happen your end I can't think, it would almost be a case of letting the 'bog' take care of its own. Anyhow you must decide. This is about your birthday time and I have done nothing at all. Suggest you cable any wants of things, food, etc. required against the winter and I will try and obtain and send, tho' don't know how it is to Eire. Your letters have been awful. Please, please, put dates as they all arrive in different order and I just don't know what is going on at all. My mail did start to catch me up here at the time, but nothing for the past fortnight and I get so downy. This is a horrid letter but I am no longer any cop without you – it gets worse and worse.

Love to Grey and Skimper and thank former for his prayers and other spiritual and moral assistance. This will probably be late for his third birthday but I will try and write him a letter when I am in better heart.

Love and all the thanks in the world to G, PM, and His Reverence. More nor life (tho' that means little now), Pat

PS. The address at the top of letter is new censorship for Eire. Bloody aggravating as it makes things twice as long. Perhaps that's what's happened to all yours. B——the censor!

The last letter from Pat was dated 20 November:

From 1 SAS Regiment, MEF
   Sent c/o Mrs Fleischmann, Chetwode Manor, Buckingham

I am writing to you this way 'cos censorship regulations to Ireland now are so complicated and I never can remember what I am supposed to do – also this is the only paper I can lay hands on. Darling, I have been awful about writing lately. Life has been so truly hectic and will probably be even more so from now on. That old Herm, bless her, has reappeared again down here and will pass on any bits when I can get in touch with her. I am so happy in my new 'home' with lots of friends – the most wonderful lot of men that have ever been got together, I am only a captain again, but have a splendid command, the sort of thing that I have always hankered after. Vivian Street is my squadron leader and is such fun to soldier with. After Henry Browne was killed I felt rather lonely with the 1st Battalion; nobody there of my real friends.

Things are so dramatic out here I feel we are moving on the watershed of History, and it is a stirring time to be alive. I have been awful about letters but opportunities have not been frequent, but am not ever very far away from you now – much closer than in the Beyroutling days just after you left. I always think I am nearer to you when I am racehorse fit and in this very, very intensive and physically exhausting life, the spirit so often has to subjugate the body, that physical separation becomes relatively unimportant. All this sounds rather nonsense I fear and is badly expressed and I do long for you at times in a really bodily way.

There is so much I would tell you if I could – this horrid censor-ship takes all the fun out of letter writing.

I hope your men are looking after you well – I really must write to Grey on the subject of filial piety anyhow towards mothers. Tell him I am very much looking forward to meeting him and perhaps one day he will see me arriving like this, which isn't a very dignified parental entry.

I love you very, very much and always will whatever happens, Pat

PS. Vivian sends his love.

My last letter to Pat was an immediate response to his of 25 October, received on 22 December and replied to on the 23rd, the day before Christmas Eve 1942:

My heart,

Your October 25th letter came yesterday. I suspected it was this from your first cable, then lulled myself into a false sense of security. Now I am peacock-proud and travel all day with my head in the air, watching the clouds and the rooks on the wind. I am bothering about your head, and how it stands parachuting. (Grey has no heads for heights, either – you see, he knew all along – he thinks of you always as an aeroplane coming across to him from the desert.) Then I go down to your poor ankle, and wonder what it thinks about, and the badly-treated collar bones. Do you remember the picture I have of you falling off Bucksbrook? Of course you are right – poor PM looks ten years older since I read her your letter – like the Holy Ghost, P of O can't be gainsaid. I am thankful there are friends – I wish you could keep some kind of diary or record for the boys' sake. And the cuttings you sent have made me go singing.

Well it's wonderful news, and I can't believe you have all got so far. The Russians are profiting and Smuts's words keep recurring: 'One day we shall awake, and like the dawn, victory will be there!' I have great belief that these years are only your beginning – just as Himself never started till Omdurman. We'll have to have great patience with the eldest pig. I know [that] give him his head and time, he'll carry on. I think that unlike many families the Ruthvens and Gowries are staging a great come-back. Sheela had great faith too in your survival of this war. She has made you her heir to CM [Castle Martin] after the others. I saw Percy when Skimper and I were luxuriating at Cappagh. 'Fraid he's no good – out of the army, and this awful Dicky who has encouraged it is obviously 'a lover'. I can see he means to stay over here. I told him how I felt about it, but we remained friends. He has a little money now . . . Great Christmassing here. Diana (in great heart and may come your way); Rom, very unlike herself and feeling awfully rotten owing to a pig in the early summer, and [her husband] Richard Dreyer – whom I know you will like. He is most attractive and Scandanavian-looking, 6 ft 4, but small bones . . .

A letter came from Herm[ione] saying she had given up her job. I hope she goes nearer you. Look now: I am still feeding Skimper but nearly finished. I propose to start haggling for the permit to get over: visit M of Information to keep in touch and take over flat for Mother which has had untidy friends in it. Then she can come over if necessary for Ex's pig's arrival. I shall try, probably in vain, to find a house near Calne to settle into and stay with Ex and possibly the parents, which would be the only way financially. This would mean that any outlay would not be wasted as it would serve [as a] temporary roof for Themselves should they return in '43. (Richard, by the way, is going to sea next month.) Once some such roots are established I can make plans to leave Grey and Skimper, but as long as *they* are in this country it is impossible to leave them. Ange has twenty waifs and strays in her war nursery, so perhaps she'd take in two stray Ruthvens. Don't you agree that it would be nice for them to be near their cousins. Anyway somehow we'll get through to next summer and then one day I'll probably turn up. If I return to Freya at that salary and conditions I'd have to stick it for the duration. We've done one year apart and it is never for more than eighteen months, is it? . . . All the love in the world. God keep you, my heart, and I believe He will. And please, please try not to be downy, if only to help me here.

Pam

PS. 'Poor Old Grey' gets so muddled, he is set on hanging dead *owls* on the Xmas Tree!

In January I received a message from Australia to say that Pat had been reported missing, presumed taken prisoner. For several weeks, right into February, I planned to send him parcels, hoping the Irish Red Cross would somehow manage to circumvent the war restrictions. At first I greeted the news almost with relief. I think I imagined, having seen Pat survive so many bad falls racing and hunting during the 'crash dash splinter' years, that he was liberally endowed with what his father called 'the luck of the race'. I could see him getting on well with his Italian captors; moreover, the worry of trying to get back to Cairo and Freya, of having to leave Grey again, with Malise not yet a yearling, was temporarily abated.

As the days went by, the picture seemed to become unreal and confused. From Australia the Gowries had made contact with the Lampsons in Cairo, the Vatican and the International Red Cross. When I asked the Reverend, 'Do you think there is any hope?' he denied it in a burst of anger, exploding as he had done so many years earlier when he denounced the treatment of the Germans at the Treaty of Versailles. In the end, it was through Jacquie Lampson's father, Sir Aldo Castellani, who was with the Italian Army in the Western Desert, that we heard how Pat died from his wounds on Christmas Eve in the Italian hospital at Misurata, following his capture in a commando raid. On 13 February 1943 a cable arrived at Government House, Canberra, containing this message from an officer of the headquarters staff, Misurata being by then to the rear of the lines of the advancing British forces:

Passing through Misurata on my way here I discovered Patrick Hore-Ruthven had died of wounds in Italian hospital on 24 December. He is buried Italian cemetry at Misurata Marina. I visited both hospital and cemetery. I saw doctor who appears to have nursed him. I feel sure they did everything possible. He was wounded through lung and died of pneumonia. May my deepest sympathy be conveyed to family.

The suspense was ended, not by relief, but by the certainty of sorrow. Following the arrival of the confirmation from Sydney, I had taken a solitary walk along the banks of Lough Derg, northward under the bare winter trees. Soon I heard padding footsteps behind me. It was Mr Jim, come to see I 'came to no harm'. Regretfully I returned with him to the hotel. I shall never forget the kindness and compassion written across his broad country face.

Grey expected his father with every plane flying to or from Shannon Airport. He had to be told. Skimper, still at the breast, cried little and smelled sweet; only when left naked on a bed or free of his napkin on the floor would he bicycle frantically, showing the whites of his eyes as if in a rage. I was fortunate to have the Giant and the Reverend, tactful, loving, understanding *croyants*. Grey's thwarted tribal instincts now had to be content with waving goodbye to the sun as it sank in the west behind the mountains of Clare, on its way to Australia.

My first official notification from the War Department was a buff envelope containing a curt demand for the return of the family allowance paid since the death of the late Captain Hore-Ruthven deceased.

As to triumphant arms
Life leaps to death,
And ends her daily harms
With quiet breath.

She brings earth-gifts as dower,
Where strong death waits
Life, fragile as a flower,
Unlocks the gates.

The hard gates barely swing
So slim she goes,
Lightfoot as wind of spring,
Transient as rose.

The dull gates open free
To zodiac height;
Like a wave to its waves of sea,
Like a star to its night.

Like a maid, but enriched with desire,
Like a summer's breath,
Life flees to her funeral pyre,
The bride of death.

Freya Stark
February 1942

9

The Ingathering

Lord Clanmorris had three dashing daughters: Matilda (known as 'Maud'), Rose and Florence Bingham. Florence in time became 'the Honourable', while Maud and Rose married respectively Albert Brassey of Heythrops and General Hugh McCalmont of Mount Juliet in County Kilkenny. Rose and Hugh's son, Dermot, established the legendary Ballylinch Stud at Mount Juliet just before the First World War. The foundation of his stock was The Tetrach, perhaps the fastest horse in the history of the Turf, passed on to him by his cousin 'Atty' Persse. Atty's fellow trainers had thought him out of his mind when he paid 13,000 guineas for The Tetrach as a yearling, but the story went that he knew it was the only colt that could keep up with the deer in the deer park.

When it was confirmed that Pat had died of wounds, I took the children first to Mount Juliet. There I wrote all my sad letters, which Dermot insisted on stamping for me. Grey was blissful, with a whole small world of estate workers to chat up and waste their time with. The house was full of servants under the kindly capable steward, and outside there was a forge, sawmills, a carpenter's shop beside the kennels and stables, and a famous water garden where I spent many hours. A tale was told of Mount Juliet that it had been protected from the forays and burnings of the Troubles, maybe because it employed such a vast number of citizens.

For the Gowries in Australia, private grief deferred to public sympathy as dignitaries and delegations arrived to make their condolencies. Letters described Zara most unusually wearing dark glasses, but available as ever to all comers at Himself's side. The thought of their grief, and their courage in facing it, helped me to forget my own. Among the first to call at Government House had been the Irish nationalist, Archbishop Mannix of Sydney. Sandie once aroused the ire of certain Sydney Protestants by visiting the Catholic archbishop in his home. When he got there, he had been surprised find a photograph of himself riding in a race.

Besides being Governor-General, Sandie was also Commander-in-Chief of the armed forces of a country whose northern coast lay virtually defenceless against a Japanese landing. He had welcomed General MacArthur and the US troops, despite the headaches they brought with them. It now seemed doubtful whether Sandie could be released until the end of the war.

I resolved to wean the baby so as to be free to make plans for us to join them in Australia. Since this would entail frequent visits to London, I decided to move with the family, May, the boys and the Giant, closer to Dublin, to Castle Martin. 'If you ever lose me,' Pat had once written, 'go to Castle Martin, I know every stick and stone.' The old house stands on a bend of the river Liffey near the village of Kilcullen on the Dublin to Waterford road: a large, square house with a stone portico and steps climbing up over a huge basement, which helps to keep it dry. There is a lime avenue to the house, but the drive doesn't use it; narrowed by grassy verges, and pot-holed, it commences with magnificent Italian wrought-iron gates, only a short walk from the village. It was a boys' house: there were boys living there ever since I first knew Pat: Zara's nephews, Percy and Ian Blacker; then, during the war, cousins on his father's side, John and James Malcolm, who came to stay with their mother Mary after their father Billy was taken prisoner.

Before the war I had usually stopped at Castle Martin on my way to and from England. Uncle Freddie, left utterly distraught by the First World War, and overcome with the sadness of the world, had by then taken more or less permanently to his bed. He had made a foray to London for our wedding, but suffered a mini-breakdown during the service. In the room above him, his old Aunt Louisa lay in another big bed and shouted for the attentions of Katie, the elderly housemaid. Katie brought brass cans of hot water for everyone's washstand; furniture and bedding would be moved from one bedroom to another according to the status of incoming occupants. Up to Katie's height, everything was scrubbed and clean; above that, the spiders and dust reigned undisturbed.

The dining room at Castle Martin had large rectangular windows looking towards the Wicklow Mountains. They dropped to the floor on rope sashes, so you could step over a low wainscot and down a short flight of steps on to the surrounding rough grass. Their red-felt curtains had been chewed by generations of dogs; now they were ragged, but out of canine reach. In the hall, the heads of African game, from a huge wildebeast to the smallest, neatest gazelle, covered the walls; between them a wide stone double staircase led up to the high bedrooms and the corridors connecting them. The rooms were mostly furnished in eighteenth-century Irish mahogany, bleached to a lovely colour by the sun because of curtains that could no longer be drawn, or shutters that refused to shut. Many were the struggles May and I had to darken a bedroom to lull the Ruthven babies to sleep.

The old stables, where Pat and his cousins had kept their hunters, were now full of Aunt Sheela's war effort – pigs. The boar and his sows roamed free. The boar had been reared by a priest, and when the Reverend arrived he was literally greeted by a standing ovation as the animal rose up to place its front trotters on his shoulders in welcome. The stable yard enclosed a vast mountain of manure, sprouting stiff blades of grass. It was always going to be, but never was, taken out to be put on the land. By now it would have needed a Hercules to shift it. In her widowhood, Aunt Sheela spent all day outdoors, or chopping wood for the fires or collecting turf, tasks that her son Percy seemed incapable of doing for her. Percy had been to England to join up or find some war work, but nothing much came of it, so he returned. An Austrian refugee named Franz Ofner had meanwhile arrived to help with the pigs, however, and was a great success. Sheela could communicate with him as she and her sisters had had a German governess. For a period the pig yard actually paid its way. Franz worked hard for Castle Martin. He had decided to stay in Ireland and farm there after the war.

In a cottage in the yard lived Mr and Mrs Morrisey, their two daughters Peggy and Phoebe, and their son Johnny. Johnny was on the backward side, but good with pigs and horses. When the moon was full, he was liable to 'streak', as the practice later came to be known: running stark naked round the outside of the house, to the alarm of any strangers or cousins at the dining table, on account of the curtains which no longer drew. Old Morrisey, his father, had been the groom all through the days when Freddie Blacker was Master of the Kildare Hounds and kept a small stud farm. Though completely blind, he knew the paddocks, gates and fields so well that he continued to lead the horses in and out of the stables by touch. The remaining presence of a few mares and yearlings entailed occasional trips to Dublin and Newmarket. Mary Malcolm's younger son, John, rode to school on whatever Castle Martin horses were available.

From time to time Ian would come home on a short leave from the Rifle Brigade, in which his father Freddie had also served. I was aware that he paid bills and made plans, and generally put heart into Sheela and Mary. Percy, of course, was heir to Castle Martin, but Ian was fairly well-off. He had inherited two properties from his grandmother's family, the Lawlesses. When Grey was three, he gave him, as his godson, a splendid feast in Jammet's restaurant in Dublin.

Percy, with the local bar, the Hideout, handily situated just down the road, found life at Castle Martin more or less tolerable. Sometimes I managed to persuade him to help me chop wood in the shed. He was well read, and enjoyed talking poetry and books. He even wrote quite well, though the pen, to borrow Percy French's phrase, 'never worked for him'. Once he began drinking down at the Hideout, Percy could become extremely argumentative and aggressive. On more than one occasion I had to drive down to the village and pick him up. The landlord, Jim Byrne, used to lay him out with a massive vodka cocktail known as a 'Moscow mule' whenever he became impossibly abusive: this rendered him in a fit state to be put in the car and dragged off to bed. If he left the Hideout mule-less, the consequences were apt to be dire. There was one night when the Giant was awakened by a terrified Franz, who jumped into her bed and cried, 'Save me, save me, PM! Percy's trying to kill me.' The heir to Castle Martin had chased him round the corridors, brandishing an axe. In the old days, Pat had been Percy's boon companion, Ian being considerably younger. Years later, Phoebe Morrisey, who by then worked for the Dean of Kildare, told me Percy's mother had 'spoiled him rotten', whereas Ian had been brought up with the Morrisey children in the yard.

My mother fitted into life at Castle Martin, as Mary Malcolm had done after Sandie's nephew Billy was taken prisoner. But there was never much to eat, especially after Snell, the butler turned cook, retired to his cottage and Peggy Morrisey took on the cooking. The Giant and Mary used to store food for their boys – big and small – in special caches. Mary took on the old walled kitchen garden near the farm buildings. It was a lovely warm sheltered muddle of old roses and fruit trees, and Mary's vegetables grew well there. Despite this, the bareness of the larder continued to worry me when I was away, together with the fact that Skimper was changed from a relaxed enchanting companion to become a rather tough, disturbing character who had learned that spittal was a highly effective means of protest. All letters between May and myself bewail this metamorphosis from infant to problem child. To Zara I wrote in January 1944:

> To quote Jim Barry, Skimper is loose and careless, he doesn't try to talk, cries at the least thing but not for long, tries to run everywhere and is quite happy out in his pram for hours alone. I hope he isn't stupid in the head. Grey adores him with the same Mediterranean affection he bestows on the poor Giant. He cries when Skimper cries, has toothache at the same time and won't let May scold him ever: 'Sure May, you have to pity a little feller like that.' The worst of it is that Grey loves his horrid little ugly face when he cries.

Early in 1944, I therefore decided to take a wretched small house above Greystones, on the coast between Dublin and Wicklow, while my parents rented a primitive but far nicer cottage, inland up the hill in the lovely village of Delgany. Grey would stand for hours at the gate of our rented home, hailing the schoolchildren as they went by, gossiping with the tradesmen. Ireland loves her children; she doesn't find them the nuisance that England does. Neither are Irishmen too proud to be seen doing things with children. After I sacked a not very suitable gentleman's gentleman whom I had hired as a cook, Ted, the garden boy, took on the job of nursemaid along with a whole lot of other household duties.

One morning the postman brought a postcard from Percy, written by his spluttery, disobedient pen. He suggested we should marry. Grey missed him: in fact it was partly because he used to say he

wanted to grow up to be just like Percy that I didn't care to leave
the boys at Castle Martin while I was away in England.

It was the Timor Sea that defeated me in my determination to
get to Australia. No one, at the London end, could have been
more helpful than Tommy Lascelles, the king's private secretary, the
Dominions Office and Lord Salisbury; but the US Command refused
us a passage, saying that travelling with two young children would
be far too dangerous. It was as well, perhaps. By February the
Gowries had announced they would be returning to England later
in the year. Sandie had a tired heart, and the Duke of Gloucester
had been appointed to take over as his successor in November 1944.
It was a real problem to decide where our first meeting should occur.
With Grey now four and Malise coming up to his second birthday,
I thought that Ireland would surely be better for us and Sandie's
strained heart, before the Gowries became involved in the official
world, their financial problems and their dream of a home near Bath,
where violets and pigs were to provide a livelihood. Grey was already
excited about the prospect of the encounter, as I told Zara when I
wrote to her on the 20th:

> He talks a lot about Pat. He says he sees his father's hand in the
> sun and whenever he goes up the mountain on Polly, the donkey.
> Once he told May, 'Grey eats raw carrots like his best relation.'
> When she asked, 'Who is your best relation?' he said, 'My Daddy,
> Lord Gowrie's son, in the name of the Lord God of Hosts.'
>
> I had a tea party which Grey attended, very gay and flirty with
> one of the guests. We were talking as usual of the cost of living
> in Ireland. He gave her a sidelong look and said, 'Happy Christ-
> mas in the workhouse, Mrs Plunkett.' She was very tickled; he
> manages to be most apt and generally brings a hint of the indelicate
> for a formal gathering. Ted took him to see the ewes with their
> new lambs on the golf links. He said they were 'the dead spit of
> Mummy and Malise at the Lakeside Hotel'. He is busy composing
> a Gloria in Excelcis Deo which he sings to his own accompaniment
> on the piano and holds the most horrible hot gospel services on
> the Delgany golf links, with 'confessions' and long invocations to
> 'Owen' (Noah) and Mount Ararat. Did Pat get religion at this age
> too?
>
> My lease ends in June, and it would be silly take on this horrid

little house if you have decided on Calne. Alternatives are Castle Martin – could Aunt Sheela face us all? – apartments at Headfort which Elsie Headfort has suggested – she has been terribly kind. Terry H. Marquess of Headfort has just been appointed manager at Foynes airport. Or there is an Irish hotel in a lovely position in the Glen of the Downs half an hour from Delgany . . . no chance of a private sitting room and of course there is a bar. I can see you there, but not Himself. Perhaps you and he could stay in comfort at Kilrudery (with the Meaths) and drive over to see us.

The day after I wrote this letter, on 21 February, David Gray, the American representative in Dublin, delivered what became known as the 'American Note' to the Irish premier, Mr de Valera – a request for Ireland to expel the members of the German and Japanese legations. The Taoiseach saw it as an ultimatum from the Allies, and reacted indignantly, only strengthened in his determination to preserve the integrity of his country's neutrality.

I had become involved in discussions with the Irish Red Cross over the possibility of bringing refugee children from Greece to Ireland, and thanks to Sandie obtained a long interview with Mr de Valera about the starving Greeks. Dev, it seemed, admired Sandie: I expect he had received favourable reports from Archbishop Mannix. At the end of our interview he nodded and said, 'Poor people, poor people.' He gave me the sense of being a very friendly neutral, an impression evidently not shared by Mr Churchill.

On a personal level, the American Note raised the spectre of complications to my plans. As I wrote to Sandie:

Well, you know about the latest developments here. The whole thing seems a pity when Eire was just beginning to feel some real friendliness and gratitude to England. Maybe it will give them a jolt. They seem to have no conception of the outer world. I have made friends with the Ryans who live here (Minister of Agriculture), he is rather an old slob but she is very intelligent. I thought I had persuaded Judge McGuire, Chairman of the Irish Red Cross, to come to London in April to see some of the British and International Red Cross people, now I wonder if either of us will be allowed to go . . . I can get no assurance from Dublin that I will be let back to Eire if I go to London next month.

The Fletchers would never forgive me if I got stuck over there. I feel the risk should be taken since [receiving] your letters and cables; 'specially as I know Sir Ernest (Fisk) and the rubber boots and mackintosh [presents from Australia] are there. I am still trying hard to get the British to allow the Irish Red Cross to achieve some active relief in Europe . . . e.g. sending canned meat to Greece. They have lots of money but are out of all UN plans. I feel it is more than ever necessary now that they take some part like Sweden and Switzerland.

Alas, the Germans have turned down the children scheme, that will now have to a post-Armistice offer. I wish the Irish Red Cross could have a ship of their own, like the Swedes, to carry food to Greece . . . I feel sure Lord Cranborne [Secretary of State for Dominion Affairs] would think kindly about this, he seemed so keen that good feeling should exist. They are rather pathetic, so keen and incompetent and entirely ignorant of the way things are done outside Ireland. Two set-backs are this old American Note and the new Archbishop McQuaid. He is reactionary and non-cooperative in every way besides making it a mortal sin for Catholics to attend Trinity College. Nearly every food kitchen has been closed down. There is real hardship: a family of four cannot possibly afford to buy butter at 2/4d per pound.

In March I wrote again to Zara about the housing problem:

We all hate Greystones. Even the seashore is smug and Protestant and un-Irish. Most of the Anglo-Irish do nothing to help the country they live in. Grey has far more public sense of duty, tho' since he heard talk of the American Note and Dev's reply he has started to say he is Scotch for the first time. I see a lot of Percy. Ian is home on leave. Uncle Val came to lunch. When I took him into the nursery afterwards I said, 'Come along, Grey, and give Uncle Val some coffee.' He took a long look and said, 'I am sorry, Mrs Hore-Ruthven, Uncle Val looks to me the sort of man who would like a little whiskey or sherry, not coffee.'

There are horrid rumours that the mail boat may be stopped and no travelling to and fro in the spring and summer. I thought I ought to go to Calne and give Ange a hand if you are going there, and I adore staying with Bets [Somerset]. My baby-doctor,

Ninian Faulkner, has insisted on my seeing another [doctor] to find out why I don't quite get fit. He seemed to think it might be the climate. I have some sort of streptococci in my throat, nothing to worry about. The men are magnificent, Grey still mad about Skimper and calls him 'the little dote'.

Whenever I was back in London, I stayed at the dirty but unscathed 87 Cadogan Gardens. I slept in my old room, where a picture in coloured silks of Fred Archer hung next to the now moth-eaten mask of the fox I won the day my mount led the master over the dark snow-covered walls in Northumberland. As in Ireland, I was beginning to feel alien. For the first time I heard myself referred to as a 'widow'. 'Unconditional surrender' was back in the vocabulary: two words which had bred Hitler. I began to wonder what Pat and his kind had fought and died for in the Western Desert. Was it for overland routes to India, or shipping lanes, or oil? Hadn't the amiable US Ambassador Fish and Roosevelt's special envoy, the cheek-to-cheek dancing Colonel Donovan, been busy stealing our oil concessions in the Gulf while we fought alone?

It seemed to me I had joined company with the invaders and settlers, the Normans, Vikings and Huns, plundering lands not rightfully theirs, then setting up armies of occupation, erasing sacred landmarks, retaining the profits of annexation in the name of progress and the defence of world resources: Churchill, Roosevelt and Stalin each playing the old, old game in his own way; but always, as I had learned in Egypt and Ireland, leaving a deep distrust which is never erased. In the Middle East, it has happened from the collapse of the Ottoman Empire. As T. E. Lawrence had written to the *Sunday Times* in the summer of 1920:

> Our government is worse than the old Turkish system. They kept 14,000 local conscripts embodied, and killed a yearly average of 200 Arabs in maintaining peace. We keep 90,000 men with aeroplanes, armoured cars, gun-boats and armoured trains. We have killed about 10,000 Arabs in the rising this summer. We cannot hope to maintain such an average: it is a poor country, sparsely populated.

During the First World War, fearing that the Ottoman Turks might start a holy war against us, which could implicate India, we had made promises of independence to the Hashemite rulers of Mecca and Medina if they joined us in the war against Germany. The pledge was unambiguous. Then came the Russian revolution of October 1917, partly instigated by its Jewish citizens, which the Foreign Office feared could have influence on those other powerful Jewish citizens of America. Hence the more ambiguous Balfour Declaration within the month. Ben-Gurion was prepared to settle for boundaries drawn west of the river Jordan; it was Jabotinsky and his so-called 'Revision-ist' group who insisted on Eretz Israel, stretching to the Euphrates and beyond.

All of this I had learned, listening to Freya and her circle of Egyptian intellectuals – the British Orientalists and the young effendis – while Pat and his comrades sweated it out in the Western Desert, fighting the Great Satan of Fascist brutalism and Nazi anti-Semitism. But when portraits of Churchill were handed out to the troops in the desert, Pat had refused to have one displayed in his vehicle, saying indignantly that it would be the King or no one.

During that spring of 1944 I found myself stranded, as feared, by the aftermath of the American Note. The British government, with D-Day and 'Operation Overlord' looming at the start of June, had been progressively tightening communications and travel restrictions aimed at placing Ireland in a state of total isolation. I was forbidden to return to my children.

One day, while travelling on the Underground, I ran into Vivian Street, who had been Pat's squadron commander on the last fateful mission. Vivian's group had been taken as prisoners to Tripoli follow-ing a long trek without petrol in the desert. He then had a remarkable escape when he was picked up in the Mediterranean after the veteran submarine taking him to Italy was attacked and sunk by a British destroyer. Subsequently he parachuted into Yugoslavia, and now he was back in London with Fitzroy Maclean, who was busily consoli-dating his *coup* of having sold Tito to the prime minister. Vivian said, 'I simply have to get some leave. Couldn't you look after Fitz for me for a couple of weeks?'

I jumped at the chance to be in the swim again. Fitzroy had been lent an office at Combined Operations in Whitehall, a pretty smart set-up with a green scrambler telephone connecting directly with the PM and No. 11. What began as a fairly hilarious fortnight

stretched into six weeks. Fitzroy had left Randolph Churchill with
Tito, living in a cave. This gave him the perfect excuse to talk direct
to the PM, recounting some successful or unsuccessful action while
reporting on Randolph's well-being. Otherwise he would stride
about London, a kilted colossus in his uniform: a ruthless and glamorous personality, throwing parties at the Ritz, courting newspaper
proprietors, and otherwise delivering nudges to the course of history.
There were fearsome arguments with Anthony Eden.

Fitzroy and Vivian had brought back with them a young Yugoslav
partisan, Vladco Velebit. Churchill finally said he would see him one
day at 3 p.m., but the Yugoslav was nowhere to be found. Fitz sent
me off to scour London and get him to No. 10 by three o'clock
sharp. All I had to go on was his habit of disappearing with Tom
Driberg and other lefties and the fact he was staying at the Savoy
Hotel. I chased around London like a demented bloodhound, even
peering under the tables in the Savoy, and in the end I got him.
Rather incongruously, we then took a 'bus to Whitehall'. 'General'
Velebit was most charming – sensitive and well read. I gave him a
copy of *The Ballad of Reading Gaol*, which delighted him, in the best
edition I could find.

While in London I was also engaged in a struggle over Pat's life
insurance policy with the Legal & General. They had refused to pay
up over some small print to the effect that he never told them he
had joined the army. I wrote Sandie:

> Re General. I am refusing to accept their offer (amount of annual
> payment made). The Public Trustee won't agree to my fighting,
> since Counsel's opinion is against it. I saw helpful Mr Banks at
> Drummonds (Bank). He told me in confidence that he asked a
> KC about my case, who said, 'If there is lawsuit, I shall probably
> act for the General, but I think that if I were to act for Mrs H.-
> R. I should win that suit.' Meanwhile, Quintin Hogg, MP, a friend
> of Pat's and mine, is looking through the papers, and I have been
> advised to keep the thing open for a few months.

The Legal & General never paid up; I heard that Bruce Ogilvy, a
cousin of Sandie's, had resigned his directorship in protest. Coming
on top of the War Department's demand for a return of Pat's marriage
allowance for the months he was presumed missing, it left a bad taste.

On 6 June the Normandy landings began. Within a week the first V–1s were making their appearance in the London skies. They flew overhead, then their engines cut out; next came the collapse of a distant or near-by bit of the capital. I continued to sleep at night in my old room, never bothering to go down to the basement. A spirit of fatalism was general by that stage of the war.

One day, soon after D-Day, I was asked to lunch at the Allied HQ at Kingston upon Thames, to meet General Eisenhower, the Supreme Commander of 'Operation Overlord'. Whether I was invited as a blonde rather than a guest of note or promise I never did discover. 'Butch', the rather brash character who drove me down, gave the impression of placing me in the first category. It was a very small party and I was seated beside the Supremo. Twice we had to abandon our cold meats, salad and asparagus, washed down with milky coffee, to troop below as the air-raid sirens sounded.

Eisenhower struck me as humble, open-minded and most endearing as he spoke of his momentous touch-and-go decision to launch 'Overlord', governed by the moon and the short-term weather forecasts. As he talked backwards to the American War of Independence by way of military alliances, he revealed a profound apprehension of the resentments among British troops to his GIs as richer late arrivals. It seemed to be much on his mind. Later I learned that he or Roosevelt had prevailed on Churchill and General Alexander not to exploit recent successes in Italy and drive on to Vienna, even as O'Connor had been halted in the Western Desert. It was the same old story, I supposed: wait for others to pay the price for the first defeats and victories, then take command and rise to glory. But Eisenhower was a good soldier and wise man and I felt proud to have met him.

I decided eventually that the children and May must cross the Irish Sea, and settled on a small house to rent in Porlock. Aunt Etta, the widow of Henry Hodgson, generously footed the bill. There I installed Hope Bruno, unmarried, a friend of Moushill summers, devoted to my mother and the Fletchers. It was Hope's two-seater Morris I had frequently borrowed for pre-war expeditions to Cambridge. One hot summer day in that August of 1944, I left to meet off the Irish ferry the little party, none of whom had ever before quitted Ireland and whose combined ages barely added up to twenty-one. The long, crowded discomfort of a war-time train journey back to Somerset followed, and at the end of it there Hope stood on Minehead station platform, tall and smiling and as excited as if these were her own: Grey atop the luggage trolley and May and Skimper with the white 'V8' perambulator. (It is, today, an exhibit in David and Rosemary Verey's unique country museum at Bibury in Gloucestershire.)

We stayed at Porlock for the rest of that long hot summer. When it ended we moved, to await the Gowries' arrival, to the laundry cottage at Bowood, a fine Adam house at Calne in Wiltshire, belonging to the Fitzmaurice family. Charles, the seventh Marquess of Lansdowne, was killed in action in Italy, only a few days after his brother Ned died in a blazing cornfield in France. Their father died in 1936, but their mother had since remarried, to Lord Colum Crichton-Stuart. When I arrived at Bowood with my party of refugees, I found Lord and Lady Colum, her daughters, Kitty and Elisabeth, and Kitty's three sons. The younger daughter, Elisabeth, was still being educated. The boys were Richard and David, and Andrew, at four a year older than Skimper. They had a nanny of rare understanding with eyes like forget-me-nots. As the lovely autumn afternoons shortened, May and I used to join her in pram-pushing convoys under the golden beeches.

During the mornings, Skimper and I picked up sticks for a bonfire we were making while Grey roamed free. He would enter the long orangery and creep silently into Lady Colum's boudoir, where she wrote her letters. It must have been the first time in his life he came close to beautiful pictures and furniture. Lady Colum's sad and dignified beauty communicated itself to children. If Lady Colum was around, Grey behaved with unusual decorum and would return to the laundry quiet and content – having, I expect, interrupted many letters.

Lord Colum used to bring bunches of grapes to my door – English hot-house grapes, which have no rivals under the sun. He must have been a great comforter to that truncated family, bereft of its sons; he was to me. He had a unique way of speaking with immense deliberation and courtesy. Never once did I feel an intruder. I had seen Charlie in Cairo, so far from Bowood; I had come from the same war. Their sadness was mine; but unlike me they had to pursue the endless wartime duties on the estate and in the county, with all the problems of keeping a great house going. (In an astounding act

193

of aristocratic vandalism, the eighth marquess pulled Bowood down after the war. Only the stables and orangery remain – and the dining room, improbably reconstituted as the boardroom at Lloyd's.)

Vern Leaze, where the Hore-Ruthvens lived, was just outside Calne and not far from the gates of Bowood. Here Ange and Malise had given sanctuary to the evacuees of the Waifs and Strays Society, who were now able to return from whence they came. They therefore offered half the house to us and the Gowries. There were endless deliberations. Bill Stirling, brother of David, offered me a farmhouse on the Keir estate, near Dumfries, and I have often wondered since whether I was mistaken to turn it down: it would have meant the boys growing up in Scotland. I was sad at the idea of leaving Bowood. I would have preferred to stay on there while the Gowries planned their future. I knew I would miss its space and beauty, the lake and the temple – even the sorrow of the family who had given refuge to a complete stranger. I sensed that, if we left, I would never again be able to live such an intimate nursery life with only May and my sons, in such perfect surroundings, in a part of this great country seat of the Fitzmaurices, whose roots were originally nourished in the mountains and bogs of County Kerry.

But I was overruled. Ange and Malise prevailed on me to move to Vern Leaze with May and the two Ruthvens. They felt the Bowood laundry to be unsuitable for visits from Their Excellencies. The former waifs' wing was scrubbed and disinfected and prepared to take us and the incoming Australian party of five – the Gowries, their two 'faithfuls' and a butler (soon to depart), plus an honorary travelling ADC. Sandie's doctors had recommended a return by sea, on account of his tired heart. When the ship was due I travelled to Liverpool by night train to greet them with General 'Lummie' Lumsden, a charmer who had been head of the military mission in Australia. A representative from the Dominions Office, an admiral of senior rank, also came. Unfortunately I mistook the door of his sleeper for mine, and discovered him in his underwear – so much less dignified in men than total nakedness. It put rather a frost on our meeting at breakfast the following morning. If I had invaded Lummie's privacy, he would have made a great joke of it.

Grief, and the stress of war, had aged Themselves. It was no doubt their determination to make us a family that finally influenced my decision to go and live with them; the boys would be a consolation for the loss of Pat. When at length we arrived back at Calne, it was late. Skimper was asleep, but Grey had lain awake, waiting to see these two Beings who had been part of the setting sun at the Lakeside in Killaloe as it made its way to Australia.

It was good and brave of Ange to take in the Gowries: she had loved her evacuee babies, with their wet bottoms and nit-ridden heads. Having nursed heroically in France during the 1914 war, she knew how to look after people. She taught her waifs and strays — many of whom had suffered shock during air-raids — how to relax by turning their limbs into falling leaves. Now she was reduced to keeping hens while Malise continued to run his small farm — definitely a duty towards the war effort and not his true *métier*. Nancy and Sally, their two teenaged daughters, attended St Mary's, Calne, daily; James, their son, was still at home. He had reached the stage small boys sometimes go through when they busy themselves with office work and pin officious notices on doors. His father could not understand why he didn't ride the pony or go bird's-nesting.

Ange was angelic; her sense of humour coped with the transformation of her house from a children's home to a mini-Commonwealth headquarters. Mrs Donald cooked, but Ange ordered the meals, one of which was high tea — anathema to Zara. But Zara always said that Ange Manners was the best intake the family ever made. Their regard for one another overcame all the everyday irritations and necessities of war-time living.

I always enjoyed the visits of Ange's cousin Letty, who lived at Stanway in Gloucestershire and was married to Guy Benson. Her first husband, Lord Elcho, the father of her two eldest sons, was killed in action in 1916. She and Ange and Zara had all been young women during the First World War, when so many lovers and brothers were killed. I sat and listened to them talking; because they had grown up together, and their present lives were restricted by war, their talk was of their youth.

They spoke loyally of their parents; but in other ways seemed closer to my generation, having grown up and married before the slaughter of the trenches. I felt a special tie with Letty, who had been married to Elcho only a few years longer than I to Pat. She had a wonderful sense of colour: the way she decorated Stanway enchanted me. She could never have been as lovely as her sister, Diana Cooper, but hers was a face of great understanding born of sorrow. Ange, who was round and very fair, sat in an arm-chair, always with a vast bundle of mending beside her. She was more intellectual than Zara, very *croyante* and high church. Zara was dark, slim and chic by comparison.

I never heard any of those three speak bitterly of the war, as if it might have been prevented. They were critical, but without envy or unkindness. I thought how unspoiled they were; that even without the six years of war, Zara, Ange and Letty would have reacted against the self-deprecating irony of their late Victorian parents and the almost incestuous flirtations and love affairs that went on in the great houses in between the games of charades and consequences. Women of their generation tended to marry in their late twenties men a few years older; they turned their marriages into working partnerships, even in field sports. During the horrific battles in France, they got nearer to their wounded than any of us were able during the Second World War. As I watched Ange carrying buckets of mash for her hens or sitting behind those formidable piles of mending, it was hard to remember she had been one of Maurice Baring's sweet peas giggling at the lizard's ball.

The nagging ache of Pat's absence as the armistice in the West was declared was eased by the ingathering of Themselves and the start of planning for the future. The house near Bath was to be found; I was to live near by; Zara was to keep pigs and grow violets. Friends were already sending her advice on these activities. Sandie would meanwhile return to his first love, the Turf. He had already been invited to become senior steward of the National Hunt and a steward of the Jockey Club. The Cavalry Club had kept a room for him whenever it was needed. Poverty, as always, was top of the agenda, so some directorships needed to be found for him.

Yet before any house could be found or decision taken, a royal offer came for Sandie to take over the post of Deputy Constable and Lieutenant Governor of Windsor Castle in succession to Lord Wigram and to make the Norman Tower his home for as long as he wished. The friends and relations all approved of this as a marvellous solution. I had my doubts and wondered how Pat would have felt about such a turn of events. It seemed to put me in the position of being unfaithful to Castle Martin: Sheela had offered us Kinneagh, the farmhouse attached to the estate; but my parents had by now returned to London. They had born the brunt of rearing Grey in exile, as well as some quite harsh criticism from friends in England for escaping to neutral Eire, and did not want to lose us now. I suspect that Sandie also harboured reservations of his own: now over seventy, he would be unlikely ever to find his peaceful backwater near Bath. Doubtless, in their discussions, Zara's will prevailed. Sandie would have a soldier servant when his valet, Tom Manion, returned to Australia. (In fact the Welsh Guards, of which he was colonel, would lend him two, a driver and a valet-cum-butler.) Windsor would provide a ready-made home for us all within easy reach of London for Sandie's directorships and the House of Lords, a garden with gardeners, and, above all, the wherewithwal to repay Australia some of the friendship, love and sympathy the viceregal couple had received there. Zara was not yet ready for pigs and violets.

Soon after Sandie's appointment was announced, we were invited to call on Queen Mary at Badminton, where she had spent the duration of the war. May was on holiday, and in her place I had an older English 'temp' who drove me mad with her excitement as we got the Ruthvens ready in sailor suits to meet that most stately and regal of old ladies. The gathering was on the formal side, but Grey's imagination was already leaping ahead to our future life. 'We'll have great jokes together when I come to Windsor Castle,' he declared during a royal lull in the conversation.

Queen Mary made no reply, but later a postcard arrived for Grey at Windsor with a portrait of herself, bejewelled and becrowned, ropes of pearls about her neck, that showed an appreciation of his effort. 'I wonder what jokes he is thinking of,' she commented. So far as I know they never met again.

10

The Norman Tower

The Norman Tower at Windsor Castle was a somewhat rambling dwelling, consisting of one of the twin towers that flanked the old Norman gateway, plus the upper half of its companion, joined on to a Georgian house overlooking the moat – now a garden – that had been built in front of the stairway leading up to William the Conqueror's original Round Tower. During the reign of George IV, Sir Jeffry Wyatville had added crenellations to the towers and adjoining buildings, along with medieval-style arrow slits and stone facings to the Georgian house to make the whole look more castle-like. The actual affect was rather dour – to live in I would much have preferred the old Georgian edifice, which had been painted pink and stuccoed, like the buildings that huddled beneath the castle walls.

One wintry day I set off to begin moving in. The prospects of the first cold nights at Norman Tower were daunting. Austerity still reigned; household wares and furnishings could be bought only with coupons; butter, sugar, cheese and meat were rationed. The royal residences had to set an example, so only a minimum of decoration and improvements could be carried out before we took occupation. A few pieces had been shipped from Australia. Uncle Louis Fleischmann lent valuable objects, as well as sofas and chairs from Chetwode Manor; and I was allowed to choose some items from the royal stores in Windsor's cavernous basements. Foolishly I had sold my few rather pretty pieces collected in Ireland; my only contribution was a four-poster Hepplewhite bed from K.'s house in Prince's Gate that she gave me, and a vast dinner service of old Masonware, some of which survived ten years at the hands of successive Welsh guardsmen. My bedroom was in the outermost tower, overlooking the river. The Hepplewhite four-poster took up most of the space. This round room had a fabulous view, however, and the bed made a seaworthy ship for my sons' piratical period as Captain John Saar and hs mate Billy Bones.

Lady Wigram, the wife of Sandie's predecessor, who had been private secretary to George V, told me there was no better place than Windsor Castle to bring up boys, but Lady Morshead, the musician wife of Sir Owen, the King's Librarian, warned me I would have to choose between the world of the court and my children. While her husband browsed over the treasures under his care, Paquita kept goats in the large garden of their red-brick house, and reared hens and rabbits to feed her family. Among his other scholarly accomplishments, Sir Owen managed to log every train journey ever made by Queen Victoria. 'O Lord Our Governor,' he wrote to Sandie on his birthday. 'How excellent is thy name in all the world.'

On Dean Randall Davidson's appointment to Windsor in 1883, Queen Victoria wrote that Windsor was 'a place of rather a gossiping nature, requiring tact and judgement'. Our Dean, Bishop Hamilton, and his wife Jessica, was also newly appointed. As with the Gowries, Windsor was their only home. The Dean was very handsome and ascetic-looking; his wife had a soft, low voice and, I imagine, an infinite capacity for the 'tact and judgement' required by women espoused to the Cloth. Canon Arthur Crawley, a charming elderly priest of the Lower Ward, the father of a distinguished family, had failing eyesight at the age of seventy-eight; yet the senior canon, Anthony Deane, six years more aged still, forbade the lectern to be lit when Canon Crawley read the lesson. No wonder the King once told the Gowries that he found it difficult to pray in St George's Chapel. Instead, Sunday morning prayers were often held privately in the royal apartments.

When the King was absent from Sunday morning services, Sandie usually occupied his pew, leading the procession of Military Knights with their dark-blue and scarlet tunics and cocked hats into the choir. Formerly there had been Naval as well as Military Knights at Windsor, but the brawling between them spread into the chapel itself. The Governor of Military Knights, from 1932, was General Sir Charles McMurrough Kavanagh, himself now over eighty. His was the tallest in the row of grace and favour residences facing St George's Chapel.

His wife was Irish, from County Tipperary, a splendid, tall and very talkative lady who could be relied on to lighten any occasion. She had rather a Wellingtonian profile and always wore a little floating chiffon scarf around her long neck. In later years, whenever we saw Errigal Mountain in Donegal with a cloud floating around its pointed summit, we would nod at each other, 'Lady McMurrough Kavanagh has come.' One day, shortly after our arrival, Lady Kavanagh had occasion to ask Grey why he did not stand up when the National Anthem was played. 'Because my flag is the green and the gold,' he declared. Grey Fitzpatrick had crossed the Irish Sea to be with us. Skimper, meanwhile, regularly needed to be retrieved from within one or other of the sentry boxes dotted around the castle. The unfortunate young soldiers on duty had no standing orders on how to deal with such intruders.

Once the Gowries were settled into the Norman Tower, Their Majesties came to call. Grey was on the stairs as they were stepping up to the drawing room. Taking a long look at the King, he asked, 'Is your crown very heavy?'

'Sometimes,' answered the King.

As Lady Elizabeth Bowes-Lyon, the Queen had been a friend of Betty Somerset, Sandie's niece. They had grown up together, and 'come out' together, and we thought that it was perhaps as a result of her personal influence that Sandie got the 'double jump' to an earldom when he left Australia. He looked upon this as wiping out the 'sentence and Doom pronounced by the Lords and Estates of Parliament for High Treason against Alexander and Harry Ruthven' in November 1600 after the so-called Gowrie Conspiracy. There followed much correspondence with Lord Lyon, especially as to what I should call myself as a viscountess, since Sandie's brother, Gerry Ruthven, already had a daughter who inherited the Scottish title in the female line. Gerry's wife, Aunt Sis, complained that there might one day be no less than four Lady Ruthvens.

In the tower below ours, the Henry VII Tower, over the entrance to the Lower Ward, lived Sir Alan and Lady Lascelles. Tommy Lascelles, as he was universally known, had succeeded Lord Hardinge as the King's private secretary, and was popular and astute. His wife Joan was a kind person who helped me in my confusion with the castle minions and general pecking order. One of their two daughters,

Caroline, studied the violin: arpeggios and double stopping used to float to us out of the high, narrow windows of their tower.

Among the curates and others in the Lower Ward was Mrs Ford, the widow of a bishop, and the tall, outgoing, outspoken mother of three sons: Neville, in the Household Cavalry, who had come through the war in northern Europe; Arthur, in the Royal Navy, who had joined the Church; and Edward, former tutor to the young King Farouk of Egypt, who was now assistant private secretary to His Majesty under Tommy Lascelles. Edward, often at Windsor, became another true friend. He would toil up the winding stair to the boys' nursery at the summit of our round tower to read to them at bedtime.

One day Joan Lascelles introduced me to a small boy walking with his nurse beside a baby sitting up in a pram in the Lower Ward, saying she hoped we'd all make friends. She explained that his parents had just come to live at Adelaide Cottage – a fanciful miniature Gothic villa with diamond-laticed windows, built as a summer-house for Queen Adelaide, that stood in the Home Park below the castle in a garden of trellises and lawns. The children's father, recently appointed equerry to the King, was a Battle of Britain hero called Peter Townsend.

After the war the King and Queen – having shared the suffering, despair and rejoicing of the Battle of Britain, clambered indefatigably over the rubble of British cities, comforted the injured and dying – chose to have around them at court young men who had seen active service. Peter Townsend, Oliver Dawnay and George 'Toby' Martin represented the three services of air, land and sea respectively. Peter had won DSO and DFC, having served throughout the war with Fighter Command.

Peter was idealistic, very good-looking and sensitive; but he lacked the kind of humour I had been used to from Pat and his friends. He had a feeling for country life, however. Sometimes we used to exercise the Princesses' horses together in the Great Park. He was deeply conscientious and serious about his job. At one stage he called to consult Himself about his future. Sandie's advice was that in due course he should emigrate and take the chances then going for young ex-servicemen. It was advice he turned down, saying that his wife Rosemary would never adapt to life in the new world.

Rosie Townsend, popular, attractive and lively, was much in

demand at parties during those years, when everyone was determined to forget the war and enjoy themselves. There was plenty of racing and polo close to Windsor; you could reach the Four Hundred or just about any other London nightclub within the half-hour at night time. I also came to find myself quite in demand as duenna or chaperone at dances, and remember my humiliation at one London ball when one of my débutantes, dressed in a checked cotton crinoline dress, escaped, withdrew the wires from under her skirt and was spotted in a nightclub with a Pole. I believe that the parents of that generation of young – including the royals – wanted their children to enjoy themselves in the way they had been able to after the First World War; they often spoiled them. Some of this seeking for pleasure and fun rubbed off on us who were older.

Since the Townsends and I had two small sons of about the same ages in common, I came to know them best within the Windsor environs. As soon as he was old enough to ride his first bicycle, Skimper would frequently visit Rosie and her boys at around lunchtime. Because Mrs Donald retained most of the ration cards for the Sunday lunch and tea parties Zara insisted on holding at the Norman Tower, the nursery fare at home was somewhat spartan. 'You are such a motherly mother,' Skimper once confided in Rosie as she tidied up a grazed limb. 'My mother isn't really a motherly mother.'

Yet the wives of courtiers often came to resent the refined living their husbands enjoyed and the hours they spent away from the necessarily restricted post-war home. At the Norman Tower we began to see the Townsends less and less together, with Peter often in London. As her boys started school, so Rosie took up painting. She had talent and worked hard, and eventually acquired her own studio and held exhibitions, with landscapes as well as portraits.

Most of the charm of the Norman Tower lay in the garden, which formed a half-moon in what had once been the moat of Duke William's original Round Tower. A single bank flanked by pathways and rockeries fell steeply to the bottom of the old moat, now planted with shrubs and herbacious borders and well-tended lawns, with a magnificent walnut planted during the reign of Charles II. At the very end of the garden was a curious summer house, inscribed with mottoes and verse. A path leading up to the top of the bank directly beneath the Round Tower hid behind a rosemary hedge. It led to King James's Bower, a seat in a pergola of roses and honeysuckle –

the only place where one could relax unseen by the crowds, who could otherwise gawp directly into the garden over the parapet wall.

Zara, who had made a substantial contribution to the private and public gardens of Australia, took up the refurbishing of the half-moon garden with great enthusiasm. She inherited an elderly gardener, Harbord, who only acquired an assistant when the steep banks below the fortress needed scything at the close of the daffodil season. Eddy Lloyd, who had charge of the Home Park, became a friend and devotee of Zara's up to the day she died, but her affection for him tempered any admiration she might have had for Eric Saville, the deputy ranger, who lived with his mother in a charming house near the entrance to the Great Park among ancient oaks, already fully grown in the days of Shakespeare and Herne the Hunter. Zara thought that Saville was cruel to his underling, a bachelor like himself, who was never given tenure, but worked on a temporary basis, at Saville's will. Saville created great dells of azaleas and rhododendrons with water gardens of primulas and irises under the tall beeches near Virginia Water. Perhaps the deputy ranger was stingy with funds for the Home Park and the Norman Tower, preferring to channel them into the gardens that came to bear his name. Whatever the reason, Saville never made it into the special place Zara reserved in her heart for gardeners.

There was an encounter with him one afternoon, as she and I were walking around the walled garden near the Royal Lodge. True to form, Zara was taking cuttings from various shrubs; all at once the tweedy knickerbockered figure of HM's deputy ranger appeared around a corner. Zara, unabashed, held out her ill-gotten bouquet under his nose and challenged him to confiscate it in her charming, soft voice, which never cracked with age. Nonplussed, the deputy ranger capitulated. In the Moat Garden itself, Zara always had her way. New Dawn and Albertine roses were wired to romp over the severe granite walls and enliven the austere circular paths and lawns; flowering shrubs and trees were planted. In summertime, the crowds began to gaze in admiration over the encircling wall.

Sunday lunches, regardless of rationing and staff shortages, but augmented by a continuous series of gifts of wine and victuals from Australia, became an essential feature of the Gowrie reign at the Norman Tower. At the top of the worn steps, the heavy front door stood open to welcome visitors, among them world leaders the

Gowries had known in wartime Australia. At the round table in the bay window overlooking the garden, Mrs Donald's superb fare was served up to Australian prime ministers, American generals and Zara's special favourites, including Ruth Draper (who came to stay), Malcolm Sargent (a regular) and Joan Hammond. These, and a host of other celebrities (Mrs Eleanor Roosevelt among them), intermingled with visiting relations from Ireland and Scotland.

Along with the kindly minions we inherited at the castle – the minister of works, who took care of the fabric of the old buildings, the gentle upholsterer, Mr Lucking – was 'the Burg': Miss Margaret Burgogne, the Lieutenant-Governor's private secretary. She arrived each morning to serve Sandie in the prison room, which straddled the archway leading to the library and the private apartments. Despite its gruesome history, the prison room was his *carenza*, where he worked behind a huge desk made for him by Australian ex-servicemen, held any tricky interviews and dictated to the Burg. He pronounced her very good.

Zara, a great delegator, soon had the Burg behind a teapot on a Sunday; then she started staying to lunch, and was to be seen nipping behind the leather screen in front of the pantry for second helpings. She was the daughter of a housemaid in the royal household, her youth spent educating herself for higher rank. 'And I never went dancing!' she would wail. She dressed with taste. Only her accent betrayed her 'below stairs' upbringing. 'I *don't* talk like that!' she shouted at the boys when she overheard them speaking Burg language. She entered into the Gowrie's Windsor life with relish and devotion. It still shone from her face when Zara and I last visited her in a home before she died.

Among relations who came often to the Norman Tower was Sandie's niece, Bettine 'Bets' Somerset, though she did not much like the tower itself, finding it oppressive. Her over-sensitive spirit sensed all the cruelties and injustices, imprisonment and torture that must have taken place within its walls. Bets was the nearest Gowries came to having a daughter. Her mother, Beatrix, known as 'Trix', had been, according to the family, 'too pretty for her own good'. She had married C. J. Orr Ewing, but then ran off with C. E. Malcolm, nicknamed 'the Mole'. When Sandie was nineteen, at the start of the 1890s, he was sent to Europe to retrieve his errant sister and restore her to her husband and children. He only succeeded in running out of money and having to touch the Mole for the fare home. Trix in due course married the Mole – reputedly an exquisite dresser and a member of White's – and had three children by him: Honor, Bettine and Billy.

Trix's last exploit was to fall in love with Tommy Sopwith, the aeroplane entrepreneur, and something of a national hero, with whom my Uncle Arthur Hodgson once worked. Although her new flame was twenty years her junior, she duly became the Hon. Mrs Sopwith, but took only her son Billy to live with her in her new home. Bets instead grew up in Scotland with her beloved grandfather Rivvie Ruthven, until Sandie returned from Gallipoli with a leg wound, when she made her home with the Gowries. I never knew Trix, but after I married I often came across elderly gentlemen who, on hearing my name, would pause with a remembering look and a sigh. One even pulled a faded photograph from his wallet to show me. It seems that she too was not a very motherly mother.

Pat kept a little photograph of Bets always when he was in the desert, but it was never returned with his effects, so I expect it was tucked into one of his pockets on that last raid. Bets's own son, Johnnie, was killed right at the end of the war. I imagine the celebrations of peace were even more hollow for her than they were for us.

Bets and her daughter Annabel usually stayed with us during Royal Ascot week, when I would ride with Sandie in the last carriage of the royal procession before losing him to the Jockey Club box. One year Anne was recovering from polio, contracted while staying with the Buccleuchs at Drumalrig – an event which caused great consternation within the royal family, Princess Margaret also having been among the guests. Another year she brought her escort William Douglas-Home, playwright brother of Alec, the future prime minister. He stayed at the Norman Tower in one of the little bachelor rooms – the very room destined to be converted into a bathroom for the exclusive use of a later visitor, General Omar Bradley. I reported to the castle that William was with our party, and could he come with us to the Ascot ball? Everyone would be delighted to see him, I was told, the Princesses especially.

William had been a reluctant warrior, hoping to stand for Parliament before his call-up papers arrived. Too intellectually honest to become a conscientious objector, he was eventually obliged to enlist and accompanied his regiment to France in 1944. In September he was ordered to attack Le Havre when it was still full of civilians, the Allies having rejected the German commander's offer to evacuate them. William refused to carry out the order, and his colonel denied him permission to resign his commission. He was placed under arrest, court-martialled, cashiered and sentenced to a year's imprisonment with hard labour. He received a good deal of hostile publicity in the press, but was a hero to those of us who shared his doubts about Churchill's policy of unconditional surrender. Many who had been in the Western Desert, where armies fought without involving civilians, sympathized with William's views about Churchill's famous exhortations: 'Medieval stuff with one of two thinly disguised falsehoods about equipment.'

As our party arrived at the ballroom, where the dancing had begun, it was as if a black cloud descended. The Master of the Household, Sir Piers ('Joey') Legh, took me aside and berated me for having brought William along. He absolutely refused to accept that I had consulted Sandie and the Princesses, or that Princess Margaret particularly had said she would be delighted. Joey's American wife, Sarah, the daughter of a Tennessee judge, who outshone all the other ladies with her Paris clothes and costume jewellery, was more incensed than anyone. Poor William retreated across the quadrangle, his visage blackened by rage or humiliation, I knew not which. The evening turned completely sour. Despite the encouragement of youthful pleasures, a residual British stuffiness had survived the war.

The incident was long forgotten by the time, years later, that we met at a luncheon at Dorneywood, when William's brother Alec was in residence there as Foreign Secretary. Bob Menzies and his wife were over from Australia for a Commonwealth Conference, and Bob and William stopped the conversation with their wisecracks, egged on by Zara. The double-act was upstaged, however, when Alec asked Bob, 'Why don't you pronounce your name properly, Mr Mingyz?'

'I'll look into it when I get Hume,' said Bob.

Overseas royalty and potentates sometimes called at the tower as part of a visit to Their Majesties. One evening the Shah of Persia came, and after his reception by the Gowries, Caroline Lascelles and I were detailed to take him to dine and dance beside the Thames at Skindles along with a company of his uniformed officers. It wasn't exactly a festive occasion – we hardly fitted the role of good-time girls. But the Shah was easy to talk to and he had a certain charm and good looks. He told me that some men were destined never to be happy, and he was one of their number. When he danced, he held one so tightly it was impossible to move to the music. I asked him why his uniformed escort did not dance. 'Dance!' ordered the Shah of Shahs, and instantly they sprang to their feet and marched whichever of us came to hand about the floor.

One summer's afternoon I was invited to tea at Royal Lodge in Windsor Great Park. The King and Queen preferred to spend time there, at a slight distance from Windsor with its bickering underlings and tiresome protocol. I drove myself alone through the white gates by the Ranger's Lodge into the park, and found them sitting at a small table on the lawn. We were quite alone. None knew better than the Queen how to put people at their ease. Tea arrived, and with it the silver kettle of hot water on its tip-up burner. A plate of delicious-looking fluffy cream buns made me wary. The King tackled his impetuously, precipitating a royal explosion of bun and language. Then he explained how they hoped the young King Feisal of Iraq would come to Eton, rather than follow other members of the Hashemite family to Harrow. They thought this would make it easier to get to know him; he would be able to come up to the castle and, more frequently, to the Norman Tower. They seemed very well informed, far better so than many of the people in government ministries Freya and I had visited.

Pat's first commanding officer, Callum Renton, Grey's godfather, was a clever and enlightened man, nicknamed 'Wingy', having lost an arm in the First World War while still in his teens. He had retired as a major-general, having carried out a brilliant saving action at Alamein, for which he was duly sacked by Monty, and then succeeded the polo-playing General Bromilow as head of the British Military Mission in Baghdad. He lived in a large Victorian house in Sussex, where he would have the young Iraqi king and the Regent to stay. Callum was undoubtedly a snob. The walls of his loo at Billingshurst were covered with fading sepia photographs of royalty. As a confirmed bachelor and Old Etonian, he may have played some role in the plan to divert Feisal from Harrow to Eton. It went so far as Feisal coming to the castle and lunching with us at the Norman Tower.

Sir Owen Morshead took him to the library and was much impressed by his appreciation of the miniatures.

But the royal hopes faded. The then headmaster of Eton, Claude Elliott, turned King Feisal down, refusing to countenance any pupil doing Arabic instead of Latin. Perhaps it was an excuse not to have on his hands the worry of a king who had already been deposed once; we never knew. When I asked Elliott's successor, Robert Birley, some years later, what he would have done, he said he would most certainly have taken the young Iraqi monarch. In the event, Feisal went to Harrow, his mother renting a house near by.

I suspect that Claude Elliott's rejection of Feisal was an aspect of an on-going rift between Eton and the castle which the King hoped the Gowries might help to mend. This they assuredly did, entertaining not only the headmasters and provosts, but numerous 'beaks' and dozens of boys – sons of friends and relations, and friends of their friends – to lunches and teas. Sunday tea at the Norman Tower ended with a mad scramble down the Hundred Steps and along the High Street as the bells tolled for Evensong.

Like the celebrity Sunday lunches, it was all made possible by the workings below in the vast kitchen, where the redoubtable Mrs Donald continued to perform wonders with rations and an assortment of kitchenmaids recruited from Ireland. One of these had to be returned to County Limerick for wearing trousers. Others fell in love with the two soldier servants lent to Sandie by the Welsh Guards, who washed up, cleaned the silver and grumbled endlessly about the 'bloody Eton boys'. Skimper, like his father before him, became the life and soul of 'the room' – the staff hall, as we had now learned to call it – showing off his new pyjamas or insisting that everyone kiss his tummy good night. Once he was heard outside the door of the cloakroom, shouting, 'Can you manage?' to the Lord Mayor of Sydney, having only lately learned to manage his trousers himself. When Grey first discovered the 'Ode to a Skylark', it was to Mrs Donald that he descended, enraptured, for an audience.

Despite the fact that Windsor Castle, standing just above the silvery meanderings of the Thames, made such an easy target from the air, the Princesses had more or less continued to live there throughout the war. This gave rise to the institution, one morning each week, of Miss Vacani's dancing class for them and other young ladies of Windsor. The time arrived for Grey and Skimper to begin acquiring social graces. The turn of the under-tens came when Miss Vacani's older pupils had finished; they were allowed one dance with the seniors. Each week my sons rushed on to the floor, vieing to capture a princess to tread on her toes and whirl her around for a brief span.

Those years were hard on Sandie. It was true he had a lovely grace and favour house, but he was obliged to collect a whole raft of directorships to maintain it. Three days a week he was driven to London by one of the soldier servants. He attended board meetings and lunches, which he did not enjoy; since being wounded in Gallipoli, he had drunk nothing other than an occasional glass of port. Most of those London afternoons he went on to the House of Lords, where he sat on the cross-benches. He thought it wrong for anyone who had served as the King's representative to return to take sides with government or opposition. Afterwards he would often wait for Zara to pick him up at my mother's flat in Cadogan Gardens. He admired her brother Walter Hodgson as a horseman, as 'the perfect image of a cavalry officer'. I find the relations of men who have served in the forces and war together touching and enviable.

His relaxation continued to be going to race meetings at Windsor and other near-by courses, in the cause of which we braved the winter fogs of the Thames Valley. At the National Hunt meetings he and his old friend Freddie Withington would be up in the Stewards' Box, binoculars trained on the race, two amateur riders of former days, ever ready hotly to defend the jockeys in any argument with less experienced judges.

Perhaps 'pigs and violets', with a comfortable home outside Bath, might have granted Sandie a less stressful old age. He would be eighty by the time he left the Norman Tower in 1952, with a mind already beginning to wander. His duties at Windsor were not arduous, but they were often tiresome. Such little quarrels and feuds broke out as those concerning the Military Knights' dogs in the Home Park, or the privacy arrangements for the royal family during their rare residences. Lord Athlone, the Governor of Windsor Castle, took little or no part in these responsibilities, leaving all the official engagements, like inspecting the Boy Scouts or parading at the head of the Garter ceremony, to Sandie. It was not easy on an old man who had no ADCs and no son to help him.

11

The Wander Year

As the boys grew out of the nursery, I decided that if they were to learn foreign languages they ought to hear them spoken. It was possible to obtain a travel allowance in foreign currency provided a doctor's certificate was produced. Windsor and the Thames Valley being famous for stuffy noses, there was no difficulty here. So early one morning in 1947, in the midst of a spring snowstorm, we set off with May in my white Bedford van to stay eventually with Freya at Asolo. Sandie insisted on my taking Tom Steely, one of his Welsh Guards batmen, to see us safely across the Channel and on to the Continent.

Calais was still in shambles. No cafés or restaurants were open, and we waited at the docks for hours in the bitter cold for Tom and the van, which had to travel by another boat. Grey was seven, Skimper four: the most unwarlike of children, they strode up and down the dockside setting mantraps.

The night before Tom Steely returned to England I had night-mares, fulfilled when we reached the Julia Pass over the Alps, where the car became stuck in the snow. A young Swiss baker offered to drive the van up and over the dangerous summit. May and Grey tramped behind, while I carried Skimper piggyback behind the skidding Bedford. That night we reached Flims Waldhause, a tiny village in the Engadine, near Schuls Terasp, where I had spent that sad October with K. and Moggie after Tim was killed. There was a school near by for Grey: the Institute Briner, recommended by Dr Reuger of the International Red Cross.

Our little pension was really a farmhouse built above the barns in

Granny Hodgson with her family, *c.* 1905 (see page 354 for key to identities)

Granny Hodgson in a pony carriage at Bolney

Giant: hunting with the Crawley
and Horsham

The Reverend: the Rev. A.H.
Fletcher

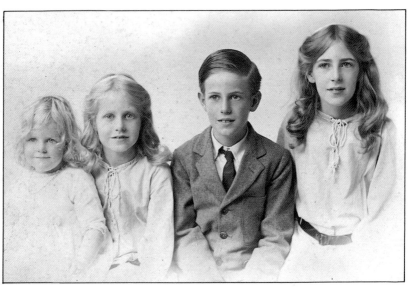

My family: (*left to right*) Romola, myself, Michael and Diana

Godmother 'K': Kathleen Rees–Mogg (portrait reproduced by permission of the Hon. G.R. Wills)

K.'s son, Tim Doughty, at Clifford stables

Myself at Petra

Zara with Pat

Pat: cartoon by his friend Taffy
Nicholls

Myself in my
wedding dress, 1939

Pat in India with Nahoo, Sandie, Zara and
Miss Stacey

Pat in Jerusalem, 1941, drawn
by Leo Arthur Robitshek

Myself with Greysteil at his
christening

Anthony Eden on his mission to Cairo in 1941 to prepare
the way for the ill-fated Greek campaign. Directly behind
him (*right to left*) stand Wavell, Longmore, Cunningham
and Lampson, with Dill (*extreme left*)

Myself riding at Gezira racecourse

Pat in desert order

Pat's grave at Misurata

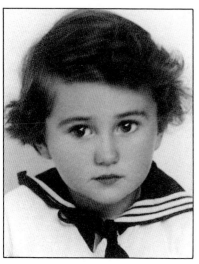

The photograph of Grey first walking, sent by Giant to Cairo from Ireland

Grey, aged two

Grey and Skimper with a wheelbarrow in the garden at Casa Freia, Asolo, 1947

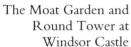

The Moat Garden and
Round Tower at
Windsor Castle

Sandie with his grandsons at Windsor: Grey
on his left and Skimper on his right

A 'New Look' dress for a garden party, designed for me,
in shot silk, by 'Harald'

Bobby Somerset on his yacht

Bets Somerset in her portrait by
de Laszlo

Moushill: the Giant
in her garden

Castle Martin: the
Irish home of the
Blackers (photograph
by Ianthe Ruthven)

The home at the head of the
glen: Dunlewy

Derek and Doherty at Dunlewy

Skimper: portrait by Derek Hill

Grey with his son Brer on his shoulders

Skimper's daughters: Chloë and
Orlanda Ruthven

Myself (drawing by my granddaughter, Chloë Ruthven)

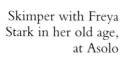

Skimper with Freya Stark in her old age, at Asolo

Derek with Mary Hawkins in
her kitchen at Andau

With Derek and the Land-
Rover, *en route* for the
Hungarian border, 1956

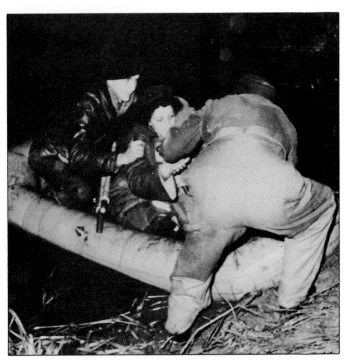

Alex France (*left*) and Einar Roos help refugees out of a
dinghy at Andau (Associated Press photograph)

Sacher's Hotel, Vienna; the champagne party to celebrate the return
of our captured aid workers: (*left to right*) Paul Metternich, myself,
Evan Carl Eltz, Tatiana Metternich, Dick Rorabach, Derek,
unknown lady and Paul Heber

Tony Dulverton's Piper Comanche on desert duty in Jordan in 1960;
Tony unleads the plane behind Mary Hawkins, myself and members
of the Jordanian desert patrol

Facing the century: the child of the rectory and (*below*) a small refugee like my water-carrier in Beirut, 1982 (UNRWA photograph by Munir Nasr)

which the cows, goats and fowl lived. Each morning Grey set off through the snow to the school, while I lay in bed until the stove in my room was lit with wood chips, followed by rolls and hot coffee. It was Lent and there were *Fasching* parties in the school and village, the children, in fancy garments, with painted faces and masks, being licensed to go wild and make as much noise as they liked. We stayed with the peasant family until the snows began to melt. Then I hired a local driver to take us as far as the Italian border. From there we next drove on to Merano, a town that had been established as a hospital and convalescent centre for the Italian army, especially for TB cases. I therefore opted to stay at Hotel Savoy, owned by a Swiss friend I had made in Schuls. From the hotel I wrote to Zara:

> Well, here we are safe and sound. The journey out of Switzerland was history. The Bedford cleared the Offen Pass in great style in a snowstorm. Skimper was sick, but at his greenest was asking the name of each mountain range. Grey sat in the back and read Dryden and Keats to May all the way to the Italian frontier. I don't think he looked out of the window once. We hired a charming young Swiss to take us that far, but it was a great moment when we set off on our own to the actual frontier. The Italian officials were kind and courteous and never opened a thing, and seemed pleased to see us. Everyone in the villages looks so much poorer than in Switzerland, and ragged, but far gayer . . .
>
> The fruit trees are in blossom, the vines just budding, the Dolomiti still snow-capped. The Adige runs noisily over its pebble bed below the hotel, and gives us nice little trout for dinner. A long walk, the length of the river right up to where the mountains meet the town, goes past the promenade and the Casino; all the way stand great trees with stout old trunks, which all the children, including ours, hide behind (only no one else rushes out with the ferocity of Skimper). We live in this Claridge's, which Grey aptly calls the Savoy Hotel, for six bob a day. I am called *Excellenza*, there is always a waiter or a concierge for the children to play with, since there are far more staff than guests. The hotel has only just opened, having been closed all through the war, being neutral property. There seem to be no actual shortages, but without rationing the cost of living is far too high for the poor. We get nearly 2,000 lira for our pound, so my Swiss francs go a long way.

Everything was in short supply in post-war Italy: the Marshall Plan would not be passed by the US Congress till 1948. Long afterwards one of the children told me how they used to tear off toilet paper from their private bathroom and give or sell it outside; but neither will now confess to remembering this act of mercy and profit

Our stay at Merano was a lovely restorative interval in my life. I sat by myself at a window table in the dining room, while the long-suffering May presided at another, her charges learning Continental manners and a taste for *haute cuisine* they never lost. There was a cable car to carry us to the pine forests high above the plane and chestnut trees. After the deep, plodding snow of Switzerland, the boys were able to run free. We discovered pools made black by mating frogs, and came across tortured German crucifixes in wayside shrines. 'It's not a bit like Him,' I heard Skimper arguing.

In Merano, the old Austrian spa of Meran, the shops crouched under arched passageways and the people still preferred to speak German and to dress in lederhosen. They had lost none of their national identity, despite our efforts to turn them into Italians, as a reward to Italy for having joined the Allies in the First World War. They were resentful of Italian rule, rightly fearing that the post-war government would maintain Mussolini's policy of flooding their town and neighbouring Bolzano with workers from the Mezzogiorno to work the new factories already springing up in the valleys. In Merano today only the riverside walk and a few small corners remain of the past. The town has been opened to automobiles and their cargoes of tourists. The post-war apprehensions of the South Tyroleans are manifest everywhere: hideous new haphazard buildings and factories, and, in neighbouring Bolzano, numerous swarthy operators from the south.

As we finally made our way to Asolo and Freya we drove light-heartedly along the erratic unfrequented ways, skirting the Dolomites, following river beds where the women still gathered for laundry and gossip, where villages roofed with rough slate tiles remained inaccessible and prosperity had not yet laid its ugly paint-brush on mountains and plain. We found the Casa Freia in a state of reorganization. Its rooms were being renovated to accommodate, not just Freya's literary contacts and admirers, but the company of friends and associates she had made during the war in the Middle East and then in India with the Wavells.

The silk factory, started by Flora, her mother, where the girls of Asolo wove silks on wooden hand-looms, had been revived with financial help from Mrs Beach, an American who sheltered Flora Stark in her Californian exile until her death in 1942. The looms in the *tessoria* clattered incessantly, weaving the raw silk fabrics from which Freya had her curtains and upholstery fashioned, or providing the materials out of which her dressmakers made copies of the exotic Eastern dresses she had brought back from her travels in the Hadhramaut valley in southern Arabia. Elsewhere in the town, craftsmen and antique dealers reopened their shops, to be patronized by Freya and her clientele of wealthy foreign friends.

That spring and early summer would shape our lives. We had escaped an England snowbound for almost twelve weeks following the first blizzards in January; and which was still in the toils of post-war austerity, with fuel shortages and frequent power cuts. We had arrived, by contrast, in a little Renaissance hill-town beneath the empty Romanesque shell of its *rocca*: two ragged walls descending the abrupt hillside to encircle the town's steep, twisting and collonna-ded streets that converged upon a wide and sunny piazza of chestnut trees. We stayed in the house called La Mura, formerly lived in by Mrs Bronson, friend of Henry James and dedicatee of Robert Brown-ing's last published work, *Asolando*. The greatest of Italian actresses, Eleanora Duse, had also briefly stayed there, soon after the First World War, when her health was deteriorating, before buying a permanent home on the other side of town. 'The scant strength at my command,' she lamented, 'makes it a great effort to *climb* and *descend* the stairs between the third floor and the ground floor, where there is situated that requirement of our physical health – the Water Closet.'

La Mura and Casa Freia stood opposite one another on either side of the town's southern gate. Our sitting room, more like a conserva-tory, with one whole wall consisting of window, hung above a steep, sloping field of grass and vines dotted with haycocks. A friend of Freya's faithful maid Emma prepared delicious meals over a petrol stove, for having spent most of the war in the comparative luxury of Egypt and Ireland, I had still not yet learned to cook. Large dishes of meat or fowl surrounded by a variety of beautifully cooked vege-tables seemed miraculous, with everything done on the single ring. Grey was accepted as a pupil at the Instituto Phillipino for boys, a short way up the hill. He trotted there alone each morning and was thoroughly indulged.

The boys played in Freya's garden, as she and her sister had done at the turn of the century. We found it just as Freya described it in the preface to her mother's *Asolo Diary*: 'The garden was quite small, but it had all that a garden needs, a pleached alley of hornbeams over-arching, a statue of Bacchus under dark laurel boughs and masses of irises that seemed to focus the colours of the plain and of the far Eugenean hills. The wall of the house was heavily clustered with a rose called Fortune's Yellow.' Freya had added some lilies and a pergola of roses down the street side of the garden, used as marriage beds by a most noxious bug. The Ruthvens played their games, regardless of who took tea or drinks under the great ilex tree – Steven Runciman was incorporated as the witchman; Stewart Perowne was a library of myths and ancient tales.

Skimper celebrated his fifth birthday at Casa Freia – a very Oriental affair, just the four of us and May. Freya donned her finest Hadhramaut robe, and we sat on cushions, burning incense sticks, consuming a cake Emma had made. One present was a rather dog-eared copy of Gelett Burgess's *Lively City O'Legg*, a favourite of the Stark girls long before. Soon afterwards Lord Iveagh, meeting Skimper in the garden with a stern, absorbed face, a bundle of paper under one arm, asked him what he was up to. 'Writing books, of course,' said Malise. 'We all write books here.'

I took the boys to a Venice still uninvaded by tourists. They carried their bags of corn for the pigeons to the roof of the Duomo and made libations to the bronze horses. I bought a painted white chest in poor condition, but with lovely gilded scrolls, for the equivalent of 15s. (75p) in the sad debased Italian currency, and we carried it off in a gondola.

Later Freya and I stayed together on the Grand Canal in a tiny pallazzo painted inside in gentle pigeon colours. She was still on the job, working for the Allied Military Government. We visited Palladio's Villa La Malcontenta near Mestre, which Bertie Lansberg, an American of rare taste and knowledge, had bought, undaunted by the deplorable state in which the Russian soldiers left it. He did not have much money to do it up with, but plenty of knowledge and patience: nothing utilitarian or ugly intruded. We often sat outside in the cool of the evening, dining with him and his wife under a huge tree. One day he took me on an extraordinary jaunt up the Brenta Canal: we pried and peered in and out of the kitchens and bedrooms of the fine old villas, looking for traces of murals. Bertie was a great raconteur. He had been a sailor in the US Navy and loved to shock us with bawdy tales. The boys would straddle his rotund stomach. 'But were you born in Great Britain?' they asked.

By the time we were headed for home, the late cold spring had given way to a very hot summer. We spent some days at the Villa Taranto, at Pallanza on Lago Maggiore, where Zara's friend Neil McEarchen had created one of the finest gardens in Italy. Neil had been in Australia, where he inherited a shipping fortune and married Imma, a German neice of Princess Alice, in order to save her from internment – or that, at least, was how he explained it to me. He brought her once to the Norman Tower – a tall, strange, rather attractive woman; but suddenly she died. The family of Sardinians who took care of the villa throughout the war, headed by Tonino, Neil's secretary, were now running the villa and Neil's life.

The garden was still in the charge of Mr Cocker from Kew, and Neil had an English chauffeur, who once a year drove the Rolls back to England, where it was registered. I was assailed by tales of Sardinian chicanery from these two British guardians of Neil's, who suspected rightly that they were fighting a losing campaign against the Sardinian faction. Toni, who must somehow have evaded military service to protect the estate, had married plump Maria from Sardinia. She was kept out of sight. The pearls around her neck were said to have been Imma's. More and more jobs were found for members of her family above and below stairs.

Some days we drove across the border into Switzerland, where we lunched and Neil collected money. A motor-boat took us to the islands; I had never before seen the exquisite little palaces on Isola Bella, which belong to fairy tale rather than reality, making our British stately homes seem clumsy and dowdy. In the evenings, Neil and I ate alone, waited on by two young footmen in scarlet livery – the nursery party having supped earlier, also waited on by the footmen. After dinner he and I sat together over his excellent wine and liqueurs, following a meal too rich for either of us, while he told me about his short life with Imma, his deep affection for the Gowries, his flirtation with the idea of accepting a papal title as a *quid pro quo* for giving the glorious garden around us to the Italian nation. In the end the ghost of a Scottish forebear must have vetoed this idea.

Summer is a time of great storms over the Italian lakes. The clouds, dense and grey, hung above the villa without movement before the thunder came crashing like gods at war, signalling the downpour to follow. All the luxury and intrigues surrounding the elderly million-aire with his overloaded table depressed me: I can only hope our long têtes-à-tête of an evening gave him pleasure.

I stayed two or three times with Neil, Pallanza being close to the frontier and easily accessible from winter holidays in Switzerland. In 1949, there was a semi-official house party, including the Caris-brookes and a young Italian government minister and his family. The Villa Tarranto was already being put to much civic use: after ceremonials in the Pallanza, the mayor was toasted, and local notables were invited to meet the British royals and the minister from Rome over elaborate meals.

It was all rather exhausting. Neil's Italian was fairly limited; the minister and his wife seemed preoccupied with their baby. Outside the gilded gates of Villa Tarranto lay a different world sorely in need of Marshall Aid. Lady Carisbrooke told me sadly of their daughter Iris, living in America and already divorced. She gave me a precious and rare gift of nylon stockings brought from the States. Among the neighbours was General Cordona. He had joined the *partigiani* in the north of Italy and been, he said, the last person to see Mussolini before he fled, dressed in a German uniform, lying in the back of a truck. I have often wondered why I never cultivated that friendship and heard more stories.

In that same year, still pursuing my children's European education – much, I fear, to their grandfather's disquiet – I had taken Skimper off to the Bernese Oberland to search out a pre-prep school. Switzer-land was still a haven of health and stability in that post-war time and I rather dreaded the long years ahead at private and public schools in England. Gstaad was one of the many mountain villages considered healthy for the young. After inspecting several schools, I decided on an old and pretty chalet up the hill, not far from the Palace Hotel. It was run by the renowned Tante Flora and her mountaineering husband, Herr Wurstel. Many children at her school were refugees from the Eastern bloc who had been separated from their parents by war: those – I later learned – whose parents were unable to pay the fees were subsidized by those whose parents could afford them.

Having deposited Skimper with Tante Flora, I dallied awhile to see how he settled in, finding Nancy Astor's daughter, Wissie Ancaster, and Doria Montagu-Douglas-Scott, sister of Earl Haig, to hobnob with. When I finally went to say goodbye, Skimper was playing with some other children and didn't even look up. I still wonder how I could have left him there. Long afterwards he told me he used to fantasize that his furry animals – 'Monk Somerset' and 'W. Bun', his koala bears, and 'Flook' – would march over the mountains to rescue him.

He came back barely able to speak English, with a crew-cut, tough and bronzed like a mountain child, singing charming little French country songs. 'Il est si celtique,' wrote Tante Flora, concerned at his tendency to daydream. I think he was only very homesick.

Another two years on, in the autumn of 1951, I was writing to Themselves from San Remo, 'I believe, more than ever, that now is the time to make these trips, not when they are bigger.' I had begun to suspect that some of the teaching at Hawtrey's, Grey's prep school, was not very inspired, while he seemed to have been spending much time in the san with what he termed 'constant nazo'. Despite the fact that his common entrance for Eton was looming, and there was a prospect of him captaining the cricket XI during his next and last summer at Hawtrey's, I had therefore borne him off on the humble post-war version of the Train Bleu, to alight at Morandi's Hotel on the seafront. Miss Morandi, of my youth, was still in residence, and gave us close attention.

San Remo was still largely unchanged since its pre-war days. The casino looked the same, but I never went back inside. Grey would hurry me past that place where I formerly danced, dined and sang 'To My Sweetheart', feeling an antipathy he was too young to explain. Maybe he sensed the terrible toll the Casino had taken of the local young men, designed, as it was, to entice. We met an old acquaintance, one of three Italian brothers, and heard nothing but sad stories of family fortunes come to grief at the gaming tables.

Where Grey was concerned, as I told the Gowries in an attempt to allay Sandie's anxieties, the education looked likely to be fairly successful and was costing a fiver a week. Grey was particularly taken with one of the instructors, a *colonello di artilleria*, and had even asked for an extra maths lesson on Saturdays.

It is all carried out in French and Italian; I saw them doing the most horrible things on paper and Grey's face was radiant! . . . The nazo we hardly notice. I believe the sun and my drops are prevailing and he is much fatter. I find him most anxious to work; I don't think the standard at Hawtrey's can be very high. Grey has always had good classical reports but he is rather behind for three years' work . . . I read him French and a most interesting but quite difficult theological book . . . The following day he can repeat the jist of a whole chapter, never missing any salient points . . . He learns by heart with the greatest of ease, and I feel sure, had he been made to, he would have all his Latin grammar and half his Greek in his head by now. The *colonello* says he is by no means stupid at maths.

On 26 November, Grey's twelfth birthday, we boarded the tram outside Morandi's Hotel and rattled off along the promenade, past the casino and the gaudy Russian church, under the overhanging tasselled plane trees, and into the country. Alighting on the farther side of a many-arched old bridge, which straddled a mass of round grey boulders awaiting the melting of the oncoming winter's snow-falls, we climbed a steep and twisting route through the olive groves, to reach a little white chapel, built in the last century to thank the Madonna of Lampedusa for delivering the crew of a shipwreck. A smelly old priest with a bristly stubble of beard greeted us, and directed us to a wash-house and lavatory the like of which Grey had never before seen, let alone made use of. I seem to remember that he was suffering from a touch of Italian tummy that day.

The old priest gave us water and coffee, and sweet vanilla cakes, and showed us round the tawdry little chapel. As we left we offered alms, which Gray wanted me to insist should go towards the cost of an improved lavatory. He also endured a warm embrace from the badger-like cheek. Following a scramble back down the mountain-side, we finally celebrated the birthday in a small restaurant beyond the bridge. Then, with the sun hovering ever lower above Corsica, we rattled back to dear Signorina Morandi, alongside the dull seashore and the railway, the mimosa and palm trees, and everywhere the terraces of artichokes and carnations.

The second part of my plan was for Grey to spend the spring term at the Chalet Flora, the school to which Skimper had been so cruelly sent at the age of seven. In December we headed up into the Alps, hoping for a fall of snow. At the Brenner Pass the train loitered a long time, where Hitler and Mussolini had gone for their meetings during the war, their railway carriages parked in a siding. It was a gloomy station, and Grey had a slight temperature. As he lay along one seat in the compartment he said sadly, 'We are two carnations picked in the sun and sent off to the snows.' In fact the snow was non-existent at Saalbach, where I had visualized that Grey would ski and play with the local children, so we repaired higher, to Lech.

After Christmas I went on with him to Gstaad, intending to deposit him in the care of Tante Flora and her mountaineering husband. In fact he refused to be so deposited, for was he not now twelve years old? He drove alone to the school above the Palace Hotel, wrapped in sheepskins in a local fiacre.

★

Freya provided a coda to these excursions in 1959 when, nearing seventy, she bravely took a small party of young friends on a culture holiday to the Greek island of Mykinos. The group included another of her godchildren, Simon Lennox-Boyd, Henry Berens and Grey – all three set to go to Oxford that autumn. Simon Lennox-Boyd didn't manage to fill one ticket, so consulted Grey, who recruited Selina, 'a pretty and nice Irish girl with blue eyes and golden curls', as Freya wrote to Sydney Cockerell on 23 August.

The four young ones have never been east of Italy and it makes me happy to see how this East is ravishing them. To come here with the Classics fresh inside one, at the age of nineteen, one cannot tell where a thing may lead one!

To me she wrote next day:

I can't tell you darling Pam what happiness it is giving me to be able to open this Greek world to these four young pairs of eyes and to think that *something* I have been able to give will go on spreading and unfolding in their lives, Grey's especially, for he and Skimper are my two dearest children and still play on the Asolo grass in my heart.

12

Slightly Perilous Parties

Duff Cooper, who visited Australia following his war-time tour of the Far East as Churchill's special envoy, wrote in *Old Men Forget* that, 'Lord Gowrie was [then] still Governor-General, and I should say that he was the best-loved Governor-General Australia has ever had.' Sandie and Zara retained this esteem. Quite apart from the hordes of Australian dignitaries and friends who used to call at the Norman Tower, groups of Australian tourists, ex-servicemen among them, would gather to lean over the parapet and cheer, 'Hello Guv!' if they managed to spot Sandie in the garden. I suspected that it was the Queen's regard for Sandie which lay behind the invitation I received in 1948 to become an Extra Woman of the Bedchamber, with a view to accompanying Their Majesties on the royal tour of Australia planned for 1949; though Lady Spencer, who delivered the invitation, tried to tell me I had been chosen for myself, not for who I happened at the moment to be.

Cynthia Spencer was an enchanting person, one of the three daughters of the Duke of Abercorn, brought up at Barons Court in County Tyrone. Despite all the grandeur of the Spencer possessions, and being married to the seventh earl, Cynthia had retained her Irish gaiety and a certain simplicity; with her very elegant slender figure, it was easy to see the girl she had been.

Every summer holiday I used to take the boys to Ireland, to Castle Martin, where Pat had known his happiest moments, and leave them safe in the custody of May and Aunt Sheela. This set me free to visit friends and relations. From Bishops Court, Straffan, I wrote to Sandie back in Windsor:

Darling GP,

I knew you would be pleased – it seems to me quite incredible, and I wonder if I will ever stay the course. How queer life is. To think that those funny mad days with Pat among the Fitzwilliam roughs and toughs should land me into HMS *Vanguard*. I shall have to have a terrific potsdam with you. Would it be possible for me to have a very secret card index of importants in each state? I shall never remember names and personalities. I could never take Stacey away from Herself, although I know she would be valuable all round. Who could I find to replace her at the Tower? . . .

I hope Grey is learning a little about economics through the allowance. It causes awful heartburnings, the purse is always being mislaid but he is too killing trying to pay for Aunt Sheela and me when we are out . . . Skimper has been so wild and cheeky, but May is back – I couldn't have stood him a moment longer; but Aunt Sheela says he is the best man on the place for getting a pig into a lorry . . . Much love and enormous hugs.

Lady Delia Peel it was who tried to teach me the courtly ways and manners necessary for an Extra Woman of the Bedchamber. The sister of Earl Spencer, she was my favourite kind of Englishwoman: kindly, unsmart and shrewd. She would put little test questions, quite artlessly, or ask me to glance through lists of guests to be invited to one of the royal garden parties. Being a Woman of the Bedchamber was, as Lady Katherine Seymour commented, 'a wonderful job for widows', the court was welcoming and understanding as generosity and humour suffused downwards from Their Majesties, through the courtiers and secretaries and the courteous and fatherly pages who signposted the corridors of Buckingham Palace.

You would have had to have sniffed its fragrance to comprehend it. Like Zara, Ange and Letty, the older ladies of the court had no jealousy of the younger generation, only offers of help from their own richly lived lives. The one person to be critical of my new position was Freya, who stated her views in no uncertain terms. I had turned her down when she wanted me to join her in India in the summer of 1945 for what she described as 'a happy unproductive year with the Wavells'. The very idea, of course, had been hopelessly impracticable at the time.

When Their Majesties were together, the Queen was accompanied by a Lady-in-Waiting; a Woman of the Bedchamber accompanied the Queen when she was alone. I remember an enchanted evening sitting in the front row of the stalls, singing our part in the story of the little sweep in Benjamin Britten's *Let's Make an Opera*. The private dinner parties and lunches at Buckingham Palace were also truly enjoyable. Sitting beside someone like Sacheverell Sitwell was far more interesting than chaperoning the young to a dance or nightclub – the boys growing sleepy after a day's work and another ahead of them, the girls happy to stay on until the small hours, or, if Princess Margaret was there, until she decided the night was over.

Other than a slight nag over leaving the boys once the tour of Australia started, it was an exciting time. There was an added bonus: the royal yacht was to be commanded by Romola's brother-in-law, Commander Desmond Dreyer. Between my fortnightly tours of duty at Buckingham Palace, I had to devote much time and thought to gathering a trousseau together. I discovered that Harald, a coutourier in Curzon Street, had a Nordic model exactly my size and a friend who invented hats. Sometimes he lent me clothes to wear at Ascot. Together Harald and I conspired over my skeleton: we chose fabrics in rare and wonderful colours – true emerald taffetas, silks like faded ponticum rhododendron, satins in *crème de menthe*.

As it turned out, all the effort and expense put into these prep-arations proved fruitless. That October the royal tour to Australia was postponed on the advice of the King's doctors. He was already suffering from the illness, brought on by the stresses of war abetted by excessive smoking, that would kill him at the age of fifty-six in 1952. All I have left today of that time of heady anticipation is a drawerful of long kid gloves in shades of white, grey and cream.

I made one of my jaunts to Paris at the end of 1949, and took Grey with me. We stayed with the Malcolms. Billy was combining his duties as a military attaché at the Embassy with a long-standing role of golfing companion to HRH the Duke of Windsor. The Minister at the Embassy was William Hayter. Grey was sent up the Eiffel Tower with Teresa Hayter, and there, he tells me, kissed her when they reached the top; later their political interests diverged as she turned with passion towards the left.

The Malcolms and I were invited to dine one night at the rue de la Phaisandrie. We were piped into a very excellent dinner and I sat next to HRH. Such are the myths of history that I had the strangest sensation of his being one of the annointed – something I had never felt in the presence of any archbishop. We spoke of the war, of Germany, of the missed opportunities for peace, the folly and the tragedy; once, raising his voice, he broke into German. I mentioned my brother Michael Fletcher, then running the Berlin Airlift to the humiliated and defeated people he too loved.

The rest of the evening was more difficult. I was taken off alone to drink coffee with the Duchess: narrow and immaculate like an Oriental woman. Obviously my connections and recent royal appointment led her to think I might have some influence at court. Her theme was that HRH must be given a job, a worthwhile position, where his talent and charisma could operate. As I sat and listened in that beautiful costly drawing room to what was virtually a plea for her man and for understanding at home, I could only think how Pat's quick mind and wit would have lubricated the situation.

In 1950 Freya mounted another campaign for me to join her; this time in Cyrenaica, where Stewart Perowne, whom she had married in October 1947, was appointed an adviser. The bait this time was that since I had acquired royal manners, I should make proper and serious use of them by helping her with the Emir Idriss's ladies. Once again, the moment was hardly propitious, but Freya was seldom out of sight for long. One of the rewards of living at the Norman Tower was its proximity to Cliveden, where she stayed with the Astors even more often than she did with us.

Nancy and Waldorf Astor and Zara were the same generation and had known each other down the years. At the first wedding party Pat ever attended he escaped from the nannies' table to listen to 'the wonderful jokes that lady over there is making' – Nancy, of course. On Christmas Eve, the Cliveden party would come with us to the service of carols at St George's Chapel, while the Norman Tower had standing invitations to send any visitors to Cliveden to take part in the traditional charades and games. David Astor remembered someone telling him: 'Your family are like street musicians, they perform whether you want them to or not.' Nancy's spirit was infectious: I recall a Christmas when the Deputy Governor of Windsor Castle wheeled his wife across the Cliveden library by the ankles wheelbarrow fashion, while Skimper flew around in sheet wailing like a banshee. Michael and Jakie Astor talked gobbledegook to each other as two envoys to the United Nations: Michael slowly picked his nose, inspected the result and wiped it on his lapel. Nancy's eldest son, Bobbie Shaw, gave a heart-rending rendition of 'My Souvenirs', holding a clutch of letters bound with a blue ribbon. But the star performer was always Nancy herself.

As Chiquita, the daughter-in-law who was married to Jakie, wrote: 'She was amazing, not only with her agility and energy, but also her shape, that strongly built little body, tending to thrust itself forward . . . probably [not] noticeable with the bustles and the long skirts of the Gibson girl, but now the shorter ones made her look sometimes like the imitations she was so fond of doing.' This was particularly true of her take-offs of the ATS or the WRAFFS on parade. She kept herself extraordinarily fit. I once saw her in her long white knickers lying on the bathroom floor, her toes touching the floor at the back of her head as the window, wide open, blew in icy air. Another time she forced poor Archie Wavell, when he was getting pretty stiff with age, to scramble across the hedges in front of the house where she continually practised her golf strokes.

The company at Cliveden, Sir Charles Barry's magnificent Italian-ate villa set on immense terraces among the woods that overlook the Thames near Maidenhead, was always varied. It ranged from the mighty like the Wavells, ex-viceroy and vicereine, to politicians of all colours and intellectuals like Laurens Van der Post and Fitzroy Maclean. Nancy was trying to coach the latter, back in the House of Commons after his gallant, remarkable war, into becoming a demagogue, a role completely foreign to his nature. Beside the enor-mous log fire in the hall, Lady Alexandra ('Baba') Metcalfe, elegant and beautiful, stitched away at her embroidery. Stanley Spencer came up from Cookham looking like a cartoon child drawn by Giles; he then sat at the piano playing most unmusically, refusing to give way, whereas Nancy's great-niece, Anne Wyndham, played with a lovely touch but needed much persuading. Another niece, Elizabeth Winn, was a brilliant performer, who would improvise little soliloquies of Americans doing their downtown shopping. Curiously her cousin Joyce Grenfell 'had to wait', according to Michael Astor, 'until she could appear as a professional artist before her talents were given, by us at any rate, the recognition that was their due'. From her own childhood visits to her Aunt Nancy, Joyce remembered Cliveden as a restless, anxious place, 'always lively, always a party – if a slightly perilous party'.

In the summer the boys and I could sit on the banks of the Thames at Cliveden, so escaping the ubiquitous crowds we faced at Windsor. One warm afternoon, as we lay on the grass under a great plane tree next to the boat-house, Nancy approached, beautifully dressed under a parasol and accompanied by a high-ranking American admiral. She always became provocative with small children, testing them after her own fashion; children picked this up and reacted according to their natures. 'Why don't you get up when I come to see you, bringing an important admiral with me?' asked Nancy.

'Because I never get up for witches,' answered Grey, sensing a primal magic beneath the smart clothes.

An asset Nancy and Zara had in common was not being pro-fessional beauties, nor were they vain. The same age, one fair, the other dark, their pretty clothes, gay hats and veils, furs and kid gloves were worn for a purpose: the job they had to do at state occasions, charitable functions or fêtes, church or memorial services. Nancy most wisely invented for herself a becoming political uniform: black coat and skirt, tricorne hat. But (and a big 'but' it is), both, one rich, the other poor, had personal maids, even as their immaculate husbands left their extensive wardrobes, shoes and boots (some, for London wear, with felt uppers instead of spats) to their valets. With no thought needing to be given to what to put on and how to arrive anywhere – clean and nourished, supplied with pocket handkerchief, necessary papers in handbag or briefcase and money – it was surpris-ing the extra hours there were to a day, and what a release of mind and intellect followed. No one now has the 'B echelon' to sustain the sartorial style of their forefathers, as the televising of the Houses of Parliament has demonstrated. At the Norman Tower there were soaring laundry bills, discovered to be because the Deputy Governor never donned a shirt twice.

Nancy loved lame ducks and hard-luck cases. Maybe I owed the instant acceptance and friendship I found from Nancy and Waldorf at Cliveden to the sympathy she felt for war widows. It was not a happy time in their life. Waldorf had suffered a slight heart-attack in 1941, and with the approach of the first post-war election in 1945, he and the family persuaded Nancy not to contest her Sutton division of Plymouth. No one could therefore ever know whether she might have done the improbable, gone against the trend of a Labour land-slide and held the constituency that launched her political career in 1919 – the first woman to take a seat in Parliament. But the worst thing for her was to feel out of things. Nancy became resentful. Many times I would hear close friends or relations criticize the way she treated the husband who so clearly adored her; not to mention Bill and his brothers, her daughter Phyllis, known as Wissie, and her daughters-in-law as they in turn came within range.

Occasionally Nancy took me to the Christian Science church in Maidenhead, or to the one behind Sloane Square. I used to admire and enjoy the *Christian Science Monitor*: John Cooley, its corres-pondent in Beirut in 1982, was valiant, honest and perceptive. But I could never make head or tail of Mary Baker Eddy. Churches for me mean the old liturgies and candles, choirs chanting plainsong with its narrow intervals – ladders by which even the humblest among us seek to reach the God we love but can never comprehend. When I go to church I prefer to hide behind a pillar. It is quite hard to creep unnoticed into a Christian Science church or fundamentalist place of worship to bring 'humble and hearty thanks' or just to offer up the sadness and sorrows of the world. I was thankful to notice that when Rosie Townsend became a 'lame duck' in a blaze of national publicity, she too was made to sit down with *Science and Health with Key to the Scriptures* to learn all about 'Mr Jesus'.

Sometimes I drove down with Nancy to her house at Sandwich in Kent. She would curl up on the back seat of the Rolls in her golfing kit with a little navy-blue jacket and cap, and sleep the whole way. Once I contracted a ferociously bad sore throat. Despite her attempts to convert me to Christian Science, Nancy summoned a doctor. It was there, among the Edwardian white-painted furniture and the blue china, that she had recovered from her own illness as a young woman. Her eldest son, Bobbie Shaw – the only child of her short-lived first marriage – often came to stay with her in Kent – away from Cliveden, which made him depressed. While Nancy played golf, Bobbie and I would do the rounds of the Sandwich antique shops.

Bobbie had terrible black moods, especially at Cliveden; he could hurt his mother like no one else. But he could also be a charming, perceptive companion, and very funny when in good heart. He used to love taking the Ruthven boys to the theatre. Once I went with

them to see a show by his friend Max Adrian. Bobbie just sat in the
box, enjoying the boys' hysterical laughter; then he took us all back-
stage to meet the cause of it. Before long a message came from
Waldorf, warning me against letting the boys see too much of Bobbie.
Rightly or wrongly, I must contrive to be around too when the boys
were in his company. Once or twice he invited me to his 'little Irish
rectory' off the Fulham Road. It had pillars topped with pineapples
behind a high brick wall flanked by pleached limes. The only resemblance to any Irish rectory I ever knew was its dark-red walls and
sporting prints. Bobbie had twice won the Grand Military at Sandown while in the Blues, and been a gentleman rider of some repute.
Many ladies had been in love with him. His subsequent life was a
tragedy for him and his mother, despite the forbearance of his stepfather and step-brothers.

Our friendship ended abruptly. Later on, when I was living in
Ireland, he invited me, along with Mark and Anne Wyndham, and
Frank, his lover, to dine at the Café Royal. It was a merry evening
until, towards the end, Bobbie overheard me inviting Frank to call
on us in Donegal the next time he was over. Then and there he
accused me of trying to seduce Frank. My protests were ignored; I
was never forgiven. For all his early charm and good looks, Bobbie
had a demon which was never exorcized in this world. After Bobbie's
suicide Frank inherited the 'rectory' and all Bobbie's money. He
continued to sponser a steeplechase at Folkestone as Bobbie had
done, but refused to present the cup the year a girl jockey won the
race.

In 1949 I went by train to Plymouth with Nancy's personal maid,
Rose, who never drew breath the whole journey. We stayed at the
Astor house in Elliot Terrace. Jakie, who was nursing the Sutton
division, hoping to reclaim it for the Astors, had sense as well as wit.
He forbade his mother to speak on his behalf, insisted on doing
things his way. He was right; her time was past. The people of
Plymouth had loved her and Waldorf and had survived the war with
them. But to be up on the rostrum again, dressed to kill, would have
gone to her head. Goodness knows what words might have tumbled
out. It proved an exhilarating few days for me, but I daresay they
were agonizing for Nancy, witnessing the son who most resembled
her stepping into her shoes; and also for Jakie's beautiful wife,
Chiquita, whom she used to belittle even in front of myself. Jakie

lost that election in 1950, but won in 1951. When I returned from my week in Plymouth, Sandie said in the nicest possible way that anyone connected with the royal household had better not take sides in politics.

Nancy kept telling me I was wasting my life; she went so far as to suggest I stand for Parliament. Failing that, I must marry again – if not Bobbie, 'who had plenty of money', there was always the elderly Swiss Ambassador. She assured me that the first time one married for love; the second time for position and security. While one of these admonitions was in progress in front of the fire at Cliveden, Archie Wavell chimed in, 'Don't listen to her. If you want another husband I'll find you one!' He still looked as Pat had described him in the desert, 'like a terrier who's been down after every badger in the county': a lovely man, permitting no sorrow or disappointment to harm or corrupt his soul. It was about this time that his only son Archie John died in Kenya in a Mau Mau ambush.

Nancy need never have married so much money. Great wealth cottons its possessors from the world. It is the object of adulation or envy and causes isolation, as I saw when living with K., my god-mother. This is especially the case in England, where people are subservient to wealth and privilege, yet at the same time envious of them and prickly when it comes to accepting charity. Nancy had no regard for such complexes. 'Have you got less than £3,000 a year,' she would ask, ''cause if you have I can give you some money and it won't cost me nothin'.' She would have made a stir in the world regardless of her money. Shortly after Waldorf's death in 1952, Zara managed to catch Nancy to attend the Victoria League Fair in Belgrave Square, a Commonwealth get-together to which Herself, the Duchess of Devonshire and Lady Dulverton gave much time and energy. Nancy walked round the fund-raising stalls, chewing gum and cracking jokes. 'They say I'm the richest widow in England, but I'm not allowed any cash,' she declared as she opened and displayed an empty purse.

At the Canadian Hospital at Cliveden, which had been fashioned out of the big covered tennis court at the end of 1914, Nancy once insisted on taking me into one of the men's wards, which was full of pensioners. 'Don't any of you old fellers want a wife,' she shouted to them, 'because I hate bein' a widow.'

As Zara used to say: 'Who would ever have heard of the Astors if it hadn't been for Nancy!'

Cliveden was like a small principality. As long as Nancy and Waldorf were there together, the formal atmosphere of a well-run large establishment by a competent staff never seemed oppressive, for Nancy never allowed the weight of the Astor millions to dampen her spirits. Being a great one for sharing, she treated her guests in the same way as Arabs do: her house became your house.

The last time I saw her at Cliveden was after her son Bill had inherited the title and moved in. Nancy threw a children's party, which she conducted in her own subversive fashion, undermining nanny-power. The first to roll down the grassy bank in a pale-blue frilly dress was Princess Anne with her yellow curls. At tea-time, in the ornate rococo dining room, Nancy admonished the large group of children, 'Now you eat your tea and no one is to pull a cracker until I get back!'

When we returned the table was littered with pulled crackers. Only Prince Charles, sitting with his back to the tall windows overlooking the terrace, was able to show her his crackers, untouched, in front of his plate.

13

The Second Dilemma

They say that Ireland is a sponge, absorbing the warm wet winds of the Atlantic before they reach the rest of the British Isles. Whenever possible I continued to escape into that magic never-never land, which sucks up the Gulf Stream, shielding the English from its dangerous romantic vapours. Among my fixtures was the annual tribal gathering of the Anglo-Irish, the Dublin Horseshow.

During my years as a widow at Windsor, I spent several horseshows watching with increasing distress the drama unfolding at Castle Martin without Ian or Pat to sustain Aunt Sheela. Percy had finally taken a wife from the Aran Islands, but she never stood much chance, with Aunt Sheela holding all the purse strings and Percy incapable of any action beyond literary conversation in between puffs from his cigarette. Around the lovely gaunt denuded house beside the Liffey, other studs and mansions meanwhile awoke to a new and prosperous dawn. Americans with money to spend, and a number of fox-hunting English, were finding in Limerick and Galway, Carlow, Meath and Tipperary, a countryside unspoiled by the necessity to supply food for a large urban population. Here the enthusiastic horsey community could again ride to hounds, even as they had dreamed in the Western Desert, or in the fields and forests of northern France.

Life at the Norman Tower, with its 'open-door' programme for Commonwealth and American visitors, had left me little space for self-pity. My contemporaries were busy with their own lives, but among many of my friends a blight appeared on their marriages as it does, however hard one tries to prevent it, on roses. There weren't the war widows around as in the post-1918 years, and sometimes an

231

unreasonable bile of jealousy and criticism would rise inside me against those reunited couples who, despite children, couldn't 'make it' again together. Two quite separate men, one from the RAF, the other from the army, spoke of the problem in almost identical terms to me: 'There they are, with Nanny, a daily and a nursery party; I feel like a bit of unwanted furniture.' Down at Adelaide Cottage, Peter Townsend spent more and more time at the palace and the castle; Rosie attended more and more parties.

One particular Dublin Horseshow, in 1949, I bought a little motor-scooter, such as paratroopers used to jump with, which they then assemble on landing before scuttling into enemy territory. It lived mostly in the boots of the cars of people who gave me lifts or at the side-door of the Shelbourne Hotel. Post-war Dublin was welcoming back its own heroes, returning to their ancestral homes, and it was the Galway Blazers Hunt Ball that year which led me into the Second Dilemma. I joined a party of people, most of whom I didn't know. While the others danced, I found myself stranded with a tall, slim Life Guards officer whose pale unhappy face stood out against the mirthful figures surrounding us. He had recently returned from Palestine, to find that, like Peter Townsend and so many others, he had become a stranger to his family. I don't remember him saying anything remarkable, but in dancing Derek Cooper passed the test. The evening culminated in a proposal by Dennis Daly that we drive all the way to Galway to see his mother Diana at Dunsandle. We had only got as far as Lucan when Simon Galway, brandishing an umbrella at a passer-by, insisted on making a refuelling stop. Since there was no whiskey to be had at that hour, the men ended up drinking milk. With them sobered up perforce, we headed back for Dublin.

Before long I was taking Derek to stay with the Somersets in Mallorca, where, I wrote to Zara, Bets was living on the boat with her 'strange untamed Jumbly', Bobby Somerset, her famous yatchtsman husband. They had their eyes on a 'little honey-coloured peasant's house which they could convert and build on to, just above the port where the terraces and olive trees give way to the rocks and pines'.

Bets is so happy here, years of being alone crouching or wandering in her garden have built up a great store to feed on. I have loved being with her, I find she has a magic of no one else I ever met.

She should have inspired poets and painters not Jumblies and Dukes. Bob is utterly married to his boat and he now has no imagination for anything else. I only pray he will let Bets have her way with the house. I fear he irritates the Duke [Derek] vastly, whose attitude to life is entirely chivalrous like Himself's and sees Bets as a pathetic figure, but he [Derek] has been good and hasn't shown it. They have an amazing selection of yachting friends here; I love to watch Bets delving into them all and they falling under the spell. Oh, I hope a little of this wonderful Ruthven selflessness has filtered to the men through my egotistical blood.

Bets told me how, one night, she had found herself sitting next to Bobby Somerset at a London dinner. He had been at sea and smelled of fish, and was about to sail for New York. When he arrived in America, he remembered the evening, thought that surely someone would try to marry her, took the next boat home and proposed. Derek was just the sort of man Bets loved. I am sure that in the endless discussions provoked by the Second Dilemma, this carried weight. To me it was the gossip they all minded, not that he was a divorced man with two children.

On 28 July 1951, Freya, on one of her visits to Cliveden, wrote to Stewart Perowne:

Nancy not peaceful! I think she is desperately unhappy inside. She had gone for the public things and now begins to find them dust and ashes I suppose, and here is Pam on the edge of a penniless marriage with the only person she has ever felt like loving since Pat died. Everyone is at me to dissuade her, but I can't find it in my heart to do so. All I suggest is to live in sin for a couple of years before deciding, which is advice that none of these old ladies would approve . . .

Nancy says she wants to become a saint so that everyone may feel her influence when she comes into a room. I told her I have only known two people who gave this impression of making a room different, one was Gandhi and the other the Mufti and neither were saints!

That November I took Grey to San Remo for his twelfth birthday and, as already described, we came back up to Lech-am-Arlburg in

Austria in search of the snow. My sister Diana, Skimper and Derek all joined us there for a Christmas made doubly memorable when Skimper did the unforgiveable. Thinking a shop had ill-treated Derek, he wrapped a rude and outraged message in a snowball and sent it hurling through the shop front with all the might of his nine years. Likewise in a rage at being unable to control his skis, he would fall face forward on to the snow, like a fainting guardsman at the Queen's Birthday Parade. These were early manifestations of an uncompromising indignation which still occasionally overwhelms him. On Christmas Eve there was mass in the old onion-domed church, where the skeleton of a popular and presumably saintly bishop reclined, uncomfortably hung with red velvet and jewels.

Anita Leslie, whom I had known in the Middle East, was now married to Bill King, another intrepid yachtsman, and writing tales about her family at Oranmore, an old granite castle they had bought, with its toes in the Atlantic a few miles from Galway City. One day I had been lunching with Anita and her two brothers, Desmond and Jack, at Prunier in London. We were thoroughly enjoying our fish when the men started a silly argument about flying saucers, Desmond having just published a highly successful book about the men from Mars he claimed to have seen. 'Come on, let's leave them,' said Anita. 'I want to go and say goodbye to someone who's leaving for the States.'

We walked up St James's to the Berkeley Hotel, once a place of rendezvous for Pat and me. In Suite No. 1 we found two American gentlemen, the elder sporting a wide fedora on his very curly hair. I discovered I was being introduced to Henry P. McIlhenny of Glen-veagh Castle in County Donegal, who welcomed us in the Philadel-phia drawl still imitated with nostalgia and affection by his friends. He had been in Donegal refurbishing the castle, which he had bought while serving in the US Navy. Now he was returning to his native city of Philadelphia, where he served as curator of the Museum of Arts and lived in splendour in Rittenhaus Square with a magnificent collection of nineteenth-century English and French paintings begun as a young man at Harvard. We did not spend long over our farewells, but he insisted that whenever I was in Ireland I must come up and stay with him. Glenveagh had always belonged to Americans. The nineteenth-century Gothic castle, built by the Adare family on land from which all tenants had been evicted, stood in the most romantic of glens near the head of a lake surrounded by steep granite hills.

One day, some months later, Henry drove me along a bumpy mountain road from Glenveagh to see the neighbouring Dunlewy estate, which he had bought for his widowed sister, Bonney Winterstein, and her three sons. The house was situated beside a deep lough directly beneath Errigal, Ulster's highest mountain. A short salmon river, and about 4,000 acres of hills, lakes, streams and bog, led up to the Poisoned Glen below Sleive Snacht where Dunlewy marches with the Glenveagh deer forest. The house was a Regency lodge with Victorian additions: a gable, a bay window and a castellated single-storey section containing what had once been a billiard room. The fine old stable block, at some distance from the house, was mostly in ruins. The purlieus were flanked by rough woodlands, where fern and rhododendron luxuriated under larch, mountain ash, alder and Scots pine.

Bonney and her sons had first stayed at Dunlewy while Henry was still in Florence. It had been a bad period for them. Her husband had lately committed suicide; only one of her boys, Jimmy, really liked the place, making friends with the men who worked outside, and sleeping with fishing worms under his pillow. That summer was unusually wet, even for Donegal, and there was trouble with the governess. When Henry returned from Italy, he found that Bonney had already taken her family back to Chicago, so shattering his dream. For a few years he let the house, along with the fishing and stalking, to the redoubtable, eccentric Lady Londonderry, known as 'Circe' from the snakes she had tattooed up her legs. The estate was now an encumbrance to him, and he was ready for a congenial neighbour.

For the first time in my life I had some money of my own. Aunt Etta Hodgson had left half of her estate to me along with jewellery and small sums for the boys. Henry was quite persuasive. His Scottish factor would help with the deer; his housekeeper, Mary Ferry, who had looked after Dunlewy House since she was fifteen, would stay on; while the O'Donnell brothers, who lived in the two cottages along the avenue flanking the lake, would step into the shoes of their old father, Paddy Pat. Henry dropped the price as I hesitated over his elaborate drapes and antique furniture.

Still I hesitated, and later, on a day when the rain turned to yellow foam as it hit the brown mountain streams, took Derek along to see and advise. 'It's a dream place,' he challenged me, 'but you'll never buy it.'

When I returned to the Norman Tower I found Nancy and Zara in the drawing room. 'Have you bought it?' shouted Nancy.

My Christian beliefs, neglected as they were, allowed me to take rash decisions, sudden deviations and directions, knowing that the affairs of this world are only the prelude to eternity. The contracts for Dunlewy were exchanged on 28 March 1952. The same Christian beliefs meanwhile became a considerable complication in the matter of the Second Dilemma.

That Royal Ascot week in June Sandie told me he had decided he must leave the Norman Tower. He sought my help in persuading Zara. Nancy had offered them Parr's Cottage in the grounds at Cliveden, overlooking the stud paddocks outside the entrance gates. The cottage was named after an Astor butler who once lived in it. Paul Phipps, Joyce Grenfell's architect father, had converted it in the 1930s to make a home for Joyce and Reggie Grenfell at the time when she was working as a radio critic on the *Observer*. But Herself would hear nothing good of Parr's. 'It wouldn't contain Himself's boots,' she said.

Zara, having adored her lovable man during their life together, now seemed unable to understand that he must be put out to grass. The anxieties of war, with Australia potentially so vulnerable, and the responsibilities of a lifetime of public service, together with those involving the castle and the company directorships he had needed to take on to sustain the public life to which Zara was addicted, had all taken their toll. Sandie's official duties were being carried out by his reflexes.

It went without saying that my Second Dilemma, coming on top of the problems caused by Peter and Rosie Townsend, and following on from the King's sudden death in his sleep on 6 February, was doing nothing to help Sandie's health. Inevitably Lord Athlone, brother of Queen Mary, Governor of Windsor Castle and Colonel-in-Chief of the Life Guards, became involved. Princess Alice, the wife of 'Uncle Alge' (pronounced 'Algy'), was, in Tommy Lascelles's phrase, 'a lady with a long tongue'. There was a sticky interview, to news of which I responded in a letter to Zara:

Darlings, I am so sad about all this botheration I have given you . . .

Poor Himself and poor Derek, it must have been a dreadful little interview for both and all because of that tiresome Princess Alice. I shall never feel kindly towards her neat coiffe and straight back again, she has caused such unnecessary bother and worry.

One day, after a walk in Hyde Park discussing Peter and Rosie with Sir Arthur Penn, the Groom in Waiting to the Queen's Household, I wrote to the Queen Mother asking to be allowed to resign from my duties as an Extra Woman of the Bedchamber. Sandie told me I had been hasty. Derek's divorce had been made absolute the previous year and his wife was remarried, to a brother officer, Tom Fairhurst. His regiment, and even the court, would therefore be happy to depict her as the scapegoat, provided I made 'an honest man of him' – as Julian Gascoigne, commanding the London District, expressed it. The way would thus be open for Derek to succeed Jackie Ward as colonel of the regiment, which would have been unacceptable had he remained merely a divorced man.

I went on with trying to explain that, so far as I was concerned, Derek was unmarriageable: the Church's teaching against divorce and remarriage was unambiguous. The Reverend, alas, was no longer there to give an opinion, having died in 1949, the year in which the drama began. Only Lady Gascoigne, the Dean of Windsor and Bishop Cuthbert Bardsley, a friend of my father's from San Remo days, seemed to understand my scruples. Bets Somerset thought I was utterly mad; Nancy Astor hoped in a letter that I was regaining my reason. The pressure on me to 'make an honest man' of Derek continued, not least from Themselves. Derek was particularly sweet to them both, winning Zara's heart and when in Windsor acting as an unofficial ADC to Sandie.

When not in Windsor Derek was in Germany, where his regiment was with the BAOR, stationed at Wolfenbüttel. From there, in the end, I reported to Zara:

I have told Derek I will 'marry' him. 'Legalized lust' the Church of Rome calls it. I don't look upon it as marriage, nor do I really want to. But he won't contemplate giving up seeing me, and I see I am doing him great harm because of 'great guns and women's tongues'. The trouble is, he inspires affection, especially from men, and his life is obviously more useful than mine . . . So there it is.

I think he has been passed over for command as the War Office pressed for a decision; or maybe it was something else. He must mind dreadfully since the regiment moves, after being flown home for the coronation [in June the next year]. But Derek has no pettiness of character and has taken it very loyally . . . the funny and most ironical thing is that he has to host the Athlones on a visit in August.

In another letter I told Zara:

Derek has some awful decisions to make and wants to see the Military Secretary. I think he may leave. I had a dreadful evening with Jackie [Ward]. He is heart-broken and very bitter. He said, 'Derek has so much to give the regiment' . . . D. would have commanded [at the coronation], Jackie Silver Stick. He says it is entirely because of me . . . If only the War Office would refuse to pass it there would still be a chance. The change-over doesn't take place till January. No one knows bar Derek and Jackie. Anne [Somerset] and I have been riding each day – I do love her, she is unlike any of the girls and a wonderful companion.

Back at the Norman Tower one morning in July 1952, Zara poured a whisky into a cup of Bovril and gave it to me to drink in the tiny writing room I had overlooking the garden. Then I left for London. That afternoon, with despair in my heart, I signed away all my beliefs in the Westminster Register Office. Everyone heaved a sigh of relief, except the Giant. 'You should never have consented in the mood you're in,' she said.

The truth of it was that my hesitations had already cost Derek his career. The Life Guards had put him on ice, and spoiled his chances of becoming one of 'Glubb's girls' in the Arab Legion, which he had put in for; he was passed over as commander of the regiment. He took it with dignity, and never lost the respect and devotion of the younger man. He was good with the men: as Anne Somerset observed: 'You can see the sentries actually *like* saluting Derek.' In the end even his good humour was overcome by exasperation. He resigned his commission. During what we anticipated as 'Black Week' at Wolfenbüttel at the start of November, Derek handed over his duties as second-in-command. But, as I wrote to Zara, it really 'went very well':

> I do so admire D. for being really Big and unbitter about it and so nice to them all. We gave a Guy Fawkes party which broke the ice. We asked the whole regiment – doctors, padres, WVSs; all the morning the boys came and fixed the most terrifying rockets and fuses up in the garden, which is tiny, surrounded by other houses. They made a guy which I couldn't help thinking looked exactly like Uncle Alge, who lurked in the cellar until it was time to burn him. I did the downstairs like an Austrian café bar with Tannenbaum and putti and red paper hearts and candle-light. We had a band dressed in lederhosen and little tables with bottles of wine and everyone came in ski clothes: thirty hilarious young men and only nine women. Simon [Galway] and Sunny [Blandford] looked quite fantastic. Nicky Beaumont, whom I love, came as a mountaineering lady. After the guests arrived and were sipping hot red wine with lemon and cloves, there was a ghastly bang from the cellar, two officers dashed down and brought the life-sized guy. He was rushed through the assembled company and taken to the bonfire. More horrible explosions as the fire was lit and 'Uncle Alge' went up in a blaze which nearly reached the house. I fully expected to read in the papers next day that he had dropped dead.
>
> When it was over we danced madly till dawn. The Colonel completely forgot himself and stayed very late. The next day I had the most touching little note saying they never had such a party in BAOR. The only blot was when the older officers, emboldened by warm red wine, tried to tell me what they felt about Derek leaving and one started on Derek himself . . . but Jackie has asked him if it is possible for him to stay over the General's inspection . . . O Mumps, Pat would so enjoy it out here, so many old Eleventh [Hussar] friends. The way Nicky and Sunny go on reminds me so much of the Cambridge days, the queer nicknames and the same silly words flogged to death . . . Forgive me for being such a bother, you have been the loyalest mother-in-law in the world.

I didn't tell Zara the half of it. They carried Quartermaster Bates, tied in a chair and swathed in Bronco, on to a hedge in the garden.

The grandfather clock was loaded with other belongings from Derek's house and seen walking down the street. They cut the telephone and rendered the house uninhabitable for the incoming second-in-command. As the sky lightened, Derek and I drove away towards the mountains. With his decision taken to leave the army, Derek knew that Dunlewy was what he wanted and needed. In the bathroom of a pension in Lech, I sold him a half-share in the Dublin company, Terry's Murphy Limited, through which I had bought the estate.

When we finally reached our haven of Dunlewy I wrote again to Zara:

> We have slept and slept, both exhausted I think. Derek looks very nice on the pillow. Bets says so many men turn into butlers when asleep . . . I am sure Mr Lee looks delicious asleep, in fact I saw him once on a hard chair in the garden at Cliveden. Pat seems so close here. Our game book is a continuation of his, so many records of Castle Martin days, always very candid, are written in it. Giant wrote a 'second thoughts' and much happier letter. New handmaiden just arrived. Very chic.

Zara, whenever boy-friends were being discussed, always used to ask: 'But is he a pillow boy?'

My crisis of conscience was not yet done with. After a while Tom Fairhurst died suddenly from a heart-attack in the west of Ireland. Derek's daughter Jennifer was just growing up, and his son Michael was five years younger. For months I felt desperate about them, despite the fact that there was no financial problem. I lunched in London with Cuthbert Bardsley to discuss the situation. He said quite unequivocally that Derek's first duty was to his former wife and family: that was the teaching of the Church. I had put my head into the sand during many phases of my life, from teenage onwards, then had refused almost to acknowledge Pat's departure; now I likewise ignored the realities of this world when my turn came to confront life as it was, not how it might be, and the terrible power of human gossip. The distress I was causing to the Gowries, who became convinced I was determined to leave Derek, surfaced in an exchange of letters with Bets, who wrote to Zara:

> My brain simply won't take in any more of her reasoning, it does

not seem to make a word of sense . . . I talked to Derek too and he said it made no sense to him either, but for the past year she has been in such a state . . . that the only thing was to let her do what she liked about it . . . It is all this hideous Church upbringing.

Grey and Skimper wrote: 'We will never give up Derek.'

I changed my name, by deed-poll, back to Hore-Ruthven, convenient for trusts and so on, but there was no reward. Not long after Jennifer married, her widowed mother, Mrs Fairhurst, became Mrs Cyril Heber-Percy, so providing her and Michael with an excellent stepfather in the colonel, another extended family and the best kind of sporting holidays in Scotland. If left to myself I still believe we would all be better off if there were no such thing as divorce. But who am I to judge?

14

The Group and the Glen

It was Derek who made for us the enchanted home at the head of the lough west of the Poisoned Glen. He set the tumbled lions back on their pillars, which in turn supported the iron gates half-way up the front avenue. 'I thought we were modest people,' said Skimper when he first drove through them.

Derek had been reared in County Londonderry, and for a short time before the war had managed his mother's estate at Garvagh. Now he threw himself heart and soul into managing Dunlewy. We bought a tractor, and a Land-Rover; and some black-faced sheep that were dipped or sheared in the old stable yard. Derek's mother was a First World War widow: his father had been killed in India. When she drove over from Garvagh, stiffened by arthritis, he set her up in a chair in a trailer behind the tractor and drove her around the mountain lanes, looking for stray ewes. She sent him £2,000, because, 'Dek will never waste money.'

Paddy O'Donnell took the sheep to market in the trailer after Derek has taught him to drive. Paddy would remark that 'the tractor's all annoyed this morning'; he called a light breeze 'a girlish wind'. We acquired our own sheep collies and learned to work them. The most expensive of them, Tam, was deeply affected by the phases of the moon: he had to be shot when he ran amok and killed some of our neighbour's ewes. We experimented with pigs and poultry and spent backbreaking hours cutting and stacking turf. We supplied sand from a beach by the river to the local builders, and sometimes to the undertakers, who used it for lining graves: people did not always like the idea of their kin being preserved in the bog until the Resurrection.

As Derek worked a full day alongside Paddy and Johnny O'Donnell, they cleared ditches, built fences, felled timber and planted trees. Many of the great larches for which Dunlewy was famous in that otherwise treeless landscape had fallen across the steep banks of a river gorge in the woodlands behind the house. They had to be cut by handsaws and pulled out with picks. Large silent men from the coast and the islands who were building new houses with grants from the government insisted on Dunlewy larch for their joists and rafters; and when, years later, a group of young men rowed themselves across the Irish Sea to Scotland wearing rough homespun wool in emulation of St Columba, we were proud that the timbers of their craft were from Dunlewy trees.

While Derek worked, I came to know the people of the Glen; the O'Donnells, the Ferrys, the Roartys, the McGeadys and their co-lateral branches. All were unstinting in their welcome and acceptance. Old Paddy Pat, father of the O'Donnell brothers, had been the gillie and stalker in charge of the estate long before Henry McIlhenny bought it from the eccentric Nellie Crankshaw. Taller than either son, he still dressed the part of an ancient retainer, in tweed jacket, shooting breeches and waistcoat. He regaled us with tales of Dunlewy's past and its previous owners: of the drunken butler drowned crossing the lake; of Nellie Crankshaw's husband, who saw a mysterious Green Lady while out on the hill the day of his death; of the evangelically minded Russells, who built the granite and quartzite Protestant church at the head of the Glen, with the aim of seducing the locals away from their Catholic faith; of the Mr and Mrs Ross, good Catholics, who built the Gaelic-style chapel at the lower end of the lake.

The Protestant church was now almost roofless, but the pews were still inside, with rotting dog-eared hymnals and Books of Common Prayer, while in the almost empty graveyard the Russell and Crankshaw headstones listed drunkenly or lay flat on their faces. Annie-the-Milk, who lived in a cottage just below the church, was its self-appointed warden. She was a small, round, highly intelligent widow who lived a hard peasant life with a few cows and hens and occasionally supplemented her income by selling hand-knitted sweaters. She kept the gate locked and pronounced it sacrilege to graze sheep over the bones of the People of the Big House. But at times when sheep had to be brought down from the mountain a large hole would appear in the wall at a convenient corner near a bend in the road, and the hallowed precinct be filled with ewes and lambs. The church-yard made an excellent sheep-pen. Perhaps the failure of its prot-estantizing mission endeared the people of Dunlewy to the old church. When it was suggested that it should be pulled down and re-erected somewhere else, in the Six Counties or even the United States, there was an outcry in the Glen. The Church of Ireland compromised, allowing it to be stripped of its roof and pews and preserved as a ruin. Today the village holds an annual ecumenical service there, as part of the Dunlewy Festival.

As a family we used to worship in the little Protestant church at Bunbeg, about six miles away, near the coast. The vicar, Canon Watson, was a lean, intense chain-smoking bachelor who conducted services in a raw Belfast accent and accompanied our hymns on the harmonium with all the fervour of a football coach. A man of quite remarkable erudition, he was reported to have been offered a fellowship at Cambridge but failed to turn up. His sermons, delivered without notes, with eyes tightly closed and hands locked in a butcher's grip, never lasted longer than fifteen minutes. They were peppered with citations from early church fathers and references to long-forgotten controversies. They were received with rapt attention by his small flock of fisherfolk whose forebears had been transplanted from Scotland by an improving landlord a century earlier. Whether they followed the threads of his arguments, or were simply impressed by his learning, was impossible to tell. The Padre, as we called him, sometimes came for high tea. He prepared Grey for confirmation and helped Skimper with his Greek. He was fond of racing and could discuss the details of form with as much knowledge as he could the heresies of Nestorius (for whom he confessed a sneaking sympathy) or the niceties of the Chalcedonian controversy. One Sunday we invited him to join us at some flapper races being held on Bunbeg strand. He shook his head, looking bitterly disappointed. 'Any other time,' he said. 'Sunday's my bad day.'

Later, as we became more established in our little community, I sometimes attended mass at the chapel at the far end of our lake. Annie-the-Milk told me my presence made her nervous; she was anxious lest some priest from the coast launch a diatribe against the

Church of Ireland and its congregations. But I enjoyed sitting among and praying with the people who had become our friends. We formed the Country Women's Association, a kind of Women's Institute which met in the billiard room: we learned how to make lumnar rugs out of the daggings of wool left by the sheep on brambles and bushes, using crochet hooks. At the end of these sessions we would sing to an accordion and dance into the night.

The Gowries were our first visitors; they had left Windsor Castle and moved to a house in Charles Street, Mayfair, lent to them by one of the companies of which Sandie was a director. They embraced Errigal and its kingdom and took the people of the Glen to their hearts, as they had taken the people of Australia. Zara was having terrible back trouble, but refused to rest. She sat in a wheel-chair as she applauded every salmon caught by Derek (christened by her the 'Duke of Dunlewy'), every trout caught by the boys in the lake. The fish were cooked by Mary the housekeeper, or by Nellie, her successor. Himself was fading rapidly, his mind wandering restlessly over past wars and half-forgotten campaigns, recycling the anxieties he must have faced before attending meetings or making public appearances.

Our parents' generation was passing one by one. The Giant, too, visited us, but was already suffering from the cancer that would kill her three years later. For the Reverend there had been, unlike Sandie, no anxiety during his decline, and though he gave up reading and talk, he had continued to sit at the piano, playing a hymn or baby Bach, till a natural death visited him at 87 Cadogan Gardens in 1949. In May 1955 Themselves were staying with an old friend, Eny Strutt, at Hodges Barn, near Tetbury in Gloucestershire. There Sandie's brave and restless spirit came to rest at last. His body was taken to the churchyard across the fields in a farm estate car by Dick Wintour, one of the Wintour twins, who both served with Pat in the desert.

After being badly wounded, Dick had gone to Australia to be mended, become Sandie's ADC and been with the Gowries when news came through of Pat's death in hospital. Boon companions, he and his brother carried on as honorary ADCs to Sandie at the Norman Tower before they both found charming wives. Sometimes, after a night out in London, I stayed with them in the latecomers' suite at Claridge's; nothing was very expensive just after the war. The game was for one of the twins to go down to be shaved, and half an hour later the other would descend to lambast the barber for giving him bad service and leaving him with such a rough beard.

I recently found an old undated newspaper cutting, a chatty piece from *The Times* about the difficulties of being a Governor-General of Australia, where such authority as the holder of the title possesses needs to be wielded with the utmost discretion. The prime example, it said, 'was Lord Gowrie who died in 1955, the very model of a modern Governor-General. As an aristocrat, a VC and a shrewd politician, he had ideal qualifications: his public speeches were bromides, but his private dinner parties were fraught with power.'

After Grey had, as a lanky fifteen-year-old, inherited the title, Ferry-the-Tailor, the most prosperous man in the village, solemnly congratulated him on 'coming into his estates', little knowing that what Sandie had to leave his grandsons was probably rather less than he, old Ferry, kept under his bed.

Our social life in Donegal centred on what Zara called 'The Group', most of whom were bachelors, gay or otherwise, who settled there after the war when old houses could be bought for next to nothing. The Group's unquestioned leader – nicknamed by Zara the 'Monarch of the Glen' – was Henry P. McIlhenny himself, a descendant of Donegal Presbyterians who had gone to America in the great migrations after the famine, and made several fortunes: in the South, they patented a highly successful recipe for peppery Tabasco sauce; in the North, they invested profitably in gasometers. Henry, the great aesthete and art collector, told me he never passed one of the huge cylinders which so disfigure America's cities without raising his fedora to it.

Henry spent most of the year in Philadelphia attending to his duties as museum curator. But once spring had laid its laggard fingers on Donegal – not before late May or early June – he arrived to indulge his passion: to create a series of gardens out of the bog and mountain behind Glenveagh Castle. Adjoining the castle was a large walled *jardin potager*, where vegetables and fruit for the table grew among herbacious plants and box hedges. Behind it a twisted stairway of granite steps rose steeply to the top of the mountain under a canopy of ancient oaks and holly trees, planted with azaleas, lillies and ferns, with platforms for statuary brought in from Italy and beyond.

Henry had only one criterion by which he judged his guests:

whether or not they 'made fun'. They came from a wide assortment of backgrounds, first the Philadelphians, some of them benefactors to the museum, others simply neighbours or friends. Some came only once, either because they couldn't stand the weather, or because Henry decided they didn't 'make fun' after all. Others were annual fixtures, such as Mrs Henry, who travelled with a trunkload of evening dresses from Paris and handed out boxes of cigars or bottles of scent to members of the Group. She admired Derek, whom she used to called 'the Shape'. On Sundays, at the Protestant church at Churchill, which many of the Group attended, a small boy would sometimes stand outside with a collection box marked 'Jubilee Nurses'. Into this receptacle Mrs Henry would stuff dollar bills. On its reverse side, presented to worshippers leaving the Catholic chapels, it bore a very different legend.

As we soaked away the day's work at Dunlewy in hot baths of soft brown water and dressed ourselves up – Derek in his velvet smoking jacket, made for him by Ferry, myself in the raw silk Arabian dresses run up for me by the *tessoria* in Asolo during grander days; and as we trundled in the Land-Rover over the wild bog road, with its puddles and ruts, and up the six-mile Glenveagh avenue through storms and gales in the long summer twilight, it seemed we had become part of the exotic landscape Henry was inviting his friends across the ocean to see. We willingly entered his Victorian Gothic fantasy, 'making fun' in homage to our Monarch, for the splendid fare we would find at his table, beneath the disturbing scenes of carnage – dying stags, dead ptarmigans – in the Landseers adorning the walls. Before dinner we would gather in the great hall, where, whatever the weather, a turf fire glowed beneath George Stubbs's painting of a hunt servant wearing a green coat, standing between his hounds and a dead hind, while old Irish mahogany furniture and silver candelabra from extinct Irish regiments gleamed in the lamplight.

Every kind of warming or cooling drink was laid out under the tall bookcases. In earlier years, under the relatively austere governance of Mr and Mrs Whiteside, dinner was served at nine o'clock sharp. Later, when Patrick Gallaher from Dunlewy took over, with his sister Nellie as cook, the regime became more relaxed. We succumbed to the transatlantic habit of downing iced drinks on an empty stomach, and when dinner was eventually served, some of the guests had

difficulty negotiating the passageways into the dining room, or reading the cards in Henry's florid hand that told them where to sit.

Later in the season the sportsmen arrived, with guns and fishing
rods: Randal Dunsany, Major 'Killer' Palmer and Bill King. They
stalked and shot the stags, or fished for sea trout in the lake. We used
to hear the gossip from the stalkers and household staff, most of
whom came from Dunlewy families. Lord Dunsany, being a famous
shot, insisted on shooting standing up, and sometimes he missed;
Mrs King (Anita Leslie) arrived with a laundry basket full of her
children's dirty clothes, and with a charming smile would ask the
maids to wash them for her. The culling of the stags – picking out
the weaker males or 'switches' – was a necessary task which Henry's
more artistic friends were too squeamish to perform. The Monarch
himself was said to have abandoned stalking after a stag greeted him
on the drive by raising its forelegs, like some heraldic beast.

I had one hunting box available with Anita, when I went to stay
with her and Bill in the old castle and keep they had bought and
half-restored on the coast outside Galway City. In some ways the
Galway Blazers country was a mug's paradise: 'You'd be saysick with
lepping,' was the caption to one of Snaffle's hunting pictures. To the
south were the Black and Tans, and in Zara's old country to the north
and east the East Galway and the inimitable Mollie O'Rourke's
Birmingham Hunt. Lovely country it was: flat with a great skyscape
above the grazing black cattle and the limestone little fields of good
grass and wild flags.

Other possibilities came up with Derek's former brother-in-law,
Pat Herdman, who before the war inherited Zion Mills at Strabane:
a red-brick settler village and a large factory that provided linen for
the famous Belfast shirt trade. Derek was still very young when Pat
married his sister Mary. One winter Anthony Powell arrived to stay:
a visit immortalized in a chapter of *Afternoon Men*. At the start of
the war Pat volunteered for the Life Guards and Derek arranged all
his interviews, but at the last minute the War Office asked if Zion
Mills could convert to manufacturing 2-pound ammunition for
armoured cars, so Pat made that his war effort instead. For years after
the war the mills prospered, Pat buying on the Continent when the
North of Ireland could no longer supply enough flax. It employed
maidens from Donegal and was never a target for the Provisionals.

Pat was accustomed by choice to hunt in County Meath, but once he was tied to the north he busied himself with transforming the Strabane Harriers into fox-hounds. It was rumoured that fox cubs were captured in the Poisoned Glen, bagged, taken to the Strabane area and released. To encourage us to become subscribers, Pat would offer to mount us and hold out the prospect of a comfortable bed and bath and an excellent dinner. The kennels were at his home, Carricklea, with quite good rough mountainy country round about, though the hunt also went farther afield into Donegal across the border. One day, when the meet was south of Dunlewy in Donegal, he rang me to say he had a mount for me which I would find there. I arrived to be met by a country boy wearing a large floppy cap leading up a young mare with little more than a donkey snaffle in her mouth. She was obviously just off grass. The boy gaped at me in alarm. 'I never thought t'would be a lady,' he said.

My usefulness, it transpired, was to try out the mare for Pat, hunt her across the border into Ulster and land her at the hunt stables at Carricklea without paying a toll. Surprisingly we had rather a happy day together; she was sure-footed and a good buy.

Sadly, in the long run, we found Strabane too long a journey from Dunlewy. Pat had married a second time, to a couturière from Dublin, known as 'Miss Dorothy' to the Group; she made a lot of fun. The other members of the Group repaid Henry's hospitality as best they could, with luncheons, dinners or picnics. At Dunlewy we could seat up to twenty. Knowing how many Dunlewy families had members on the castle payroll, Nellie and Mary never faltered when the Glenveagh party came to dine. Our social arrangements would be known all over the village: as there was no telephone, we communicated by telegram. Seamus, the postmistress's son, would bring them up on his bicycle from Gweedore, six miles away, and await a reply. Sometimes the postmistress would save her sons the long bicycle ride by answering a telegram for us. Once, when Kitty Nairne telegraphed to ask if she could stay a few nights, she received the instant reply, 'DELIGHTED STOP PAM'. When she arrived she was greatly disconcerted to find us away: the postmistress, mistaking a car she had seen for the Major's, assumed we were back from our travels. But Nellie looked after her as beautifully as if we had been there ourselves. The postmistress belonged to a well-known republican family: when it was Seamus's younger brother, 'the wee fella', who brought the telegrams, we knew that Seamus must be out on some operation and trouble afoot in the North.

As Henry did in his bothy, so we gave ceilidhs in the billiard room, dancing the local dances, 'The Waves of Tory' and the like, to a local fiddle and concertina. None jigged better than Padre Watson and Patrick O'Donnell, both maintaining the professional straight face and torso and the high-stepping legs. Despite our dictum, 'by invitation only', strangers would turn up from the coast or having crossed the mountain between us and the Finn valley. One small mountainy man, who wouldn't leave the kitchen, replied when interrogated, 'M'name is O'Toole and I take a long while to drink me tay'; it had to have whiskey in it. Skimper held up one evening with his demands for a vet. He was drying out some half-drowned gosling in the airing cupboard. He would search the Glen on his bicycle for bargains in ducks.

Beyond Glenveagh, towards the country town of Letterkenny, where we did our shopping, lived two other Donegal bachelors, Sir Anthony Weldon and Derek Hill. Tony Weldon, 'The Bart', had been one of the most sought-after young men during the 1920s. His Punch-like profile features prominently among the Bright Young Things in the frontispiece of Patrick Balfour's *Society Racket*. His mother, Winnie, had known Sandie and Zara during the days of their courtship in Ireland, when Zara was forbidden to attend any ball if it was thought likely that Sandie would be there. Winnie had been famous for her talent for whistling: her after-dinner performances must have made a welcome change from the sentimental ballads that usually went with the coffee and sweets. Tony had inherited some of her irreverence and sense of fun. He was particularly fond of telling risqué jokes, and even his Christmas cards would be pregnant with double-entendres. He owned a cocker spaniel, named Elvis, who took a lascivious delight in men's legs while his master looked on, indulgently.

Tony's house, Rathdonnel, was a Georgian town-house, with steps up to the front door and railings, set improbably on a hill next to an ancient rath or ring-fort, as if transplanted bodily from Dublin. The dinner parties he gave were generally more stylish than ours, though the guests would always arrive by the kitchen door, to be welcomed first by Hannah, his elderly cook, and whoever happened to be taking tea with her in the kitchen.

Derek Hill's housekeeper, Gracie, also liked to receive his guests, but preferred to wait until dinner was over. She made wonderful soups from wild sorel or home-grown herbs and was endlessly inventive, never tiring of trying out new recipes given to her by Derek. His house, St Columbs, next to Lough Gartan where St Columba had been born, had once been a small hotel. It was filled with his collection of paintings – including works by Renoir, Mary Kessel, Victor Pasmore and Keith Vaughan – as well as an enormous collection of old postcards and memorabilia from his frequent travels in the Middle East. When dining with Derek we ate off plates designed by Picasso. Derek loved opera and used to play his favourite arias over a hi-fi system run on car batteries – a great novelty in the days before the ESB brought electricity into our valleys.

We bought a black pony from the tinkers at a local fair – unwisely. She wasn't an easy ride and had surely been ill-treated. Grey was undaunted, however. With a sandwich in a rucksack, he rode her across the bog to the cultivation and Lough Gartan on an expedition to see Derek Hill's pictures. He returned late in the evening with a small Henry Moore bronze in the rucksack, which, he assured me, had been lent for the holidays, because he loved it so.

The Bart found D. Hill a bit too bohemian and democratic. Derek went to great lengths to cultivate local people and dignitaries, and I have no doubt that, had his offer to advise the tourist industry been accepted, Ireland would now be the pride of the European Community. Bart's relations with local farmers and tradespeople were rather more paternalistic. Our Monarch did nothing to ease the strife that grew up 'twixt St Columbs and Rathdonnel. He delighted in teasing D. Hill, who nearly always rose to the bait; and when Derek turned up at Glenveagh looking grumpy, Henry would say, with a dismissive sweep of his hand, 'Well, my dear, I don't think he makes fun at all!' When Zara was old and unwell and staying with us at Dunlewy, she tried to prod Henry into negotiating a Monarch's peace between Bart and Derek. 'What do you do,' she asked slyly, 'if two of your neighbours don't get on?'

'I fan the flames, Lady Gowrie,' said Henry, giving his famous shrug and inimitable chuckle. 'I just fan the flames.'

Most of Donegal had been so poor that Anglo-Irish landowners were more than usually absentee. Only two members of the Group were truly indigenous. The first, Anne Leitrim, the widow of Lord

Leitrim, lived on an estate overlooking Mulroy Bay, the most gentle of the sea loughs penetrating Donegal's northern coast, with tame-looking fields and islets that contrast with the savage cliffs of neighbouring Lough Swilly. Her husband had been a descendant of the so-called 'Wicked Earl' murdered on the road between Ramelton and Carrigart, not far from his estate: reputedly a harsh landlord who abused the local maidens. His assassins are believed to have escaped across Mulroy Bay by boat; they were never apprehended. Anne Leitrim was a tiny bird-like person who always looked cheerful, even after undergoing a series of fearsome operations for cancer. A passionate gardener, she did not appear despondent or cast down when a hurricane utterly destroyed her collection of rare rhododendrons and azaleas. She was Henry's closest gardening friend and mentor. They would stroll round the grounds together, Henry with his secateurs, Anne turning over the plants leaf by leaf, intoning the Latin names that gardeners use but no Roman ever spoke.

Rosapenna Hotel, on the sand-dunes near Mulroy, had been built by Lord Leitrim: a rambling overgrown chalet with golf course and tennis courts, and fabulous views of the Muckish mountain, which had greeted my eyes when we were being chased by the U-boat on my way home in 1941. The hotel was noted for giving extra helpings of its sound country fare without any extra charge. It had a landing strip and good harbourage with fishing, and we used it a lot in the early years. But it burned to the ground. Derek Hill, who painted on Tory Island, was staying there at the time, and so was Bobby Somerset's uncle, 'Obbie' St Albans. The old man wouldn't leave the doomed building, and kept shouting for his toast. 'Your Grace's toast is burnt,' answered the terrified waiter. Obbie had a villa in Andraix, Majorca, where Bobby Somerset kept his yacht. It was when we were staying there one year that to our delight we overheard Lady Dashwood's pronouncement to another villa owner: 'If you want to have people like us, you cannot have people like them.'

The Group's other indigenous member was Lionel Perry a former 'golden boy' at Oxford during the 1920s who now lived with his elderly mother, a native of Donegal. In her youth Mrs Perry had driven by pony trap as far as Lisadel in County Sligo, home of Eva Gore-Booth and Constance Markievicz. Now she was confined at home with arthritis. There was a Gertrude Jekyll atmosphere to the house and garden near Milford on Mulroy Bay, and on the walls idyllic watercolours of Lionel and his brother by Æ (Russell), two small boys with golden curls dashing into the Atlantic waves. After working in Intelligence during the war, Lionel had returned to Donegal, his golden curls receding, his girth expanding to the contours of the Laughing Buddha. He never overcame the stammer which afflicted his youth, but always his humour and jokes bubbled through. After evenings at Dunlewy or Glenveagh, when he tended to consume considerable amounts of whiskey, there was always a worry about returning him home in his battered old car. He knew the country like no one else in the Group. When people bought houses, he knew all the best shops in Derry or Strabane for antiques and furnishings. Unable to entertain at home because of his mother, he repaid hospitality by arranging picnics and outings. It was Li who organized crabbing expeditions at Marble Hill strand on the first night of the new moon, when the tide was extra low and the smooth round domes of the crabs could be felt and yanked from crannies under the rocks before the claws severed one's fingers.

Ricki Huston came into our lives about this time, when she was staying at Glenveagh. She had abandoned a career as a ballet dancer to become the fourth wife of the film director John Huston, and mother of his only children. She lived at St Clerans, the house the Hustons bought near Galway City and the ruins of Lismany, where Zara had spent her childhood. It was also close to the kennels of the Galway Blazers, of which John became joint master. Ricki created for herself a little home in the steward's cottage in the yard at St Clerans, and here brought up her two children, Tony and Angelica, while John came and went about the world, making such films as *Moby Dick* and *The Roots of Heaven*.

Ricki's father, Tony Soma, had been an Italian New York restaurateur since Prohibition days – the proprietor of Tony's Place on West 52nd Street. John first met her in the restaurant when she was thirteen and he promised to take her to the ballet. The promise was never fulfilled, but she reminded him of it when they met again some years later. 'I never did get to the ballet with Ricki,' he wrote in his autobiography, 'but I did marry her.' Ricki showed me her father's way of mixing a salad. Despite her romantic looks, she was a good housewife and homemaker. She had black hair, a lovely pale skin and the largest imaginable pair of dark blue-grey eyes.

At one time when she was very unhappy she came to stay at

Dunlewy with Angelica, Tony having gone off to boarding school. The time must have been nearing Christmas, for when I asked Angelica what carols she knew, she replied that she only knew one, 'Rudi the Red-nosed Reindeer' – at which point I twigged Ricki's background was Jewish. She wore becoming country clothes and rarely went out on the blustery mountain; instead she sat beside the turf fire, recovering from I know not what tragedy or love affair. It seemed that John was just a father figure for her and her children, and before long there was a legal separation. Derek and I grew to be closely attached to Ricki: it was through her that we first heard of the work of Amnesty International. Hers was another soul that cared about the world's injustices.

Once, when we were staying with her at St Clerans, word came through that John would be arriving with his entourage to stay a few days. Under Ricki's direction, the big house was aired, the bedrooms prepared, the larder loaded. In due course we sat down to dinner by candlelight with the whole Huston circus at a long mahogany table. Outside, seen through the great glass windows, the moonlight shone on the walls, fields and dykes that lay beyond St Clerans. John sat at the head of the table, a welcoming expansive host, as if the only life he ever knew was that of a master of fox-hounds in the west of Ireland. When a big dog fox crossed the lawns outside, our host jumped up and led the Americans in a chorus of hunting halloas which culminated in drinking the animal's health – to the astonishment of some of the other guests, who included visitors from the Far East. Next morning, as he was walking around the estate with someone I took to be his man of finance, I heard the adviser utter twice, 'All I can say, John, is, keep working, keep working.'

Ricki seemed happier among the snows. We found her at Klosters, and again at St Anton, skiing as I had always longed to do: with the best of the private guides to carry skis and fasten boots. The last I saw of her was at her house in Little Venice in about 1964. She seemed to be happy, with her new baby, Allegra. When I asked her whom it was like, she said, 'Like you.' It was not John's, but she bears his name. When Allegra was about five, Ricki died in a car crash in France and John brought the little girl back to Ireland.

The Giant had finally succumbed to cancer early in 1956. I had stayed over in London to help my sister Diana and the devoted Alice during the last stage of her illness. Michael flew over from Germany, a brigadier resplendent in scarlet, khaki and gold braid. We buried her beside the Reverend in the little churchyard near Moushill cottage, just next to the London to Portsmouth road. Seeing her slight, unaged shell, with its mane of thick blonde hair, left me feeling sad and remote, lonely and guilty.

When I arrived back in Ireland, to meet Derek and the boys at the Shelbourne Hotel in Dublin, they could talk of nothing but a sealed bid Derek had made for Knockalla, one of six naval forts on Lough Swilly, originally built against a Napoleonic invasion and now offered for sale by the government. During my absence in England, Derek had taken the boys for picnics there. All three had fallen in love with the old ruined fort, with its banana-shaped tower, clad in soft sandstone to withstand French or German shells, its crumbling barrack buildings, its gun emplacements and its massive ramparts surrounded by pounding seas and gannet-crowded cliffs. In the event, we lost Knockalla to an English general with a Gaelic-speaking wife. Disappointment was mitigated when a slightly larger offer – all of £70 – was accepted for Fort Macamish, a Martello tower farther up the lough near Rathmullen, the port whence the O'Neill and the O'Donnell, earls of Tyrone and Tyrconnell, the last independent chiefs of Ulster, fled to France early in 1607 – the so-called 'Flight of the Earls', clearing the way for the 'plantation' of the six counties with Protestants.

Paddy O'Donnell brought timber and other materials over from Dunlewy by tractor, a journey that took him three hours or more: his wife Nora suffered dreadfully every time he ventured on to the open road. The work of restoration was backbreaking: it seemed that everyone in the vicinity, grown-up or child, had spent many happy hours tipping stones from the fort into the sea below. Fortunately we found a brilliant mason, Tommy Deaney, who lived in a cottage near by. Using block and tackle, Derek, Tommy and James, Tommy's mate, raised most of the stones needed to construct a causeway across the dry moat between the fort and the little peninsula on which it was situated.

We restored the guardroom next to the old drawbridge, and the magazine, with its thick sandstone walls set below ground level to contain any explosions. Then we got to work on the tower itself, which, though damp, was in fairly good condition. There was a large basement where the soldiers had lodged. This we made into a bedroom with a bathroom *en suite*. A corkscrew stairway set in the thick sandstone walls led to the officers' quarters above, which hung with stalactites caused by more than a century of damp. We never quite defeated the stalactites and weeping walls, but the upper floor provided us with a crescent-shaped kitchen and large living room, punctuated by slit windows and deep wall embrasures. There was no ground-floor entrance: the soldiers had reached the upper floor by a ladder drawn up at night. Li Perry solved this problem in the local pub one evening, designing an external cantilevered staircase that we built out of concrete.

The restoration of Macamish caused much excitement among the Group. Henry would bring over the whole of his current house party, along with lavish picnics, which Patrick laid out, weather permitting, on the grassy ledges beneath the tower. When the work was finally complete, we threw a huge party of our own. Nearly a hundred people turned up, to drink black velvet (Guinness and champagne) after climbing the steep stone steps to face the turbulent winds at the top of the tower. There were duchesses and poets, artists and masters of fox-hounds, sportsmen and aesthetes, writers and couturiers, as well as Tommy and Fanny Deaney, James and their friends.

During the summer holidays, when Errigal was shrouded in mist and the midges became a torment to us, we would flee to Macamish, where the weather was usually better. Skimper was in heaven there, piloting the small motor boat we used to fish for mackerel and collect lobsters, or simply gazing at the cormorants and gannets diving off the rocky pinnacles beneath the gun emplacements. Grey, who was having problems with mathematics, used to take an open boat from Rathmullen to Fahan, on the opposite side of the Swilly, there to catch a bus to receive tuition from Mr Gillanders of the Londonderry High School for Girls. The mysteries of calculus continued to defeat him, but the hours he spent waiting for the bus back to Fahan, when he would walk around the old city walls, and inspect the Bogside graffiti, no doubt stood him in good stead when he became Minister of State for Northern Ireland.

At Macamish we became friendly with a new neighbour, Circe's eldest daughter, Margaret Vane Tempest Stewart, known as 'Lady Peg'. She had bought the near-by Drumallagh House, a Regency shooting lodge not unlike Dunlewy, set amid beautiful trees, with a delightful garden. Lady Peg, however, never became sufficiently organized to live there, and like so many Irish houses it went into a steep decline. Instead, she converted a cottage next to the beach into a Spanish-style studio where she gave parties lasting late into the night. Lady Peg cooked supper, which sometimes took rather a long time to arrive, but seldom partook of it herself. Before her guests had finished eating, she would be ready to perform one of her 'cabarets' – really improvised ballads celebrating recent events or topics in the manner of the Gaelic bards of old.

There was one about the spy for Russia, Klaus Fuchs, whose name was back in the news with his release to go behind the Iron Curtain; another about Diana Dors, whose buxom movements, 'in the doors and out the doors', Lady Peg mimicked between puffs of her cigarette. My favourite, 'The Good Ship', commemorated a drama which nearly cost Derek and me our lives, when our spaniel Doherty fell overboard and almost drowned in the Swilly's turbulent waters, before Derek managed to rescue him by plunging overboard himself. The three of us eventually fetched up, dripping, shaken and exhausted, on Lady Peg's beach. Even as the hot whiskeys were reviving us, we saw the episode transformed into Art, in an epic that came to bear frequent repetition. Not everyone appreciated Lady Peg's cabarets, but they fulfilled an important need for someone who, in Sandie's phrase, had not enjoyed 'the luck of the race'. She bore the scars of a less than happy life. Her former husband, Hugh Falkus, who had briefly resided with her at Drumallagh, was once reported to have attacked her with a salmon he'd just caught in the river.

On the mountain behind Dunlewy we kept a flock of 'hornies', black-faced sheep tended by Johnny and his collies. Among them was a black ewe known as Granniepack (a 'granniepack' being a term used in Zara's family to denote a letter written to one member, which could then be forwarded to any others who might be interested; thus it might travel the world). Like those steers on the Bogong high plains, Granniepack was uncontainable and would break out from any flocking, dipping or clipping occasion. We decided to bring her to graze the lush, overgrown grass of about a quarter of an acre within the sea-wall at Macamish. For company, Paddy provided young Ram O'Donnell, equally black. We looked forward to a black family and a woolclip for spinning and knitting into sweaters by Fanny Deaney. I got one sweater from the ewe: it smelled fiercely and was dirty-grey in colour. But one day Granniepack heard a dog and, already tired of her confinement, jumped the sea-wall by the old garderobe and fell to her death.

Dominic, our butcher, was a powerful cattle men and sold excellent meat. He said the secret was never to kill a beast when it was frightened: not only was it cruel but the meat would not taste right. He had a notable flow of oaths, but was shy. At the kitchen door he would preface every sentence with, 'Ah, cheese,' bridling like a girl and chewing anything to hand – a cow's tail, when inspecting the beast, and once he downed a whole daffodil while talking with me. His wife looked like Mrs Bull the Butcher's Wife in 'Happy Families'. She sawed, cut and served in the shop at the little port of Bunbeg, along the coast. When she was out of temper, they said, she attacked Dominic with the cleaver. He often tipped the boys half a crown, which pleased them greatly.

Altogether we spent four or five pleasant summers at Macamish, until the boys were grown and other concerns began to interfere. Eventually Derek sold the Martello tower to Arthur Pilkington from Cheshire for £4,000. The Pilkingtons, who had been at the famous party and fallen in love with Macamish over a jar of black velvet, were able to use the glass they manufactured to defeat the wind and weather in a way we could never have afforded.

Our sojourns in Rathmullan had taken us closer to the tensions brewing in the six counties, though in the late 1950s an uneasy calm spread across the province after the collapse of an earlier IRA campaign. The borders at Strabane or Bridgend were merely symbolic: there were no delays as one entered the richer farmlands of Ulster. A shopping expedition to Derry, where goods were cheaper and more plentiful than in the protectionist Republic, was a special treat for Nellie and Mary, and for Nora, Paddy's wife. All the people of the Glen had relatives in the city. Men found employment in its mills and factories; and now that the naval base had been reduced to a shadow of its wartime presence, Derry was a safer city than Dublin for the daughters of the Gaeltacht, who could train as nurses or find jobs without danger to Catholic virtue.

At the ends of holidays I often sent the boys back to school from Letterkenny, or even from the cross-roads a mile beyond the Catholic chapel, where the bus picked them up, with absolute confidence. From Letterkenny they took an antiquated 'bus-train', actually a bus sitting on train-wheels, that ran on a remnant of the old Lough Swilly railway; at Strabane, the kindly Corporal Shearer (late of the Irish Guards, now a porter) would place them on the train to Belfast, where they caught the night ferry to Liverpool. The greatest danger they faced was losing their tickets, or an excess of Guinness in one of the pubs they visited to kill time before the boat.

'We intend nothing with greater earnestness than the plantation of Ulster with civil men well affected in religion shall be accomplished with zeal and integrity,' proclaimed King James I and VI in 1609. His policy is still seeping its poison into the land, like the spurge in the Poisoned Glen. After the earls of Tyrone and Tyrconnell had fled, two fifths of their forfeited landed estates was granted to the 'undertakers', the Scotch and English settlers, one fifth was given to the Church and education. Once the Crown had also taken its whack, there was little left for the indigenous population of native Irish. Only Trinity College, Dublin, the Alma Mater of my grandfather, the Reverend and his three brothers, received any benefit from the reign of King James. To this day, few British leaders have shown any understanding of the hopes and fears of the native Irish.

Despite this, the community in Dunlewy seemed to accept us as both familiar and foreign: the distinctions of rank and the privileges of ownership were acknowledged, but counted for less than in England. Long after we were married, I remained Lady Ruthven, while Derek was always 'The Major', except to some of the older men, who addressed him tersely as *Kuperr*. Dunlewy folk were mostly Fine Gael supporters: the big man in the area was Pa O'Donnell, a kinsman of Paddy and Johnny's, whose network of patronage extended from the Rosses to Gweedore. As heirs to the pro-Treaty faction in the civil war, Fine Gael supporters tended to be less 'republican' than the rival Fianna Fáil, the party of de Valera.

Nevertheless there were certain rules to be observed, and Derek, having been brought up in the North, understood them well. With the salmon fishing, it was sometimes expedient to turn a blind eye to strange rods, especially when they belonged to locals; while the affable Father Sharkey from Falcarragh, who loved to fish, was welcome to borrow our boat. Sophie Ferry, the unmarried sister of Ferry-the-Tailor, who lived with two other bachelor brothers on the other side of the lough – the whole family were weavers – said the salmon didn't belong to the Major, even though he paid the rates. The Major, unabashed, would watch from his dressing-room window for the first salmon to rise at the head of the lough. Sophie had a wonderful sales blarney. She sold tweed to the Group and their house guests, and arranged for the cloth to be made up by Ferry-the-Tailor.

Dunlewy was to remain the haven we returned to from our travels, to be succoured by Nellie, with her simple country cooking and wonderful home-made bread, in safe seclusion from the madness and cruelty of the outside world.

15

Hungarian Winter, Arabian Spring

Hungary

There wasn't much mud in north-west Donegal in the post-Suez autumn of 1956. Great stair-rods of rain hit the thin coating of soil cladding its ancient rocks, and except for the unnegotiable bogs, the water hurried down into the lakes and rivers. But it was mud we were thinking about as the newspapers and radio told of an uprising in Hungary against its secret police and their Russian masters. As the Russian tanks stormed in, many Hungarian families and young people, encouraged by the strident American accents of Radio Free Europe, began to flee the country. What they encountered as they attempted to cross the border into Austria was mud, the mud of the still unfrozen marshes and swamps. Foreign correspondents told a piteous story. We had just bought a new long-wheelbase Land-Rover.

I crossed to London, my task to listen, weight up the need and the opportunity to help, then telephone my findings back to Derek in Dunlewy. Many discussions and planning meetings took place in Patsy Jellicoe's handsome drawing room in 20 Chapel Street, Patsy having brought together a group of friends who mostly knew one another from the campaigns in the Middle East. 'What would you do,' I asked Alan Moorehead, 'if you'd just bought a new Land-Rover to get in turf and wood for your fire?'

He didn't answer immediately, but walked away past the piano. Then he turned and looked at me with his huge navy-blue eyes. 'I'd get hold of a load of what's needed and go. If I found there was nothing I could do when I got there, then I'd come back.'

So it came about that Derek left Paddy and Johnny to look after
the old woods and the new plantations on the mountainside, for-
sook the loving care of Nellie and Mary, the big turf fires and his
little kingdom of lakes and rivers watched over by Errigal mountain,
and hurried to London in the brand-new white Land-Rover. My
embryonic plan was transformed into precise preparations and we
became part of a team whose members would include, at various
times, Bill Astor, Mark and Annabel Birley, Celia Monkton and Jane
Willoughby, from the English side; and, from the Continent, Count
Geza Andrashy, Evan Carl Eltz (a German Knight of Malta) and,
working for the Austrian Red Cross, Tatiana and Paul Metternich.
We picked up a mound of relief supplies from the Save the Children
Fund, at the time under the outstanding and imaginative direction
of Brigadier Boyce, and left London on 29 November.

On 2 December we drove into Vienna, laden down with one ton
of bedding, clothing and socks, medical supplies and dolls. After
reporting to the Austrian headquarters of Save the Children – Rettet
das Kind – we delivered our load to the cellars of the Hoffburg
palace, the enormous basement of which was full of blankets and
camp beds, and every kind of clothing, from knitted jumpers to
boiled shirts and evening gowns from Paris. It was all being sorted
by Austrian helpers. The Russians had only quitted Vienna the
previous year, after seven years of wearisome bargaining to wrest
from Moscow a settlement founding the new Austria. Within a few
hours of the last foreign soldier leaving her soil, Austria's government
passed a law which 'Freely and voluntarily' proclaimed her 'perpetual
neutrality'. She undertook to join no military alliances and to forbid
foreign bases on her territory. But when neighbouring Hungary
erupted, Austria, struggling after so much suffering into her new
national costume, had opened heart and purse to the *flüchtlinger*
(refugees) two months before any of us from the West arrived to
help.

In Vienna we met Count Trapp, prior of the Austrian Grand
Priory of the Sovereign Order of the Knights of Malta, whose history
went back to the eleventh century and the founding in Jerusalem by
Italian merchants of a monastery with a hospital and rest-house for
the pilgrims to the Holy Sites. The Hungarian uprising had con-
fronted the Austrian Grand Priory with the task of meeting the
desperately urgent needs of the hundreds of thousands of refugees

who were streaming into the country along the length of Austria's eastern border, stretching from Czechoslovakia in the north to Yugoslavia in the south. Its response included setting up round-the-clock first-aid stations at various points close to the frontier to provide shelter, food, warm clothes and medical aid for fugitives, to bridge the gap between their arrival on Austrian soil and their reception at one of the big camps prepared by the authorities farther inland. After talking to Count Trapp, we decided to work for the Order in conjunction with Rettet das Kind, our first assignment being to collect a ton of sugar from a warehouse outside Vienna and deliver it to the cellars of the Lichtenstein palace. There we had a call from Count Trapp's office asking us to drive south to Oberpullendorf with a cargo of apples, chocolate, sanitary towels and rum. On the way we caught our first glimpse of the *flüchtlinger*. They were gathered in small groups, having crossed the frontier some six kilometres to the east. The next day our contact in Oberpullendorf, the flamboyant Count Pallavicini, told us our Land-Rover was not needed there as they already had two Italian jeeps, and most of the refugees came in to their centre on foot anyway. Wondering despondently if the whole venture mightn't have been a mistake, we studied the map and decided to head north to Andau, where a number of aid agencies, including Rettet das Kind, Samarita Bund (the Samaritans), the Knights of Malta, and the Austrian and German Red Cross, had set up forward reception centres.

Andau was very close to the frontier, which to the north ran as a fifty-metre ploughed strip marked on one side by the red and white flags of Austria and on the other by Russian-built watch-towers. To the south it veered to the west, and here it was marked by the Torf and Einser Canal running through desolate swamps and marshland. On the canal's southern, Hungarian bank loomed the dark Kapuvar Woods. We drove at dusk into a village whose low houses stood back from the main street and turned their backs on its deep cart-ruts and huge, icy puddles. Introduced to the Samaritans, we asked a man called Ricard, wearing a dark-blue uniform, if they could use a Land-Rover. He almost hugged us. Allotted a pair of camp beds with grey blankets, we were served with supper and a bottle of wine.

By half past seven it was dark and time for our first patrol. It was heavy going, through the deep mud of ploughed fields, steering round haystacks. Ricard told us to stop beside a well. He got out, sniffed the air and put an ear to the ground. When he heard something, he took off his peaked cap and stood in the beam of the headlamps. 'Hier Österreich,' he whispered loudly into the darkness. Figures approached across the fields – two families, fourteen people altogether, one a very shaken old lady. We all shook hands excitedly before bundling them into the back of the Land-Rover. Ricard stayed behind on patrol as we set off back to Andau with our first load of *flüchtlinger*. Mercifully Derek had memorized the route. Shuttling back and forth till 4 a.m., we brought in a total of eighty *flüchtlinger* on our first night. We snatched only an hour's sleep in our camp beds, waking to a room crowded with refugees gnawing on *würst* and sipping sweet lemon tea. We gave up our beds to two pregnant women and spent what remained of the night in the Land-Rover.

The Land-Rover proved perfect for the job. By now sporting a large Red Cross flag as well as the cross of Malta on its bonnet (vital for getting into the frontier zone), it was a thoroughbred among the motley collection of Volkswagons, jeeps, ambulances and local farm tractors ferrying in the *flüchtlinger* at Andau. The weather grew steadily colder, the work more demanding. The sea of mud froze over and became covered with heavy snow. Adjoining the Rettet das Kind *lager*, in the nuns' schoolhouse, was the kitchen where Mary Hawkins, a nurse who would become an important figure in our lives, held sway. A small bird-like woman from Plymouth, and a descendant of the seafaring Hawkins, Mary had devoted her life to children of every nationality. After serving with the troops in North Africa during the war, she volunteered for Palestine, and then Korea, where she ministered to the needs of refugee children. British Aid to Hungary had sent a mobile canteen for her use at Andau.

Mary's kitchen was never empty, even on a quiet night. The village inns were dirty and closed early, leaving nowhere else for the frozen drivers to rest and thaw out. The kitchen became Andau's heart. Here we forgathered as the cold intensified. The room would be swept and scrubbed, water put to heat on the stove in a corner. The copper urns brimmed with lemon tea and cocoa, and great piles of ryebread sandwiches lay freshly cut on the table. Nappies, socks and baby clothes were stacked everywhere in the little room. Inside, all was warmth, light and order; outside, the darkening night, frozen snow and bitter cold. In Andau's ill-lit street the Land-Rovers and Volkswagens assembled; and after a hurried consultation, their polyglot assortment of drivers set off for the border, lurching and skidding towards their appointed rendezvous, by haystack and lonely well, around the outlying farms and marshes – Albrechtsfeld, Hansaghof, Pumpstelle, Kanal. Many tracks were becoming impassable. Vehicles bogged down in snowdrifts, and hours were wasted pulling them out. Soon only the tractors and Land-Rovers could make it. The road to the canal was ten kilometres of potholes and ruts that even the heavy snow could not fill. It narrowed dangerously where it left the ploughland and became a causeway across the marshes, ending abruptly at the frontier and the canal.

A long wait in the bitter cold stretched ahead of the volunteers as they combed through the frozen marsh, ears straining for footfalls, voices, a child's cry. If it rained or snowed or blew, the *flüchtlinger* would usually come in small groups; if the moon and stars were bright above the frosty world, they would still arrive, but more scattered, and many would be caught. When the Very lights flew up and exploded like fireworks in a lovely spray of white and red, we could make out huddled figures trying to cross the ploughed strip which stretched like a flattened snake along the frontier, or others chancing the canal on bundles of straw, home-made rafts. Sometimes we towed them across with a rubber dinghy brought from England as, all the while, the guards searched for them with flares, dogs and rifles.

By the lonely haystacks and wells or in the ice-bound swamps, we met them with handshakes, hugs, kisses, tears and laughter, or just a frightened scramble into the back of a truck. Baskets of food and a few pathetic valuables were heaved in after them. Deadweight rucksacks dropped from aching shoulders. One refugee refused to loose his pack. It had two holes cut in the bottom, out of which stuck two small, stiff legs. Heavily drugged, a blue woolly cap pulled over its face, the baby lay like a tiny St Andrew's Cross. Older children stood silent and polite, solemn eyes reflecting their parents' courage.

One woman was shot crossing the canal on an inner tube. She reached the shore, where she lay and died in the snow in a pool of blood, far from the track. Alex France, a young American who should have been studying in Paris, watched over her body until the others were free of the living. Later a young girl crossed over all by herself, panting like a hunted animal. She had become separated from a party rounded up by an AVO patrol. A few hours before she arrived, we heard women's voices pleading with an officer. A baby cried ceaselessly until they were marched away. The girl explained she had made her desperate escape because her fiancé had already managed the crossing. As she hid in the bushes, a guard had shouted, 'They won't help you on the other side.'

One by one the overloaded cars grumbled and reeled back to Andau, and drove first to Mary's kitchen. The big room, smelling strongly of mud and wet wool, was already half-full. Behind the Christmas tree a baby was being bathed. Two small brothers stood staring at the lights and parcels as layer after layer of clothes were peeled off. We handed the rucksack baby over to Mary. The agonized father leant over the inert little shape as she tried to discover from him how many tablets it had been given.

Mary darted hither and thither, directing her workers and carrying the badly drugged babies over to the doctor, who injected them and ordered cold douches. They had to be kept awake for several hours to prevent them getting pneumonia. Having served its purpose, the drug began to irritate the babies' nerves; they rolled and squirmed like kittens, moaning as if in pain. Once Mary spotted a group of pressmen armed with cameras standing by the Christmas tree. They were flashing at a sick baby and trying to talk to the sleepy mothers. She descended like one of the furies, abusing them in three languages. They remained obstinate and mannerless while she sent for the police.

Christmas Eve, and the flat plain of the Burgenland was deep in snow. The farm trails were slippery with ice, and a bitter, freezing wind penetrated duffle-coat, sweater, flannel shirt and woolly vest as if they didn't exist. A small group of us huddled by a wall, stamping in the snow. A watch-tower, fortunately unmanned, loomed in the dark sky. 'What a silly time of year to have a revolution,' grumbled Einar Roos, a Red Cross volunteer from Norway. 'The French are logical, they think of everything. They had theirs in July.'

The night stretched away indefinitely, its darkness broken only by occasional Very lights over on the other side, like a small, sinister Fourth of June celebration. Beyond the Hungarian patrols who'd fired them off were two lines of Russian patrols. Suddenly scurrying shapes detached themselves from the dark of the scrub of the Hungarian forest. Our little group on the Austrian side leapt into action and launched an inflatable raft, paddled by a tall boy. Three at a time, the fugitives were pulled across the water and hoisted with difficulty up the icy, slippery canal bank, then hustled into the Land-Rover and driven the eight miles to the village. Working through the night, we brought in about a hundred refugees that Christmas Eve: a mother with a frostbitten baby; frozen, exhausted children who had walked many miles with their parents through the deep snow; old women; peasants; gipsies; the odd intellectual; whole families and lone individuals. It was a risky affair. A few nights later, there was machine-gun fire and the raft was lost.

Christmas Eve was also the night Bill Astor arrived from England with his chauffeur, George Chapman, an ex-commando. Bill had already donated a second Land-Rover after reading one of our letters home to Zara, and now he was to spend the next two weeks helping us on the frontier. He became an enthusiast, excited rather than daunted to come under fire one night for the first time in his life. He declared it the most worthwhile Christmas he'd ever spent; it certainly made a change from the splendid parties of Cliveden. For us, Bill's presence was a blessing – it meant a thorough servicing for our Land-Rover and some much-needed sleep. After he returned home, leaving Chapman and the Land-Rover, Bill threw himself into fund-raising for the Knights of Malta. He went to the United States, where he extracted one large contribution by pleading with Cardinal Spellman that 'even the Jews and the infidels have helped me'. The Jews in this case referred to his friend Eddie Warburg of the banking family; the infidel was Aly Khan, who said, 'Of course, Bill, but you must lend me the money for the moment.' All told, he succeeded in raising $100,000, producing two more Land-Rovers, among other things. With the loan of another, complete with crew, from British Aid to Hungary, our team became five vehicles strong.

By the New Year, conditions were so bad that regular servicing was essential. We always tried to have one vehicle in Vienna to be checked over. Each carried tow-ropes and shovels: there was one two-week period when we had to cut through snowdrifts every night. Snowploughs were in constant use keeping the roads to the village open, and we lived in dread of the bottleneck that would arise should the buses could not get through to take out the night's crop of *flüchtlinger*.

Groups of refugees wandered the frozen marshes, not knowing whether they had reached the safety of Austria. They would mistake

the lights of our cars for Russian or AVO patrols, and turn back –
so we tried to use more Red Cross markings and flags whenever
possible. Often we had to cross into Hungary, as when a child who
had not been drugged began to cry loudly. We found an utterly
terrified old couple crouched by some bushes. With them were two
small children, and a baby in a laundry basket. It had been turned
on its face in an attempt to stifle its cries.

The worst crossing place was always the canal. Since the formidably
potholded road out to it was in full view of a watch-tower, it had to be
negotiated without lights. But despite the dangers the canal crossing
remained popular with the *flüchtlinger* because of the cover offered
by woods and reeds on the Hungarian side. Towards the end, it was
mostly young men who braved it, fleeing the mass deportations
eastwards being carried out by the new Soviet-backed regime in
Budapest. They paddled over on makeshift rafts, or walked across
when it froze sufficiently. Some of the hardier ones swam to freedom,
especially if they were fired on, and at least two contracted pneumonia as a result. Eventually Derek acquired three small rubber
dinghies and two large army-type landing craft, but the latter needed
at least four people to operate and were too cumbersome to move
quickly. Two of the smaller boats were captured – the first while
bringing over a party of about fifty, mostly women and children. A
Hungarian patrol stumbled across them when half were still waiting
on the farther bank, and they were marched off into the woods.
That night the border guards, using police dogs, began crossing to
the Austrian side of the canal, which was technically just inside
Hungary.

With the canal half frozen over, we did our best to get messages
through, warning the refugees to avoid this route. But still they kept
coming. It was impossible not to go down to meet them, however
risky, and the night Derek lost our second boat, two of our student
friends went with it: Einar Roos, our Norwegian, and Dick Rorabach, an American. Derek watched helplessly from the opposite bank
as they were led away by border guards. After three anxious weeks
of trying everything we could think of to secure their release, they
were taken out of their Russian prison in Budapest and deported to
the West. Paul Metternich came from Germany and laid on a champagne supper, after which they promptly returned to Andau.

It began to be a commonplace to be fired on by the Hungarian patrols. As these encounters grew grimmer, we resorted to counter-measures. One was to fire off our own Very lights at some deserted spot to draw away the soldiers from the real crossing. Another counter-measure, fortunately for all concerned nipped in the bud, was the over-rash dispatch of a telegram asking for the 'long wooden green box' at Parr's Cottage, Cliveden, to be sent out to us in one of the new Land-Rovers. When Zara was asked how, as a respectable, impoverished widow of seventy-eight, she had come by the ex-Life Guards tommy-gun and 1,000 rounds of ammo that lived under Mrs Donald's bed, her only rejoinder was, 'Don't forget I'm Irish!'

Some time after all these incidents we made a return trip to Andau, but by then the frontier had been completely sealed by a regular spacing of watch-towers on the farther bank; the village school had been rehoused in the Rettet das Kind *lager*. We made our way home via Schloss Johannisberg and stayed several days with Tatiana and Paul Metternich, tasting wine and inspecting its culture. One evening a neighbour was invited to dinner: a quite young Panzer Grenadier colonel. Afterwards Paul put on the gramophone to dance, but then mischievously selected a recording of 'Colonel Bogey' and asked Derek, 'How do you feel when you hear it?'

To Paul's delight, Derek launched straight into the ribald Second World War version:

> Don't throw the lamp at father,
> Wait till he gets into bed:
> Hitler has only got one ball
> Göring has two but they're very small,
> Himmler has something similar
> And Goebbels has no balls at all.

The Panzer Grenadier stiffened with shock and bewilderment at this response to a famous British patriotic march by the Household Cavalryman.

Jordan

After our adventures in Austria, we kept in touch with Mary Hawkins through Bill Astor, who was on the Foreign Relief Committee of the Save the Children Fund. By 1960 she was back in the Middle East, working among children in the Irbid area north of Amman, as part of a team which included two other nurses, a woman doctor and an administrator. Through Bill Astor and Baba Metcalfe, who chaired the Foreign Relief Committee, we heard there had been trouble among the team. Relations between the medical staff and their administrator were at breaking-point. When the administrator offered his resignation, Derek agreed to go out and hold the fort until a new one could be found.

Grey was now at Oxford, reading English at Balliol. He was making a name for himself as a poet and journalist, editing *Isis*, the literary-political magazine. Skimper was still at Eton, preparing for his A-levels. Zara remained ensconced at Parr's Cottage, safely in the care of the two Faithfuls, Mrs Donald and Auntie Stacey. Winters at Dunlewy were long, dark and gloomy. Thanks to Derek's training, the O'Donnell brothers now had things well under control, and we were ready to escape again.

We bought a new Land-Rover with a long-wheelbase, loaded it with medical supplies and left England on St Valentine's Day, taking the night ferry from Dover to Dunkirk. Unfortunately the French customs insisted on impounding the whole cargo: after arguments that went on from eight in the morning till three in the afternoon, interspersed with lengthy telephone calls to the SCF in London, we gave up and had the consignment sent back to London by rail. We consoled ourselves with delicious garlicy *escargots* in a one-star Michelin restaurant, then proceeded to Domrémy, where I appeased my fury by lighting candles to Joan of Arc. At Basle we stayed at a four-star hotel and dined on *poulet duc de Chartres* and *marrons*. Next morning we found the road to Winterthur completely blocked by an accident. Derek drove the Land-Rover through a field of beet, leaving the traffic jam behind. The following day we crossed the Brenner in thick fog, and eventually arrived in Cortina where a nice lady found us some rooms. We telephoned Freya, who demanded imperiously, 'Come at once!' but we decided to spend a few days skiing.

When we finally arrived at Asolo, Freya was decked out like a bride, in white and gold, and smelling delicious. After dinner she brought out the maps for our journey across the Balkans, Turkey and Syria. I started reading the typescript of the second volume of her autobiography, *Dust in the Lion's Paw*, which covers the period when we worked together in Cairo and Baghdad. It was enthralling, but brought back agonizing memories. Derek was blissfully occupied with Freya, planning a journey to the Euphrates and eastern Turkey for September. Asolo was wonderfully peaceful, filled with spring sunshine and birds. Everyone in Italy was talking about the engagement between Princess Margaret and 'Il Fotografo'. The Italians were rather disgusted, thinking it a waste of a princess.

We left Asolo on leap-year day and headed off through Yugoslavia and Bulgaria. A week later we had crossed the Anatolian plain. Syria seemed lonely, cold and empty until we reached the flat cultivation, where the ladies wore pantaloons and every car was a Mercedes or Land-Rover stuffed with country Arabs. The flowers were all coming out. I watched a little girl in long frilly pantaloons under her smock picking asphodels to give to her cow. The cattle were pathetically thin, as were most of the horses. 'I get the very British feeling to save them not the children, of which there are far too many,' I told Zara in one of my letters. At the Lebanese frontier we had trouble with an amorous customs officer. As soon as Derek had gone into the office with the passports, he jumped into the Land-Rover and began stroking my legs, saying how 'beatful' I was. He stayed there even when Derek returned, and had to be gently persuaded out of the car. He was still making mournful cow's eyes as we drove away. Beirut's reputation as a city of vice was confirmed after a night in the St George Hotel. At 8.30 in the morning, when we were still lying in bed, exhausted from the journey, Derek picked up the phone to hear an unknown female voice: 'I have seen you many times. I like you. I am brown and skinny and very clever. Will you come and have a talk in my hotel?'

At 2 p.m., after meeting the director of UNRWA, Mackenzie Pollock, we set off for Damascus, and the next day crossed the Jordanian frontier at Deraa with a stiff wind blowing. At Irbid the manager of the only hotel immediately took us down to the SCF headquarters, two modern houses at the edge of the town. The welcome was terrific. Lord Dulverton, of the Wills dynasty, had recently been out on a lightning visit and presented the team with a new Land-Rover. With our vehicle added to the two they already had, they were now in a position to expand the clinics and feeding centres in the surrounding villages.

Compared to Syria, its northern neighbour, where there had been several *coups* since it gained independence from France after the war, Jordan was fairly stable as a monarchy under the relatively benign rule of King Hussein. Although, during the build-up to the Suez crisis in 1956, the young Hussein got rid of Glubb Pasha, he was still well-disposed towards Britain and enjoyed a certain amount of protection, direct or otherwise. The British military mission in Amman was headed by Vivian Street, Pat's old colleague in the SAS, now a general. His deputy, Paddy Bowden, had also been a friend of Pat's. They enjoyed close links with the officer corps, which came under the control of Habes Majali, brother of the prime minister, Hazza Majali: both were members of a prominent East Bank family that had controlled the town of Kerak for generations. The British ambassador still occupied the former high commissioner's residence inside the palace compound on Jebel Hussein. A more direct form of protection was provided by the King's British chauffeur, Maurice Rayner, a former garage-owner who had befriended him at Harrow. During our sojourn in Jordan, Syrian agents made several attempts to assassinate the King. While I was staying with the Streets in Amman in August 1959, a bomb went off, killing the prime minister, Hazza Majali. Thereafter the King regularly slept in the Rayners' house, since the palace staff were not always to be trusted.

The King's enemies were mostly Arab nationalists, led by Gamal Abdel Nasser; but the Palestinians – as always – were at the heart of his problems. His grandfather King Abdullah had been assassinated before his very eyes as a result of a plot by disgruntled West Bankers who blamed him for trying to reach a peaceful settlement with Israel. Egypt's failure in the war in 1948 had been responsible for the *coup* that brought Nasser to power in 1952; while nationalist resentment over the loss of Palestine contributed to the murder of Hussein's Hashemite cousin, the young King Feisal, in the bloody Iraqi revolution of 1958.

Through Hussein the people of the West Bank who had their homes and lands incorporated in Jordan, or who fled as refugees in 1948, were now bound up with the peasant and desert people of the East Bank. They brought many skills, some even brought money, but they also produced the insoluble problem of how a poor country, most of which was unproductive desert, could absorb a sudden addition of 650,000 to its population of nearly one million. UNRWA (the United Nations Relief and Works Agency) was the child of the United Nations, set up with the mandate of looking after the Palestinian refugees. For years it had been trying to find an answer, not always with the co-operation and gratitude of the refugees themselves, whose one wish, emotionally and politically, was to return to their lands and homes. UNRWA provided basic subsistence for refugees. Many people in the northern villages near Irbid had UNRWA cards, legally acquired or otherwise. The indigenous farmers, though ineligible, were often in as much need of help as the bona fide refugees.

It is pouring with longed-for rain [I wrote to Zara from Irbid], so I have finished early and can get a letter off. We went to a far village this a.m. with Margaret Wigley, the beautiful lady doctor, and Mary Hawkins. Duke said bar the war it was one of the worst drives of his life. The track was steep and horrid, skidding in liquid mud. He was anxious for his cargo of ladies. We have now been to all their five villages and seen the clinic and welfare at work. They are really a remarkable little team. Michael Wilson is the administrator, ex-Somaliland, and the fourth is a sweet little Dutch girl, Joop Bronsema, who does the welfare, teaching the mum's to look after the babies and to sew for them. Soon they will start feeding centres. The Jordanians are, if anything, worse off than the refugees as UNRWA can only give rations to refugees. They have had a bad drought and half the fields not even sown. The animals look awful.

We drove Mary Hawkins up to Jerusalem via the Jordan valley and stayed the weekend at the American Colony Hotel. The garden reminded me so much of La Graziella and Giant. Stocks and hyacinths and freesias and jasmine all smelling their hearts out. The South African chief UNRWA doctor was charming to us. His wife took us round Old City, it is very moving and fascinating. It is nice to have a historical religion. It was lovely and warm that weekend but is cold again here. I do hope it won't be too hot when the Men [Grey and Skimper] come [out in the summer]. We get up each morning at 6.30 and leave the house at 7.30 and often the team don't finish till three. Sometimes we picnic under the olives on the way home among the anemones and irises and wonderful views all round us towards Galilee and Syria. It is heart-rending to see a country cut in two and little Jordan left with no port. It is all so like Ireland. Bitter prejudices, high walls going up in Jerusalem so that you can hear the Jews talking on the other side but can't see them.

I think we will go down to the much discussed Southern tribes. They are in great need but being bedouins and not refugees UNRWA can't help them. The SCF were asked to go but this team thought it too much to take on as distances enormous and the medical team are all women. It is really a matter of getting supplies to them, so Duke says he will have a look, but he is walking cannily. The whole thing is mixed up with politics.

Duke wants me especially to tell you that he is now an expert on breast feeding. He hears the Mums being ordered to give a two-year-old something stronger, and is fascinated by the ladies squatting around him with a bundle at the breast. They do look terribly poor but not all are undernourished. The worst diseases seem to be impetigo, bronchitis, TB and worms. I think if they can train a few Arab orderlies – the girls are not generally allowed to do the work – and start nurseries where the mothers can leave the children for an hour or two and the orderlies can administer the ointments and rations and injections during that time, they would be killing several birds with one stone and starting something which might go on. The difficulty is to get the Jordanian doctors, who have large private practices, to co-operate.

Duke could get a job with UNRWA I think, but he doesn't want to be stuck in an office. The main thing is to learn Arabic, it is coming slowly, and I can already shop a little on my own. What a fool I was not to have lessons in Cairo. We must force one of the men to tackle it.

Love to Bill if he hasn't gone to US, and all relations and friends, and as much to you as the sands of the desert.

The Irbid team's work expanded to six villages. About 4,000 children attended the medical and welfare centres each month; and about the same number were given a daily meal at the feeding centres. As the SCF operation became established, the numbers tended to increase. Unbeknown to the doctor, mothers were walking all the way from Irbid to the nearer clinics. The rumour had got about that the king had asked for the best pediatrician from England and had got her.

Towards the end of March we left Irbid for our fact-finding tour of the south, where there was a similar anomaly to that which prevailed in the north. Only the Azzazmih bedouin, who formerly grazed their flocks in what was now Israel, were technically refugees and entitled to UNRWA rations. Other bedouin tribes, notably the Huweitat, were no better off and were suffering badly. The decline of the camel trade, the suppression of the old way of life – really a form of highway robbery – and the droughts of recent years, had decimated the flocks on which they depended for food and drink, transport, tents and income – in fact their whole way of life. They were now in a condition of abject poverty and malnutrition, though it was hard to assess the needs of a people too proud to beg and constantly on the move.

The doctor in charge of the whole district between Ma'an and Aqaba was youngish, trained in Cairo, and after talking to him I understood the difficulties the SCF doctor and administrator had foreseen during a reconnaissance in the Ma'an area a few months before. The doctor thought the terrain would be difficult for a team of four European women: distances were so enormous that 'the journey would hardly be worth the aspirin'. The team had said they found some of the local doctors uncooperative. There were only four of them in the whole of the south and I guessed this was one of them. Yet it must be very trying, I thought, however desperate your need, to have 'do-gooders' descending on your country, wanting to spend money and hand out supplies you could never hope to get hold of otherwise.

In the middle of his recital of the activities of the Jordanian health services, a large pair of scales was set in front of us. At first I thought there was about to be a baby-weighing demonstration. But then five policemen came in with a large sack containing a quantity of small flat canvas bags, each stamped in purple with the name of Allah. They turned out to be a consignment of hashish found hidden under a tree, Ma'an being on the main smuggler's route between Lebanon and Egypt. The haul, headed for Aqaba, would have been taken in small boats to Sinai. The flat packets could easily be concealed in a camel's saddle-bag or a person's shoes. There was a long ritual while each packet was weighed and signed by the doctor and five officers before being returned to the sack for official burning. Derek begged a small token for his pipe.

This seemed to put us on a more familiar footing. The doctor immediately became friendlier and suggested we had supper with him, although, being unmarried, he said he had nothing prepared, though he did have a servant. He would also invite the commandant of police. Over supper, which consisted of a *mezze* with little bowls of peppers and laban balls, with cheese and olives and unleavened bread, the atmosphere mellowed considerably. We all sat round a small table in our host's bedroom, the party dominated by a cousin of the doctor's, the *mukhtar* of his village, who could neither read nor write but was a celebrated wit and personality and immediately took on Derek. He rolled his own cigarettes and offered D. one. (The old brute must have put hashish in it, for there were disastrous results in the early hours next morning, under the formidable eyes of Lord and Lady Willingdon, Viceroy and Vicereine of India, whose imperial picture adorned the wall of our hotel.)

By now any remaining pomposity had left the doctor's speech. He spoke candidly and touchingly about the needs of the desert people, the impossibility of getting married in Jordan for under 1,000 dinars and of his ambition to do a year at a London teaching hospital, though he knew he would have to live as a student. The commandant discovered that he shared a mutual friend with Derek, and there followed a lengthy yarn about how the pair of them had outwitted the Jews. The faithful servant brought in a hubble-bubble. Derek had a go, and so did I whenever it was free.

The next morning there was a very correct farewell coffee in the office of the commandant. He assured us that we would have every assistance from the police all over the south should we start a mobile clinic. They would give protection for our stores, I would be lent horses to ride and a house could easily be found for the team.

At Wadi Rum the bedouin police came out to welcome us, dignified and courteous with no unnecessary words, using charming expressive gestures with their hands. They led us into a high walled courtyard, whitewashed and flagged with stones. Two trees grew out of the paving, a pepper and a eucalyptus; in the corner was a stable where the police hung their bright woven saddle-bags. We drank coffee and, explaining our mission, asked about the number of bedouin in the district. They sent for their 'health officer'. He arrived most suitably dressed, in white from top to toe except for the jacket of a blue lounge suit. He explained he had been trained in first aid at Amman. He toured the tents by camel and reported to Aqaba if a doctor was needed. He was enthusiastic over the possibility of a mobile clinic, but said the tents were too scattered for him to be able to bring the sick to the police post. A mobile clinic would have to travel round a radius of about twenty kilometres from the post, visiting each tent where there was need.

It was the usual story of depleted flocks, with no milk for the children. There had been a delivery of flour some months back, but they desperately needed oil and sugar, tea and dates, and possibly vitamin tablets. There was a good spring so that most of the bedou came there at some time or another to collect water; they all belonged to the Huweitat tribe. But we left Rum in high heart. It seemed that some form of medical help and relief was possible there, combined with a near-by clinic; we would have the help of the 'health officer' and his camel. Aqaba and Ma'an were only two hours' distant.

Nearer to Aqaba the mountains closed in steeply and became rather forbidding, with wide bands of black granite painted across them at an oblique angle, as if to convey some ominous message. After the open desert we penetrated the narrow defile in the mountains through which Lawrence and Audah Abu Tayi, chief of the Huweitat, surprised the Turks to secure Aqaba as the port of supply for the Allied advance. Ahead we saw the gleaming cylinders of the new petrol refinery. It grew stiflingly hot.

Aqaba's famous beaches came under military control, cut in half by the Israel-Jordan armistice line. The new Israeli town of Eilat could be seen most clearly at night, brilliant with green and blue neon lights. We turned seawards just short of the forbidden area, past mounds of white potash, old petrol cans and lorries, following a notice in English marked to 'Lighter Berths' and 'Rest House'. We pulled up short between an extraordinarily beautiful tree with yellow flowers and two dejected-looking doors marked WC. The one advertised for ladies seemed in spate. We found a long low series of buildings, loosely connected, built on the beach under straggling tamarisk trees: a sort of miniature shanty town, with small bungalows thatched with palm fronds and colonial-style verandas. Everywhere were signs of the plumbers fighting a losing battle against the sewers.

Our hearts sank as we contemplated Aqaba as a possible headquarters, *plage* and playground, but we were boarded, 'first class', in the manager's bungalow with a private veranda and two new deck chairs and our own lavatory and shower. By striking up a very exhausting friendship with the youngest of three waiters, from the local 'reception office' of Air Jordan, we managed to keep him for ourselves. Ahmed used this intimacy as an excuse to visit our bedroom via the veranda at any hour of the day or night. Very early one morning, his tousled, unattractive head peered through the mosquito netting: 'Friend, do you want I wash the WC before or after?' When we left he gave me a coloured postcard we had refused to buy for a shilling and an unsolicited kiss on my left ear. He wasn't our only visitor. One night we found a donkey investigating the contents of our wastepaper basket. Rummaging was a common habit in Aqaba. In the *bidonville* of little huts made from petrol tins filled with earth, the inmates were to be seen at dawn and dusk searching for food among the garbage heaps. At the refuse dump on the outskirts we saw a small boy with his herd of goats, each animal with its head in a tin or chewing paper. There were a number of sheep and goats in Aqaba, but I never saw a blade of grass or herbage.

On Good Friday, at 6 a.m., our escort called to take us up the Wadi Araba to investigate the numbers and conditions of the tribes there, then on to Gharandal. We were placed in the middle of a convoy consisting of ourselves and two open Land-Rovers, the leading one manned with a driver and three bedouin police with Bren guns mounted in front and behind; the rear vehicle had three men armed with rifles and pistols. All belonged to the special border militia. We set off at a brisk pace up the wide river bed which runs north and south parallel to the Israeli border. As we trundled bumpily along, we could clearly see traffic moving much more speedily along the surfaced road to Eilat. There was no shade in this pitiless land, apart from an occasional umbrella pine where groups of blackened stones indicated that fires had been lit. We saw a family using one of these trees as a tent, their cooking pots and cloths hanging from the branches out of reach of the goats. The track was almost invisible, and with our heavier vehicle it was hard to keep the leading car in sight.

After some distance the stones gave way to sand-dunes and we had to increase speed to avoid becoming stuck. The steering wheel shuddered and vibrated as Derek worked incessantly to prevent the tyres sticking. The red and white *kaffiehs* of the border guards bounced and nodded far ahead in the most abandoned and heartless fashion, but we were lost in admiration at the way they seemed to ride their Land-Rover as if it were a living creature. After about an hour we began climbing a rockier surface and, turning towards the line of mountains on our right, saw the 'Beau Geste' turrets of the Darba police post. Our leaders circled the post, then continued up the mountain with cries and waving of arms and weapons.

At Wadi Araba, we learned, there were about sixty tents gathered around the spring within an area of three kilometres. Normally there would have been 200, but most had left for Wadi Musa, near Petra, to find grazing. All were Huweitat and would return to Darba for winter. Only nine or ten sheep and goats remained to feed the families. The last visitor had been a police officer several months ago. The bedou were enthusiastic over the idea of a visiting clinic; unlike Wadi Rum, they promised they would be able to collect the sick for the day of its visit. They asked particularly for a midwife. Mortality among mothers and babies was high and death generally arrived before the doctor.

We had as far again to travel to reach Gharandal, so we once more turned northward, left the wadi bed and took a route across the sand-dunes. The country became more attractive, with tamarisk bushes and apricot-coloured sands that had blown into lovely dimpled humps, creating the most exciting obstacles. Derek made for every old root or bush to give the tyres something to grip on. The leading jeep stuck three times, and each time had to be lifted bodily by its crew. The car behind was discovered not to be following and we had to turn back. It was embedded, and when all hands had finally lifted it out, the driver confessed his doubt of ever making Gharandal and turned back to Wadi Darba. The pace became furious. There were no longer any backward glances from the vehicle in front. If it stuck, we skidded and roared past for fear of doing the same. Once ahead, we had no idea where were were heading for, yet did not dare pull up.

Finally, driving into Gharandal, a long-established gathering ground for the Beni Ariyah tribe, we found a hidden oasis among high sandstone rocks. Palm trees grew around a pool, into which tiny rivulets of water trickled from a piped spring. A tangle of barbed wire encircled the plantation, with a crazy gate of beaten-out petrol tins serving as an entrance. There were signs of human habitation. A patch of thin barley, a straggling of wheat and a few lettuces and onions had been planted. On the north side a wall had been built. It had the air of pathetic endeavour and subsequent neglect.

Our men described how the police post and near-by school had been attacked by the Israelis in 1958. Eleven policemen were killed and the buildings completely destroyed. There was now no police post, but since Ghirandal lay on a route through the jebel from Ma'an to Darba and Aqaba, trucks sometimes passed that way. The deserted oasis and its unhappy story dampened our spirits. The driver who had led us with such courage and daring was so depressed by it that he had to beg for an aspirin. Then he pronounced, very seriously: 'We see you follow your leader.' 'It wasn't at all easy,' Derek replied. Our interpreter explained that they were talking, not of our just completed journey, but about Good Friday and the Way of the Cross.

Presently, from under the green branches, came Robinson Crusoe in person: an Old Testament figure, in threadbare creamy robes, with bright sunken eyes and handsome features polished like ebony. He saluted us gravely and squatted beside the Land-Rovers. He looked very old and was short of breath. He explained that the tribes had all moved with their flocks towards Wadi Musa. He, a slightly younger companion and a nine-year-old boy had been left behind as guards. They had no tea or coffee; and we saw no animals or any food beyond what was growing, but as the old man baked bread for the three of them on an open pan, they must have had flour. He puffed away at an ancient pipe and offered us a kind of tobacco made from herbs he dried in the sun. He said he had been ill, but was a getting a little better. From his description he may have been suffering from bronchitis or influenza. We gave them a packet of tea, some cheese, two oranges and all that remained of our chocolate biscuits. The old man clung pathetically to the policemen, kissing their hands as they said goodbye. The boy stood beside his father, delicately opening up a chocolate biscuit and eating it with curiosity. Feeling inexpressibly guilty, we followed our leader back down the Wadi Araba.

The less said about our return to Aqaba the better, but our trip to the south did succeed in opening the way for a permanent SCF presence in the area. After tortuous negotiations with the Ministry of Health over the disposal of some unsightly pit latrines in the garden, the old quarantine centre at Ma'an station was made available. A second doctor, Richard Cleave, travelled out from England, while the redoubtable Mary Hawkins came down from Irbid. Weekly clinics were held in temporary buildings at El Jafr, El Qweira, in Dilagha above the Wadi Araba, and at Ras el Naqb, a village that sits on the edge of the plateau overlooking Wadi Rum, with a spectacular view of its lunar landscape. Skimper settled in with Mary and Richard, helping to organize the feeding centres. His progress in Arabic endeared him to the bedouin. When Derek turned up at one of the feeding centres, one of the fathers put him firmly in his place: 'You are a relict of Glubb Pasha,' he said. 'We only have faith in Mister Skinder.'

Tony Dulverton, who had meanwhile wandered into a massively publicized divorce, cabled Derek to offer help and ask if there was anything in particular we wanted. Derek replied in jest that we could really use an aeroplane as the distances were too great to cover in Land-Rovers. Within a month Tony arrived in a four-seater Piper Comanche, piloting it himself. We had no idea he possessed an aeroplane, let alone knew how to fly one. He spent four months with us in the *quarantina*.

With his old tweed jacket and Highland thumbstick, Tony was instantly recognized by the bedouin sheikhs as one of their own. The distribution cards, with their murky thumb-prints, became known as the 'Lord's Cards'. After being treated to a view of his mainly black basalt estate from the air, Sheikh Khalaf of the Huweitat was presented with a tractor. Near Mafraq, north of Amman, Tony contributed to the digging of a well and irrigation scheme set up by Miss Coat, a retired English nurse, with the help of an Armenian water diviner whom none of the other charities had been willing to sponsor. The result was a flourishing orchard and market garden.

With a determined if somewhat lugubrious efficiency, Tony organized a comprehensive food-distribution campaign to the southern Huweitat, using his plane to get medicine and some food to distant groups along the Saudi Arabian frontier, to be collected by camel transport. The country was ideal for flying: apart from the occasional sandstorm, the weather was usually clear. The mudflats, whose mirage-smooth surfaces stretched for dozens of miles, made perfect landing-strips. He came close to disaster one day, however, when a dead camel lay across his line of landing. There was a fear that Tony was dicing with fate after his recent experiences, and the only evening when he was missing and we had no news was the night his mother, Victoria Dulverton, phoned from England. It was the one occasion on which he had needed to ditch the plane and take to a camel train.

Realizing that many children would fail to survive the winter unless supplied with emergency rations, Tony raised £10,000 from Oxfam. He systematically worked out, with the help of our doctor, a precise ration for each child in lentils, rice, sugar and dates, placing orders with wholesalers in Amman. The main food distribution was conducted by the bedouin police – Glubb's famous 'girls', who wore ankle-length khaki robes – using convoys of army trucks. Skimper travelled with them for several weeks, sleeping with them in the black goats-hair tents. Each family was given flour, dates and pulses, according to the number of children. To ensure fairness, each child had to be identified individually – with an allowance made for those guarding the flocks.

Concerned about the longer-term future of the southern tribes, Tony sought an audience with the King, to whom Derek introduced him. The young monarch decided, at their prompting, to come down and see things for himself. One day in January 1961 we had a telephone call from Amman to say he would like to visit us next day to discuss our work. The King arrived by plane in the afternoon, accompanied by twelve-year-old Prince Hassan. His first words were, 'What can I do for you?' Then he sat with a millboard, making notes and asking questions. He thanked us for the work we were doing and for pointing out the serious plight of the southern tribes. He said the bedouin were a proud people who would not ask for help or expose their poverty. We confessed that we had somewhat exceeded our mandate from London, which was to work in the country south of Ma'an, by attempting a distribution for children in nearly the whole of south Jordan, but explained that the governor of Ma'an had asked us to go to the villages in the hills overlooking the Wadi Araba, where there were 6,000 needy children rather than our original estimate of 2,500. The cold there was intense, and the children had no warm clothing.

The King asked if we had any special needs. We said we could do with a tent for our clinic at Wadi Rum. Two new tents arrived within twenty-four hours. We were promised all the electricity and water we needed for the *quarantina*. Before leaving, the King handed us an envelope containing 500 Jordanian dinars in five-dinar notes as a personal contribution.

The royal visit had an electrifying effect. The following day we received an urgent message to go to the camp: the King was arriving at 10 a.m. with the prime minister, the whole Cabinet and the chiefs of the army and police. A conference took place at which HM presided and spoke at length in Arabic. Finally he turned to Tony and Derek and said: 'We owe you a great deal for showing us the situation in south Jordan and we are ashamed that this has come from people outside our country. We shall always be grateful.'

After the King's departure there was much shouting and waving of arms. A sack containing 7,000 dinars raised in Amman for relief of the south was produced and pushed around the floor amid laughter and ribaldry. At one moment it was almost presented to us, but somehow we failed to consolidate our claim. Later it was distributed in cash to the bedouin by the army at the rate of 500 fils (half a Jordanian dinar) per head, along with ex-army greatcoats and battle-dress and shoes. The next day Jamil Pasha, the minister of health, arrived, along with several parliamentary deputies. We were invited to a *mensif* at the mayor of Ma'an's house, where again we had to submit to words of thanks and a cross-questioning about the future of south Jordan. We were beginning to feel exhausted and rather foolish.

Jamil Pasha came on to tea at the *quarantina*. He offered us new buildings and a cut in a hundred tons of cement alloted to the south. A few days later, the British and American ambassadors and their wives arrived with the chief of Point Four, one of the US aid agencies. They gathered at the *quarantina*, then drove in a convoy of sedans and Land-Rovers for Ras el Naqb, El Qweira and Wadi Rum. We were questioned very closely about the relief we were doing, what was to happen after we left in May, the best way of carrying out distribution and the best food to give these people. We stopped at our clinics at Naqb and Qweira, where they interrogated the medical orderlies and complimented the cleanness of their clinics. Tony used to hum: 'What is queerer than Qweira? What is rummer than Rum?'

No doubt the concern of the diplomats and aid workers was entirely sincere, but it was strange that it took a personal visit from the monarch to alert them to the needs of the south, and even stranger that it took the prompting of an English lord to alert the monarch.

16

The Village That Sat Down on Its People

The Iranian earthquake struck at eleven o'clock during the night of Saturday, 1 September 1962. It lasted about forty seconds, measuring 7.5 on the Richter scale. The epicentre was just west of the village of Cheskin, thirty-eight miles from Qazvin. The effects were devastating: at least 20,000 people were left dead, smothered under the mounds of clay that were formerly their houses. Some 430 villages were destroyed over an area of 23,000 square miles. About 50,000 survivors were left without food as many animals also died.

The Donegal season was at its height, the Monarch of the Glen in residence. The Group was hard at it, stalking, fishing, sailing to the islands, picnicking by sea, river and lough, and entertaining anyone who 'made fun' from Ireland, the British Isles or across the Atlantic. At this point the Save the Children Fund cabled Derek to ask him if he would represent them in channelling help to the earthquake area. Within a few days he was in Tehran. There were plans for me to join him a few weeks later.

I arrived in Tehran to find that Derek had two residences: the tented camp at Cheskin and a room in an old house not far from the Embassy, belonging to the redoubtable Miss Palmer Smith. PS, as she was known among the expatriate community, must have been well into her eighties, although she took pains to conceal the fact by painting her face, dying her hair with henna and sporting an astonishing variety of hats, which she used as weaponry, carefully chosen for the campaign of the moment. I feel sure she had love affairs, but she never married. When she was very young she lost her parents in a railway accident. Well-educated and adventurous, she had flown with

some of the earliest British aviators before ending up as governess to
the daughter of Sir Robert Clive, the British Ambassador in Tehran.
After the Clives left, PS stayed on with an Iranian family with whom
she lived until her pupils were grown. Afterwards she continued to
teach English language and literature: I doubt there was an Iranian
of rank or importance who had not at some point encountered her
astringent wit, her indomitable Britishness and her sympathy for
the poor and truly deserving. The current ambassador's wife, Lady
Harrison, was a former pupil of hers.

PS knew practically everyone in the government and at the court.
She was still teaching English to a number of exalted pupils of all
ages, but her real passion was a nursing scheme with dispensaries.
This she had started in Shiraz in 1902, and it had gradually spread
all over the country. By now age had restricted her ability to travel
and she was unable to supervise the dispensaries as before, but the
British centre at Cheskin, of which she heartily approved, gave her
a new interest. Thus she absorbed Derek into her ancient little house,
with its unreliable roof, its courtyard with fluttering pigeons, Vali,
her man-servant, and a friendly Alsatian dog.

She did not treat me as an intruder. By the time I arrived, Sydney
Watson, the military attaché – a first cousin of Tony Dulverton –
had already become ill from overwork and she was growing anxious
about Derek. I soon understood why. The long rough, dusty drive
back and forth from Cheskin, the endless discussions and dilemmas,
were punishing, especially after Sydney could no longer get to Cheskin. Derek was becoming very tired and not sleeping well. With his
curious blend of conscientiousness and flair, once he has hatched a
plan he is incapable of relaxing the pace. Within the Embassy compound, behind its high wall, everyone seemed devoted to him.

I was taken up to Cheskin fairly soon after my arrival. We drove
across the wide plain with the snow-capped Elburz mountains, which
hide the Caspian, always in view. There we were to live for most of
the next six months, in the village that had 'sat down on its people',
as a Persian friend described it. The peasants lived mainly on bread.
Apart from a few root vegetables grown in the large walled garden
shared by the village, a few raisins and nuts, they ate little else. Their
chickens and eggs, their cheese and butter, the by-products of the
flock of sheep and goats that passed my tent each morning and

returned by the same route from the bare pasture each night, were all sold in the market or paid in kind to the landlords as rent.

The army and rescue teams had already done a magnificent job, and the Save the Children Fund had sent Derek a medical team from Jordan. At first they all had to help bury the dead, burn the carcasses of the animals and erect whole villages of tents, the larger ones housing several families. The Iranian Red Cross Society, known as the Red Lion and Sun, with the American agency CARE, then undertook a survey of 280 villages in varied conditions of destruction. At first the people had been stunned, with no will to do other than pick over the ruins, seek their dead and their belongings or set their tents as close as possible to where their homes had been.

Relief supplies from all over the world were funnelled through our camp, our main problem being to prevent these gifts from more fortunate countries being sold back to the city or to other less severely affected villages, so enriching the middlemen at the expense of the victims. It was this concern over the final destiny of our relief that decided us stay on throughout the winter, until the people could be rehoused.

Soon after his arrival in Tehran, Derek had been summoned by Mr Alam, the prime minister, to have an audience with the Shah. Mr Alam escorted him into the Imperial Presence, then left him alone with the Shah. His Majesty wanted to know about malpractices – pilfering or swopping of blankets, thefts of milk and food. He asked about the reputation of the Red Lion and Sun. Despite Derek's protest that he was a foreigner operating only as a guest in Iran, he was pressed to follow up the interview with further reports. He sent two letters to the Shah, via the prime minister. One outcome of this meeting was that a member of the *gendarmerie* arrived to pitch his tent not far from the Cheskin camp.

As well as food and clothing, we were to distribute 12,000 blankets, 23,000 gallons of kerosene, 16,000 pairs of shoes. The National Iranian Oil Company ran a shuttle service for us. The convoy's arrival would be heralded by a cloud of dust, which could be seen for miles across the vast desert plain between the two mountain ranges where the earthquake had wrought its devastation. In Cheskin and adjacent villages, such as Danisfahn and Rudak, which were totally destroyed, with half the population killed outright, we were able to set up milk centres and teach the women how to make *mast* from the powdered milk. I watched the condition of the children improve within a few days. They came each morning for a drink of malted milk or cocoa sent from England, the boys waiting on one side, the girls on the other. Even the tiniest girls were draped in cotton chuddors, held in their teeth. Boys and girls alike were liable have a baby brother or sister strapped to their backs for the day.

We got to the mountain villages up river beds and goat tracks in our trucks. The approach to one part of the country was through Rudak, which seemed to me the saddest village of all. It was built at an idyllic spot along the banks of the river, with fine poplar trees and good fields. The road wound its way through the village above the river bank. No one who passed that way after the earthquake could ever forget it. On either side of the track were great mounds of tumbled clay walls and sickening cavities. The wooden poles, cut from the poplars, that had once upheld the walls and roofs criss-crossed at random, as in a game of spillkins. Where the dead were still buried under rubble, the families had tied black flags; above them a community of rooks, which still lived in the poplars, circled the sky in ceaseless mourning.

We became devoted to the people of Rudak; they were always courteous and grateful, the first to appreciate the dried milk. They had a colony of shepherds who watched the village flocks from caves or dug-outs in the near-by hills. As the earthquake had happened at night most of the animals were in these shelters and the toll on livestock was exceptionally heavy.

The people of Cheskin and most of the surrounding villages were Azeris or Turcomans, whose languages are a dialect of Turkish. The people of Chulambar, farther up the river into the mountains, were Kurds. Some of these had never seen a motor vehicle before. They sprinkled our Land-Rover's wheels with a kind of local incense in special welcome. Always we would be offered a meal from their frugal store: rice, if the headsman was better off, or eggs fried in the delicious mutton fat they all prize. Even the most rural people understand good living. When a sheep or goat was to be slaughtered, they would sit solemnly about together with an air of sacrifice. We would be brought gifts, or bribes, of sheep, chickens, eggs or mutton fat, and a home-brewed firewater similar to poteen, by fathers whose children had hardly tasted these foods and suffered severely from malnutrition.

The success of a distribution in a village depended largely on the *khatkhoda* or village headman. Sometimes there would be more than one and fighting would break out before the family cards we used had been sorted. In the larger villages on the plain we could often only function if the *gendarmerie* was there to restrain the people with batons. Among the younger men, *gendarme*-baiting became a recognized sport. But it was the grandmothers who were the most rapacious and intractable. The children were nearly always well-behaved and decorous, whereas their elders displayed a savage cupidity and lack of self-control. A friend who had spent many years in the Middle East once said to me, 'I'll tell you how you can help these people. Tuck a pound note under the tent flap now and again and they'll help themselves.' Sometimes I felt he was right. But it was easier said than done. I have witnessed a cash distribution with both army and police in charge, and it was still quite a tricky operation.

A young mullah from a near-by village was constantly with us, bringing and introducing men from other villages and helping to mark up the family cards. It was a long and tedious business. In some cases we had to place unmarked villages on the map, which few could read. Spotting forgeries and false entries was also a problem, though alterations to the cards were as a rule pathetically crude.

Derek sent word through the infallible bush telegraph that anyone who could reach Cheskin could collect supplies for their village so long as they brought the family cards with them. They came by far more direct routes than we could use, with camels, donkeys and on foot. A small tea-house or *khan* sprang up where the visitors mostly stayed the night, sleeping beside a fire of camel-thorn on a raised platform spread with kelims woven in the village. I believe they paid about ninepence for a night's lodging, and I hesitate to contemplate what bargaining and deals were arranged over our wares, within those mud walls.

The strangers would set off the following morning, their beasts bearing striped saddle-bags bulging with kerosene, tea, sugar, lentils and atop, most coveted of all, the quilts. We had decided to spend a considerable portion of our funds on this uniquely Persian article, since it was seldom sold and benefited the whole family. Made from coloured cotton, it was stuffed with wool or floc, then quilted by hand. It could be spread over a *khurseh* – a low table set above a charcoal fire. When the sun went down and the bitter cold descended, the whole family would sit around the *khurseh*, eating from it and later sleeping beside it, covered with the warmed overlapping quilt. No sooner had our store of quilts been replenished than it would be exhausted again. The trucks had a tough time getting through from Tehran, where night shifts were working in the bazaars to keep us supplied.

We were grateful for the cases of excellent clothing which reached our rusty and battered old store tent from all over the world, but the native trousers, chuddors and sweaters we had made in the bazaars of Tehran were less marketable, this helping to ensure that they got to the people who needed them. They also made their wearer feel less self-conscious.

When the snow fell and winter gales blew down our tents, the tracks and river beds became impassable for our trucks. We were cut off from the mountain districts by floods and snowdrifts. Our last distribution before winter closed in was made after a hazardous journey to a destroyed village built on the mountainside. In a snowstorm we gave out clothing and food to families who had only thin white tents for protection. The headman of the village, whom we lunched with afterwards, had lost four children. Two very small girls were running around who, he said, had lost both parents and they had been adopted by him. Orphans were nearly always kept in their village; the homes prepared for them in Tehran were never used. We found the villagers loath to allow even blind children to leave home for training. In Cheskin, however, which had never had a school, we opened one with a young volunteer aged nineteen. He appeared to have no difficulty in keeping order. The children showed a passion for learning, and held classes among themselves when he was absent.

On 26 November, I had noted in my diary, 'Grey's birthday, and he is love.' The next day we had driven back to PS in Tehran after making a delivery to a village called Danisfahn, and had gone out to dine at the restaurant Auberge. That night we feasted off a kebab of sturgeon – excellent, like tender lamb. The following afternoon I went up to Solhak to have tea with Sydney Watson and his small daughter. Sydney's health had improved, though he still seemed frail and nervous. When his wife, Diana, came back, I stayed on to dinner and we spoke of Ireland among other things. Then they told me about Grey's engagement announcement being in the previous Saturday's *Times*.

On 20 December we flew back to England to stay at Cliveden, and on the 21st motored to Gloucestershire with Zara, whose back was still giving her trouble, for Grey's wedding to Xandra Bingley at Hatherop Castle. But I felt torn and bewildered and of little use to my family. I knew I must return to Cheskin after Christmas, Derek having been asked to take on the Red Cross aid in addition to the Embassy distribution. It would be the middle of March 1963 before we finally pointed the bonnet of the Land-Rover towards Europe and began the long trek of our homecoming by way of Asia Minor.

As the winter receded and the days grew longer I liked to watch the families in those villages not entirely destroyed as they carried out their household goods, their bedding and children on to the flat roof-tops. Another dimension was added to their lives until next winter. But the new houses being built for them by the government, the charitable societies and the business firms all had narrow sloping roofs. There were no mellow surrounding walls to keep lambs from straying or to preserve the privacy of every-day life; no evening roof-top sessions above the dust and clamour.

When the British Red Cross Society offered to rebuild our village and seven others, the people at first showed some interest. But then the word came down that there was to be a completely altered town plan. The new houses would be set along wide boulevards, a certain distance from the walls which had sheltered them and their flocks for centuries from wolves and human marauders. The people suddenly became morose and showed the age-long antipathy towards the city one finds throughout the Middle East.

The villages which were destroyed may have seemed primitive, but they were still beautiful. Most had walls with rounded battlements of yellow clay, many with domed roofs, a communal bath-house (alternating days for men and women), a simple mosque, a *qanat* or underground water course bringing water to the walled garden, cleansed by small fish, where corn and vegetables grew under almond trees. All of this may have been arcadian: perhaps it was. There are still villages standing in that vast plain between two mountain ranges where the water runs clear beside the silver-barked poplars and the bath-house furnace is fed with camel-thorn from the surrounding desert, where the children's hair is hennaed against bugs and their parents are led by a wise mullah and fatherly *khatkhoda*. These people accepted with dignity the gifts from other lands, and in exchange would offer us bowls of precious mutton fat, sun-dried raisins and walnuts, each one moist and sweet.

But outside the crumbling walls of the destroyed villages the oil companies, the international companies and the charitable societies built houses of indescribable ugliness, vulnerable to prowling wolves and jackals and the raids of envious neighbours. We were altering the subtle accents man had added to the landscape. Left to himself the Persian creates charming shapes and colours. Watching the men set to repair the mosques of Isfahan, sitting cross-legged in an unused corner, following drawings of leaves and flowers, chipping and working them into jigsaws to complement the ancient tiles, I came to realize that we had no business telling them how to organize their lives. The men I liked to think of as my friends must have watched our activities with amazement and distrust. I remember one of them stirring a vast bowl of milk made from the contents of a paper sack bearing US lettering. 'Is it too thick? I think it is OK. Ask Major Cooper, he knows about milk.' Yet what did Derek have to tell a farmer whose family had for generations been making yoghurt or *mast* out of local cows' milk? What arrogance to insist on putting up houses with pitched roofs, when the flat roof of the traditional dwelling was essential to so many vital activities. It was those of us who were privileged to help during someone else's crisis who learned the most important lessons.

In London when Richard Dimbleby (a nanny to the British public if ever there was one, who told it what to think about world affairs or how to comport itself on royal occasions) made an appeal for the earthquake victims on behalf of the British Red Cross, the donations poured in at an unprecedented level. But in the wake of the generous impulses, there was no proper consideration given to how these funds of £400,000 would achieve their urgent aim. Channelled through the Red Cross and Save the Children by way of the British Embassy, their distribution created intolerable burdens for those who had the task. Sydney Watson became ill and Derek found himself virtually responsible not only for delivering supplies to the teams but for rebuilding eight villages.

Along with our persons we brought all the paraphernalia of our own land: large sums of money to help the hapless victims, but also preconceived ideas and even terms and regulations for how that concern and cash must be administered. If it was often frustrating and bewildering for us to have to organize transport and purchases and such things as milk and feeding centres in a strange land, how much more disturbing it must have been for our hosts. The English are not very sensitive when action has to be taken; perhaps this is why they relish emergencies. Even when our efforts prove fairly efficacious, as in wartime, there is always a feeling of the schoolroom in the way we handle a crisis. Our Embassies have this quality, likewise the army. I remember having to apologize for it during the Hungarian revolution, but my Russian friend, Tatiana Metternich, laughed and said, 'Don't worry, I was brought up by an English nanny.'

Not that the attitude of Nanny Knows Best is exclusively British. Persia had survived many earthquakes, but this one aroused consciences throughout Europe, and donations poured in. Couples who knew Iran only through Fitzgerald's translation of one of its minor poets, decided they must adopt a Persian orphan. In Italy a sum of nearly £2,000 was collected for a small boy whose picture was published in a daily paper. I was visiting the Tehran headquarters of the Red Lion and Sun the day the child's parents, both alive and unhurt, were protesting that nothing would induce them to allow him to travel to Italy to collect the money. Letters of abuse arrived from Germany when people were told there were no homeless or unwanted orphans to be sent to the Fatherland.

When one knows neither the language nor the history of a country, and has never before met its people, it is rather like being introduced to a large family for the first time. All generations have a similitude of feature, voice and gesture, engrossed in a common way of living. Later, when one becomes personally involved, then the differences between family members, in morals, tastes and personalities, become apparent. It is no longer possible to use thoughtless generalizations. They become part of the human race, busy weaving the same old patterns of love and hate, unselfishness and greed.

I blush to think of the toes I must have trodden on during that winter in Iran, tramping into government offices, demanding this and that, intent on getting my way in order to carry out the job as I saw fit. But the Iranians are an old and civilized race, and they possess a great sense of humour. The smile was all; they did not mistrust the humourist, nor did they offer advice or help where it was not sought. But they understood courtesy and a good deed.

One morning before we left Iran, we called on a Qajar prince with an introduction from PS. The prince was receiving homage from friends and neighbours, it being the end of Ramadan and the feast of Id al-Fitr. Everything about our host belonged to another regime: the house like a Regency house in Europe; himself tall and spare, who could have passed for a near relation of Sandie Gowrie. His princess, close to his own age, was equally welcoming, and we talked as if our friends were their friends, our ways their ways and the paths we trod the same. We sat a long time, drinking coffee and nibbling Persian petits fours while others came and went as if they were his subjects, bowing and honouring him as some Austrians and Hungarians might a Habsburg. As we took our leave, he confided that he was having to forgo his annual trip to England in March, for he had heard that something was wrong with the heating at Claridge's and there was no hot water. Only when we returned to PS did she tell us that the charming princess was not his wife but his favourite sister, and that he had, on his father's instructions, murdered his mother for her adultery.

Years later I wrote to Sydney Watson in Tipperary to see if he could recollect the name of the Qajar prince. He could not, but he did remember from those days what he called 'the two most memorable sayings of the Coopers':

Major C.: 'You're a very naughty mullah.' He was too.
Mrs C., at one of my dinner parties: 'I used to live in Windsor
Castle, but found it too small during the holidays.'

★

On the day we began our departure from Iran, 12 March 1963, we 'left PS at her threshold with Vali', I recorded in my journal, 'a very poignant farewell'; then drove out of Tehran and headed for the filling station at Qazvin. It was the start of our greatest epic in a Land-Rover. My diary takes up the story:

At Qazvin we received a civic welcome – both of us dressed for the road in white Arran sweaters, with Derek in jeans and me in the ubiquitous dark-green kilt. Governor, *gendamerie*, army and the new RL & S [Red Lion and Sun] director. Our reception is no doubt a result of Derek's confidential reports to the Shah and the PM. Once inside the town hall there was an hour's sit, a good Nestorian interpreter provided, followed by a vast spread of chicken soup, rice and kebabs, salads and fruit. The governor made a long solemn speech when we had fed, full of literary allusions and references to Great Britain and old ties and friendships, interrupted by the arrival of Chuck Hancock of CARE looking cretinous, his hair growing over his eyebrows and the school colours on his white cricket sweater running. He was accompanied by two new Peace Corps youths, bewildered, lower lips drooping, but polite, listening while their dinner grew cold.

A great send-off, but we somehow had to find the mausoleum of Soltaniyeh before dark or else lose cast with Derek Hill when we return. Already the pigeons were gathering round the great dome for the night. A nest of owls with young clung to the outer wall on which the dome sits like an egg in an egg-cup 170 feet above ground, constructed entirely of brick, a 'dome which simply stands by virtue of a perfectly conceived and constructed profile'. The minarets at its eight corners are now in ruins. Like the dome, they were covered with turquoise tiles. Had we been travelling along the road from Qazvin to Tabriz a few centuries ago, it would have stood proudly above the city founded by the Mongol ruler, Arghun Khan. His son Oljeitu planned to bring the sacred remains of Ali and his son Hussein from Iraq to rest among devoted Shi'as. We were told there was a royal city at Soltaniyeh, but I believe it was sacked by the Timurids at the end of the fourteenth century. The baby owls and the pigeons looked better off and better fed than the inhabitants of the small mud villages near by.

Our next stop was Zanjan. We drove straight to the hotel, both longing to wash and have something to drink and I to exchange the kilt for a light garment. A kilt is really not the slightest use to do anything other than dance or walk in. In a car you are sitting on a bodge of material, and it's no use for riding a horse or donkey. I don't know why I brought it with me, although it was wonderfully warm during the hand-outs at Cheskin and in the mountains. Most unsuitable for civic receptions. Hardly had we reached the hotel when a RL & S spy chased us and insisted we turn around and follow him to their headquarters. Ritual ablutions conducted by

Muslims seems to preclude any thought that some folk need to attend to their persons at other moments. He was excited at having traced us and there was no gainsaying him. This time we were lucky. Two couples greeted us, the district attorney, whose wife spoke quite good English, having been to university; and Herr Schmidt and his *Frau*. There was the usual long 'sit', tea was served and we were asked if we liked vodka. We said very much indeed, but it never came. About 7 p.m. I boldly asked where we were to sleep. I was taken to a suite near by. I changed and washed as hastily as I could, knowing that until I had appeared again and done another broody 'sit', no dinner would be prepared. After a whole hour there were signs of dishes being carried back and forth but still no vodka. When Mrs Schmidt disappeared into what I guessed was the kitchen, my spirits rose. Not too long afterwards we were ushered in to a huge spread, joined by other notables and sat down to a very hilarious meal discussing politics and land reform and community life in Zanjan. 'We are more active than Qazvin,' they all said. We retired as early as possible after such lavish hospitality and asked if we could leave unfarewelled in the morning.

13 March

Our wish respected, we moved off at 8 a.m. for the long dusty stretch to Mianeh. We must be nearly half-way to Tabriz and the frontier, even farther. I can't believe we are actually leaving. Wherever we stop there are these smiling faces of all ages, in and out of uniform, offering us rest and sustenance, little human settlements linked in endeavour to the Red Cross in country places at home. Whatever its failings in the capital, these outlying centres of the RL & S in the little market towns we stop at is deeply touching. South of Mianeh we crossed another wonderful-looking half-busted bridge across the river Qezel Owzan. Couldn't some great consortium like Alexander Gibb repair and restore the ancient bridges of Iran in return for the millions they earn here?

A *gendarme* spotted us at the entrance to Mianeh and directed us to where we were very obviously expected. A crowd of men and boys gathered around the door of a building where the gutters were overflowing after heavy rain. Led through a yard to a nice old house. The local notables thronged the doorsteps. The chief, our host, has not much English. He looks very Turkish, with huge bristling eye-brows and twinkling blue eyes that watch every word and movement. He leads us up a broad flight of stairs. At every turn a young girl stands in the RL & S uniform: royal-blue woolly trousers and hat with white overalls. Two school-mistresses have been detailed as interpreters, so the school has a holiday. We sit in a long narrow room on comfy sofas, an old 'Nafto' burning merrily in our midst, along with the army senior officers and much-decorated chiefs of *gendarmerie*. No 'broody' sitting this time, but discussions regarding our journey. The director of education was introduced. He had good French. Later the governor walked in, extremely suave, luscious looking and well-dressed but also surprisingly warm and friendly. Once it was accepted that we could not stay the night, they unani-mously counselled we should leave by 1.30, but no lunch was served until nearly two o'clock. Like most Persian meals, it was delicious, served with a rather sweet red wine. We sat side by side, as at the Lord Mayor's banquet, with an enormous bottle of Glen Avey whisky set before us. As always, and so sensibly in the East, no conversation is expected during the tucking-in.

The governor made a long speech which the poor little fat teacher had to translate at one go. She got very out of her depth once or twice, and had to resort to friendship and the depth of Iranian-British togetherness. Finally we were presented with a pair of hand-made vases, fashioned from poplar wood and fired with the national colours. The two teachers told me of their difficulties, needs and aspirations: always the need for books and the Red Cross instruction manual. Couldn't we stay with them, or return?

A brave show was put on through the order of Mr Hamami and Princess Shams, but what they really needed was those wonderful knights of the British Council in Tehran, an ABC on wheels dispen-sing words and ideas and friendship, exchanges of history and poetry. All along I took addresses and made promises I was unlikely to fulfil. Freya had an idea after the surrender of the French in Syria, when we were dispensing tractors and trucks, some without instructions in Arabic, that each petrol station along the desert roads should be manned by an educated and cultured young man or couple who could also dispense language and learning along with spare parts, tyres and lessons in maintenance. Each was to be well paid and not left in any one station too long. Some of our garages might profit from the idea. No wonder it is school-teachers who lead revolutions.

A very touching if far too tardy farewell; then up and away through chocolate hills to Tabriz. We were late and found the RL & S with some difficulty. No one knew we were coming, no civic welcome on the door-step, only one tired girl in a white apron. Eventually a nice warm room upstairs was prepared and a whole roast chicken and fruit brought to the room. A wonderful, wonderful sleep.

14 March

Two thin wolves look over their shoulders above the roadside as we approach the frontier late in the afternoon. It is wild, lonely country, but we have been assured that there is a comfortable hotel on the frontier where we must spend the night before completing formalities of transit. Before we left Tabriz in the morning, we called on the British Council, who also had never heard of us. In charge, a charming couple expecting Dervla Murphy on her bicycle. We think now of this intrepid Irish lady, heading for Afghanistan. She had been attacked by a wolf, we were told, had shot it and found it very emaciated.

Mount Ararat comes into view, its snow-covered cone shining with the harsh sunlight and dominating the landscape for miles around. The new hotel is built like a coaching house over the arch above the customs post. We hope to get our documents passed tonight so we can make an early getaway in the morning, but no one seems interested. We obtain a room from the hotel manager, who bears a strong resemblance to Emlyn Williams, the actor. The hotel is modern, but already beginning to disintegrate. The hall and dining room are thronged with young men and a few girls in jeans, the young women's bouffon hair-styles dyed in bright colours. They tramp up and down the stairs and sit along the passages. A few lucky ones can be seen stretched out on beds through open doors. A radio blares and the whole place is thick with tobacco smoke. The restaurant is shut, but Emlyn W. brings us some tea and white cheese. He explains that three buses bound for Turkey have been held up by the weather. They will have to stay overnight, though he has no room for them.

15 March

The stranded passengers are still there when we leave. In Persia we found that a smile accomplishes many things; but it takes a display of temper to rouse the Turkish customs at 9.30 a.m. They wave us through without examining anything. We speed along lightheartedly, thankful for the car's efficient heater, through a landscape where myth merges with history. Looking at Ararat I make a note to find a Noah's ark for a godchild. We gaze across the rough terrain leading up to the mountain, wondering if the archaeologists are still searching for relics. A couple with a pony comes into view. The woman, who dutifully walks behind her husband and the sleek, well-fed animal, is most unlike the wooden Mrs Noah of my nursery. She wears a bright cotton dress which makes her look as though basketfuls of red and yellow roses have been spilled over her. Her head is wrapped in a huge red turban. There is a bright sash about her waist. Her bodice is neat and intricately tailored. Her skirt sweeps the ground behind her in a cascade of rose-covered frills. The man wears wide baggy jodhpurs, a navy serge European jacket and a flat navy cap that sits like a cowpat on his neat Turkish head. This extraordinary headgear, worn solemnly without the jauntiness with which caps should be worn, is the strangest of all Atatürk's legacies. One of the first things we notice with thankfulness on reaching Turkey is the condition of the stock. All ponies and donkeys look sleek and well-fed. Even the cattle, which in Iran drag their bones painfully through the spring sunshine after the starvation of winter, appear healthy.

Before climbing the Taher pass, we slow to watch an eagle picking at a dead dog. The road has suffered from the winter, and potholes cut our speed by half. The pass rises steeply between high cliffs, the country is lonely, cruel and barren. Although we are crawling, none of the buses or trucks has caught us up. While lunching in a biting wind at the roadside, we see a small grey car coming from the west towards Iran. A smiling, round elderly face peers out at us. We wave as it approaches and, spotting its GB plate, expect it to stop. It slows, but picks up speed again, and we gaze with amazement at the backs of two white-haired heads as they disappear towards the dangerous pass and a gathering blizzard. An English professor, with wife in tow, on his way to give a lecture?

At Erzerum we will decide which route to take to Ankara. We will sleep there in the best hotel before making our decision in the morning. The snow drifts half-heartedly as our wheels slide through liquid mud down the steep hill into the city. We make a complete circuit before finding a Snow Cat parked outside a likely looking hotel. The reception is in the café-cum-bar. The two young men dressed in khaki do their best for us, but there is nothing to sustain us except hard-boiled eggs, a piece of bread and a bottle of raki.

16 March

An Armenian who speaks faultless English advises us to put our car on the train. He is sitting in the café in a huddle of flesh, his young, yellow, heavy face creased with tiredness, the immense dome of his forehead showing through ink-black hair. He arrived at 3 a.m. in the only bus that has so far got through, twelve hours behind us. We wonder how the English couple of the day before fared. When we say we think the train will be too expensive, the Armenian consults a truck driver, who advises the northern route, via Trebizond and the Black Sea coast. The direct road by Sivas is snowbound. 'You won't get through,' says the Armenian. He turns and addresses an elderly man in Farsi.

'How many languages do you speak?' I ask.

'About ten,' he says. 'I can learn any tongue. God has given me the talent.'

Soon after turning off the main Ankara road, we start to climb. We overtake an open lorry overburdened with hay and listing heavily. I shut my eyes until we have negotiated the narrow space between it and the edge. One snowy bend succeeds another. The road narrows. It has the wrong camber, tipping us towards the increasingly precipitous fall on our right: this is all the more unnerving since ours is a right-hand-drive vehicle. We ought to be in a sleigh with horses, not in this filthy overloaded Land-Rover, which is already exhausted from making too many journeys between Cheskin and Tehran. Derek, who has a poor head for heights, becomes rather silent. I prattle on about Rose Macaulay and the delights of Trebizond. The sun shines over snow-lit country as spectacular as the Bernese Oberland. Below us the valleys lie under a floating veil of pearly mist. We negotiate hairpin after hairpin, a dog ever chasing its tail.

We meet a snowdrift, come to a halt and have to dig ourselves out. The listing hay wagon comes up behind us, blaring its horn.

We are suddenly unnerved by a spread of fresh-looking fish on the road: another truck, doubtless travelling south, has shed a load destined for the tables of Erzerum. We make the summit in the lowest gear and slide cautiously down the other side. The descent is not so steep, but very twisty. 'Look at the birds on that roof!' I cry.

D. looks up and the Land-Rover slides slowly but determinedly into the ditch and heaves over. Luckily this is a less lonely part of the mountain. A grader comes into view. The driver gets me out of the Land-Rover and puts me in his cabin. He tows out Derek, then leaves him to collect his wits and his gears. Derek speeds after us, fearing I have been abducted. Fortunately our rescuer drops me and all is well. He refuses to accept any payment – only our heartfelt thanks in an unknown tongue.

The next pass takes us up to 8,000 feet. The mist has cleared. A beautiful mountainous land is revealed sparkling below – enough to make one sing for joy. Suddenly, rounding a bend, we encounter a sight that almost stops us in our tracks. Hundreds of feet below there is, clearly discernible, a glistening pile of fish. Next to it, lying as helpless as a beetle on its back, its wheels skyward, is the truck. There is no sign of its occupants, nor of any rescuers. Yet the fish we saw earlier looked definitely fresh, not frozen. Reduced to silence, we drive on as the mists enclose us again. We come to a hotel. It is closed because of the snow, but there are trucks parked outside a near-by hut.

Faces appear at our windows. It is the roadmen's hut. There are two shovel men, four grader men, three lorry drivers, a cook and two *gendarmes*. They take us in like two lost children. A meal is prepared – soupy white beans in tomato sauce, fresh bread, a dish of rice and tea. It is a merry evening. We communicate by signs and drawings. The oldest man leads the evening prayer in the kitchen. We are able to use a tolerable lavatory and then repair, exhausted, to a dormitory of double-decker wooden bunks. I am put to sleep above the elderly prayer leader. Derek is in the farthest corner of the room, along with the grader drivers. All the men sleep in the pyjamas they wear under their day clothes. Despite the closed windows, there is no smell. After the lights go out, one man begins to snore. There are some jokes about the *zelzel*, and he is speedily shut up.

17 March

We are all woken before 6 a.m., when my guardian on the bunk below starts to offer his morning prayer. I lie anxiously waiting for him to finish, so I can scramble down and visit the lavatory. But he has much to say to Allah, and I can only offer prayers of my own and contain myself.

Breakfast is served by the cook – one of the shovel men – who lights the stove while the others scrape snow from the doorway. Each man takes a turn to greet us formally. We are given tea with toasted bread and black olives – a little dish of fresh butter provided for the unexpected guests. When we try to inquire about the fish lorry we meet evasive replies. We say goodbye with full hearts – looking into each pair of black, smiling eyes and shaking each pair of hands, helpless in our ability to convey our thanks and appreciation. I shall never forget these hosts of one night. Thank God Atatürk did not succeed in fully westernizing his country.

The descent, all in low gear, is slow and perilous. After two or three bends we again collapse into the ditch on the mountain-side. An upcoming lorry pulls us out after frantic digging. We proceed once more along precipitous slopes, now sprinkled with chestnut-trees, leading down to the immense snowy plains. A team of graders waves us on, and round the next bend we run straight into an avalanche. As Derek starts to dig again, I walk back to the graders and lead them to the avalanche. Together we clear the road and we drive on, with ropes tied to our wheels in lieu of chains. I am now at the wheel. The road winds steeply downhill between cliffs. The snow turns to slush, then to amber mud. As I spy the first green leaves and shoots of grass my muscles begin to relax. The sky is overcast and a fine drizzle falls. We cross and re-cross a mountain torrent, and after a while find a petrol pump under a grand old plane tree. There is a small café with tables and chairs. Maybe the fish lorry stopped here for petrol before climbing to its disaster.

We pass villages filled with waving children, through markets where women in shawls and aprons are selling luscious vegetables, freshly killed lambs – and fish. Livestock is being driven and loaded into wagons. Outside the villages, the road is lined with violets, primroses and helibore. Numbed by exhaustion, we slide into Trebizond. We welcome the red-tiled roofs of our familiar civilized world – the churches converted to mosques, the narrow cobbled streets leading to the scruffy little port. We are flagged down by a scout from the Hotel Beuli. After a rest we descend to a very different meal from the one we had last night – coley fish. We meet a weary American, disillusioned after four years in Trebizond. 'Take the boat to Samsun,' he says. 'There are wolves on the road. A boy who left his Land-Rover was eaten last week.'

18 March

We leave early, unable (alas!) to linger. The coast road runs with liquid yellow mud, between rocks and stones and islets of broken asphalt. The buses and lorries crawl along at a patient 5 m.p.h. There are snow showers all day. The country seems made for children and fairy-tales. We splash through high banks of wild wanda, primroses, cyclamen and helibores, shaded by neat bushes and little pruned briars.

The bridges that span the noisy torrents which dash into the sea consist only of wooden planks, one for each wheel. The engine stalls and won't start. Again we are rescued by truck drivers – the Turkish Knights of the Road. We come into olive and orange groves. The women look bent and bandy, with legs thickened by work. Wearing striped aprons, they carry heavy baskets of tobacco. After sixteen hours we make it to Ordu – about half-way to Samsun. The hotel is the worst so far. The lavatory stinks and overflows. We eat kebabs and sardines at the Haji Baba restaurant. The night is broken by unfamiliar noises and the whistling of the night watchman.

19 March

Another early knock. Coffee with a friend from last night – such intimacy and companionship, never to be met with again. Always the same joke: D.'s height and lantern jaws – 'You must be Gary Cooper!' The Land-Rover is fed up and won't start. But the scholars are on their way to school and give us a mighty shove till we splutter down the street – and away to Samsun. The day is brilliant, the sea a Caribbean blue. Rivers tumble from the mountains under frail-looking bridges. The beaches become less black – there are headlands with rocks and tiny Byzantine churches. Not far out of Trebizond a boat glides gracefully by – leaving us to toss and heave along the muddy disappearing roadway. At Samsun we head inland across the central Anatolian plain to Ankara. When I finish my stint at the wheel I collapse into a bent lump of sleep. It must be some little fever – a legacy from Cheskin. I remember only the great spaces and countours of that land, infrequent halts in the biting wind.

Ankara is snowbound. We find a hotel of no great distinction or comfort. I ring the British Embassy. The Ambassador, Bernard Burroughs, whom I know from Cairo days, is there. 'Come for a late supper,' he says. 'It's Nanny's night off and we have to put the children to bed.' We bathe and begin to enjoy our metamorphosis. But the taxi gets stuck on a hill, and has to deposit us back at the hotel. D. pulls out the brave little Land-Rover. This time it consents to start and carries us up to the Embassy on its hill. We are given the warmest of welcomes, without reproaches. It is a wonderful evening – just the four of us. We drink consommé and eat sole off gold plate, served with delicious wine in a charming room, with two intelligent, kindred spirits. It is the start of our homecoming.

17

Pink Clouds

Age was tightening its hold on Zara. Her indispositions were becoming more frequent. She had in the end capitulated to Parr's Cottage, and it was a comfort, during my absences abroad or in Ireland, to know that Bill Astor was near at hand. Unless he, too, was travelling, hardly a week passed without him calling to see her. She also continued to be well looked after by her two 'faithfuls'. After more than twenty years' service together at Government House, Norman Tower and Charles Street, they still addressed each other as 'Miss Stacey' and 'Mrs Donald' – the latter a courtesy title, since both were unmarried. A true perfectionist, Mrs Donald paid as much attention to the small lunch parties Zara gave in the cramped confines of Parr's dining room as she had to those in the more glorious surroundings of Canberra and Windsor. Zara's taste in people remained as eclectic as ever, mixing the humble with the mighty, Irish wit with English decorum. Nancy Astor was a frequent visitor, lavishing tips on the faithfuls, chasing Zara round the table after some argument over politics or religion. Zara would tease Nancy about Christian Science, and once got her to drink a whole glass of Dubonnet, claiming it was non-alcoholic. Nancy, who originally lent Parr's to Zara, invariably responded by 'throwing her out of the house'.

Once I arrived at Parr's to find Mo O'Brien, Hugo Brassey's lovely sister, now fallen on evil times, entertaining the somewhat prim Eddy Lloyd, head gardener at Windsor Great Park, with her famous imitation of a loose horse at the meet – tail up, breaking wind, unprintable comments from the foot followers of the Limerick Hunt. Poor Eddy was puce, torn between outraged indignation and respect for the 'quality', but Bill found Mo amusing and would ask her up to Cliveden whatever luminaries were staying. On one occasion it was Bob Menzies and Dame Pattie. Bob was well up to Mo's antics. Had not Hermione and I escorted him round the Cairo nightspots during the war, and had he not thoroughly enjoyed himself without embarrassing us?

When Sandie died, Zara had insisted I take Frank, his Polish valet, to see if he would look after Mo. We arrived along a road that ended at a charming old house between Oxford and Burford to find terriers on every chair, dozens of pictures stacked against the wall and nothing organized. On the way back Frank said to me, 'I think I can help Mrs O'Brien,' and so he did for several years, cheerfully keeping the chickens, growing vegetables and telling her when her fly-buttons were undone. He seemed to find the life a happy relief after the constrictions of the Norman Tower and Charles Street. Frank's own extraordinary story reached a culmination when his wife and daughter, whom he had not seen since the child was a baby, suddenly appeared in England. They all lived, I trust, happily ever after.

Staying at Parr's I would sometimes exercise Bill's hunters along the wide avenues where beech leaves lay thick on the ground and golden pheasants crept like small fireballs from under the azaleas and rhododendrons; or else I walked them down the steep chalky tracks leading to the river, under the ancient yews. The cottages along the river were being modernized. Bill at one time offered us the largest, which was somewhat bigger than Parr's and had room for us all. But Zara insisted Parr's was to be her 'deathnest': 'I'm waiting for my pink cloud,' she used to say. Anyway, I told Bill, I couldn't take on his cottage as well as Dunlewy, quite apart from needing to keep the occasional eye on Castle Martin. So instead Bill offered it to his osteopath, Stephen Ward.

I never found Stephen attractive, but he was amusing to talk to and always appeared anxious to please. He was a brilliant manipulator – of backs if not, as it eventually transpired, of people. After a weekend lunch at Cliveden, he would come up from the cottage to massage Bill's back, then do anyone else who wanted it. He did my spine so much good that I took a course of treatment with him in Wimpole Street – all highly professional and correct. In his character, however, there was something not quite right about Stephen. He could not rest content as a good artist and excellent osteopath, and

he presumed on Bill's generosity. Many of Bill's friends did the same
– except that Stephen wasn't really a friend. Bill once asked me if I
thought Stephen was a spy. I couldn't imagine he would have asked
such a question about a friend. Bill was quite snobbish in an English
sort of way, and Stephen had many other prominent patients. It was
convenient to have him near to the palace for treatment at weekends.

I came to know Bill very well at this time when Zara was growing
more delicate – though her mind was always alert – and the two
faithfuls were losing their stamina. Thus I frequently found myself
crossing from Ireland. Bill was lonely after the failure of his marriage
to Philippa Hunloke and would often walk his dogs down to Parr's.
During Ascot week he would play host to the younger racing crowd.
The regulars included Virginia and Richard Sykes – Richard being
the elder brother of Christopher, whom the family wisely chose to
write their mother's biography. Virginia Sykes, as bright and gay as
anyone, lacked that cultivated indifference to social niceties one finds
among the British upper classes. After one Ascot week, Bill told me,
she was the only guest to give Chef a *pourboir* – in Ireland he would
have been toasted after an extra good dinner. British boorishness,
alas, seemed to have survived the Second World War. It was curious
how, when overseas visitors arrived and Bill wasn't actually in the
room, the house guests would continue to sit around flirting or
gossiping in the great hall at Cliveden, as if they were staying in a
hotel.

Despite all that has been written about Stephen and his girls, I
doubt whether their visits to the big house were all that frequent.
I only met Christine Keeler once – and that was down by the
river. I remember the smell of lavender as Stephen and his friends
relaxed by the cottage on a summer weekend. One evening Derek
sat next to Mandy Rice Davies: afterwards he confided that it seemed
odd that Stephen should produce such mediocre fare.

While we were working in Jordan, Zara's letters were full of Bill's
latest romance – with Bronwen Pugh, who became his third wife.
Zara called her 'The Pencil' in not very flattering tribute to her
wonderful legs and shape. Bill and Bron came out to the Middle East
during their honeymoon, and stayed with us at the old quarantine
centre at Ma'an. Grey, too, was with us at this time, but became ill
and had to return to England. For Bron he wrote a 'Semi-Spiritual
Poem':

Pink Clouds

Looking for Damascus
we have flown over much dry land,
and a few clouds wake
our river memories.

Somewhere underneath
the Princess came
with camels, no doubt, and eunuchs,
looking for Damascus,

a husband, more riches and a green garden
all to herself. But these were
the fabled, dusty
days before aeroplanes.

History has it
no one was allowed to see her
except black girls and the eunuch
of longest standing,

but does not say
if she succeeded,
whose tracks are patterns now
in the dry land.

Our Lebanese pilot
has no use for them:
since each in his own way
finds out Damascus,

maps and radar
will lead him where
St Paul needed visions
as we do – only

ours are filigree and tug the eye
of re-enactment. The hot browns
and purples of the desert, the places where
all but flowers last a million years,

grant their peace and memory to humans
homing on Damascus. Clouds may
obscure our landing, but rumour goes
it's raining over there.

We visited Wadi Rum with Bill and Bron, and accompanied them
to Petra before sending them on their way to look up some of Bill's
wartime friends in Jerusalem and Beirut. I see Bron on the terrace
at Cliveden, swinging those famous legs — she had been Balmain's
favourite mannequin — and saying: 'It's all too good to be true.' In
the summer after our return from Jordan they brought Emily — Bill's
daughter by Philippa — to stay with us at Dunlewy.

We had lingered some weeks with Freya on our way home from
Iran, and arrived in England to find the papers full of what was being
called the 'Profumo affair'. The Profumo we knew was Philip, the
attractive younger brother of John (Jack) Profumo, the Minister of
War in the Macmillan government. Philip had been master of the
Galway Blazers, and later of the Fitzwilliams in County Wicklow,
but he'd never seemed the ordinary run of an MFH. Derek, who
had known him in the Life Guards, said he wasn't the ordinary run
of a Household Cavalry officer either. When we stayed with him in
Wicklow we could lie in bed and have music by Beethoven piped
into our rooms.

I never ran into Jack at Cliveden. Evidently he met Christine
Keeler swimming at the pool with Stephen and others after he and
his wife had been dining with Bill. It was his lie to the Mother of
Parliaments — that he had never had a relationship with Christine —
which caused the first crack in the Macmillan government. The
Cheskin earthquake came at night, swallowing most of its victims as
they lay in their beds; the Profumo earthquake at Westminster was
in its way as destructive — spewing out some of the nastiest aspects
of British life, with its extraordinary and prurient obsession with sex.

Poor Stephen became the universal scapegoat: security risk, pro-
moter of orgies for the rich and powerful; consorter with racketeers;
pimp who lived off the immoral earnings of the prostitutes he introduced to his clients. Like the medieval church, which outlawed then
hunted lepers, witches, Jews and prostitutes, the press promptly set
itself up as the protector of the Ordinary Decent Folk of England
against the licentious aristocracy and governing classes — or what

remained of them after the Second World War. Even the most peripheral families, like the outlying villages beyond Cheskin, felt the tremors and quaked.

Since Derek and I had hurried home to a neglected Dunlewy for the late spring planting, we missed most of the witchhunt. When Neily the postman brought the papers – a day late – I tried to hide them from Nellie, knowing she would be agog. For some reason the Astor lawyers advised Bill to go about his normal social life as though nothing had happened – and this he valiantly did, with Bronwen at his side. It is hard to conceive the suffering and hurt they had to endure from men and women who had accepted their hospitality and whom they had thought of as friends. When I read how Stephen, abandoned by his friends, killed himself with an overdose, I was left with unresolved feelings of personal discontent and distrust for authority. Did he believe that, because the witnesses had lied, he stood no chance of a fair trial? The girls he lived with – Christine and Mandy – were not prostitutes, just good-time girls wanting a life-style they could obtain only through their bodies. Throughout the time she lived with Stephen, Mandy was being paid £100 a week by Peter Rachman, the slum landlord, and there is no evidence that Stephen took money from Keeler. Was it lies that killed Stephen, or was it shame, remorse or an appalling isolation? Or was it simply the hounding of the gutter press? I still feel guilty and bewildered when I think of those days.

After I began this book, I met Peter Smithers, a contemporary of Pat's at Hawtrey's, their prep school, who was the Parliamentary Undersecretary of State in the Foreign Office in the Macmillan government. He recounted how another Hawtrey's boy, Dorian Williams, later prominent in the horse world, had a remarkable gift for story-telling. Once he spun a yarn so terrifying that, as it passed from mouth to mouth, virtually every boy in the school was reduced to a state of panic. The headmaster summoned the whole school to explain to his doubting audience that the story was nothing more than the product of one boy's imagination. The same spirit overtook the House of Commons when the Profumo scandal broke. 'I use the word panic,' Peter said, 'for panic it was. Every MP remembered his own transgressions, great or small, past or present.'

The lie Jack Profumo told the Commons when he denied sleeping with Christine Keeler was the only matter of substance in the whole affair. Ivanov, the only real spy in the case, made this clear in a recent interview. Admitting to being implicated in the Portland spy ring, Ivanov, who had shared Christine's sexual favours with Profumo, knew he was being watched by MI5, who hoped to 'turn' him. He would never have dreamt of using anyone as naïve as Christine to winkle secrets out of the Minister of War. Like Julian Critchley, Peter Smithers blames the whips, especially the Chief Whip, Martin Redmayne, for not alerting the prime minister to the possibility that Jack Profumo's protestations of innocence were false. Harold Macmillan seems to have been weirdly unworldly in sexual matters: perhaps he found them too painful, given his wife's long affair with Bob Boothby.

There were two centres of panic in the Houses of Parliament, said Peter: the Smoke Room, where everyone wondered who was 'going to be next'; and the Press Bar downstairs, the principal rumour mill, whence an astonishing variety of lurid tales emanated. Practically every member of the Cabinet was reported to have indulged in some sexual extravaganza – everyone, of course, except the prime minister. The scandal became the catalyst for events that were asking to happen: not only was the Labour party waiting to pounce, but a number of Tory backbenchers, men who felt themselves excluded by Macmillan's preference for appointing people with titles or good social connections to the junior posts in his government, found in the scandal an opportunity to air their resentments. 'On the back benches,' said Peter, 'there were many Tories who had not been to Eton, Harrow or Winchester, who felt themselves to be second-class members of the party. They had no sympathy at all with Harold or his friends.' Not only was Macmillan destroyed, but the Tory party too, as it then was. It wouldn't be too much to say that the Profumo scandal was the necessary prelude to the new Toryism, based on meritocracy, that would eventually emerge under Margaret Thatcher.

After Stephen Ward, it was probably Bill Astor who paid the heaviest price. Apart from Bronwen, who remained by his side throughout, and his brothers, Zara remained his most loyal and stalwart supporter, but she was growing ever more frail. She dug in at Parr's Cottage – tight-lipped and angrier than I had ever seen her as the hypocrites and pharisees rounded on Bill. In the unkindest cut of all, Ange and Malise, who had joined the Moral Rearmers after the war to save the world from Sin and Communism, urged her to leave Cliveden's den of iniquity to ensure that her grandsons would not be corrupted by its depraved atmosphere. During Royal Ascot week, Dermot McCalmont, our favourite racing cousin from Mount Juliet, smugly announced that he had refused to shake hands with Bill and that many in the Royal Enclosure had also cut him dead. A leading newspaper refused to publish a letter from Bill advocating the co-ordination of voluntary organizations dealing with the victims of disasters, refugees and displaced persons, along the lines devised by him and Derek after the Hungarian revolution. I have no doubt that the whole experience aggravated the heart condition that killed him three years later in 1966.

After Bill's death, his brother David wrote to me:

I think that expedition to Austria was literally the most valuable thing that ever happened to Bill as regards his happiness and moral strength. It not only pulled him up at what he always said was his all time lowest point, it also gave him something to use as a lifeline. When his second, worst calamity occurred, the Profumo one, thank God he had this.

Zara went before Bill, but only just. One day, when I took her to see Pat's name engraved on the new war memorial at Eton, she suffered a pain in her arm in what, with hindsight, was probably a mild heart attack. In the summer of 1965, while waiting for a car to take her to see a specialist in London, she fell down and died. Her mind had been fully alert to the end. 'What will Pat and Himself think of her?' asked Grey in a letter to me. 'From the way she talked of Stevenson's death [the week before], I should think she'll make straight for Adlai!'

Pink cloud beyond all expectations! H. God's acknowledgement of a terrestrially-orientated (very unspiritual? – perhaps not – who knows?) but unique life. Saw her the night before mercifully and Bill cracked with her two hours before she was due to go to London to get massage for arm agony (obviously heart) which came in spasms: Talbot was ordered when she died. Am going ahead with plans: cremation (only me and perhaps executor attending). Memorial service prob. St George's Chapel (King couldn't say his prayers there but we can say ours at Hodges later) and probably next week – if you *must* come cable *Parr's instantly* you read this: suggest you don't come as we can keep Gran's urn in Cliveden chapel (*à la* Aunt Nancy and it's so reminiscent of Gran's taste in matters visual) until your pleasure and return for final rest by Himself at Hodges . . . What about Skimp? Bill cabled him but no word yet. Sweet personal telegram from the Queen to me! Mrs Donald ran weeping after the undertaker but Stacey there now and both are flushed with enjoyment of drama.

Bill let her body rest in the private chapel at Cliveden. Together her grandsons took her to be cremated quietly at Slough, according to her wishes. Later, after the memorial service at Windsor, we took her ashes up to Gloucestershire, to be placed in Sandie's grave.

Earlier that same year, Bets Somerset's Jumbly died at sea. I later learnt the full story from a précis of the testimonies of witnesses. At 11.15 a.m. on 27 February 1965, Bobby had sailed his 22-metre yacht out of Casteloriso, an Aegean anchorage, and headed for the island of Rhodes. There was no doubting Bobby's experience as a yachtsman and ocean racer. Indeed, he was at this time commodore of the Royal Ocean Racing Club. On board was his crew of four seamen and two girl passengers. When they set sail there was very little wind, and they needed to rely on the engine, but later in the afternoon the wind increased from the east. By dusk it was blowing a gale and Bobby reduced sail considerably; but he maintained his south-westward course towards the north point of the island of Rhodes, just to the south of which lay the little harbour of Mandraki below the city of Rhodes itself.

Mandraki harbour is V-shaped. It faces north, with all the jetties on the west side of the 'V' and a long pier on the east side. At the north end of the pier the St Nicholas lighthouse flashes a white light, and north-west of the pier a tongue of land sticks out eastwards and ends in jagged, half-submerged rocks. According to Bobby's chart, this dangerous point carried another lighthouse with a flashing red light, but Bobby's chart had been printed in 1945 and that light had disappeared in the late 1940s. Unbeknown to him there was now a quite different flashing red light on the very northern tip of Rhodes island.

At 21.00 hours, when one of the crew sighted the flashing St Nicholas light, it was still very rough and visibility was difficult. They looked for the red flashing light and, as they thought, sighted it to starboard, thereby setting a course too far west and on to the treacherous rocks. The crew managed to swim ashore through the breakers, but Bobby stayed aboard to help the girls below decks. He went below, where they were all three trapped and drowned.

I remembered the summer Derek and I took the boys to Andraix when the Somersets borrowed their Uncle Obbie St Albans's house. Derek felt seasick, but Bobby pronounced him a yachtsman manqué. We sailed all round the island, anchoring at the still secret little ports and bays, but the Jumbly soon tired of the little booths and tavernas we loved and pointedly stayed on board, recalling us impatiently from our dallying. Lately, he said with scorn, he had had two Eton boys on the boat who never got out of their dressing gowns but lay in their bunks talking. Perhaps, it occurred to me, they had felt too seasick to do anything else. The Ruthvens did their best to present a better Etonian image. They let themselves be lowered into the warm but buffeting waves at the stern, with a rope each to hold on to. I felt a slight alarm, though never having reared sons before, somehow agreed, under pressure of the Jumbly's dominance, that it was all part of sailing on the *Iolaire*. The Spanish crew told Derek he strongly disapproved, and Derek himself was most apprehensive and stood watch at the stern over the adolescent, half-submerged bodies, lest they go under the hull and suffer a keel-hauling *à la* mutiny on the *Bounty*.

Most of anyone I think I enjoyed that trip. Up in the prow, riding the waves of the sea, seemed the greatest escape we could hope for in this life till we gain heavenly wings. Bets sometimes drove round the coast to meet us with picnics; Bob's rations aboard were spartan and wrapped in newspaper.

During those years I often came alone to Castle Martin, where the situation grew to be an increasing preoccupation. Aunt Sheela became ever more difficult and obstinate with time. For years, following the death of Ian Blacker in 1943, members of the family had tried to persuade her to sell the estate and ensure a comfortable old age for herself. With its virgin pastures, never turned by the plough, right next to the Curragh, its eighteenth-century stabling and the perfect site it occupied on a lovely bend in the Liffey, the old mansion had long been eyed by wealthy race-horse owners. Raymond Guest, the US Ambassador to Dublin, once tried to talk the old lady into selling the place to him, and seemed to be making some headway – only to fall at the last hurdle when he made the fatal error of speculating on how he would replace the old iron fences and barbed wire with brilliant white stud fencing. 'Mr Guest, there will be no white fencing at Castle Martin,' declared Aunt Sheela, and that was the end of the matter.

Aly Khan, who owned the neighbouring stud, had been equally unsuccessful, and out of affection for Zara, Bill Astor had offered to buy the estate and lease it back to Sheela at a nominal rent for life, so she could have enough money to live on respectably. But this plan went the way of all the others. With Percy and Anne at Kinneagh a constant drain on her resources, ever-declining rents and a Quixotic insistence that horse-breeding was the only activity that might properly be conducted at Castle Martin, the estate fell ever more deeply into debt. As she became steadily more remote from the real world, good standing trees were sold to local woodmen, who brought her cooked chickens as 'luckpennies'. Many family treasures were sold at knock-down prices to dealers from the Quays in Dublin.

I tried to discuss the future for herself, Percy and Castle Martin. I even called on her solicitor in Dublin, but discovered he no longer acted for her. Eventually there was so little cash that Peggy, daughter of old Morrissey, the groom, and Aunt Sheela's only domestic, had to be let go. Peggy went to work as a cleaner at the convent up the road, but so worried was she about Aunt Sheela's condition that she spent half her wages buying food in the village and smuggling it into the fridge. By now virtually all the rooms in the house had been abandoned and Aunt Sheela reduced to living in the library. On the last occasion when guests were entertained at dinner – just before Peggy's departure – we ate at the round table in the hall, in front of a massive log fire that roasted those who sat next to it while those opposite almost froze to death.

Then, in the spring of 1967 – that traumatic, extraordinary year which saw the eruption in June of the Six-Day War in the Middle East – Anne Blacker died. Percy found it convenient to move back into the big house, to be looked after by his mother. The old routines began again, with Sheela often lying awake in her bedroom above the front door, waiting for the midnight taxi to bring Percy back from the Hideout or the Red Cow at Naas. The old lady, already penniless, was hardly in a position to cope. By July she was seriously ill, and had to be taken to hospital in Dublin. She never returned to Castle Martin, but died the next month. Derek by then was back in Amman, working with the British Ambassador to distribute the British Aid to Jordan Fund for the victims of the Six-Day War.

I remembered one evening when Aunt Sheela and I were alone at Castle Martin and she said, with her enchanting smile, 'They say that I am Jim's child.' Then she told me the story of a small girl and her governess going along the Bois de Boulogne to an appointed rendezvous near where the carriages drove by. A phaeton drove up and a man strode towards them. He stood looking at the little girl, gave her half a crown and, without a word, drove away again. I always saw the scene as one of those early Victorian question pictures: the governess in black bonnet and tight-waisted dress holding by the hand the little girl in a sailor suit, whose thick dark-blonde hair hangs to her waist. In the background the smart phaeton and high-stepping black horse pull up and the man alights, the tall trees above them.

In November 1939, awaiting my first-born at Ongar, in the little study allotted for my use – looked down on by Binghams, Persses and Clanmorrises in hunting coats, with horns tucked between their two top buttons, on either side of the turf fire – I found in a drawer some old newspaper cuttings reporting a Dublin scandal, when John Pollok horsewhipped Jim Barry outside the Kildare Street Club. I left them where I found them, but when I returned from the Middle East just in time to buy in the sale the old rocking chair in which I had nursed Grey, Aunt Ruby had been through everything and every trace of evidence of the break-up of the Honourable's first marriage had been burned.

At John Pollok's house at Ronachan, the eldest son, Alan, had slept in his parents' dressing room and heard the terrible rows that went on despite the nine children born to them; it was the reason he never married young, and disliked his father. Zara, on the other hand, remembered clinging to her father, her arms around his neck as he swam towards the islands. Later she and Ruby and their young brother Valentine went to live with their mother at Scriblestown, not far from Dublin, while John Pollok took his eldest sons to Ronachan. Sheela was born at Ronachan, but John Pollok lived only two years after he suspected she was not his child, and conveniently died before there was a divorce. Gwan would then have needed to wait two years before being able to marry Jim.

On the day of Sheela's funeral I arrived late from the airport, and was summoned by Percy to the Hideout, where funeral meats awaited a small gathering of Blackers and Goschens and Sheela's surviving siblings, Aunt Ruby and Uncle Val. Percy took me straight into the back parlour to meet Mr Osbourne, the new lawyer, who read out the will to the two of us alone. Castle Martin was to be Grey's, while to Percy there went Kinneagh, and an income for life from the Castle Martin estate. Yet there were no trustees or legal provisions – only debts. I walked back dumbfounded into the adjoining room to meet what I felt, quite wrongly, must be the accusing eyes of Uncle Freddie's relations. The house had been in the Blacker family for generations, but Aunt Sheela, who owned it outright, had bequeathed it to her own not her husband's kin.

Percy seemed content, even happy, to be entrusted to his much younger cousin, with whom he shared a taste for poetry, and who now had the responsibility of supplying him with all the drink and cigarettes he required. With the old lady dead, however, the banks were likely to threaten to foreclose. The young Gowries were in Cambridge, Mass., with their small son, Leo Patrick Brer. Grey, doing a PhD at Harvard, knew nothing of farming, still less about horses. The academic side of his life was taking off, and Xandra, in a prestigious job, was immensely popular. It was true Xandra had a country upbringing and showed early prowess as a horsewoman, but the couple were obviously far too young to think about settling in Kildare and making a living from its land.

I felt bereft: the one person in the family who understood estate management was helping with the aftermath of the Six-Day War in Amman, where I planned to join him as soon as I could. I came to believe that Aunt Sheela had seen in Grey the one person who would look after Percy, and felt desolate that she had never been able to tell me. Then there was Brer, only two, but she kept a snapshot on her desk of him and his nursery dog, nose to nose, sniffing one another.

The situation was before long alleviated, if not resolved. Poor old Percy walked out of the Red Cow one night after a row with the landlord and was killed by a passing truck. Grey was thus freed from his obligations to Percy, but the estate was still in massive deficit. Kinneagh, whose acres might have made Castle Martin viable, was lost for ever: because Percy died intestate, the property was sold and the proceeds divided between his elderly next of kin, his uncle and two aunts. The problem of what to do next with Castle Martin therefore remained.

With Grey back in England, starting on a political career in the Lords, Skimper and I took charge of Castle Martin. We made the house habitable and spent money on furnishings to make it attractive to tenants, and we had Peggy with us. For a brief period I wandered along the river banks and through the old walled garden, tangled with outrageous growth, and dreamed we might have found the solution. First the singer Donovan, then the rock star Mick Jagger rented it for a year each, but in the end Grey took the only sensible decision and sold the old house to Tony O'Reilly, the Irish rugby star, who became president of Heinz foods and owner of the *Irish Independent* newspaper.

Derek's passionate and chivalrous sense of the injustice done to the Palestinians sprang at first from everything he saw as a young officer serving in Palestine at the end of the British Mandate. After the Six-Day War, the Palestinian dispossession finally became the focus for all the concern he had felt and channelled into his work with the relief agencies. As our turbulent century continued, there was little sign of the world knowing, or wanting to know, what to do about the scandal of the hundreds of thousands of Palestinian refugees, living in camps and shanty-towns for generations. The Israelis meanwhile knew exactly what they were up to, as they had from the beginning. Derek's outrage was to be the driving force of all our work during the years that followed, and it would lead us into many more adventures together. They are mainly the subject of another book – Derek's story – at present being written. They clashed, sometimes agonizingly, with Grey and Skimper's unfolding careers, even embarrassing them. When Grey became Minister of State in the North of Ireland, his Secretary of State, Jim Prior, referred bemusedly to certain of these exploits, commenting that his family had some strange friends. 'You have to realize, Jim,' replied Grey, 'ma' folks are the PLO.'

The better-educated of the Brethren, the young effendis Freya set such store by, told me with charming frankness that the education we gave them, such as that of the excellent Read's School in Cairo, was only cosmetic: they resented and hated the British during their schooldays; why should they have to take sides in our quarrel as we fought over their land, motives disguised in the cause of democracy, Western values and, in the case of Palestine, quoting dubious stories from the Old Testament?

During the war we all had theories as to why the British government and the prime minister appeared progressively pro-Zionist. One floating around was that Jewish publishers had advanced Churchill large loans for his books; or was it because of his friend of the famous bench in the park, Barney Baruch? Between the wars he wrote a collection of essays, *Thoughts and Adventures*. In a piece called 'Moses', he describes him as one of the 'greatest human beings' and identifies him with 'the most decisive leap forward descernible in the human story', going on to argue the beliefs so dangerously endorsed by many churches today, yet more and more queried by scholars and archaeologists, that 'we may be sure all things happened just as they are set out according to Holy Writ'. He did, however, concede that the ancient Hebrews made terrible claims on Jahweh or El, rendering him revoltingly partial to the Chosen People: all divine laws and ordinary equity were suspended when they applied to a foreigner, especially to a foreigner whose land and property they required. I enjoy reading some of the Old Testament as myth and poetry, as jumbled-up history told and recited, as with the old sagas, but I rebel in church when, after a lesson, a priest says, 'This is the word of the Lord.'

I also have a quarrel with borders. Harold Nicolson was there, at the Treaty of Versailles, watching, appalled as the Reverend, as the three heads of state ruled arbitrary lines through the Balkans and the lives of millions. He was there in Parliament to speak passionately against the Munich Agreement and continued to be there, at the Ministry of Information, through the worst of the blitz. He was there, too, for the birth of the state of Israel, though he sadly predicted in a letter to Vita Sackville-West that 'instead of being a nice comfy little home like Luxembourg, it will be a fierce camp, riven with hatred and red with blood'. Zara and the Reverend, both born in Ireland on 20 January, never accepted the partition of Ulster as a solution. To them, Londonderry not Dublin was the capital of Donegal. The people of the Glen had close relations bred in Ulster; you can separate a people but you can't slice through a land mass.

Dunlewy remained the warm Irish heart round which our family life was centred. After Derek's daughter, Jennifer, married Jeremy Altamont and was taken by him to live at Westport House in County Mayo, they brought their children to stay as they arrived – five in all. When Leo Patrick Brer was born at Harvard, Derek ran out to the yard and pealed the old bell that still hung precariously at the entrance, while every light in the house shone across the lough to tell the good news to the Glen. Dunlewy and Donegal provided the backdrop to Skimper's early romance with Tiggy Hodgkinson, once they had discovered each other at Cambridge. Here their daughters, Chloë and Orlanda, learned to walk, and ride the pony Porridge, lent by the Guinnesses.

But it was Derek's son Michael who stayed the longest – a year, while we were mostly in the Middle East. He had married Carol, the daughter of the youngest of the three Garland sisters, well known in the racing and hunting world. One day Derek Hill's artist's eye spotted some Dürer-like hands, carved by Mick from logs of firewood. He returned to England to become a sculptor of repute. After Carol died tragically, leaving him with two very small daughters, Padre Watson scattered her ashes around the oak we planted for her in Pan's glade, because Mick said their year at Dunlewy had been their happiest. As Padre Watson prayed fervently, frowning as he did in church, the midges buzzed him and the 'girlish wind' blew the ashes about. It was a scene Carol would have enjoyed. She was sorely missed from the family, especially by me.

As with the rest of the world, Dunlewy was not immune to change. In the contentious matter of the fishing, the choice had been taken from our hands when the Electricity Supply Board took over the Dunlewy and Nacung lakes as reservoirs for the Gweedore hydro-electric scheme. Though a salmon-ladder was fitted in the dam, the fish never returned to spawn in the same numbers as before. The upper end of Dunlewy lake was wrecked. By the old estuary a wonderful copse of Scots pines where the herons nested was felled. Most of the families in the old village below the Protestant church were evacuated and provided with new cottages above the road. They were infinitely more comfortable than their former homes, but the Glen lost its wild beauty. The level of the lake now rose and fell according to the needs of the turbines twelve miles away, leaving a no mans land of mud and rotting stumps, looking like Ypres or the Somme. Electricity came to the Glen, marching in pylons across the wild and boggy waste that separated us from the farmlands of the east, closely followed by the telephone. The ancient bog road was repaired, asphalted and widened, making an ugly scar across Errigal's lower flank.

With the arrival of civilization, the Troubles too came closer. The Provos began training in the forestry land above the Lower Nacung lough, hiding their arms in remote beaches, or on deserted islands. Once, while we were away in the Middle East, a carful of strange men drove up to Paddy's cottage and asked in menacing tones if there were any guns up at the big house. 'I'm sorry, boys,' said Patrick, 'you're too late. Didn't the Major hand them all to the Garda before he went off foreign!' The men took some convincing, but eventually departed empty-handed.

When old Paddy Pat grew truly old he went to live with his daughter, Nora McFadden. There, beside the fire, this tall unbowed man – ghillie, stalker and estate guardian – took up the grandfather's role of what is now called baby-sitting to his two grandsons. He died several years later; the boys helped to lay him out and prepare for the wake. As was the custom, only the neighbours attended the first night, quietly slipping across the river at dusk, along the road past Errigal. Myself came down the long avenue, carrying a small contribution for the hospitality.

At the door of the low house, set back among the stunted firs, the fuchsia and the hydrangeas, old Paddy's sons and son-in-law welcomed those who arrived with the courtesy phrases translated from the Gaelic that came easily to them and, as among the bedouin, are a blessing on formal occasions. I passed through the doorway into a back room. There in an open coffin lay old Paddy, dressed in his best; four candles which burnt beside him gave the only light. I crossed myself, said a prayer, took the chair offered by his daughters and joined the little gathering of women. We talked in low voices about his life, his going. It was the first wake I had been to, and I wondered at its dignity, its unhurried simplicity. After a while, invited into the kitchen for tea, I joined those who had already paid homage. The men did not stay so long beside the coffin. They were to spend the rest of the night reminiscing, discussing the price of a lamb or ewe or wool, drinking tea and whiskey and waited on by the women of the family. As I saw from my window after I walked home, the lights burnt long into the night.

Pink Clouds

The following day a continuous stream of cars bumped up to the little house. They came from the coast and over the bog road from Letterkenny and Glenveagh. All night again the lights shone out, as Paddy Pat's descendants followed the custom of their ancestors, until, after the third night, he was carried by the men of the Glen to the chapel. His grave, dug from the heathery, stony soil, was lined with sand from our sandpit.

The same three days had to be gone through by the stricken family of Nancy Ferry after she died suddenly from a heart attack in the old house facing Dunlewy House directly across the lough; only then could they be alone with their grief. Nancy it was who had been the life and soul of our early days at Dunlewy, who had found Skimper's ducks and geese for him, who had lent us her eldest daughter Mary for so long, and who had, I feel sure, promoted out acceptance within Dunlewy Far.

Not even Henry McIlhenny and the Group could hold together for ever. Henry, with his connoisseurship and illustrious contacts, was far from being a snob. George Melly wrote in an obituary for *The Times*:

Unlike so many rich men he never confined himself to the company of those equally wealthy, nor did he choose to surround himself only by the famous and distinguished. Anyone he took to was welcome, and while not uncritical and something of an inspired gossip, he remained profoundly loyal to those he considered to be true friends.

His one criterion for his guests continued to be whether or not they 'made fun'. Glenveagh Castle was even so capable of including living legends among its fauna. Almost our last alfresco meal with Henry was outside the stalking hut at the head of the lough. As we arrived, a slight figure, grey hair blowing with the wind, came swinging down the track, which narrowed where the mountain river met the sandy beach. It was Greta Garbo, staying at the castle incognito as 'Miss G.'. We sat down to an Irish stew, ministered to by Henry's men-servants in traditional Austrian kit, and two hand-maidens in white blouses and dirndl skirts in the Irish colours of green and gold. There was much of the laughter and wisecracking so dear to Henry. Miss G.'s companion, Cecile de Rothschild, dressed in loden green, sported a badger's brush in her trilby. Already we were planning to sell Dunlewy, and Henry was manoeuvring the handing over of Glenveagh to the Irish government.

Some time after we sold Dunlewy, we went back in June 1982 to stay with Henry at the castle during his last weeks in occupation. Grey's second wife Adelheid was with us. In the evening I was out fishing on the lough when I saw a cavalcade of cars approaching along the winding avenue between the shore and the rhododendron bushes. It was the Minister of State for Northern Ireland. He had picked up an escort of Garda at Letterkenny, had already called at the cottages in Dunlewy Glen and now was here to spend an evening where he had shot his first stag as a boy. Later I spotted him in conversation on the keep with Patrick the Butler, known to have IRA affiliations. It seemed a fitting end to the ambivalence of the Group in Donegal and the nonsense of the border. If the night's menu was not quite up to standard, it was because the baron of beef was being served to Grey's escort and security men below stairs.

Epilogue: A Beirut Diary (1982)

> 'The only lesson History teaches is
> that History never learns the lesson
> History teaches' – Arnold Toynbee

1 July

Our plane is, alas, a Boeing 707, so I suffer excruciating pain in the ears as we leave the lovely cloudland and descend on Larnaca. Drove straightaway to the port and booked on a boat sailing to Jounieh, Lebanon, this evening. The *Kanah* is a cargo boat, dirty and foul-smelling; its only lifeboat, glued to the davits, might just accommodate ten, but we are thirty with a crew of four. We sleep fitfully above the cargo beneath a noisy, flapping tarpaulin.

2 July

After fourteen hours at sea, the mountains of Lebanon are in sight, but anticipation is dampened by an Israeli gun-boat patrolling the sea all round. For two and a half hours we lie there, rocking without an engine, outside Jounieh harbour.

This country, once most favoured by the gods, now has a shoreline of hate, greed and pollution from Tripoli to Ashdod. Suddenly the idea of nuclear destruction seems not so horrifying. Our taxi driver finally deposits us at the office of Cyprus Airways in East Beirut. We find an inner room housing some of the British Embassy staff. They have no news for us of our Oxfam colleague, Peter Coleridge.

We book in at the Alexandre Hotel, an unsavoury room in the

disused wing: No. 619 at the end of a long passage. We arrive with General Sharon, who is lunching at the hotel and giving a press conference. The place seethes with press and cameramen, useless to complain about our room. I foresee much waiting and sitting around in the bar and coffee shop, the only place where a meal is served, and the wide lounge and hallway: the double ever-open entrance door cannot relieve us of the prevailing cloud of tobacco smoke. We run into Uri Avnery, the Israeli peace activist and journalist. He has just been to interview Arafat and is hurrying back to Tel Aviv for a 'Peace Now' demonstration. Sad to have no time to talk. Thankful to reach our unattractive room to repair the ravages of the good ship *Kanah*.

3 July

An Israeli soldier with a huge tommy-gun, and, to me, identically kitted out as a GI, is demanding a 'good room'. He chucks a page boy under the chin; I am reminded of another occupying army in Cairo 1940.

The evening diversion is to climb to the roof and watch the other half of Beirut being shelled from the sea or hills, or bombed from the air. Some of the camera boys sit up there for hours taking pictures. It is beautiful in the moonlight, the rockets and flares denigrating the stars and planets.

4 July

Despite a quorum of maids with pails and smiling youths, the hotel is dirty and stained, we still cannot get a better room. But I begin to bask in the goodwill Derek always engenders. He looks good in his tight trousers and rolled buff shirt, he has started wearing his Knights of Malta arm-band. He won't grow a beard, it is *de rigueur* in the Israeli army, he'll struggle on shaving with dicey electric current and batteries. We still await news of Peter Coleridge and John Forsythe, the Oxfam mediaman.

5 July

Walk down to Musée crossing to prospect chances of getting across. A backing car nearly knocks Derek down; cars travel backwards as often as forwards in Beirut, whereas in Limerick, due to hunting falls or climate, hardly anyone over forty can turn their head to reverse a vehicle. A very young lolling sentry asks why we want to cross. 'Because people are being killed and wounded over there, and we have come to help.' We show our Red Cross and Malteser emblems (the latter a decoration for our work in Hungary). 'We are being killed too, why don't you come and help us?' 'You have all America helping you,' I shout, seeing he won't let us through.

We find a fairly ineffectual Lebanese Red Cross office, and then at last the International Committee for the Red Cross. Here Christine Faris promises to contact Thomas Ruegg at Jounieh regarding our problem in getting across the green line. Back at the hotel, we are moved to room 424 in the new building with the other nobs; then Christine Faris rings telling us to return to the office at 4.30 to meet Thomas Ruegg: a very young German Swiss, but informative, especially when he hears Derek knows the newly arrived field chief delegate, John de Salis. He reports segregation and camps for Palestinians, wounded PLO mostly taken to Israel but are not treated as prisoners of war, which worries them. He will ask if we can get to Ras Beirut in one of their vehicles.

6 July

Frank de Jong of UNRWA collected Derek in a small car at 7 a.m. to spend the morning in Ras Beirut.

At mid-day a number of the occupying forces arrive in the hotel, officers and men. One with a fair beard is looking for a chair and comes to my table. I tell him to sit there if he wishes. He speaks fluent English, in civilian life is a reporter with *Yediot Aharonot*. His theme is that, as a Jew in Yugoslavia, his father never felt welcome. He was born in Israel and only wants to be allowed to live there among other Jews. 'Arafat can be king of the West Bank and Gaza for all I care.' My theme is that in a shrinking world none of us can live as an exclusive theocratic state, it is a multi-racial world and we must share it and its resources; but the block is there. He says he is not religious, yet he wants to have an entirely Jewish state. Back to the old dilemma. Is being a Jew belonging to a faith or a race? This young man is very obviously European despite being a *sabra*; he has never been subjected to persecution, yet he admits Arabs are. He wants them out, his whole thinking conditioned by the tales his

325

father told him. We argue for over half an hour or more, but part amicably.

Derek and de Jong return at 2.30, no one likes to leave the crossing of the line too late. As he walks into the hallway, Derek looks different, like one who saw the hunt. For a moment I feel diminished, even jealous, left behind among the fat cats and the occupying forces, safe and bored. Then the old identification takes over as he tells me what he saw, and I am included in the visit to the Palestinian Red Crescent hospitals and Dr Arafat. The maps come out and are related to the evening's theatre from the roof; the green line, no man's land, the Hippodrome, the airport, the three crossing points. There is a chance of travelling to the south with UNRWA and there will be room for me.

7 July

A large white car called for us early with a driver and Mr Large, the most surprising dapper figure dressed as if for Henley Regatta in a cream suit with a black tie and a silk scarf, topped by a panama hat, most un-UNRWA like. At the first check-point, Mr Large is extremely polite to the Israeli sentry, almost effusive, and away we go, pale-blue flag flying. We join the coast road, the only road to the south and Israel. It is my first real sight of the Israeli war machine. The tanks, all American, are huge; behind the great guns are what look to my jaundiced eye to be hairy gorillas, each with goggles and round tin hat which make them caricatures of Manachem Begin.

Damour was a shock. This pleasant seaside town is a shambles, the road pitted with craters and shell-holes. On we go down the old Canaanite coast into Sidon. It is fairly bashed, some quarters much worse than others. Near to the UNRWA office it is bad. A block of flats opposite has been shelled, and where we park there is a piece of half-buried decomposing body. The stench is awful, the first time I have met it so strong. It stays with me all day and long afterwards.

Inside the UNRWA office, we find the field area officer for south Lebanon. He is a New Zealander, his job Herculean: the Israelis have lifted more than half his staff, mostly Palestinians; those that remain are intensely nervous. Since Israel dislikes the UN, they give very little co-operation. They are on their way to the battle for Beirut, and care little whether families they have bombed out of their homes have food or housing. We discuss the plan for an Oxfam mobile clinic. Mothers will always bring children to the doctor. A young Palestinian who speaks fluent English is detailed to drive us round the camps.

At least ten schools have been utterly destroyed. We pass a large boys' secondary where they are still digging out bodies. Not just children were buried alive under the falling buildings, these schools were used as shelters by all the camp people. As we approach Ein el-Helweh I feel the bile rise into my mouth and rage and despair fill my heart. These places are called 'camps' but are in reality small townships, and the refugees have built on to their houses, made walls and gardens. Some women are picking over what I suppose were their houses, looking either for a body or a belonging. They haven't even their men to help and comfort them; those who survived have been taken prisoner.

It is noon and stinking hot at Tyre. We stop under a cluster of gum trees at the bend of the road before it crosses the Litani river. By the river there is a group of tents: half-naked soldiers in wide digger hats bathe and rest and supposedly guard the bridge. Mr Large is reminded of Australians. I only wish they were, remembering the Aussie troops in Cairo and Alexandria and how the Egyptians really preferred them and their antics to the better-behaved homesick British. The old sea fort is intact, but a lot of the town is badly shelled.

In the UNRWA office, we have the chance of a good chat about the problems and how Oxfam can help. Morale is very low: Tyre has been longer under occupation. Rashadiyeh camp took an awful pasting. The American Ambassador is arriving shortly with the Israeli officer in charge locally; it is put tactfully to Derek that they cannot take us to the camp, Cooper being a dirty word in Israel, especially since the Israeli authorities expelled us in 1976, when we were attending the trials of young Palestinians. When those personages arrive we are kept hidden in a back room. We emerge to find the elusive Peter Coleridge there. He is driving back with us and returning to Oxford. Good-looking, but gold-rimmed spectacles give him a rather schoolmasterish air. I think to myself, he is very determined and aims to have his own way, I doubt even the Israelis can stop him when he has made up his mind. We drive away up the battered coast. They even destroyed all the fishing boats and nets; Oxfam and the Menonites will give them new ones. Outside Tyre bulldozers root up whole orange groves, banana plantations and olive trees beside the road, I suppose to widen it for their infernal war machines.

8 July

Derek says pack, we may get across today. He is going early again with UNRWA, when the night's bombardment gives way to dawn and there is a lull.

I sit restlessly in the lounge, surrounded by our packed grips and near to the telephone for messages. At last Christine Faris comes through, she is sorry but the ICRC cannot make exception and take us across to Ras Beirut. Derek will be disappointed, but he must now persuade UNRWA.

Outside the hotel a young man in jeans and a blue shirt asks me if I like him better now he is not in uniform. 'No,' I say, 'I can't like you until this ghastly killing stops.' But he does go on to say, 'Things would be better without Begin and Sharon.' His paper is more or less a government publication, though it sometimes allows people like Uri Avnery and the Opposition to put their opinions forward.

Derek comes in for lunch. No chance of getting in today, but joyous news: we are booked in at the Mayflower Hotel tomorrow night and Frank de Jong himself will collect us after breakfast.

9 July

We wait anxiously till Frank de Jong comes alone in a very small car full of eggs. We cross via the Musée. Miraculously there is no hold-up, no peering into the boot from the Israeli post. We get a friendly wave-through from the PLO post. Frank puts us down at the Mayflower just off Hamra Street. We choose a fair-sized room at the back: three beds, a desk, a chest of drawers and a built-in wardrobe; and a bathroom, which we soon learn seldom has light or water. All somewhat run-down but cleaner than the Alexandre. Our windows look on to two blocks of flats with a narrow alley to the street between.

We walk up to the Commodore Hotel for supper. The long desk in the lounge is given over to the various press agencies, each with their telex booths. I never saw the international press at work before. The bar is crowded, a paper or television man on every stool. The cameras are trooping in after the day's spying on death and destruction. Few of the press have seen the destruction in Tyre and Sidon, the south being risky regarding re-entry. Soon the Israeli bulldozers will have it tidied up, the poor arms and legs will be submerged for ever, but never that sweet stench.

10 July

A real bad night, but we slept. They fired from land and sea. Shells fell near the French Embassy and in Ashrafiyeh, East Beirut. Breakfast in a semi-basement room next to the kitchen. Most tables have a small transistor giving out the morning news in varying tongues. We'll have to buy one to hear what's happening beyond our narrow streets.

We have our local committee in the Orthodox Youth Centre. It is an old house and we climb the outside stairway to the second floor. Across the street is the Orthodox church, with smooth dome and golden cross, wide cloisters and courtyard. The priests and church workers sit and talk in the shade with a view to the sea, only a short but dangerous stroll away.

The centre is a large cool apartment. A stone balcony looks east to the sea. The Oxfam representative, Chris Damars, has organized a small band of pilgrims to help co-ordinate our aid. Each member works with a different group in West Beirut and they are of varying confessions. Yusef, behind the desk, talks to a stout man, Tariq. Both know Derek, so I am welcomed; along with the Arab courtesy, I sense an atmosphere of strain. While we settle down to business – where the need is greatest, how much to spend now, how much to keep in reserve for more evil times, what the hospitals need – I watch Yusef's good profile, the grey-blue alert eyes and thick grey hair. The room is full of secrets of past hopes and present fears and frustrations. When Yusef and Tariq hear the firing from the ships off the coast, or the planes, or the crash of falling cement, there is a look in their eyes I shall never forget.

Derek has cash now in the bank for immediate relief for hospitals and families, both Palestinian and Lebanese. The need is sheets, there is little water to launder them. Food must be distributed since, increasingly, UNRWA and the ICRC supplies are held up at the green-line crossings.

4.30 Walk round to La Houte to see Dr Fathi Arafat; we weren't kept waiting. I was more moved by him than anyone so far. His English is limited and he didn't know *our* history. He talks excitedly, waves his arms, begs us to tell the humanitarian and human rights people of the world to speak up above the deafening silence of the Arabs and prevent the genocide of the Palestinian people. He asks for sheets, generators, beds and bedding and blood plasma. The PRCS [Palestine Red Crescent Society] hospitals in the suburbs, 'Ramallah', 'Gaza' and 'Acre', and adjacent nursing school are all damaged. Tomorrow a doctor interpreter and organizer for foreign medical workers will call for us and take us round the centres.

11 July

Breakfasted with Lilliemore Ericsson, the WHO pediatrician working with UNRWA. She is enthusiastic about a mobile clinic based on Sidon and a great one for dodging red tape. It could start soon, maybe with a couple of UNRWA vehicles and supplies, a couple of Oxfam personnel and some Lebanese. This way Oxfam avoids having to obtain permission from the occupying forces.

A Red Crescent car called for us at 11 a.m. and drove us to a hospital set up in the Triumph Hotel, where we met with the receiving end of all those beautiful rockets, shells and explosions, painting the sky in blue, orange, red and yellow. On the beds young and old, men and women: legs, backs and tummies horribly burned by phosphorous shells, some with the deeper wounds of cluster missiles. The nurses looked very young and untrained, but the wards were clean and there was a caring atmosphere.

On to the requisitioned French Protestant Lycée, high on the south of the city among expensive apartment blocks and built round large shady playgrounds with covered verandas. The large airy classrooms make excellent wards where they have a hundred beds, some only foam mattresses on the floor, but clean and well spaced (need for sheets). So many pairs of huge dark eyes look at us, sometimes with a smile, some with bewilderment, none with anger or bitterness. A small boy of about seven has lost his right arm and left leg. Pathetic stumps are uncovered and the burned skin and pitted flesh displayed. Again they are mostly civilians: many Lebanese or Syrians; two Bangladeshi who owned a fruit stall.

There is some good equipment, but never enough. The hospital averages about forty patients a day, but as I listen to the continual barrage, I doubt the figures staying so low.

Today's paper says 300 young Israeli reservists have demonstrated against the war.

12 July

I was collected at 9 a.m. by a very old lady, Mme Habib Rihaye, the widow of an American University professor. She did Red Cross work in hospitals during Second World War. She said then, and says it again, 'Every young man should refuse to fight – but live for his country, not die for it!'

After a formal presentation ceremony to Lebanese Red Cross president, Issa al-Khoury, behind an impressive desk, I was led to a large room with ladies in spotless white and tasteful gold chains, all well coiffed. After a short gossip I asked what we could do – 'Stop the war first.' The smart ambulances and chauffered cars in the courtyard seem from a different world from the hospitals and ambulances we saw yesterday. Our mandate is to work across the divisions, so we descend to the dispensing room and a most confident lady compiles a list of needed drugs.

I did my usual 'protestant' suggestion about incinerators for the streets, and there was the familiar story of 'no petrol – our young people are helping'; but something is wrong with those stinking piles and their ribbon of refuse along the gutters.

At Commodore, long talk with Robert Fisk. D. showed him the evidence of the burials in south, and the informers. Fisk has sent story of phosphorous wounds and cluster bombs to *The Times* – assured us they were front-page news.

Lilliemore returned from Sidon; says it was cordoned off – the camps beginning to be unrecognizable. All those dead limbs and heads neatly bulldozed and flattened – no list, no trace, the young men rounded up.

13 July

Amal's forward post impressive, in the firing line. We drive to it along the old corniche which leads to airport. Great banks of generous terracotta soil are heaped against shelling. The long areas of flat-headed pines are tired and dying beside the blasted coast-line, and on the land side high rises still burn and smoke from Sunday's bombardment from the sea. The post is an ex-municipal building in a deep basement. Rocky descent eased for footsteps by steel rods, pots of basil for the sensitive nose.

Turn a corner and you are in a small emergency hospital – operating theatre, three efficient doctors and volunteers. Chatty Lebanese doc. showed us patients, said the soldiers know how to take shelter – casualties were mostly civilians. Those treated are sent as soon as possible to relations or hospitals in safer positions.

We came up and crossed street to church – hit over porch. On the steps saw a round ball – an unexploded shell stuck into ground and phosphorous splashes still active, even though covered with sand. The town smells are of death, sewers and stinking rubbish. I add a new one – phosphorous. What of the Yanks and the Geneva Convention?

15 July

We are to visit the forward hospitals and areas towards the airport. Unsafe up till now. Five of us in a shaky blue car, same nice driver, and another boy who spoke English. We drive through that bombed-out scary area. Dr Fathi Arafat welcomes us. We are given a great smiling *ahlan*, and me, two pink roses from the garden, tucked into my bosom. 'Acre' hospital was the pride of the PRCS, well designed and magnificently equipped. Now only the basement and ground floor can be used. Most windows are shattered, the nursery wing wrecked. 'Acre' suffered a direct hit on each wing and more in Sunday's heavy shelling. The hospital is marked with Red Cross markings on roof. All staff sleep in this most vulnerable building, 600 metres from the Israeli army.

The casualties were all civilians, Lebanese, Palestinian, Egyptian, Syrian and others. Even Jewish journalists now admit this is not war but genocide. We drove through the shattered camp of Chatila, at the far end more devastation from aerial bombing. A high rise had one façade standing – round the side it was simply a heap of rubble below. Even air-raid shelters were blown apart.

'Gaza' hospital still functions – underground. You creep down over a mound of earth into a cave among the rubble. Dr Arafat was again waiting for us. Two children were being operated on. I hate standing around with my silly little notebook, watching pain and broken bodies.

A small ward had three men desperately ill – a very young nurse pumping oxygen into one and two on drip feed. There is something especially moving, because these people, so fine and dark, have beautiful legs and arms. One face above the sheet was like an El Greco painting or an icon. Nothing coarse or brutal – indeed he was not a soldier. I think of those hairy gorillas in their vast tanks and armoured cars on the road in Sidon.

Of all the Arabs the Palestinians are by far the most intelligent – a Mediterranean people, Caananites, I suppose. Therefore after 1967 the Israelis lost a wonderful chance to show the world what can be achieved by two people. But if Irish and Scots can't do it, who can? Maybe Israel has missed the historical boat.

16 July

Down Hamra Street we collect sheets and pillow cases bought for the Palladium. The street is transformed, every café full, the sidewalks lined with stalls selling clothes, shoes, what the Americans call 'notions'. It seems there really are some hopes of a settlement, or at least of prolonging the cease-fire, and Shultz has mentioned the words 'Palestinian *patrie*' for the first time. I found a *Newsweek* of 12 July. Excellent coverage. It reports the Israelis taking up positions in East Beirut prior to moving against the west city. Horrible stories of their increasing hold on the south and use of informers. Gemayel may regret his *ahlan* to the Israelis and Haddad. Presidential elections take place at the end of this month.

At the HQ of the Secours Populaire du Liban, a small day clinic with a few beds, there are the usual complaints of the Israelis holding up supplies. Twenty-one beds are in use, half fighters, half civilians. Some, with second-degree burns, must be vaccinated against infection. Antibiotics and painkillers badly needed. We look at terrible wounds from cluster bombs, amputations and shrapnel cases. One boy has his shoulder penetrated by a flat-nosed bullet which is proving hard to dig out. All is spotlessly clean, the men in camouflage cotton pyjamas. The surgeon shows us casualties from close shelling and falling debris. The underground shelters are adequate against shelling, but not from the high-altitude deep-penetration bombing.

Such a tale of Peter C.'s getaway; on arrival at Brumana, no sign of his passport, the contact had left for London. There ensued a chase around, but he caught the Oxfam Jounieh ferry.

17 July
An endless procession of small children carries water cans up and down the stairs – there is no privacy in this building for the families. As in all the occupied buildings in West Beirut, these people come from the surrounding camps: figures given are 14,500; then there are all of us – international, the Beiruties who did not leave. So it is false of the international press to talk of West Beirut as a besieged PLO stronghold. It is a huge area – we must get this across. General discontent with BBC, Leach, etc., who never looks around.

Fighting in the south last night. Shelling seems to grow closer.

18 July
David McDowell arrived from London via Damascus. His taxi stopped at Homs demanding a further £L400. He is tired and goes to bed.

19 July
David McDowell only saw Peter Coleridge in London for one evening and left next day at dawn – he did talk to Skimper, who was anxious about us, but no replies to all our letters and telexes is rather a disappointment.

My two favourite press men are Robert Fisk of *The Times* and Phillipe Flandre of *Le Croix* in Paris. Phillipe is expert on India, where he lived a year – his mother born there and I think English, father a broker in London. His last night, we had long session at the bar. He plans to go south on his way out with Colin Smith of the *Observer*. He quarrelled finally with his Hindu friends – as I suppose he or Skimper would with any fundamentalists. He knows Persia, and met the Ayatolla in Paris and Arafat here. He will take letters.

Also drink a couple of araks on the ebullient Fisk when he finds us; we grumble together over British foreign policy. He may seem brash to some, but he has great guts and gets everywhere.

Epilogue: A Beirut Diary (1982)

20 July

I wake and stare across at the seven flats and watch the inmates creep out. The stout couple on the top have plants on their balcony and don't hang out washing, none in that building look like squatters or refugees. But those in the other yellow block I guess to be newcomers having a hard time.

At these dawn wakings, when the radio pronounces the endless talking, the timidity of the world powers in allowing this genocide to continue, having given one people's country to another, I am irritable and despairing and long to go home.

I see D's naked back sitting on the stool at the desk, as slim and straight as when I first knew him. I feel impatient and cross because it is thirty years and more since we started on this tragedy of the Palestinians and the Zionists; the former are still disposessed, landless, homeless, without passports or shelter, but strangely of use to various governments at certain times. Once I've swallowed my black coffee downstairs and seen the real workers hurrying off to the hospitals, I recover some sense of humour and historical proportion and remember *I* can go home.

Siesta at 3 p.m. The planes fly over – the small arms respond from the roof-tops very near. I am too lazy, too Lebanese to climb to the roof. I just lie there reading *The Times* and *Newsweek* on the Lebanese crisis, and I sleep.

Now I am writing again at 4 p.m. I have tried the Beckstein piano next to the dining room on the lower ground floor. It is nicely in tune but damp and sticky, like us all – so I open it and play a while.

We heard about the IRA bombs – Knightsbridge and the Green Jackets, Regents Park. So where do you take your kids?

21 July

Mr Oxfam, USA, arrives tomorrow, and Richard Grove Hills of London SCF, who have woken up at last.

I go to morning service in the new church near our meeting place. It is enchanting inside, in traditional decoration of marble, alabaster, icons and winking chandeliers. It is a World Council Ecumenical Service. We pray in Arabic, French and English, read the psalms and gospels and are addressed by a variety of bishops and metropolitans. A Swedish bishop wears a pink very ecclesiastic top, but it only extends to his waist, he continues in white jeans. Not only is the Mayflower full of these visiting clerics, but a new group of Nordics have come, leaving the last room for Grove Hills.

In the bar it is said the Israelis don't know what to do with their invasion. Mr Shultz has sent a message for the Feast to Wazzan, the prime minister, and to the Gulf rulers. General Haig would never have done that.

Euphoria reigns, the barman is very verbal, we lunch late.

Woken after a short sleep by the voice of Dan Connell on telephone – Oxfam US – straight from Damascus. I go down to fill him in and find a tall man, late thirties, looking exactly like a Beiruti with a drooping black moustache, and very quick and easy. He's a journalist and photographer, hired by Oxfam in Boston, and is here to see what is wanted – in two weeks – and he must see south and Beqaa.

David McDowell returns p.m. and the only young English doc, Paul Morris, joins us. I fear he is hard up – he brings his cup of choc and eats the last sandwich with gusto. I can't talk or listen any more, but D. sits up late with them all, joined by other Norwegians. He has learned a lot about the weapons used. Nothing excuses the wounds and burns inflicted.

22 July

No paper because of the feast, but we hear of an ambush in East Beirut and five Israeli soldiers killed. So that was why Begin makes unhelpful statement regarding West Bank. We are for it if the US parleys with PLO. Can no one topple Begin and his lot?

23 July

Derek, David and Dan collected by PRCS car to visit all forward areas and 'Gaza'–'Acre' hospitals. Then to French Lycée, where D. gave interviews with *Pravda*, sitting on bed of old lady whose legs were blown off. Dan got pictures – he is gradually catching up on his sleep. He, David and Derek make a good confederacy. He is expert on telex, thank God.

I spend a miserable morning waiting for Hills of SCF, who never arrives. An afternoon follows of watching Israeli planes flying over:

tiny white meteors in the blue sky. We note a black kite flying near by. 'Children playing with kites,' says an older man at desk. But Derek thinks it is a kite flown by IDF [Israel Defence Force] to mark non-targets.

23 July
Wake with World BBC at 6 a.m. – reports on renewed IDF attacks. BBC news decidedly slanted towards Israel. David writes a note to Graham Leach at Commodore, and we compose a telex for the Lebanese desk at the Foreign Office, asking for a copy to be sent to Douglas Hurd. A telex came asking for news on 'Pam and Derek's activities', so word has got through – probably to Grey. We reply, 'Well, hoping to return in August,' though Derek is having doubts. But I think if we stay longer than a month to six weeks in this heat and tension, Derek will fall ill.

24 July
Poor Dr Shawi has to give up his free morning to drive us, so off we go down the airport route. The hospital beds are empty but for two young Fedayeen – who will recover. Three or four young boys in camouflage uniforms sit on a bench; a curly-headed youth in jeans follows us into the ward where the two wounded lie. Dr Shawi makes him take his pistol from his hip and then says, 'Don't you remember Ahmed?' It's a boy with wounds from a splinter shell we saw before, all bandaged in pyjamas. He shows me his right hand, flexes the fingers – he is going home. Discharged? Dr Shawi says he is going back to his unit. Ahmed is about eighteen, small with a curved semitic nose and huge grey eyes. He comes with us in the car back to the Mayflower and shows me the book he is reading on Fascism. He has knocked out several Israeli tanks and is known as a crack marksman.

7 p.m. The Israeli planes come in and the shelling and bombing sound very close. I don't jump any more, only at the *rat-ta-tat-tat* when a neighbour lets down his venetian blinds. Later we learn from the BBC that the Syrians, who earlier threatened they had weapons not yet used, have shot down an Israeli plane and captured the two pilots who bailed out – God help them. It is common knowledge that Israeli soldiers have beaten prisoners to death. However, these

two, like the other they hold, will be of immense propaganda and bargaining value.

Jim Muir, who looks like an anglican archangel, has done a super report from the south on the BBC. I think he listened to what we told him about Ein el-Helweh being tidied up. He actually reports that the ICRC are worried they are not allowed to visit prisoners in Israel. God knows what happens to tens of thousands of young Ahmeds.

25 July

Just as we doze, about 4.30 comes a knock on our door. Derek, all sleepy and startled, can't get his sarong on. It is the Canadian Ambassador, Theodore Arkand; our phone was malhooked. Derek joins him downstairs. I follow, in a sudden panic that it might be news of Grey in Northern Ireland via the British Embassy. Mr Arkand is wanting information, especially from the south – anything we can tell. A brave and angry man, he is already posted to Budapest but determined to stay until there is a settlement. He has made representation to Tel Aviv and is very unpopular with the Israelis, but like the Norwegians, French and Yugoslavs he stands up to them. Derek, elated by his visit, spends the night sorting papers and evidence to take round to the Canadian Embassy.

At the Commodore bar, Phillip Dallas Saye, a young man with Associated Press, says Arafat has signed a document recognizing Resolution 242 and the other UN resolutions dealing with Palestine.

We take chicken and dried bread up to our room. I feel queer. It is the dreaded squitters. Woken in the night by bombing and shelling from the sea. Each raid grows more intense and we hear next morning they tried to land and were driven back. Israelis deny it; they also say the US Senator's signed document with Arafat is a propaganda move. Yet on the BBC's later information, the former US Ambassador to Saudi Arabia confirms it should be enough – that is, Arafat's signature – for the US to start talking with the PLO.

26 July

I feel ill, dazed, squittery, and hopeless – all the old symptoms one never grows accustomed to, though they are the Middle East norm. We take the papers to the Canadian Embassy – housed in a flat of the high-rise Étoile buildings, the security very impressive. It takes a long while to get to HE's department. A friendly, stout secretary sits us down with lemonade and takes the whole lot to be photocopied.

On the stickiest hottest day yet, the worst daytime raid yet, in mid afternoon. We climb nine floors to the roof. They seem to be using smoke bombs, which make one sick. Something with a light makes an arch like a plane exhaust, which spreads in a huge cloud above the south of the city. What a foolish way to live. Rabbit hutch upon rabbit hutch, piled to the sky. Is it better to go down from the top to extinction or to be buried by the steel and lumps of cement at the bottom? After the raid the footballers start playing below in our courtyard – it is becoming serious and professional. After a goal they run round, throwing up their arms like pros, and smaller boys have started a game around the corner, but during the raid the baby in the bottom flat cried and cried and I watched the poor father trying to comfort him.

Handsome Eddie from the desk asked to come up to see us in our room. He talks with embarrassment to Derek about the 'Islamic people' rehoused in the yellow, poorer flats opposite. It offends them to see us moving around naked. I have pleasure in saying, 'I told you so.' The venetian blinds must now stay down.

27 July

Derek went off early with Richard Grove Hills to see UNRWA; gradually they each come round to Derek's view of working with or alongside UNRWA, the only body which has saved the Palestinians of the poorer levels from oblivion. John Defrates reminds Derek that however many Fedayeen the Israelis kill, maim or imprison, it will only take one more generation of the UNRWA schools to man another army.

From lunchtime onwards the shelling and bombing hardly stopped. We climbed to the roof but the view doesn't compare with that from the Alexandre. Begin says he has the right to finish Beirut, and I suppose us. The ambulances flash and scream through the streets. We sleep through a really bad night; most of the occupants went down to the basement.

28 July

Damage from yesterday grim, a whole high rise full of displaced Palestinians and Lebanese families bombed. Two Norwegian doctors spend the afternoon and evening pulling dead and wounded out of the rubble. Two helicopters flew over and gunned the survivors as they tried to pull them out. The brave Canadian Ambassador's house was hit, and the abandoned Swiss Embassy. PLO rockets meanwhile hit the International Red Cross ship lying off Jounieh with medical supplies and blood plasma – they continually snipe at the Israelis across the green line, but why a Red Cross ship off Jounieh?

At 10 a.m. we are asked to conference at the Bristol Hotel, held in a huge air-conditioned room, which fills with 'national humans', the wording on the invitation.

We rose for the national anthem, a marching tune much resembling the 'Soldier's Song' of Ireland, and again for two minutes' silence to honour the dead. After one or two opening speeches, another two minutes' silence – I think this time for martyrs. In the front row sat a posse of Orthodox priests. One gave histrionic speech on the Israeli occupation, the altering of the Torah to suit their colonial intentions, and their hatred of Christian Arabs, whom they term 'barking dogs'. He could vouch that in Majayoum there were no weapons or fighting men when they invaded.

Dan Connell, sitting the other side of Derek, had asked to speak as an American. He took the microphone as a conductor takes his baton and made a most excellent appeal for help in his task for Oxfam US. He needed personal stories and experiences, he told of the ignorance of the American people, which he was going to try to correct. Oxfam could not have hired a more dedicated and fast-moving PR or fact-finder.

Then Derek went up, such a wonderful contrast. He tells them who he is and why he has come to West Beirut, gives a brief outline of how Oxfam is trying to help. It fascinates me, watching these two together, physically so dissimilar, but sharing an intense devotion to the rights of the poor dispossessed.

Lunched back at the Mayflower. David McDowell arrived back from the south at about 5 p.m. and sat and drank his one Campari in our room. All is changed down there. He thinks medical aid through UNRWA and local Lebanese adequate at present. His eyes filled when he recounted how there were people back at Ein el-Helweh, still trying to dig out their dead despite Israeli bulldozing. Some have made pathetic shelters from corrugated bits. He asked one woman why she was there. She said, 'I must stay, we lived here, I have two daughters in hospital, one has lost both legs and the other one.' He says he doesn't know how not to show hatred for Begin, so tries to think of him as a baby in napkins and what a rotten upbringing he must have had to turn killer.

29 July

We hear the Israelis are giving UNRWA a freer hand in the south. They have only just grasped the magnitude of the refugee problem. Having razed Ein el-Helweh camp, they now suggest those refugees not fled or killed should settle down again on top of their dead.

The young Israeli colonel who asked to be relieved of his command told Begin he had seen through his binoculars children playing in the streets.

30 July

At breakfast *L'Orient-Le Jour* has all the proposed plans in detail: much face-saving for the PLO, the four countries bordering Israel to welcome them, plus Iraq. UN resolutions conferences around the world almost unanimous in condemnation of the invasion. It all looks hopeful in print, but in the streets the horrific casualties of flesh and blood, bones and cement, steel and stone give it the lie. If they can do what they have to date, why would they refrain from finishing the destruction?

In the siesta period the sound of children playing is what is mostly heard, songs, shouts and capers. Then, at 5 p.m., that vile distant rumbling of the Israeli planes, the firing of guns warning for the streets to be cleared. I am now not frightened at all, I just loathe the idiocity of it. The PLO have said they will go. In the name of all the hosts of heaven, what is the sense of not allowing them to go with the small victory, if it is a victory? Yes, it is a victory, the longest Arab-Israeli engagement, and they have carried it out virtually alone.

31 July

4.30 p.m. Visit Mr Labib, seven floors up just round the corner. There never was such a welcome. In 1967 at the Hourani school at Marjayoun he was headmaster when we stayed in the family house in the village, cool, whitewashed and veranda'ed, with a view across the valley to the Damascus road and Mount Herman: a lovely build-ing with playing fields. We got an Oxfam grant for it, since when it has twice been occupied and looted. The last time the Israelis finished the job and took everything moveable.

Enjoying himself hugely, our host recounts how he took Arnold Toynbee to visit a tribal Druze village in the south and acted as interpreter. But Toynbee knew Arabic well. When it came to a pronouncement by the Druze leader on how happy they had been under British occupation, Labib refused to translate, and Toynbee shouted, 'Bravo, Labib.' He is lame now and cannot get up and down the four flights of stairs, but refuses to leave, come what may.

1 August

They started at 4 a.m., first the distant boom, then the rackety response, then the planes. The cock of dawning crows regardless, and as the sky grows pink we dress, climb to the roof. It is the same old pattern, the phantoms so high we see only the protective smoke they drop. The little orange stars fired are there always, way behind, but maybe they keep the planes up high. I would dearly love to talk with an Israeli soldier again. They say an older colonel has committed suicide in Israel in despair.

11.30. The planes, the bombing and shelling haven't let up – God knows what is happening. How can any human being, soldier or civilian, withstand this hellish holocaust? When they talk of a 'salami' option, they don't mean taking another slice, they mean flattening the next slice. I heard on the radio that Reagan telephoned Begin and Habib at 3 a.m., but the rockets and the bombs didn't stop until dark. A Syrian poet at the Napoleon put it well: 'It is the Israeli dialogue.'

2 August

Some of the buried were dug out last night, many had to be left until morning. Each day the pictures in the local papers are more dreadful – Israeli tanks closing in on us.

As I walk in to read the Associated Press news at the Commodore some well-dressed little girls are carrying water with their parents – they laugh and caper like colts let out of a stable. Everywhere children carry water, playing games again; I shall never forget the children of Beirut. Perhaps dodging the traffic is to them a kind of war game they are brought up on, so maybe the bombs become not too frightening.

3 August

I am told by doctors that phosphorous fragments in the body go on burning as they do in the sand or earth and are hard to put out. The patient burns inside himself.

We are to try the Galleria crossing along the road where the PLO offices were, past the half-destroyed buildings standing like giant mouth organs. Near the check-point the build-up of cars looks ominous. They are at every angle across the road, dissected by heaps of earth and shell-holes.

Cars and the foot people have been turned back. There is hooting and shouting but we press on, hoping the UN flag and my blue eyes will prevail. A huge tank sits astride half the road, a string is being drawn across. A young soldier says in perfect English, 'No crossing today.' I ask politely whether I may speak with an officer. He points out one even younger than himself, and a far scruffier figure, so I get out and again politely ask why. 'It's orders, no one crosses by car or foot.' So we have to turn about, hooting, shouting. A stout lady walks deliberately in front of all the cars, cursing them and the Israelis. Parents trudge back with children in their arms or lugging suitcases or bundles. It is hot, dusty and humiliating, and West Beirut is running out of bottled water to buy, even if you can afford it. I am comfortable in an UNRWA car, but suppose I was a young soldier with a gun and a belt full of ammunition in sight of those arrogant, dirty Israelis, wouldn't I break the cease-fire?

That thirty minutes' snub by Reagan to Shamir in Washington is going to make life very uncomfortable for West Beirut.

4 August

1.30 a.m. No planes, but gunfire and rockets. D. says there isn't so much fire from our side. I actually doze, but by five we're up listening to the BBC, which reports an Israeli advance with tanks. We pack our bags in case.

The generator is pumping, so Eddie sends off our telex to Oxfam to comfort the loved ones about returning. I hope it reaches Grey and Skimper. An incoming telex reads, 'Sons don't want you to return to Beirut,' but they think we are leaving, or have left on the 3rd; they'll be 'old hens' when they hear of this attack. We brave the shells to the Commodore and drink its excellent free coffee. Suddenly, from behind the swimming pool, comes a terrific explosion. No panic, but very frightened faces and much scampering into the hall. Derek says head for the Mayflower, so we run down the street, dodging into doorways during bangs, emerging for another dash during silences. One doorway has camp people's sons, another Fedayeen – all very friendly. We jump over the garbage dump, over the rope and into the Mayflower hall. A youth in blue shining running shorts carries a tommy-gun and ammo upstairs and comes down empty-handed, but somehow this old building seems safer than the vast concrete ceilings of the Commodore.

At 12.30 suddenly a blessed lull – another cease-fire? Alas, I hear a distant rumble.

To bed supperless. Derek can't eat and has acute diarrhoea – his usual response to the Israelis seeming victorious.

5 August

5.30 a.m. and no sound. A very pale waiter manages to bring us, later, bacon and poached eggs, our one meal of the day – but no bread. There is no *L'Orient-Le Jour* to read, it was bombed. The ambulances bring in the wounded and dead from the front.

Richard Hills wants the SCF to help over the 'brown maggot' children of the mental hospital.

Derek walked up to UNRWA, found only a PLO guard on the

gate, a night guard, two shell craters in the yard, and devastation all around. We thought UNRWA would be a non-target.

The hotel is out of drinking water. I ran on a long hot search to find kaolin for Derek's tummy, and water. Water is all we think of. Boys trundle barrows of 7-Up, and all the water points that UNICEF fill have the usual queues.

The cratered roads make it impossible for the ambulances to approach the destroyed buildings. Last night how many died in a tangle of mortar and steel, a few kilometres from us in our beds?

6 August

Quiet night and dawn, but I think Derek is rather ill, he looks feverish. I go ahead to breakfast and consult dear Lillicmore. Her face shines with real concern and we decide I will go with her to the wholesaler to try and buy the clothes for the 'brown maggots'. No one has news of whether they have been hit again. A nice US nurse sits down at our table and offers two lots of pills for Derek to take after whatever he tries to eat at midday.

Mr Begin has said 'no' to the Security Council's resolution, 'no' to Mr Reagan's plea, 'no' to the world – a feeling of doom overtakes me.

7 August

There is little of Beirut left untouched by shelling. Derek is so doped he hardly takes it in. How can I get him to leave? He looks so ill, his work is really done. He has done a wonderful liaison job. The crisis may go on for weeks, until Derek is seriously ill or Begin flattens us all. The latter ain't going to risk house-to-house fighting with the PLO, and he has to show that Israeli casualties, the highest in any Arab-Israeli war, have not been in vain. We are crazy to stay, but maybe we can't get out.

Clemenceau building is just another high rise occupied by refugees. It looks as if it was shelled from the sea. Somehow they got the 300 families down into the three underground damp garages of shelters; only one was killed, someone was blinded. The street as we approached is paved with broken glass. The building stands but one whole floor gapes empty: above it a family has climbed back and already hung out the usual multi-coloured washing on the balcony.

Most are still sleeping underground. This building is an example of wanton destruction. They must know it is only full of women and children and those new babies I went to see, cared for by my little Finnish volunteer friend.

8 August
We make our delivery of food and clothing to the mental hospital, an Islamic and government foundation. The 550 patients are now isolated in what remains of this very modern, well-planned establishment for the handicapped, disabled and aged. The fine wide hall is undamaged, but the whole edifice has few windows left. We have to start unloading the truck ourselves, but gradually other hands come to help from the staff and a few of the more active patients. By the time the unloading is through, the midday meal is being served, a savoury-smelling stew.

The women, moved down from the women's floor, mostly sit or lie in the corridors, the airy well-appointed dormitories with good beds and bedding abandoned for fear of further attacks. Some bedridden patients in rooms on the northern side are of all ages, in various stages of physical and mental disability – some just very, very old, many incontinent. They greet us with smiles and clutching hands and one hopes that however frightened they may become during the shelling, their poor simple memories are short.

The children remind me of a medieval painting of the damned, some on beds or cots, naked like a litter of puppies, others behind a low barrier, scrambling around on the floor. Obviously with the water supply cut off it is best to keep them without clothes. In a cot three look as though they have not long to live. 'They die of their diseases,' says the male nurse, and rattles off a stream of medical terms.

Climbing the stone stairway, the window frames all gone, the steps broken up, the roof gives way to the sky. The children's nurseries are totally wrecked: yellow curtains awry, good new beds covered with fallen roof. Through the breached southern wall, which had led to a large outside veranda, we look on the twisted, crumpled Sports Stadium, what is left of the suburbs of Chatila and Sabra, and beyond to the battlefield of the airport.

9 August

Pina and Marguerita of the International League of People's Rights arrive – they have heard of my idea to march and taken it up in a big way. I tell them I am an ideas person, not an organizer, but I will rouse the women I know and get them to start if they do the rest. But it has to be today or tomorrow, and the shelling is bad.

Most of the rest of the day is spent collecting women for the march. At 6 p.m. I am able to pin a notice at the Commodore and Mayflower hotels: 'The march will gather at the AUB Medical Gate at 10 a.m. on the 10th.'

Janet Stevens, an American journalist with long hair, has done much research on weapons and brings Derek her analysis. She gives us the remains of a cluster bomb to take away, and one of the small horrid objects dropped in the streets for curious children to pick up. We stumble home supperless.

10 August

4 a.m. No more sleep. I lie listening for the *boom, boom* from the sea to begin. I feel sure no one will want to march, certainly I don't feel like it.

10.30. Under the trees outside the building, and the press starts to arrive: television teams, cars. I am already wondering will I ever make the long slog? There seems to be a hold-up – the two Italians with the banners have not turned up. Others from the Mayflower, and some I have never seen, arrive in groups. The Norwegians are all in their white uniforms, and my heart lifts. I seem constantly to have a microphone stuck under my nose. Still no sign of Pina and Marguerita.

I begin to feel rather desperate. It is getting hot and late and the Israeli planes generally start their nasty sorties in the early afternoon. I beg someone to go and find the two Italians. He returns to say only another fifteen minutes, they are finishing the banners. Then they come, Marguerita chattering like mad in her extraordinary English, with paper banners written in six or seven languages, including Phillipino. I am given a huge red megaphone, which hoots and squeaks if you don't handle it with civility, and the proclamation, which is to be read out. 'Bamela, *cara* – you have to do it, it was your idea,' shouts Pina as I remonstrate.

Finally, about noon, twenty-seven of us climb into three buses, and away we go through the gates which only lately saw the kidnapping of poor President Dodge. In front of us a television van, with a cameraman on the roof, leads a horde of press cars and we take the dangerous route to the green line, lurching in and out through the streets, often meeting an obstacle and backing to take some other way. Finally we reach the wide stretch of no man's land leading to the green line. We all jump out and forthwith start our long hot march, headed, indeed surrounded, by press and television.

I do a trial broadcast on demand. Towards the end the words become incoherent on account of a dry mouth. Someone gives me a drink from a small tin of pineapple juice, and I spend the rest of the way, which takes twenty minutes at least, collecting saliva in my mouth. At the barrier, we have to leave most of the press behind, and a Lebanese soldier steps in front of the barbed wire. 'What do you want?' 'To speak with an Israeli officer,' I say. 'You cannot, there is no officer here.' We ask to be allowed to proceed and find one. 'I have orders, no one can go farther.' 'Who gives you your orders'? pipes up a young nurse. 'My boss,' says he. 'Your boss? Your boss is the Israelis,' she replies. He looks at her and draws a finger across his throat: 'Never.'

Other soldiers have gathered, and a smartly dressed police officer. He asks us to step to one side as we are holding up the traffic. We gather to the left of the road but have moved steadily up to the barrier. The border guards, initially nervous, are beginning to enjoy the company of all these young women. I lift the megaphone, pray it won't give out one of its appalling squeaks, and say the piece they have written for me.

'We, a delegation of foreign women in West Beirut have chosen to march to the green line to focus attention on the horrible situation. We women are witnesses to the destruction of Beirut and the killing of civilians. We can attest to the facts that there is an unbearable shortage of food, water, fuel, medicines and electricity. The Israelis claim that for the past two days they have allowed the passage into West Beirut of some medicines, blood and powdered milk, along with water, but there is no fuel to activate the generators to pump the water into the houses. The water is lost in the streets through broken conduits and the milk cannot be dissolved. There is no fuel to activate our generators in the hospitals, which are threatening to close. We foreign medical workers in West Beirut are witnesses to the maiming and death of a large number of civilian casualties from the Israeli use of weapons, such as cluster bombs and phosphorous bombs, and the shelling of hospitals.

'We can attest to the fact that more than two-thirds of the casualties are women and children. We beg all women around the world to use their influence to stop this crime and we beg the government and the people of the world to call for an end to the siege of Beirut which is putting a large civilian population at risk with ever-increasing possibility of widespread epidemic diseases.'

I pass the megaphone round, first to Marguerita, who begins in incomprehensible English, then resorts to Italian, ending with *basta, basta,* looking like one of the furies. In turn each group takes the megaphone and in her own language demands that civilians and children be spared, the siege lifted.

The press have been made to stand behind us, but a lovely Arab stallion with a young man on it is to our right and going to escort us back I can see. My blood is up. It is getting late, it is very hot and my Italian friends think it is time to go. 'Bamella, andiamo a pericoloso.' But I don't want to go, I want to stay, I want to go on telling what is happening, I don't care if the planes come over or the shelling starts. This is something I have been waiting to say for six long weeks. However, I am prevailed upon. We lay our banners across the barbed-wire rolls with dignity and turn and face the long slog back. I don't feel tired any more and I don't mind the hot sun. We even manage quite a few jokes, we feel rather elated; I am devoted to them all, especially to those two Italians who have driven me mad till now. Without their enthusiasm I don't believe we could ever have done it.

When I see Derek back at the Mayflower, he says, 'I think we will be able to go, it looks as though the arrangement for the PLO to leave is on course.' With the help of the International Red Cross, he and Richard Hills have brought out twenty-seven children from the mental home, all dressed up in the new clothes we delivered, and everyone helped to carry them into the cars. They are in a corner of the Secours Populaire Hospital: the old basketball stadium.

11 August

I go early to the Secours Populaire, and could never have imagined such a difference in the poor little brown maggots. They are all in the netball ground, sitting, talking, some even running around – they look far less spastic and obviously there is a great improvement already. They are being well fed now, but have no clothes on; it is still quite impossible to keep them clean if clad. No one knows how long they can stay; the hospital isn't very happy about it, but they are on a ground floor well away from the central staircase and at least are in the open air and free from shelling.

As it is rather a nice day and not too hot, I go along to the American University. After this week of intensive bombing and shelling many hospitals have moved from the outer rim and taken over part of the AUB campus.

I meet Dr Arafat walking with a small boy of four, holding his hand. The hope is that the Israelis will spare the American University complex; and that the children, wounded men and boys who are here will be fairly safe.

Only in the gardens of the AUB does one get any glimpse of the old Beirut. I walk slowly home back to the Mayflower, away from the coast and up into the narrow smelly corner which has been our home for nearly five weeks. Derek thinks we may leave tomorrow. Now the time has come, of course I want to go, of course I want to live and see everyone again, but somehow a great sadness fills my heart.

12 August

We are packed and ready very early, waiting for the UNRWA car to take us across to East Beirut. The bombing has started again and the shelling sounds very, very near. It doesn't look as if any driver will come to fetch us. Derek and I wait, our bundles beside us. Lilliemore is there, and Richard. The hall gradually fills with people coming down from their rooms. I see the despairing faces of those we have to leave behind.

Derek finally decides he will go up with Lilliemore to see if they can find John Defrates and discover what is happening. They disappear among a hail of shells and horrible noises. All day I sit and wait, sometimes I try and write my diary.

After the longest morning I remember, Derek comes back with Lilliemore. They never got farther than John Defrates's flat, where they listened to the bombs and shelling and tried to analyse how near the Israelis have come.

Dr Arafat wants to say goodbye. We are asked to go up to his apartment later in the day. We find him behind his desk, his office in a sort of wing of the hotel. He is very busy, and people come and go the whole time, but we sit down and he smiles. Eventually he makes a little speech, thanking us for all we are doing, asking us to tell the outside world what is happening to the Palestinian people. When we get up to go, he kisses me on both cheeks, and also Derek, and we part with tears in our eyes.

In the evening we sit outside for a while, and watch the Israeli planes high, high in the fading light, before we cross the street to the Napoleon, where I sit outside, listening to the bombs, the shells, the rumours of a cease-fire. A woman with a baby in her arms passes and suddenly dodges into the basement as another bang explodes.

There is no bread in the hotel, no food in fact, and most of the staff have left. Sami the waiter has gone, they say to Sidon. The dining room is in darkness, but we peer into the kitchen. The cook is there, but says he has nothing to give us.

The BBC World Service says there *is* a settlement, a cease-fire and a real one, and it will hold. Maybe we *will* go tomorrow. In the dark streets only the ambulances flash by towards La Houte or the AUB hospital, but the bombs, the shelling, the bangs have stopped. We had better get to bed.

13 August

5.30 a.m. The cease-fire still holds. Surely the UNRWA car will come. The goodbyes are moving, terrible, we are hugged and kissed by so many. At breakfast there is only the Lebanese cook, the rest too frightened or tired, but we get a cup of coffee. John Defrates is driving us himself to the Galerie crossing. A mad euphoria seizes us as we get into the car, to follow again the way of destruction. Many more landmarks have gone; more craters are in the road. It takes a long time to reach the green line. Just before we get there a UNIFIL car passes us. 'Where were you when we wanted you?' shouts John through his window.

At the barricade where our march was halted, we pass with no hinder and spot Fisk and his Danish girl-friend chatting with the frontier guard. He waves madly and shouts goodbye. John stops the car and hands us over to another UNRWA car. We embrace and watch him drive back to his lonely job without staff, to an office full of holes, but I never saw him so zestful as this morning.

We have to find the British Embassy, which is difficult. It sits over a supermarket. A tatty little Union Jack is pasted on to a glass door. I feel ashamed for my country. Only Hazel Roberts is there. She has a message from Douglas Hurd for us, but we don't get the text. We tell her that a large group of Christian Aid doctors and nurses has arrived under the auspices of the Middle East Council of Churches. Another 'goodbye' and away to Jounieh and the ferry.

All along the route we see Israeli soldiers and vehicles bogied up in the cliffs above the highway and a number of Phalange in green uniforms, their golden crosses exposed upon hairy bosoms, their faces buttoned up and unsmiling.

Not many are gathered to board the ferry, which compares well with the dirty old *Kanah*. Two little embryo tarts in the shortest of shorts prowl the quayside, smoking. I walk, still in my old blue-jean sandals, and Laura Ashley dress, up the gangway.

★

Afterwards I wrote down:

When the siege is finally lifted and the Israelis and their Phalangist allies move through the devastated streets of West Beirut, will they purposely destroy those bands of mutual trust, the fabric of social welfare and service which the Christian and Muslim, Lebanese and Palestinian men and women have woven so strongly through their suffering?

Will that sense of belonging, for which I am already lonely, along with the smelly streets, the burning refuse, the rats and broken sewers and those gallant children, daily carrying water containers beyond their strength down the streets and up the

352

stairways to their mothers and grandmothers nursing a new baby be irretrievably lost?

When we left Lebanon, we hoped we had seen the worst of it. On 1 September the last units of PLO fighters also departed. Two weeks later, on the 14th, Bashir Gemayel, the leader of the Maronite Phalangist party, recently elected President of Lebanon, was assassinated in a vast car-bomb explosion. Two nights after that, the Phalangist militia moved into the defenceless camps of Chatila and Sabra and slaughtered all they could find; the Israelis, who cordoned the perimeters, purported to know nothing of what was happening. The shock of this outrage ran round the world. In Israel 400,000 citizens took to the streets to demand an official inquiry. Begin and Sharon had finally achieved one thing: never again would international media and public opinion be as inclined to take Israeli propaganda at face value as it had in the past.

Key to family photograph in the illustrated section (from left to right):

Back row: Rev. Ben Fryer, Joan Hodgson, Uncle Walter Hodgson, Uncle Arthur Hodgson, Aunt Ettie Helme (married to Bob), Rev. A.H. Fletcher (father), Uncle Willie Campbell, Uncle Harry Hodgson

Middle Row: Uncle Ted Hodgson, Aunt 'Podge' Fryer (married to Ben), Aunt Mabel Hodgson (married to Barnard), Uncle Barnard Hodgson, Granny Hodgson, Aunt Margaret Campbell (married to Willie) holding Findlay, Uncle Bob Helme, Alice Fletcher (mother) holding Diana, Aunt Etta Hodgson (married to Harry)

Front row: Barbara Hodgson, Beryl Fryer, Gertrude Hodgson, Nigel Helme, Barnard Beckett Helme (killed in First World War), Mollie Helme, Guy Helme (killed in First World War), Rosamund Fryer

Index

British Union of Fascists, 71
Britten, Benjamin, 223
Britten-Jones, Joyce, 132, 136
Bromilow, General, 207
Bronsema, Joop, 273
Bronson, Katherine De Kay, 213
Brotherhood of Freedom, 127,
   128, 129, 130, 131, 134, 135,
   138, 143, 149, 317
Browne, the Hon. Alicia, 75
Browne, the Hon. Henry, 75,
   170, 173, 175
Browning, Robert, 213
Bruno, Hope, 192, 193
Bryant, Sir Arthur, 133
Buccleuch family, 205
Buisson, Capitaine de, 137
Burckhardt, John Lewis, 69
Burgess, Gelett, 214
Burgogne, Margaret ('the
   Burg'), 204
Burroughs, Sir Bernard, 303
Busvine, couturiers, 80
Byng, Douglas, 40, 41, 75–6
Byrne, Jim, 184
Byron, Robert, 75

Cadbury, Richard ('Dick'), 49
Cadogan family, 78
Cairo in the War (Cooper), 131
Cambridge, University of, 36,
   44, 49, 74, 76, 86, 90, 112,
   174, 192, 239, 244, 319
'Campbell Kids', cousins, 10,
   11, 12, 131
Campbell, Margaret, née
   Hodgson, aunt, 10–11
Campbell, William, uncle, 10

Canadian Embassy, Beirut,
   338–9
CARE agency, 286, 294
Carisbrooke, Marquess and
   Marchioness of, 57, 216
Carisbrooke, Lady Iris, 216
Carlisle, George, Earl of, 144
Cassell's, publishers, 36
Castellani, Sir Aldo, 110–11,
   178
Catroux, General Georges, 139,
   140, 143
Catroux, Margot, 143, 145
Chamberlain, Joseph, 42
Chapman, George, 267
Charles, Prince of Wales, 230
Charles II, 136, 202
Christian Aid, 352
Christian Science Monitor, 227
Churchill, Randolph, 191
Churchill, Sir Winston, 67, 129,
   133, 148, 151, 169, 187, 189,
   190, 191, 192, 206, 221, 318
Circassia, HMS, 97
Clanmorris, Lord, 79, 181; see
   also Bingham
Clara, nanny, 15
Clayton, Major Gilbert, 10
Cleave, Dr Richard, 280, 281
Clive, Sir Robert, 285
Cloud of Unknowing, The, 11
Coat, Miss, benefactor, 28–9
Coat, Miss, nurse, 281
Coats, Peter, 133
Cochrane, Miss Minnie, 30,
   31, 57
Cocker, Mr, 215
Cockerell, Sydney, 219

Index

Headfort, Marquess and
  Marchioness of, 187
Heber-Percy, Cyril, 241
Heber-Percy, Pamela, formerly
  Fairhurst, formerly Cooper,
  241
Helme, Barnard, cousin, 16, 17
Helme, Ettie, *née* Hodgson,
  aunt, 16, 17
Helme, Guy, cousin, 16, 17
Helme, Molly, cousin, 16, 17
Helme, Robert ('Bob'), uncle,
  16, 17, 18
Hendy, E.W., 47
Henry, Mrs, 247
Henry, footman, 1
Herdman, Mary, *née* Cooper
  (later Mrs Tony Cook), 248
Herdman, Pat, 248–9
Hetty, maidservant, 29
Hill, Derek, 250, 251, 295, 319
Hills, Richard Grove, 335, 336,
  339, 344, 349, 350
Hitler, Adolph, 137, 189, 219
Hobbs, Peter, 121
Hobbs, Sylvia, *née* Huth, 6,
  121
Hodgkin, E.C. ('Teddy'), 147
Hodgson cousins, 36
Hodgson, Arthur, uncle, 12, 15,
  205
Hodgson, Barbara, cousin, 15
Hodgson, Barnard Becket,
  grandfather, 5, 6, 9, 15
Hodgson, Barnard Thornton,
  uncle, 9, 34
Hodgson, Edward ('Ted'),
  uncle, 15
Hodgson, Elizabeth, cousin, 15

Hodgson, Etta, aunt, 192, 235
Hodgson, General Sir Henry
  ('Harry'), uncle, 31, 65,
  98–100, 192
Hodgson, Margaret, *née*
  Thornton, grandmother, 1,
  5, 6, 7, 8, 10, 13, 34, 36, 53
Hodgson, Nancy, aunt, 15
Hodgson, Brigadier Walter,
  uncle, 10, 209
Hodson, Rev. and Mrs, 43
Hodson, Avis, 43
Hoffman, Freddie, 122
Hogg, Quintin (later Lord
  Hailsham), 145, 191
Holt, Sir Vivian, 149
Hood, Miss, organist, 30–31
Hore-Ruthven, *see* Ruthven
House of Commons, 225, 309,
  310
House of Lords, 197, 209, 317
House of the Soul, The
  (Underhill), 11
Household Brigade, 10
Household Cavalry, 308; 1st,
  137
Howard, Leslie, 106
Huda, Lulie Abdu'l, 129, 135
Huda, Lima, 129
Humphrys, Sir Francis and Lady,
  52, 71
Hunloke, Philippa, 306, 308
Hurd, Douglas, 337, 352
Hussars, 11th, 156, 239
Hussein, imam, 295
Hussein, Sherif of Mecca, 62,
  67, 69
Hussein, King of Jordan, 272,
  282, 283

366

Markievicz, Constance, Countess, 252
Maronites, 143, 153
Marriott, Sir John, 131
Marriott, Lady ('Momo'), 131
Marthe, Madame, couturière, 37
Martin, George ('Toby'), 201
Mary, Queen, 197, 236
Mary, housemaid, 8, 20
Mau Mau, 229
'Maud' (Tennyson), 33
Maureen, Miss, hotelière and cook, 157
May, nursemaid, 163, 173, 182, 183, 185, 186, 192, 193, 194, 197, 210, 211, 212, 214, 221, 222
Meath family, 187
Melly, George, 321
Menzies, Keith, 48
Menzies, Dame 'Pattie', 305
Menzies, Sir Robert ('Bob'), 131, 135, 206, 305
Metamorphosis (Ovid), 39
Metaxas, Ioannis, 133
Metcalfe, Lady Alexandra ('Baba'), 225
Metternich, Prince Paul, 262, 268, 269
Metternich, Princess Tatiana, 262, 269, 292
MI5, 310
Middle East Council of Churches, 352
Middle East Intelligence Centre (MEIC), 126
Military Knights of Windsor, 199, 209
Milton, John, 21
Ministry of Health (Jordanian), 280
Ministry of Information, 126, 137, 148, 318
Ministry of the Interior (Iraq), 147
'Minnie the messy old mermaid' (Byng), 40, 41
Moby-Dick (Melville), 36
Moby Dick (film), 253
Mohammed, Prophet, 67
Mohammed Reza Pahlavi, Shah of Iran, 139, 206–7, 286, 289, 290, 294
Monkton, the Hon. Celia, 262
Montagu-Douglas-Scott, Lady Doria, 217
Montgomery, Field-Marshal Bernard, 1st Viscount (of Alamein), 141, 169, 207
Moore, Henry, 251
Moorehead, Alan, 116, 261
Moorehead, Caroline, 149
Moral Rearmament, 310
Morandi, Signorina, 217, 218
Morris, Dr Paul, 336
Morris, William, 36
Morrisey, Mr, groom, 183, 184, 314
Morrisey, Mrs, 183
Morrisey, Johnny, 183–4
Morrisey, Peggy, 183, 185, 314, 317
Morrisey, Phoebe, 183, 184
Morshead, Sir Owen, 199, 208
Morshead, Paquita, Lady, 199
Morton, H.V., 52, 59, 64
Moses, 63, 68
'Moses', essay (Churchill), 318

O'Toole, stranger, 250
Ovid, 39
Oxfam, 323, 324, 327, 329, 330,
334, 335, 336, 340, 343, 344
Oxford, University of, 17, 35,
73, 128, 219, 252, 270

Paddy, nurse, 83, 85
Pakravan, General, 289, 290
Palestine Liberation
Organization (PLO), 317,
325, 328, 334, 336, 338, 340,
341, 343, 344, 345, 349, 353
Palestine Red Crescent Society
(PRCS), 132, 326, 330, 332,
336
Palladio, Andrea, 214
Pallavicini, Count, 263
Palmer, Captain Anthony, 142
Palmer, Lady Henriette, née
Cadogan (later Lady Abel
Smith), 142
Palmer, Major 'Killer', 248
Palmer, Mark, 142
Parade, 131, 145
Park, Miss, private secretary, 91
Parliament, 205, 227, 229, 318;
see also House of Commons;
House of Lords
Pasmore, Victor, 251
Patton, Bishop Henry, 34, 101
Patton, Mrs, 35
Paul, St, 14, 59, 60, 61
Payne, May, 161
Peace Corps, 294
'Peace Now' movement (Israel),
324
Peake, General Frederick
('Peake Pasha'), 69, 70

Pearson, General Sir Tom, 98,
131
Peel, Lady Delia, 222
Peel, Lady Robert, see Lillie, Bea
Penn, Sir Arthur, 237
Pennyfeather, Harold, 148
Perowne, Stewart, 148, 214,
224, 233
Perry, Mrs, 252
Perry, Fred, 28
Perry, Lionel ('Li'), 252, 253,
256
Persse family, 90, 101, 315
Persse, 'Atty', 181
Petrified Forest, The (film), 106
Phalangist party, Lebanon, 352,
353
Phipps, Paul, 236
Philip, Aidan, 147
Picasso, Pablo, 251
Pilkington, Arthur, 258
Pina, human rights worker, 347,
348, 349
'Plantation, the', of the six
counties of Ulster with
Protestants, 255, 259
PLO, see Palestine Liberation
Organization
Plunkett, Mrs, 186
Plunkett-Ernle-Erle-Drax,
Admiral Sir Richard, 85
Pollock, Mackenzie, 271
Pollok, Alan, 315
Pollok, Gladys, née McKinnon,
87
Pollok, Ian, 102
Pollok, John, 79, 315–16
Pollok, Valentine ('Uncle Val'),
188, 315, 316

Rifle Brigade, 74, 75, 95, 96,
110, 118, 133, 141, 167, 184,
335; 60th Rifles, 112;
Support Group, 120
Rihaye, Madame Habib, 331
Rizzio, David, 89
Roarty family, 243
Roarty, Nellie, 245, 249, 258,
260, 262, 309
Roascio, Count Mario di, 35
Roberts, Hazel, Lady, 352
Rommel, Field-Marshal Erwin,
133, 137, 153, 159, 170, 173
Roos, Einar, 266, 268
Roosevelt, Eleanor, 204
Roosevelt, Franklin D., 148,
189, 192
Roots of Heaven, The (film), 253
Rorabach, Dick, 268
Rorke, Kate, 40, 45
Rose, personal maid, 229
Ross, Mr and Mrs, 243
Rothschild, Cecile de, 321–2
Royal Ascot week, 205, 223,
236, 306, 311
Royal Horseguards, 17, 130,
139
Royal Navy, 9, 201
Royal Ocean Racing Club, 312
Ruegg, Thomas, 325
Runicman, Sir Steven, 141, 214
Russell family, 243
Russell, George William, *see* AE
'Ruthven, raid of ', 106 and n
Ruthven, Alastair Hore-, 164
Ruthven, Alexander, 200
Ruthven, Alexander Gore
Arkwright Hore-, *see*
Gowrie, 1st Earl of

Ruthven, Alexander Patrick
Greysteil, *see* Gowrie, 2nd
Earl of
Ruthven, Angela Hore-, *née*
Manners ('Ange'), 49, 188,
194, 195, 222, 310
Ruthven, Chloë,
granddaughter, 319
Ruthven, Gerry (Lord Ruthven
of Freeland), 110, 200
Ruthven, Harry, 200
Ruthven, Ianthe, *née*
Hodgkinson ('Tiggy'),
daughter-in-law, 319
Ruthven, James Hore-, 197
Ruthven, Leo Patrick Brer,
grandson, 316, 319
Ruthven, Colonel the Hon.
Malise Hore-, 49, 50, 51, 88,
108, 194, 195, 310
Ruthven, the Hon. Malise
('Skimper'), son, 161–2, 163,
164, 166, 167, 168, 169, 170,
171, 172–3, 174, 177, 178,
179, 185, 186, 189, 192, 193,
194, 195, 200, 202, 204, 208,
209, 210, 211, 212, 214, 215,
216, 217, 219, 220, 221, 224,
227–8, 233, 234, 241, 242,
244, 245, 250, 256, 270, 312,
313, 317, 319, 321, 334, 344
Ruthven, Nancy Hore-, 197
Ruthven, Orlanda,
granddaughter, 319
Ruthven, Patrick, Lord, 89
Ruthven, Patrick Hore- ('Pat'),
first husband, 10, 12–13,
63–4, 74, 75, 76, 77, 78–9,
81–2, 83, 95, 109, 110, 111,